CHEQUE DISHONOUR

CASES EXCLUSIVE

"THE PRACTICAL GUIDE"

for Trial Court Practice – Complainant & Accused Side Representation

Authored by the CLC(R) Team, Mumbai, led by Advocate Vinod Kumar GB Singh Chhabra from the Bombay High Court.

KAVYA
PUBLICATIONS

Publisher:

SDR INNOWAYS INDIA PVT. LTD.
667, Rajaward, Kulpahar, Mahoba - 210426
Imprint:
KAVYA PUBLICATIONS
Plot No.107C, Hanuman Khand, Gulabvatika, Behta Hazipur, Loni-UP (Near Dilshad Garden Delhi) NCR - 201102

Mob. : 7905266820
Website : www.kavyapublications.com
E-Mail : info@kavyapublications.com

ISBN : 978-93-6431-864-8
Price : 999/-INR
Year : 2025

This book is printed at MTL and published by Ajay Agrawal, CEO of SDR Innoways India Pvt. Ltd. Kulpahar Mahoba with its imprint and centre, Kavya Publications Delhi.

DISCLAIMER

The Practical Guide For Trial In JMFC Court Aims To Provide Guidance On Practice, Procedure, Precedent, Drafting, And Advisory For New JMFC Advocates, Among Others. There Is No Intention To Criticize, Condemn, Demoralize, Or Adversely Affect Any Of Our Colleagues, Which Could Potentially Contribute To Any Negative Judgment By A Court Of Law. Therefore, The Founder, Author, And Entire Team Of CLC Submit Their Unconditional Apology If Any Such Issues Arise And Undertake To Omit, Remove, Or Modify Any Problematic PARTs At The Earliest Opportunity Upon Gaining Knowledge.

PRELIMINARY/INTRODUCTION

PREFACE "THE PRACTICIAL GUIDE NI ACT"

The Practical Guide to the NI Act.' The scope, object, logic, thrust, and purpose of writing this book, in simple language, are to inform new entrant advocates about how to handle a cheque dishonour case, even if they have no prior knowledge. This book will teach them practically how to manage a new client when they come to them, with confidence and full conviction. Your client may be the complainant, meaning the payee of the cheque, or the accused, meaning the drawer of the cheque. This guide is equally helpful for either side of advocates. As per the advice of the author, who himself is a longstanding regular practicing advocate and knows well what steps ought to be taken at any stage and scenario, you will be provided with the required guidelines through this book. 'The Practical Guide to the NI Act' is especially for law students, lawyers, and litigants: practical advice that is designed to be an essential resource for legal practitioners and students at every stage of trial court proceedings.

By providing ready-to-use drafts, notice applications, and step-by-step guidance, this book will help readers navigate the litigation process efficiently from day one until the final decision.

☞ Key Points to Highlight:

1. Comprehensive Coverage – A practical roadmap for law students, new lawyers, and self-represented litigants.

2. Ready-to-Use Draft Library – Includes drafts of Misc . Applications, notices, and pleadings to save time and ensure correctness.

3. Step-by-Step Guidance – Covers procedural and strategic aspects from filing a case to securing a judgment.

4. Courtroom Practicalities – Tips on advocacy, evidence presentation, and avoiding common pitfalls.

5. Quick Reference Tool – Designed for fast access to critical information during case preparation and hearings..

SD/-

Vinod Kumar Chhabra

Introduction & Notes

IMPORTANANT NOTES:

Just an Advice to NEW ADVOCATES HANDLING THEIR FIRST CASE ON THE COMPLAINANT SIDE:

If possible, read the whole concept OF THIS PRACTICAL GUIDE at your convenience, based on your intellect and passion. It is better to have a clear understanding the basic facts, and law applicable, then call the client to fill up the Conversant format, gather each detail and document, and after that, start drafting the notice By Following Various Formats In The Guide, In The CHAPTER **"DRAFT LIBRARY,** Coupled with Coaching Part For Better Understanding and the answers of queries from the Practising Advocates.

TERMS AND CONDITIONS

TO USE FOR ACCESSING SOFT COPIES

The "Practical Guide In short 'PG' N I Act Exclusive for Trial Court Practice" is a comprehensive resource designed for effective representation in trial courts under the Negotiable Instruments Act, 1881 (N.I. Act), accommodating both the complainant and the defense/accused side with structured, user-friendly divisions.
Guide Structure

Part I: Focused on steps, strategies, and legal resources available to the complainant in cheque dishonour cases (Section 138 trials), from inception to the logical end.
Part II: Dedicated to defense/accused support, detailing rights, common defenses, procedural safeguards, and arguments to challenge or rebut the complainant's case under the N.I. Act.
Part III: Contains material and procedural guidance relevant to both parties, such as key sections, case law summaries, trial strategies, and general trial court best practices.
Every Part Is Organized Into Main Chapters, A To Z Captions, And Sub Captions For Clarity.

1. Terms and Conditions for accessing soft copies

Individual Subscription & Access Right: Access to the conte this right is personal and non-transferable.

Strictly Prohibited Uses:

No Group/Class Use: The subscriber cannot use, share, display, or distribute the materials to or for the benefit of any group, class, Institution, organization, or multiple individuals.
No Mass Distribution: Any form of mass dissemination, sharing, Broadcasting, uploading to public/shared platforms, or widespread Distribution of the materials is strictly forbidden.

Device & Electronic Communication Terms:

Access and use of the soft copy are subject to all applicabl laws governing electronic communications and digital content within India. Relevant laws include, but are not limited to:

The Copyright Act, 1957 & other related laws : Protects the intellectual property of CLC (R)

Mumbai and entire LLP (Partners and Publisher)

The Information Technology Act, 2000: Governs electronic transactions, digital signatures, data protection, and defines penalties for computer-related offenses (like unauthorized access or data theft).
Other Applicable Laws: Any other relevant Indian laws pertaining to digital content, data privacy, and electronic contracts.

Authorized Use:

The soft copy is solely for the subscriber's own personal study, reference, and
Educational purposes . Use is confined to devices owned or controlled by the subscriber personally.

In Summary:

You buy it, YOU use it. Only the person who paid for the subscription
Can access and use the materials.

Personal Devices Only. Use the materials on your own computer, tablet, or phone.
Founder, Practicing Advocate Team C L C (Registered)

Mumbai Headed By Advocate Mr Vinod Chhabra Since 1991

****

MASTER INDEX

INDEX PART 1

(Supporting Complainant Representation)

CHAPTER-01

ACCOUNT STATUS

ACCOUNT CLOSED:

Cheque Issue: The consequences and legal implications of a cheque being dishonoured due to account closure depend on when the closure happened, who initiated it, and the intent of the account holder.

Account Closed BEFORE the Cheque was Issued

Consequence: The cheque is invalid from the outset. It's drawn on a non-existent account.

Offenses (Legal Liability):

Civil Liability: The issuer remains liable for the underlying debt/obligation to the payee. The payee can sue for recovery.

Criminal Liability (Cheque Bounce S.138 NI Act in India): Potentially Applicable. Issuing a cheque knowing the account is closed is strong evidence of dishonest intention or knowledge that it would be dishonoured. The payee can initiate proceedings under Section 138 of the Negotiable Instruments Act (or similar laws elsewhere) after following the statutory notice procedure. Courts often treat this as a serious offense.

Account Closed AFTER the Cheque was Issued but BEFORE Presentation

Consequence: The cheque will be dishonoured upon presentation due to "Account Closed".

Offenses (Legal Liability):

Civil Liability: The issuer is still liable for the original debt. The payee can sue for recovery.

Criminal Liability (Cheque Bounce S.138 NI Act): Very Likely Applicable. Closing the account after issuing the cheque, thereby preventing its payment, generally constitutes an offense under S.138. The key element is the dishonour due to insufficiency of funds (which includes nonexistence of the account caused by the drawer's own action). The drawer must have known or reasonably expected that closing the account would cause dishonour. Intent to cheat is inferred more easily than in some other bounce scenarios.

3. Account Closed by the BANK without Holder's Knowledge

Consequence: The cheque will be dishonoured upon presentation due to "Account Closed".

Offenses (Legal Liability):

Civil Liability: The issuer (account holder) is still liable for the original debt to the payee. They may, however, have a separate claim against the bank for wrongful closure/damages.

Criminal Liability (Cheque Bounce S.138 NI Act): Potentially Defensible. This is a key exception. If the account holder can prove:

The account was closed solely by the bank's action.

They had no prior knowledge or reasonable cause to believe the account would be closed before the cheque was presented.

They had sufficient funds in the account at the time of closure (or when the cheque should have been paid) to cover the cheque.

There was no intention to defraud the payee.

If these conditions are met, the mens -rea (criminal intent) required for S.138 may be lacking. The dishonour was due to the bank's unilateral action, not the drawer's fault or intent. The drawer should immediately inform the payee and arrange alternative payment.

Key Consequences for the Account Holder (Drawer)

1. Dishonour of Cheque: The cheque will be returned unpaid with the reason "Account Closed".
2. Bank Penalties: The bank may charge a cheque return fee (even if the account is closed, this might be deducted from any positive balance held or pursued separately).
3. Civil Suit by Payee: The payee can sue to recover the cheque amount plus costs and potentially interest/damages.

4. Criminal Prosecution (S.138 NI Act India): If applicable (see scenarios above), this can lead to:

A legally mandated demand notice from the payee within 30 days of dishonour.

Requirement to pay the amount within 15 days of receiving the notice to avoid prosecution.

If unpaid, a criminal complaint leading to summons, trial, potential fine (up to twice the cheque amount).

Important Citations:

****

CHAPTER-02

(A) ADVISIORY /COACHING PART INGREDIENTS UNDER SECTION 138OF THE NI ACT

When a case under Section 138/141 of the NI Act is considered "proved"

1. Ingredients under Section 138 of the NI Act (proven against the drawer) The complainant must prove:

a) Legally Enforceable Debt/Liability

The cheque was issued for a valid existing debt or liability (not as a gift or without consideration).

Example: Loan repayment, unpaid goods/services, legally owed money.

b) Cheque Issued Within Valid Period

The cheque was presented to the bank within 3 months (or before expiry if post-dated).

c) Dishonour for "Insufficient Funds" or Other Specified Reasons

The cheque bounced due to:

Insufficient Funds (most common)

Account Closed

Exceeds Arrangement

Payment Stopped (unless justified, e.g., fraud, forgery; no liability exists). Bank Return Memo (Cheque Return Memo) must be obtained as proof.

d) Statutory Demand Notice Served Within 30 Days

A NOTICE must be sent to the drawer within 30 days of dishonour.

The notice must:

Demand payment within 15 days. Clearly state the amount due.

Warn of legal action under Section 138 of the NI Act.

Proof of delivery (postal receipt, courier acknowledgment, email/SMS) is crucial.

e) Drawer Failed to Pay Within 15 Days of Notice

If the drawer does not repay within 15 days of receiving the notice, the offence is complete.

f) Complaint Filed Within 30 Days of Cause of Action

The complaint must be filed in a Magistrate's Court within 30 days after the

15 day notice period expires.

2. Liability Under Section 141 (Proved Against Company Directors/Partners)

If the drawer is a company/firm, the following must be proved to hold directors/partners/officers liable:

a) Offence Committed by the Company

(Section 138 must first be proved against the company).

b) Accused was "In Charge of and Responsible for the Conduct of Business" The director/partner must have been actively managing the company's affairs when the cheque was issued.

Mere designation (e.g., "Director") is not enough; an active role must be shown.

c) Consent or Negligence

The accused either consented to the offence or negligently allowed it.

Exception:

If the accused proves they had no knowledge or due diligence was exercised, they may escape liability.

When is the case "proved" in court

The court will consider the case proved if:

1. All Section 138 ingredients are established through evidence:

   Original cheque + return memo.

Proof of NOTICE + delivery.

Evidence of debt (agreement, invoice, acknowledgment).

2. No valid defence is raised by the accused (e.g., no proof of forgery, no material alteration, misuse of cheque, etc.).
3. Section 141 liability is proved if the accused is a company official

   Key Defences to Challenge "Proof"

The accused can argue:

No legally recoverable debt (cheque issued as security). Notice not received/properly served.

Material alteration/forgery in the cheque.

Full payment or any payment was made after the notice but before the complaint.

Accused was not in charge of the company's business (for Section 141).

Conclusion

A case under Sections 138/141 of the NI Act is proved when:

- All 6 steps of Section 138 are established.
- Company officials' liability is shown (if applicable).
- No valid defence succeeds.

Next stages in a Section 138 NI Act case after the complainant's evidence (Pursis) and the recording of the accused's statement under Section 313 Cr. P.C are as follows:

Next Procedural Stages:

1. Defence Evidence Stage: The accused is granted an opportunity to present evidence to rebut the presumption under Section 139 NI Act. This includes:

Witnesses: The accused may examine themselves or other witnesses. Documents: Submission of relevant documents (e.g., proof of no debt, alternate agreements). Failure to adduce evidence weakens the defence, as statements under Section 313 CrPC alone are not substantive evidence.

2. Cross Examination: The complainant may Cross Examination the accused's witnesses. Documents submitted by the defence are scrutinized.
3. Final Arguments: Both parties submit oral/written arguments. Legal precedents (e.g., judgments from High Courts/Supreme Court) may be cited.
4. Judgment: The court decides based on: the strength of the complainant's evidence, the accused's success in rebutting presumptions under Sections 118 and 139 NI Act. If convicted: The accused faces imprisonment (up to 2 years) and/or a fine (twice the cheque amount). If acquitted: The case concludes unless appealed.

(B) ADVISORY FOR COMPLAIANT & NEWADVOCTES

COACHING & STRATEGY FOR COMPLAINANT

FACTUAL MATRIX:

Your client's cheque, is bounced for one or the other reason , Your job is to use the law to get them their money.

Step 1: Learn the 3 Strict Rules (Before Anything Else)

This law has very strict steps and deadlines. Missing one can destroy the case.

1. The Cheque Bounces: The bank returns the cheque because of "insufficient funds" or a similar reason.
2. Send a Demand Notice: You must send a formal written notice to the person who wrote the cheque (the drawer). This notice demands payment.

- Deadline: This notice must be sent within 30 days of the cheque bouncing.
- Send it by: Registered mail or courier that gives you proof of delivery.

3. File the Case in Time: If the person does not pay you within 15 days of receiving your notice, you can file the case.

- Deadline: You must file the case in court within 30 days after those 15 days end.

Why this matters: If you miss the 30day deadline for the notice or the 30day deadline for filing, the case will be thrown out. No exceptions. This is the most important part.

Step 2: Get EVERY Document from Your Client

Your case is only as strong as your proof. Get these documents immediately.

- The original bounced cheque.

- The cheque return memo from the bank. This is the bank's official paper stating why it bounced.
- Proof that you sent the Demand Notice (post office receipt, courier receipt).
- The postal tracking report showing the notice was delivered.
- Any written agreement or MOU that shows why the cheque was given (a loan, payment for goods, etc.).
- Any other proof of the debt (emails, messages, receipts). Step 3: Draft the Demand Notice Perfectly

This is your most important document. It must be perfect.

- Be Exact: Clearly mention:
- The exact date the cheque was written.
- The cheque number, bank name, and branch.
- The exact amount of the cheque.
- The date you were informed that the cheque bounced.
- A clear demand: "Pay me Rs. X within 15 days of receiving this notice."
- Send it Right: Always send it by a method that gives you proof of delivery. This is your evidence that they received it.

Step 4: File the Case Correctly

- Where to File: File the case in the court that has jurisdiction over the place where your client's payee bank is located (where the cheque was presented for payment).
- Check the Math: In your filing, correctly calculate all the critical dates (cheque bounce date, notice sent date, notice delivery date, 15day wait period, filing date) to prove you are within the time limit.

Core Documents for Filing Complaint

1. Complaint Petition

Typed on stamp paper (value as per state rules) or plain paper with court fee. Must include:

Full particulars of the drawer (accused) and payee (complainant).

Exact date of cheque issuance, presentation, and dishonour.

Clear cause of action (nonpayment despite statutory notice).

2. Original Cheque or Certified Copy If the original is lost:

Affidavit explaining the loss (u/s 65B Evidence Act). Secondary evidence (photocopy + bank certification).

3. Bank Dishonour Memo (Return Memo)

Must bear the bank's seal & authorized signatory's signature.

If electronic: S. 65B Evidence Act certificate from the bank.

4. Statutory Demand Notice (u/s 138(b) NI Act) Copy of the notice sent to the drawer.

Proof of Delivery:

Postal receipt (Aadhaar enabled /registered post).

Tracking report + delivery confirmation (UPI/email acknowledgment if sent digitally).

5. Postal Receipt & Tracking Report

Proof that the notice was dispatched within 30 days of dishonour.

6. Affidavit of Complainant Sworn statement verifying:

Cheque issuance for a legally enforceable debt. Details of dishonour and notice compliance.

7. Vakalatnama

If represented by an advocate.

II. Additional Documents for Cases u/s 141 (Company/Directors' Liability)

8. Board Resolution (if the cheque is issued by a company) Authorizing signatory to issue cheques.

9. Memorandum of Association (MOA) & List of Directors

To establish accused directors' roles.

10. Proof of Directors' Involvement

Emails/WhatsApp messages (with S. 65B certification). Minutes of meetings showing approval of the transaction.

III. Court Fee & Process Documents

11. Court Fee Payment Proof

Chillan receipt (online/offline payment as per state rates).

12. List of Witnesses & Documents Filed

13. Power of Attorney (if the complainant is represented by an agent).

IV. Procedural Requirements (JMFC Specific)

Copies for Accused: 2+ sets of all documents for summons. Index: Page numbered bundle with a table of contents.

Verification: The complaint must end with the "I solemnly affirm..." clause.

V. Supreme Court Mandates

1. Anvar P.V. v. P.K. Basheer (2014): Electronic evidence (bank memos, emails) requires S. 65B certification.

2. Dashrath Rathod (2014): Jurisdiction is the payee's bank branch location.

3. Aneeta Hada (2012): For S. 141, the company must be arraigned as accused.

VI. Common Pitfalls & Solutions

Defect	Remedy
Unsigned dishonour memo	File bank manager's affidavit
Notice sent via ordinary post	Resend via registered post + file delay condo-nation
Cheque copy unclear	Submit certified copy + affidavit

VII. Pro Tips

Pre Filing Audit: Use the [eCourts Checklist Generator](https://ecourts.gov.in) to validate documents.

Digital Backup: Scan all documents (password protected PDFs).

Note: For state specific variations (e.g., stamp duty, notary rules), consult the NI Act Practice Manual or seek assistance via WhatsApp (9082093332).

This checklist ensures compliance with JMFC procedural rules and minimizes dismissal risks. Always verify local court rules before filing.

Court Fees For Cases Under Sections 138/141 Of The Negotiable Instruments (NI) Act,

Covering online/offline methods, fee calculation, and key procedural requirements:

I. Court Fee Calculation Court fees for NI Act complaints are state specific but generally follow this structure: Based on cheque amount (ad valorem fee) + fixed processing fee. Example Fees (Illustrative): | Cheque Amount | Approximate Fee (States like Delhi/Maharashtra) | ||| | Below ₹1 lakh | ₹500 – ₹1,500 | | ₹1 lakh – ₹10 lakh | 1–2% of cheque amount + fixed fee | | Above ₹10 lakh | 2–3% (capped at
₹25,000–₹50,000 in most states) | Note: Check your state's Court Fees Act or the
[eCourts Fee Calculator](https://ecourts.gov.in/ecourtshome/) for exact amounts.
II. Payment Methods A. Online Payment (Recommended)
1. Via State EFiling Portals (e.g., https://efiling.ecourts.gov.in): Log in → Select

"Pay Fee" → Enter cheque amount → Generate challan. Pay via: UPI (Google
Pay/PhonePe) Net Banking Debit/Credit Card

2. State Specific Portals (e.g., https://mahacourts.gov.in for

Maharashtra): Follow similar steps; fees auto calculated based on jurisdiction.

B. Offline Payment

1. Court Cashier: Submit a manually filled challan form (available at court offices) with cash/DD. Ensure the challan mentions: "Complaint Case u/s 138 NI Act" Cheque amount + calculated fee Jurisdictional court details

2. Demand Draft (DD): Prepare a DD in favor of: "Registrar, [District Court Name]" (for magistrate court) "Registrar, [High Court Name]" (for appellate cases)

III. Key Requirements

1. Attach Fee Proof to Complaint: For online payments: Print the payment receipt and annex it to the complaint. For offline: Attach the courtstamped challan copy.

2. Jurisdiction Specific Rules: Delhi: Fixed fee of ₹1,500 for complaints (regardless of cheque amount). Karnataka: 1% of cheque amount (min ₹500, max ₹25,000). Tamil Nadu: 2% (capped at ₹25,000).

3. Exemptions: Paupers: File an indigence application (Form 1A) to seek fee waiver (rarely granted in NI Act cases).

IV. Post Payment Steps

1. E-Filing: Upload the fee receipt while submitting the complaint online.

2. Physical Filing: Submit the receipt with the complaint bundle to the court clerk.

3. Verification: Ensure the court's fee register reflects payment (get an acknowledgment).

V. Common Pitfalls & Solutions | Issue | Solution | ||| | Underpayment of fees | Recalculate using state rules; pay deficit | | Payment gateway failure | Take screenshot + retry; contact helpdesk | | Wrong payee name | Cancel DD; reissue with correct details |

VI. Supreme Court Directives 1. Timely Payment: Non payment or fee defects lead to rejection (Indian Bank Assn. v. Union of India, 2014). 2. Transparency: Courts must display fee charts (Imtiyaz Ahmad v. U.P. State, 2012).

VII. Resources Fee Charts: Download from state judiciary websites (e.g., [Delhi Courts](https://delhicourts.nic.in)).

COURT FEES REFUNDS

1. General Rule: Court Fees Are Non Refundable

Default Position: Once court fees are paid for filing a complaint under Section 138 of the NI Act, they are typically not refundable if the case proceeds to trial or is withdrawn unilaterally.

Rationale: Court fees are treated as a cost of accessing the judicial system, and refunds are exceptions rather than the norm.

2. Exceptions Where Refund May Be Allowed

A. Settlement through Recognized ADR Mechanisms

The Supreme Court of India has clarified that refunds are permissible only if the case is settled through formal Alternative Dispute Resolution (ADR) processes (e.g., mediation, Lok Adalat) under Section 16 of the Court Fees Act, 1870

Example: If parties settle via court annexed mediation, the complainant may apply for a partial or full refund of court fees.

Private settlements (out of court agreements without ADR) do not qualify for refunds.

B. Compounding of Offence under Section 147 of the NI Act

If the parties mutually agree to compound the offence (i.e., settle the dispute amicably), the court may permit a refund of fees, especially if compounding occurs early in the proceedings (e.g., before the trial begins).

Key Precedent: In Damodar S. Prabhu v. Sayed Babalal H. (2017), the Supreme Court encouraged compounding but did not explicitly mandate fee refunds. However, some courts may exercise discretion.

C. Technical Dismissal of Complaint

If the complaint is dismissed due to jurisdictional errors, lack of cause of action, or other technical grounds (e.g., account frozen by statutory authorities, as held in Best Buildwell Pvt. Ltd. v. R.D. Sales, 2025), the complainant may seek a refund.

3. How to Apply for a Refund?

File a Formal Application: Submit a memo or affidavit to the court detailing the grounds for the refund (e.g., ADR settlement, compounding).

Attach Proof: Provide evidence of settlement (e.g., mediation agreement, compounding order).

Court Discretion: The refund is subject to the court's approval and may
involve partial deductions for administrative costs.

4. Key Takeaways

1. ADR Settlements: Only structured ADR settlements qualify for refunds; private deals do not.
2. Compounding: While compounding is encouraged, fee refunds are not automatic and depend on judicial discretion.
3. Technical Defects: Refunds may be granted if the case is dismissed due to procedural flaws.

For state specific variations, consult local court rules or a legal practitioner

(MCA)

MINISTRY OF CORPORATE AFFAIRS REPORT

In India, an MCA Report refers to a regulatory document filed with the Ministry of Corporate Affairs. It details a company's legal, financial, and compliance status.

Key Components:

Company Overview:

CIN (Corporate Identification Number), incorporation date, registered

address. Financial Statements:

Balance sheets, profit/loss accounts, cash flow statements. Compliance Status:

Annual return filings (e.g., Form MGT 7), audit reports. Ownership

& Legal Data:

Shareholding patterns, director details (DIN), active legal cases. Access via MCA Portal:

Public documents can be searched using CIN or company name.

Can the Complainant (Victim) Appeal Before the Sessions Court? Yes, but with conditions: Since the complainant is a "victim," they can file an appeal before the Sessions Court under Section 372 CrPC read with Section 378(3) CrPC. However, leave (permission) of the Sessions Court is required before the appeal is admitted. The Supreme Court ruling (R. Vasanthi Stanley v. State, 2022) clarified that a complainant in a Section 138 NI Act case is a "victim" under Section 2(wa) CrPC, thus entitled to file an appeal. Alternative Route: The complainant can also approach the High Court under Section 378(4) CrPC, but the Sessions Court route is now available due to the victim status. Practical Steps for Filing Appeal 1. File an appeal in the Sessions Court under Section 372 CrPC + Section 378(3) CrPC. 2. Seek leave (permission) of the Sessions Judge to admit the appeal. 3. Argue that the complainant is a "victim" (citing R. Vasanthi Stanley judgment). 4. If leave is granted, the Sessions Court will hear the appeal on merits. Conclusion: Maintainability Before Sessions Court

Yes, a complainant (victim) in a Section 138 NI Act case can file an appeal before the Sessions Court against an acquittal by JMFC, provided they obtain prior leave. This is a significant shift due to the Supreme Court's recognition of NI Act complainants as "victims," granting them broader appellate rights.

(C) STEP BY STEP TRIAL PROCEDURE FOR SECTION 138/141 NI ACT

Stage 1: Filing of Complaint (Pre-Trial)

1. NOTICE (Mandatory)

Send a 15 days NOTICE to the drawer of the cheque (u/s 138 NI Act) via registered post.

Mention the amount, date of dishonour, and demand payment.

2. Filing Complaint

If payment is not made within 15 days, file a complaint before the JMFC Court under:

Section 138 NI Act (Dishonor of cheque)

Section 141 NI Act (Liability of directors/partners) Documents Required:

Original cheque + return memo (dishonor memo from bank).
Postal receipts + NOTICE copy + reply (if any). Affidavit of complainant.

3. Cognizance & Issuance of Process (BNSS 223, 237)

The magistrate examines the complaint (u/s BNSS 233, OLD CrPC 200).

If a prima facie case exists, summons are issued to the accused (u/s BNSS 237, Old CrPC 204).

Stage 2: Appearance & Plea of Accused

4. Accused Appears

The accused must appear in person or through a lawyer (u/s BNSS 238, OLD CrPC 205).

If the accused absconds, proclamation & attachment (u/s BNSS 97, ex CrPC 82).

5. Substance of Accusation (BNSS 285)

PLEASE READ AND FOLLOW GUIDE LINES AND DIRECTIONS OF SUPREME COURT IN JUDGEMENT OF SANABIJ TARI VERSUS KISHOR S.BORCAR & ANR

DATED 25-09-2025

The magistrate reads the accusation (cheque details + dishonor) to the accused.

The accused pleads guilty or not guilty.

Stage 3: Evidence & Trial

6. Complainant's Evidence (BNSS 233, 348) The complainant submits:

Affidavit of evidence (chief examination). Cross examination by the accused's lawyer.

Witnesses (bank manager, postman) may be summoned (u/s BNSS 348, old CrPC 311).

7. Accused's Defense (BNSS 350)

The accused submits evidence/witnesses.

Examination of the accused (u/s BNSS 350, old CrPC 313).

Stage 4: Judgment & Sentencing

8. Judgment (BNSS 394, 289)

If guilty, the magistrate may order:

Double the cheque amount as compensation (u/s BNSS 398, ex CrPC 357). Jail term of up to 2 years (u/s 138 NI Act).

If acquitted, case dismissed (u/s BNSS 290, exCrPC 256).

9. Appeal (BNSS 415)

Appeal to the Sessions Court within 30 days (u/s BNSS 415, old CrPC 374).

Stage 5: Compounding (Settlement)

10. Compromise (BNSS 359 + NI Act 147)

The case can be compromised anytime before the appeal (even after conviction).

The accused pays the full cheque amount + costs.

Key Timelines Under BNSS

Step	Timeframe
NOTICE reply	15 days from notice
Filing complaint	30 days after notice
Trial completion	6 months (BNSS emphasis)
Appeal filing	30 days from judgment

Special Considerations for Section 141 (Company/Directors)

Liability: Directors/partners can be prosecuted if they were in charge of the company's conduct.

Evidence Needed: Proof of their role (e.g., GST filings, bank signato

(D) ADVISORY PART LEGAL ADVICE AND PROFFESSIONAL SERVICES: TO CLIENT/S

<u>Needful Actions:</u>

Verify Cheque Details: Ensure the cheque is legally valid (date, amount in words/figures, signature, etc.). Examine Liability: Confirm the existence of a legally enforceable debt/liability (essential for S.138). Pre Litigation Advice: Advise the client to issue a legal demand notice (if the cheque bounces) before filing a complaint. Ensure the cheque is presented within 3 months of issuance (or validity period). Documentation: Preserve all supporting documents (agreement, acknowledgment of debt, correspondence).

1. After presentation of the Cheque (Post Bounce Scenario). Needful Actions:

Obtain Cheque Return Memo: Get the bank's memo stating the reason for the bounce (insufficient funds, signature mismatch, etc.). Send Legal Demand Notice: Draft and send a 15day demand notice (S.138 proviso) via registered post to the drawer's address. Mention the amount, date of dishonour, and demand paym2. ent within 15 days. Preserve Proof of Notice: Keep postal receipts, acknowledgments (if received), and tracking details.

For Issuance of a Demand Notice. Needful Actions:

Draft a Precise Notice: Clearly state cheque details (number, date, and amount). Mention the dishonour reason (based on the bank memo). Demand payment within 15 days from receipt. Proper Service: Send via registered AD/post to the drawer's correct address. If the drawer avoids receipt, consider publication in a newspaper (in some cases). Wait for 15 Days: No legal action can be taken unless the drawer fails to pay within this period.

<u>NOTICE ISSUED, NOW FILING A COMPLAINT. NEEDFUL ACTIONS:</u>

Check Limitation: File a complaint within 30 days of the expiry of the 15day notice period. Prepare Complaint Petition: Include: Cheque copy, return memo, demand notice, proof of delivery, and reply (if any). Affidavit of the complainant. Jurisdiction: File in a Magistrate's Court where the cheque was drawn/presented, or the notice was delivered. Alternative Remedies: Consider parallel remedies (civil suit for recovery, criminal complaint for cheating if intent is proven).

2. <u>During the Course of Trial (At Any Stage). Needful Actions:</u>

Examine Complainant's Evidence:

Ensure all documents (cheque, memo, and notice) are exhibited properly. Cross Examination bank officials if needed. Defense Strategies (If Representing Accused): Challenge the existence of debt. Prove no proper service of notice. Argue the cheque was misused/stolen. Compounding: Explore settlement (with court permission) to close the case. Appeals: If convicted, file an appeal within the limitation (30 days). General Legal Acumen Tips: Documentation is Key: Maintain all records (cheque, bank memo, notices, replies). Strict Adherence to Timelines: S.138 has strict deadlines (15day notice, 30day complaint filing). Jurisdiction Matters: File in the correct court to avoid dismissal. Alternative Dispute Resolution (ADR): Encourage mediation for faster resolution. By addressing each stage methodically, you can ensure robust legal representation for cheque bounce cases.

(E) ADVISIORY AND ALERT

"Want of Prosecution" mean?

It simply means the complainant's lack of action, negligence, or failure to pursue the case with due diligence. When a complainant is absent or unprepared on multiple hearings, the court can infer that they have lost interest in prosecuting the case.

Grounds for Dismissal for Want of Prosecution

A court may dismiss a complaint under Section 138/141 NI Act for the following reasons:

1. Non Appearance of the Complainant: This is the most common groun d.

- If the complainant (or their counsel) is absent on a hearing date when their presence is necessary (e.g., for recording evidence), the court may dismiss the case.
- The Magistrate must first issue a summons to the accused. Once the accused appears, the burden shifts to the complainant to prove the case.

2. Failure to Lead Evidence: After the accused pleads "not guilty," the stage of the complainant's evidence begins. If the complainant repeatedly fails to appear to present witnesses or does not file evidence by way of an affidavit (as per streamlined procedure), the court can dismiss the case.
3. Inordinate and Unexplained Delay: If the complainant causes excessive delays without seeking an adjournment or providing a valid justification (e.g., medical emergency, genuine unavoidable circumstances), the court can dismiss the case to prevent abuse of process.
4. Failure to Comply with Court Orders: If the court has issued a specific order (e.g., to pay costs for unnecessary adjournments, to produce a document) and the complainant wilfully disobeys it, the court can dismiss the complaint.

The Legal Procedure for Dismissal

The dismissal does not happen after a single absence. The process generally follows these principles

1. Adjournment First: On the first instance of the complainant's absence, the court typically adjourns the case to a future date.
2. Costs may be Imposed: The court may impose a cost on the complainant for wasting the court's time and requiring the accused to appear unnecessarily.
3. Final Opportunity: On the next date, if the complainant is again absent, the presiding magistrate is empowered to dismiss the complaint under Section 256 of the Code of Criminal Procedure (CrPC).

Section 256(1) CrPC: "If the summons has been issued on complaint, and on the day appointed for the appearance of the accused, or any day subsequent thereto to which the hearing may be adjourned, the complainant does not appear, the Magistrate shall... acquit the accused, unless for some reason he thinks it proper to adjourn the hearing of the case to some other day."

Consequences of Dismissal for Want of Prosecution

- For the Accused: It results in an acquittal (if dismissed under Section 256 CrPC after the accused has appeared). This is a final order, and the principle of double jeopardy applies, meaning the complainant cannot file a fresh complaint for the same cause of action.
- For the Complainant: The case is closed. The only remedy is to file an application for restoration of the complaint or to challenge the dismissal order in a Revision Application before a higher court (Sessions Court or High Court).

****

CHAPTER-03

ADVISORY TO JMFC (BY HIGHER JUDICIARY)

A Judicial Magistrate's Guide to Conviction Based on Accused's Admission under Section 138 of the Negotiable Instruments Act

Advisory Note: This guide addresses the legal principle that an accused's unambiguous admission of liability is sufficient grounds for conviction under Section 138 of the Negotiable Instruments Act, 1881, even in the face of a complainant's refusal to settle the matter. The following outlines the jurisprudential foundation and a structured action plan for judicial magistrates

The Jurisprudential Foundation

'The legal soundness of convicting an accused based on their own admission, independent of the complainant's stance on settlement, is firmly rooted in the principles of evidence and statutory presumption.

To be continued The Supreme Court of India has recently issued comprehensive guidelines to streamline the trial of cases under Section 138 of the Negotiable Instruments Act (NI Act). These guidelines are designed to assist magistrates in managing the massive backlog of cases and ensuring their expeditious disposal.

The Supreme Court, in the landmark case Sanjabij Tari v. Kishore S. Borcar & Anr. (2025 INSC 1158), issued a detailed set of guidelines to be implemented by all courts.

Guideline Area Key Directive Purpose / Implication

Service of Summons Use regular modes, dasti (service by complainant), & electronic means (email, WhatsApp); complainant provides accused contact details via affidavit. Overcome evasion, expedite service of summons, a major cause of delay.

Complaint Synopsis Mandatory standardized synopsis at top of every complaint with parties, cheque, dishonour, notice & cause of action details. Quick case assessment, ensure procedural compliance, identify specific defence.

Pre-cognizance Stage No summons to accused required before magistrate takes cognizance under S.223 BNSS. Streamline initiation, avoid unnecessary pre-cognizance steps.

Trial Procedure Use S.251 CrPC/S.274 BNSS questions; record reasons for converting summary trial to summons trial. Early admission/denial, preserve summary trial nature for speed.

Interim Compensation Use S.143A power to order interim compensation "as early as possible". Provide immediate relief to complainant, encourage early settlement.

Settlement & Compounding Set up online payment (QR/UPI); encourage settlement; modified compounding costs based on stage. Promote early resolution, reduce pendency; incentivize early payment.

Monitoring Dashboards for pendency in Delhi, Mumbai, Calcutta; High Court monitoring committees. Ensure accountability, continuous oversight for expeditious disposal.

Key Legal Principles for Magistrates

Beyond procedural directives, the Supreme Court has reiterated crucial legal principles that should guide your decision-making in NI Act cases:

- Strict Adherence to Presumptions: The Court in Sanjabij Tari strongly emphasized that magistrates must give effect to the rebuttable presumptions under Sections 118 and 139 of the NI Act. The initial burden is on the accused to rebut the presumption that the cheque was issued for a legally enforceable debt or liability. Treating these cases as civil recovery suits and asking the complainant to prove the debt from the outset is contrary to the legislative intent and prolongs trials.

- Liability in Partnership Firms: In Dhanasingh Prabhu v. Chandrasekar (2025 SCC OnLine SC 1419), the Court held that a complaint under Section 138 is maintainable even if only the partners of a partnership firm are arraigned as accused and the firm itself is not implicated. This is because a partnership firm lacks a separate legal identity from its partners, whose liability is joint and several. Notice to partners is deemed notice to the firm.
- Vicarious Liability for Company Directors: The Court has concurrently clarified the limits of vicarious liability under Section 141. In K.S. Mehta v. M/S Morgan Securities and Credits Pvt. Ltd. (2025 INSC 315), it was reiterated that non-executive and independent directors cannot be held liable unless specific allegations demonstrate their active role and involvement in the company's affairs at the time the offence was committed. Bald allegations without specifics are insufficient to fasten liability.

These guidelines and principles provide a robust framework for you to handle NI Act cases effectively. The overarching judicial focus is on expediting trials, upholding statutory presumptions, and encouraging settlement, while ensuring fairness and legal compliance.

TO BE C0TINUED IN NEXT VOIME PART 2 P

****

CHAPTER-04

AFFIDAVIT FOR VERIFICATION AND EXHIBITS IN SUPPORT OF A COMPLAINT

IN THE COURT OF THE JUDICIAL MAGISTRATE FIRST CLASS (JMFC)
AT________________

CASE NO. OF____ 2025

ABC versus XYZ

AFFIDAVIT OF COMPLAINANT FOR VERIFICATION IN SUPPORT OF COMPLAINT U/S 138/141 OF THE N.I. ACT

I, [Name of Complainant (C)], S/o. [Father's Name], aged about [Age] years, and
residing at [Full Address], do hereby solemnly affirm and declare as under:

1. I state that I am the original payee/holder of the dishonoured cheque bearing No. _, dated _, drawn on [Bank Name, Branch] for an amount of Rs. __ (in words), issued by the accused in discharge of a legally enforceable debt/liability.
2. I state that the said cheque was dishonoured as per the Bank Return Memo dated _ with the reason "_" (e.g., "Insufficient Funds").
3. I state that I issued a NOTICE dated __ to the accused within the statutory period, demanding payment of the cheque amount, which was duly served (as per Postal Receipt/Acknowledgement/Service Proof). The accused failed to make payment within 15 days of receiving the notice.
4. I state that I am in possession of all original documents, including:
1. Dishonoured cheque,
2. Bank return memo,
3. Copy of legal notice,

4. Proof of service (Postal receipt/Acknowledgement), Any other relevant documents.

I state that I have not filed any other similar complaint regarding this matter in any other court of law.

DEPONENT [NAME OF COMPLAINANT

VERIFICATION

I, the above-named deponent, do hereby solemnly affirm and declare that the contents of this affidavit are true and correct to the best of my knowledge and belief, and no part of it is false or misleading

Place: ________ Date: _____

Solemnly affirmed before me by the deponent on this day.

[COMPLAINANT'S SIGNAT

AFFIDAVIT OF EVIDENCE

Along With

The Tendering Of Exhibits

IN THE COURT OF THE JUDICIAL MAGISTRATE FIRST CLASS (JMFC) AT [CITY/DISTRICT]

CASE NO. ________OF 2025

In the Title of___________

AFFIDAVIT OF EVIDENCE OF COMPLAINANT (C) U/S 145 NI ACT

(Along with Tender of Original Exhibits)

I, [Name of Complainant (C)], S/o. [Father's Name], aged about [Age] years, residing
at [Full Address], do hereby solemnly affirm and declare as under:

1. INTRODUCTION

- I am the complainant in the present case and am fully conversant with the facts of the case.
- This affidavit is being filed in lieu of my examination in chief as permitted under Section 145 of the Negotiable Instruments Act, 1881.
- I am one of the parties to the transaction and the original documents, and fully aware with My claim set forth in the complaint supra, hence the exhibits are per se admissible in evidence.

2. FACTS OF THE CASE

- That the accused had issued a cheque bearing No. _ dated _ for a sum of Rs. __(in words) drawn on [Bank Name, Branch] in my favour towards discharge of a legally enforceable debt/liability. EXHIBIT /C

- That I presented the said cheque for encashment on _ through my RESPECTIVE BANK DETAILS DEPOSIT SLIP endorsed by the Bank is also annexed herewith as EXHIBIT /C

but the impugned cheque was dishonoured vide Bank Return Memo dated _ with the reason "Funds Insufficient" (or other relevant reason). EXHIBIT/C

- That I issued a statutory NOTICE EXHIBIT C/
- dated __under Section 138(b) of the NI Act, demanding payment within 15 days, THROUGH registered AD POST , postal recipt is annexed as EXHIBIT C/

The Notice which was duly served upon the accused as per Postal Receipt/Acknowledgement/Service Report EXHIBIT/C

- That despite receipt of the notice, the accused failed to make payment within the stipulated period, thereby committing an offence under Section 138 of the NI Act.

3. LIST OF EXHIBITS & LIST OF WITNESSES/ SEPARATELY BEING FILED.

I hereby tender the following original documents as exhibits, which are admissible under Section 145 NI Act since I am a party to them:

Exhibit No. Description Marked as

Exhibit1 Original Dishonoured Cheque Ex. C1 Exhibit2 Bank

Return Memo (Dishonour Memo) Ex. C2 Exhibit3 Copy of

NOTICE (U/S 138 NI Act) Ex. C3

Exhibit4 Postal Receipt/Acknowledgement/Service Proof Ex. C4

Exhibit5 any other relevant document (e.g., Loan Agreement, Invoice, etc.)

4. VERIFICATION & PRAYER

- I solemnly affirm that the contents of this affidavit are true and correct to the best of my knowledge and belief.

- I pray that this Hon'ble Court may:

Take the affidavit as my examination in chief, Admit the original exhibits in evidence, Proceed with the trial as per law.

DEPONENT

[NAME OF COMPLAINANT (C)]VERIFICATIOI, the above named deponent, do hereby solemnly affirm that the contents of this affidavit are true to my knowledge, and no part of it is false or misleading.

Place: _ Date: __

Solemnly affirmed before me by the deponent on this day.

[COMPLAINANT'S SIGNATURE]

JUDICIAL MAGISTRATE / OATH COMMISSIONER /NOTARY PUBLIC ATTESTATION

Key Legal Points:

- Section 145 NI Act allows evidence by affidavit, and the complainant need not appear in person unless summoned.
- Original documents (cheque, memo, notice, postal proof) are per se admissible as the complainant is a party to them.
- The affidavit serves as examination in chief, saving court time.
- Ensure exhibits are properly marked (Ex. C1, Ex. C2, etc.) for identification.

****

CHAPTER-05

ALTERNATIVE REMEDIES

FOR HOME BUYERS BEYOND SECTION 138 NI ACT

Home buyer has several powerful alternative remedies beyond the standard Section 138 NI Act prosecution to recover their money and hold the builder accountable .The builder issued a cheque as buyback consideration after cancelling the allotment, but the cheque was dishonoured), the aggrieved home buyer has several powerful alternative remedies beyond the standard Section
138 NI Act prosecution to recover their money and hold the builder accountable. These remedies can be pursued concurrently:

1. Consumer Protection Act, 2019 (Before Consumer Commission)

Cause of Action: Deficiency in service (failure to deliver flat) + Unfair trade practice (issuing a dishonoured cheque for a refund).

Reliefs Sought:

Refund of the entire amount paid (principal + interest).

Compensation for mental agony, harassment, and litigation costs.

Penalty for unfair trade practice.

Costs of proceedings.

Advantages:

Faster than civil courts (though delays exist). Designed for consumer

grievances against builders. No court fee or minimal fee.

Can claim significant compensation beyond the principal amount.

Jurisdiction: File in the District/State/National Commission based on the value of the claim (Refund amount + compensation).

2. Real Estate (Regulation & Development) Act, 2016 (RERA)

Complaint Cause of Action: Violation of RERA provisions:

Failure to deliver possession as per the agreement. Misleading promises (buyback guarantee).

Non refund of the amount as promised/ordered. Unfair trade practice.

Reliefs Sought:

Refund of the entire amount paid with mandatory interest (as prescribed by RERA, often higher than market rates).

Compensation for losses/damages suffered.

Penalties imposed by RERA Authority on the Builder (fines, revocation of registration).

Direction to the Builder to cease and desist from unfair practices.

Advantages:

Most Potent Remedy: RERA Authorities have strong powers (attach property/bank accounts, revoke registration, impose heavy fines).

Builder centric focus designed specifically to regulate developers.

Mandatory interest on refunds.

Generally faster than civil courts.

Jurisdiction: File with the RERA Authority of the State where the project is registered.

3. Civil Suit for Recovery of Money & Damages

Cause of Action: Breach of contract (Agreement to Sell + Buy Back Agreement) + Recovery of money had and received.

Reliefs Sought:

Decree for recovery of the principal amount paid.

Interest (pre suit, pendent lite, future can be claimed at a higher rate than standard.

Damages for breach of contract and fraud/misrepresentation.

Permanent injunction (if needed to prevent the builder from selling the disputed unit).

Advantages:

Can lead to attachment/sale of Builder's assets (including personal assets of promoters if proven liable).

Strong discovery process to uncover Builder's finances.

Can combine with a request for interim attachment of Builder's assets during the suit to secure the claim.

Disadvantages: Slower than other forums.

4. Insolvency & Bankruptcy Code, 2016 (NCLT) If Builder is a Company Cause of Action: Builder owes a debt (refund amount) which is undisputed (evidenced by bounced cheque, cancellation letter, demand notice) and has defaulted.

Relief Sought: Initiate Corporate Insolvency Resolution Process (CIRP) against the Builder company.

Advantages:

Nuclear Option: Forces the company into insolvency. Can lead to change of management or liquidation.

Moratorium on other actions against the Builder, focusing efforts through the Resolution Professional.

Potential recovery if the company has assets.

Disadvantages:

Threshold: Minimum debt of ₹1,000/ (easily met).

Requires clear evidence of debt and default (bounced cheque)

****

CHAPTER-06

AMENDMENTS IN NI ACT

Important Amendments in NI Act from the Inception

1. Amendment Act of 1988 (Key Introduction of Section 138)

Objective: To criminalize the dishonour of cheques due to insufficient funds.

Key Changes:

Introduced Section 138 (Dishonour of a cheque for insufficiency of funds).

Provided a legal remedy (penalty + compensation) to payees.

Specified conditions for filing a complaint (demand notice, 15-day grace period, and complaint within 30 days).

2. Amendment Act of 2002 (Enhanced Deterrence & Jurisdiction

   Clarity) Objective: To reduce delays and strengthen penalties.

Key Changes:

Inserted Section 142 (Territorial jurisdiction for filing complaints).

Amended Section 147 (Offences to be compoundable).

Increased punishment under Section 138 (up to 2 years imprisonment, fine up to twice the cheque amount).

3. Amendment Act of 2015 (Clarifying Jurisdiction & Speedy Resolution) Objective: To address conflicting judgments on jurisdiction.

Key Changes:

Section 142(2) introduced – Complaint can be filed where the payee's bank
is located (if the cheque was delivered for collection).

Section 142A – Allowed pending cases to be transferred to the proper jurisdiction.

4. Amendment Act of 2018 (Interim Compensation & Electronic Cheques)

Objective: To provide interim relief to payees and recognize digital transactions.

Key Changes:

Section 143A – Court may order interim compensation (up to 20% of the cheque amount) during trial.

Section 148 – Appellate court may order the deposit of 20-50% of the fine/compensation during appeal.

Inclusion of electronic cheques (e-cheques) under the NI Act.

Key Objectives of These Amendments:

- Deterrence against cheque bounce cases.
- Faster disposal of cases & reduced pendency.
- Clear jurisdiction rules to avoid forum shopping.
- Interim relief for payees during litigation.
- Adaptation to digital banking (e-cheques).

These amendments aim to boost trust in cheque transactions, reduce fraud, and ensure quicker justice for aggrieved parties.

This is a very specific and important question regarding Indian commercial law.

The Negotiable Instruments Act, 1881 (NI Act) has been amended several times. The most significant and recent amendments pertain to Sections 143 to 147, which deal with the procedural aspects of speeding up the trial of cheque dishonour cases (under Section 138).

The key amendment was introduced by The Negotiable Instruments (Amendment) Act, 2018. This act was passed to override a Supreme Court judgment and clarify the jurisdiction for filing cases.

AMENDMENT AND MISCELLANEOUS PROVISIONS

Here is a detailed arrangement of the major amendments to the NI Act, section by section, till date:

1. The Negotiable Instruments (Amendment and Miscellaneous Provisions) Act, 2002

This was a major overhaul that added substantive provisions to make the law more effective.

- Sections 138 to 142: These sections were introduced/amended to define the offence of dishonour of cheques and the procedure for it.
- Section 138: Defined the offence of dishonour of cheque for insufficiency of funds, etc.
- Section 139: Introduced a presumption that the cheque was issued for a debt or liability.
- Section 140: Provided that the defence of the drawer that he had no reason to believe the cheque would be dishonoured shall not be accepted.
- Section 141: Dealt with offences by companies.
- Section 142: Specified the procedure for taking cognizance of the offence.

2. The Negotiable Instruments (Amendment) Act, 2015

This amendment introduced significant procedural changes to expedite trials in cheque dishonour cases.

- Insertion of Sections 143 to 147: These new sections created a special procedure for trying cases under Section 138.
- Section 143: Allowed for trial of cases as a summary trial (faster process). It also provided for the compounding of offences (settlement between parties).
- Section 144: Mode of service of summons, including service by courier, email, and FAX.
- Section 145: Allowed evidence of the complainant to be given on affidavit, saving court time.
- Section 146: Provided that a bank's slip or memo stating the cheque was dishonoured is prima facie evidence of the fact of dishonour.
- Section 147: Made all offences under the NI Act compoundable (i.e., parties can settle the matter even after litigation has started).

3. The Negotiable Instruments (Amendment) Act, 2018

This was a crucial amendment enacted to clarify the issue of territorial jurisdiction for filing cases, which was creating confusion due to a Supreme Court ruling.

- Amendment to Section 142: A new subsection (2) was inserted.
- Objective: To nullify the effect of the Supreme Court's judgment in Dashrath Rupsingh Rathod vs. State of Maharashtra (2014), which held that a case under Section 138 can be filed only in a court within whose jurisdiction the drawer's bank is located.
- New Provision (Section 142(2)): It allows a complaint to be filed in a court within whose local jurisdiction:

a) The place where the payee or holder in due course presents the cheque for payment is situated, OR

b) The place where the drawer's bank is located, OR

c) The place where the payee's bank is located.

Insertion of Section 142A: This section was added to deal with pending cases. It allowed all cases pending in any court (except those where final judgment had been passed) to be transferred to a court having jurisdiction as per the new Section 142(2).

4. The Negotiable Instruments (Amendment) Act, 2023

This is a very recent amendment that focuses on addressing the issue of delayed payments in government contracts due to cheque dishonour.

- Insertion of a new CHAPTER NO. XVII (Sections 148 to 156): This CHAPTER NO. is specifically for "Instruments issued for the purpose of discharge of legally enforceable debt or liability under a contract with the Central Government or State Government." (Note: The specific section numbers might be provisional as the act is new, but the CHAPTER NO. is dedicated to this purpose).
- Key Feature: It provides a fast-track mechanism for resolving cases of cheque dishonour where the cheque was issued to the Central or State Government or its undertakings. The goal is to ensure timely recovery of dues for public projects.

Summary Table of Key Amendments

Amending Act (Year) Key Sections Amended/Added Primary Objective

2002 Amendment Introduced/Amended Sections 138 to 142 To formally create the offence of cheque dishonour and establish the basic legal framework for it.

2015 Amendment Inserted Sections 143, 144, 145, 146, 147 To expedite trials through summary procedures, affidavit evidence, and electronic summons.

2018 Amendment Amended Section 142; Inserted Section 142A To clarify and expand territorial jurisdiction for filing cases and transfer pending cases accordingly.

2023 Amendment Inserted a new CHAPTER NO. XVII (Sections 148-156) To provide a fast-track mechanism for cheque dishonour cases involving government contracts.

Conclusion:

The NI Act has been dynamically amended, with the most significant changes focused on Section 138 and its procedural aspects (Sections 143-147). The 2018 amendment to Section 142 is particularly critical for lawyers and businesses as it dictates where a case for cheque bounce can be legally filed.

Please verify above with the official Gazettes and sources

AMENDMENT IN COMPLAINT/s

Quasi Civil Nature:

Proceedings under Section 138 of the NI Act are considered quasi civil in nature, which has led courts to be more liberal in allowing amendments compared to other criminal cases.

When Amendments Are Allowed

Based on judicial precedents, amendments in Section 138 complaints are generally permitted in the following circumstances:

1. To Cure Curable Infirmities: Amendments can be made to

correct simple, formal defects or curable infirmities that do not prejudice the accused. For instance:

Correction of typo graphical errors in dates of cheque presentation/dishonour. Rectification of company names (e.g., from 'Modi Industries Limited' to 'Modi Distilleries').

Addition of necessary factual allegations regarding the vicarious liability of partners/directors.

2. Before Cognizance: Amendments are more readily allowed if sought before the Magistrate takes cognizance of the offence and issues process. LATEST JUDGEMENT OF SUPREME COURT QUA AMENDMENT ALLOWED EVEN

AFTER COGNIZANCE C L R VOLUME 5 (DIGITAL) Citation: Bansal Milk chilling Vs. Rana Milk Food 2025

3. No Change in Core Allegations: When the amendment does not alter the basic core, crux, or tenor of the original complaint.

4. No Prejudice to Accused: Where the amendment causes no prejudice to the accused or does not deprive them of any valid defense.

5. Formal Defects: Correction of technical or procedural defects that do not go to the root of the matter.

To be continued in PHASE II

****

CHAPTER-07

ARREST WARRANT

In the trial of cheque dishonour cases under Sections 138/141 of the Negotiable Instruments Act (NI Act), the provisions related to warrants (earlier Sections 7081 of CrPC) have now been replaced by Sections 7281 of the Bharatiya Nagarik Suraksha Sanhita (BNSS), 2023, which will replace the CrPC.

Key Changes & Importance in Cheque Dishonor Cases (138/141 NI Act)

1. Earlier (CrPC Sections 7081) dealt with:

- Issue of warrants (bailable/nonbailable).
- Execution of warrants (by police/authorities).
- Procedure for arrest and production before court.

2. Now (BNSS Sections 7281) refines the process with:

- Stricter timelines for execution of warrants.
- Digital tracking of warrants (ewarrants).
- Clarity on arrest procedures (especially for directors in S.141 NI Act cases).

Execution of Warrants in Cheque Dishonor Cases (S.138/141 NI Act)

1. When is a Warrant Issued?

- If the accused does not appear despite summons (S.62 BNSS).
- If the court believes the accused is evading trial.
- In S.141 NI Act cases (companies), warrants may be issued against directors if they ignore court orders.

2. Types of Warrants (S.72 BNSS)

- Bailable Warrant – Accused can secure release on bail bond.
- NonBailable Warrant (NBW) – Requires arrest & production before court.

3. How is a Warrant Executed? (S.7377 BNSS)

- Police must execute within 21 days (stricter timeline).
- EWarrants can be issued for faster tracking.
- Attachment of property (if accused absconds).

4. Special Considerations for S.141 NI Act (Company Directors)

- Personal appearance may be exempted if a lawyer represents them.
- NBWs should not be issued mechanically – Courts must check if directors were actually in charge.

Right Perspective for Execution in Cheque Cases

1. Avoid Unnecessary Arrests – Courts should first try summons & bailable warrants.
2. EWarrants for Efficiency – Reduces delays in serving warrants.
3. Protection for Genuine Directors – NBWs should not be issued without proof of their role in the offence.

Conclusion

The BNSS (S.7281) brings more clarity and efficiency in executing warrants, especially in S.138/141 NI Act cases. However, courts must ensure warrants are not misused against innocent directors or accused who are willing to comply.

Section 90 of the Bharatiya Nagarik Suraksha Sanhita (BNSS) (previously Section 87 CrPC) deals with the "Issue of warrant in lieu of or in addition to summons". This provision allows a court to bypass summons and directly issue a warrant in certain situations, especially when the accused is deliberately evading the legal process.

1. When is Section 90 BNSS Applicable in S.138 NI Act Cases?

A court may skip summons and issue a warrant directly under Section 90 BNSS in the following scenarios:

Situations Where Direct Warrant is Justified

1. Accused is Absconding or Evading Summons

- If the court has reason to believe that the accused is deliberately avoiding summons, it may issue a warrant directly.
- Example: If the accused changes address frequently or refuses to accept notices.

2. Previous Summons Were Ignored

- If the accused did not respond to earlier summons, the court may escalate to a warrant.

3. Risk of Accused Fleeing or Tampering with Evidence

- If the court believes the accused may destroy evidence or flee jurisdiction, a warrant can be issued.

4. Seriousness of the Offence (Repeat Offender in Cheque Bounce Cases)

- If the accused has a history of cheque dishonor cases, the court may take a stricter approach.

When Should Courts Avoid Direct Warrants?

- Firsttime offenders with no prior evasion.
- Minor procedural delays (e.g., postal delays in receiving summons).
- No evidence of deliberate avoidance by the accused.

2. Procedure Under Section 90 BNSS (vs. Old Section 87 CrPC)

Aspect Old CrPC (Section 87) New BNSS (Section 90)

When Applicable If summons likely to be ineffective Same, but with digital tracking options

Type of Warrant Bailable or nonbailable Now includes ewarrants for faster execution

Judicial Discretion Court must record reasons Same, but stricter timelines apply

3. Judicial Precedents & Key Considerations Courts Must Record

   Reasons (Mandatory)

- The court must justify in writing why it is bypassing summons (e.g., past evasion, flight risk).
- Example: Satish Kumar Jindal vs State of Punjab (2014) – Direct warrants should not be issued mechanically.

Directors in S.141 NI Act Cases

- For company directors, courts must first issue summons unless there is clear evidence of evasion.
- Example: K.K. Ahuja vs V.K. Bhargava (2009) – Directors cannot be mechanically arrested without proof of involvement.

Use of EWarrants (New in BNSS)

- Courts can now issue electronic warrants for faster execution.

4. Practical Implications in Cheque Bounce Cases

- Faster Justice: Reduces delays caused by prolonged summons procedures.
- Stronger Deterrence: Discourages habitual offenders from dodging court appearances.
- Protection Against Misuse: Courts must apply judicial discretion to prevent harassment.

Conclusion

Section 90 BNSS (old S.87 CrPC) is a powerful tool to ensure accused persons in S.138 NI Act cases do not evade trial. However, courts must use it judiciously, especially in S.141 cases involving company directors, to prevent misuse.

Would you like a sample court application for issuing a warrant under Section 90 BNSS?

ISSUE OF WARRANT

The issuance and cancellation of warrants in these cases are governed by the Code of Criminal Procedure (CrPC), 1973, as the NI Act does not provide a separate procedure.

The Short Answer

- Issuance of Warrant: The presence of the accused is NOT necessary. The court can issue a warrant ex parte (in the absence of the accused) if the conditions are met.

- Cancellation of Warrant: The accused can appear through their advocate to file an application for cancellation. However, for the actual hearing of the application or for surrender, the physical presence of the accused is almost always required by the court.

Detailed Breakdown

1. Issuance of Warrant (Under Sections 7081, CrPC)

A warrant is a written order issued by a magistrate to a police officer to arrest the accused and produce them before the court.

Grounds for Issuance in a 138/141 Case:

- Nonappearance: If the accused, who has been summoned to appear, willfully disobeys the summons and does not appear before the court.
- Absconding: If the court has reason to believe that the accused is absconding or is likely to abscond to avoid prosecution.
- Risk of Nonappearance: If the accused has previously avoided appearing, making the court believe that a summons or a mere bail bond will not secure their presence.

Is the Accused's Presence Necessary for Issuance? No. The court can issue a bailable or non bailable warrant in the absence of the accused if it is satisfied that the accused is evading the process of law. This is often done when the court's summons have not been complied with.

2. Cancellation of Warrant (Under Section 70(2), 437 CrPC)

A warrant can be cancelled or recalled by the court that issued it.

Grounds for Cancellation:

- The accused appears and is ready to cooperate with the trial.
- The accused provides a satisfactory reason for their previous nonappearance (e.g., genuine illness, lack of proper service of summons).
- The accused is willing to execute a personal bond and a surety bond to ensure their future attendance.
- The warrant was issued due to a mistake or oversight.

Is the Accused's Presence Necessary for Cancellation? This is a twostep process:

1. Filing the Application: The accused can (and should) initially engage an advocate to file a formal application for cancellation of the warrant. The advocate can argue the application, present reasons for the previous nonappearance, and assure the court of the accused's willingness to cooperate.

2. Surrender & Hearing: However, in the vast majority of cases, the court will insist on the physical presence of the accused for the following reasons:

- Surrender: The primary condition for cancelling a warrant is the surrender of the accused before the court.

- Custody: If it's a non bailable warrant, the police may have to execute it and produce the accused in custody. The application for bail (and thus cancellation of the warrant's effect) can only be made once the accused is in custody.
- Court's Discretion: The court needs to see the accused to record their undertaking to appear regularly and to assess their bona fides. It is a matter of the court's authority and dignity.

An advocate can argue the legal grounds, but the court typically will not cancel the warrant without the accused personally appearing and surrendering.

Procedural Flowchart: Warrant Issuance & Cancellation

A [Court Issues Summons to Accused] B{Did Accused Appear?};

B Yes C [Trial Proceeds];

B No D [Court may issue Bailable WarrantNBW for wilful disobedience]

D E {Accused seeks to cancel warrant?}

E Yes F;

Subgraph F [Process for Cancellation]

F1 [Accused engagesAdvocate] F2 [Advocate files Application statingreasons for nonappearance];

F2 F3 [Advocate urges court to cancelwarrant & offers surrender]; F3

G {Court's Decision};

G Requires Presence H [Court directs accusedto be physically present];

H I[Accused appears, surrenders,files bond]; I J [Court cancels

warrant& grants bail];

J C;

G Cancels on Advocate's Plea K[Rare: Court may cancel based onadvocate's undertaking for appearance];

K C;

E No L [Warrant remains activePolice may arrest]; Best Practices for

the Accused

1. Do Not Ignore Summons: The first summons is a chance to avoid a warrant. Appear through an advocate and seek bail.
2. If a Warrant is issued: Immediately engage a local advocate. The advocate can:

- Obtain a copy of the warrant order.
- File an application for cancellation stating genuine reasons.
- Request the court to list the application urgently.
- Assure the court of the accused's willingness to appear and comply.

3. Be Prepared to Appear: The accused must be prepared to be physically present in court on the date fixed for the hearing of the cancellation application. The advocate can often get an assurance

from the court that the accused will not be taken into custody if they appear on a specific date.

Summary Table

Action Can it be done through an Advocate? Is Accused's Physical Presence Necessary?

Issuance of Warrant N/A (Court acts on its own) No. The court can issue it in the accused's absence.

Filing for Cancellation Yes. The advocate must do this. No. for filing the application.

Hearing for Cancellation Advocate can argue the case. Yes, almost always. The court requires the accused to surrender and be physically present to cancel the warrant.

Surrender is a personal act.

BAILABLE WARRANT ?

The word Bailable or non- Bailable warrant is not mentioned in the text of the Criminal Procedure code. However, Section 71 comes into play when the court
endorses, while issuing a warrant, that such person shalexecute a Bond with sufficient Sureties for their attendance before the court at a specified time and thereafter until otherwise directed by the court. The officer to whom the warrant is directed shall take such security and release
From custody. The endorsement is defined in section 70(2).
1. NON-BAILABLE WARRANT (NBW) means where

No sort of endorsement as discussed above is directed. Usually, NBW is issued only after the accused/person fails to comply or appear through summons and bail-able warrant, which is an alternative step in arresting a person and confining their liberty by issuing NBW from the Court of Law. Now the practical issue is how to tackle/escape once the fact of issuance of arrest warrant is acknowledged by the accused person or their family/friends and well-wisher, including an advocate. Now the question is, what should a common man do when their bailable warrants are received at their place through the police.

Read or ask the police officer concerned to make you aware of the endorsement of the court. If the person executes a bond with sufficient sureties for their attendance before the court at a specified time, the court may direct the police to take such sureties and Release the person from custody. Whether physical presence of accused is mandatory to cancel / Recall NBW? If a written application is submitted on the person's behalf by an authorized advocate for the cancellation of a warrant, logic and the liberty of law

dictate that the person/accused may have a strong presumption and reasonable apprehension in their mind that they may be arrested or taken into custody if they appeared before the court. A self-speaking and supported judgment has been passed by the Bombay High Court (Please refer to page 265 of CLR Volume 2 for the most important cases/citations). Disclaimer: The article above is for the limited purpose of

sharing knowledge without dictum on the subject in question. The author shall not be answerable if any part of the article is contrary to the law, repelled, rescinded, modified, overruled, or beyond the scope, object, and thrust of the law applicable actually, or even if it is misconstrued by the author. Complete missing of mens-rea on the part of the author shall be strongly presumed. Therefore, readers are advised to reaffirm
With any prudent lawyer or judicial authority before applying it in any way or manner.

1. EVERY WARRANT OF ARREST

Shall be signed in writing, signed by the Magistrate / Presiding officer of the concerned Court, and shall bear the seal of the Court. WARRANTS ARE NORMALLY DIRECTED TO POLICE OFFICERS,

however, the court may direct any person to make an arrest if the person is an escaped convict, proclaimed offender, or a person who is liable for a non-bailable offense and is

evading arrest.

A Warrant of Arrest may be executed at any place in India. And every warrant remains in force until it is cancelled, recalled, or stayed by the Court which issued it or until it is executed.

Any accused/person so arrested shall be produced before the court within 24 hours, excluding the time necessary for the journey.
Note: This Article to be continued in next VOLUME

****

CHAPTER-08

BNSS versus CR.P.C Key Differences

As per Old Cr. P.C (S.82/85) New BNSS (S.84/88)

Time for Appearance 30 days (from proclamation) 30 days (same)

Attachment Process Manual execution Digital tracking possible

Restoration of Property Same procedure more streamlined

5. Judicial Trends & Important Case Laws

1. K.K. Ahuja v/s. V.K. Bhargava (2009) – Proclamation against directors MCHAPTER NO. ust be based on evidence of their involvement.
2. Indian Bank Association vs Union of India (2014) – Courts should avoid mechanical issuance of warrants/proclamations in S.138 cases.
3. SC in Rajesh Kumar vs State (2021) Proclamation should be a last resort after warrants fail

Conclusion

Proclamation (BNSS S.84) & Attachment (BNSS S.85) are last resort measures to ensure accused appear in S.138/141 cases. Courts must not issue them mechanically—proper steps (summons → warrants → proclamation) must be followed.

· For company directors (S.141), courts must check their actual liability before 2ordering attachment.

Proclamation & Attachment in Cheque Dishonor Cases (S.138/141

NI Act) (Old CrPC: Sections 8285 New BNSS: Sections 8488)

In cases under Sections 138 (cheque bounce) & 141 (liability of directors) of the Negotiable Instruments Act, if the accused absconds or avoids court appearances, the court may resort to proclamation (public notice) and attachment of property under BNSS Sections

8488 (previously CrPC 8285).

Section 223 (BNSS) – Corresponds to Section 190 CrPC (Cognizance by Magistrate).

Section 230 (BNSS) – Examination of the complainant (similar to Section 200 CrPC).

Section 231 (BNSS) – Inquiry before summons (similar to Section 202 CrPC but mandates preliminary inquiry in cheque bo

unce cases to prevent frivolous cases).

Key Change:

BNSS mandates a preliminary inquiry before issuing summons in cheque dishonour cases to curb misuse.

2. Summary Trial Procedure CrPC (Old Provision)

Section 143 NI Act states that cases under Section 138 NI Act shall be tried summarily as per CHAPTER NO. XXI (Sections 260/265 CrPC).

Section 262 CrPC – Procedure for summary trials (no lengthy evidence required).

Section 264 CrPC – Judgment in a summary trial. BNSS (New

Provision)

Sections 281/286 (BNSS) – Correspond to summary trial provisions.

Section 283 (BNSS) – Procedure for summary trials (similar to Section 262 CrPC).

Section 285 (BNSS) – Judgment in a summary trial (similar to Section 264 CrPC)

No Major Change, But BNSS Streamlines The Process For Faster Disposal.

3. Compounding of Offence (Settlement) CrPC (Old Provision)

Section 147 NI Act – An offence under Section 138 NI Act is compoundable.

Section 320 CrPC – Governs the compounding of offences

(with court permission).

BNSS (New Provision)

Section 358 (BNSS) – Corresponds to Section 320 CrPC (compounding provisions remain similar).

Section 147 NI Act remains unchanged (compounding allowed). Key

Change:

No significant change; compounding remains permissible with court approval.

4. Power to Order Interim Compensation

1. When is Section 90 BNSS Applicable in S.138 NI Act Cases?

A court may skip summons and issue a warrant directly under Section 90 BNSS in the following scenarios:

Situations Where Direct Warrant is Justified

1. Accused is Absconding or Evading Summons

- If the court has reason to believe that the accused is deliberately avoiding summons, it may issue a warrant directly.
- Example: If the accused changes address frequently or refuses to accept notices.

2. Previous Summons Were Ignored

- If the accused did not respond to earlier summons, the court may escalate to a warrant.

3. Risk of Accused Fleeing or Tampering with Evidence

- If the court believes the accused may destroy evidence or flee jurisdiction, a warrant can be issued.

4. Seriousness of the Offence (Repeat Offender in Cheque Bounce Cases)

- If the accused has a history of cheque dishonour cases, the court may take a stricter approach.

****

CHAPTER-09

CHEQUE RETURN MEMO

When a cheque is presented for clearance but cannot be honoured due to insufficient funds, stop payment, or other defects, the collecting bank follows a strict, time bound process before issuing a Return Memo (also called a Cheque Return Memo).

Here are the key steps:

1. Receipt & Verification the cheque is received via clearing (e.g., physical/electronic clearing house, image based systems like CTS in India). Initial checks are conducted on: MICR code validity, bank/branch details, and formal completeness (date, signature, etc.).

2. Presentment to Paying Bank (Drawee Bank) The collecting bank forwards the cheque to the drawee bank (where the issuer's account is held) through clearing settlement cycles (e.g., T+0 or T+1).

3. Drawee Bank's Internal Checks Upon receipt, the drawee bank verifies: Funds Sufficiency: Checks account balance/overdraft limit. Stop Payment Instructions: Confirms if the issuer requested nonpayment. Account Status: Ensures the account is active, not frozen/closed. Cheque Validity: Examines for alterations, stale date (>3 months), mismatch of signature, or postdated status. Legal Barriers: Verifies absence of court orders/garnishee orders blocking payment.

4. Decision to Return Unpaid If any defect is found (e.g., insufficient funds, stop payment), the drawee bank: Flags the Cheque: Marks it for return in the clearing system. Assigns a Reason Code: Uses standardized codes (e.g., "Insufficient Funds" Code 101 under RBI India; "Stop Payment" = Code 108). Records the Decision: Logs details internally for audit trails.

5. Generating the Return Memo The drawee bank creates a Return Memo containing: Cheque details (number, amount, date). Account number of the issuer. Precise reason for return (with regulatory code). Timestamp of return decision. Deadline: Must be issued before the clearing cycle's return window (e.g., by 2 PM on T+1 day in India).

6. Notification & Settlement To Clearing House: Submits the Return Memo electronically via the clearing system (e.g., NACH/ECS in India). To Collecting Bank: Automatically notifies the presenting bank and reverses the provisional credit (if any). To Issuer: Sends an intimation to the account holder (optional but common). To Depositor: The collecting bank informs the depositor (cheque presenter) and may levy a penalty fee.

7. Physical Cheque Handling (if applicable) In non CTS systems: The physical cheque is returned to the presenting bank with the Return Memo. In image based systems (CTS): Only the electronic memo is sent. Key Regulatory Requirements Timeliness: Return must occur within 24–48 hours of presentation (varies by country). Accuracy: Incorrect returns attract penalties (e.g., ₹1,000 per wrongful return in India under RBI guidelines). Transparency: Reason codes must be specific to guide the depositor. Common Return Reason Codes | Code | Reason | ||| | 101 | Insufficient Funds | | 108 | Stop Payment by Drawer | | 116 | Account Closed | | 132 | Stale Cheque (>3 months) | | 133 | Post-dated Cheque | Outcome: The depositor's account is debited (if provisionally credited), and the cheque is returned unpaid. The issuer may face penalties from their bank, and repeated returns can impact their banking credibility. This process ensures accountability, speed, and regulatory compliance in cheque clearing ecosystems globally.

When a cheque is presented for clearance but cannot be honoured due to insufficient funds, stop payment, or other defects, the collecting bank follows a strict, time-bound process before issuing a Return Memo (also called a Cheque Return Memo).

Here are the key steps:

1. Receipt & Verification The cheque is received via clearing (e.g., physical/electronic clearing house, image-based systems like CTS in India). Initial checks are conducted on: MICR code

validity, bank/branch details, and formal completeness (date, signature, etc.).

2. Presentment to Paying Bank (Drawee Bank) The collecting bank forwards the cheque to the drawee bank (where the issuer's account is held) through clearing settlement cycles (e.g., T+0 or T+1).

3. Drawee Bank's Internal Checks Upon receipt, the drawee bank verifies: Funds Sufficiency: Checks account balance/overdraft limit. Stop Payment Instructions: Confirms if the issuer requested nonpayment. Account Status: Ensures the account is active, not frozen/closed. Cheque Validity: Examines for alterations, stale date (>3 months), mismatch of signature, or postdated status. Legal Barriers: Verifies absence of court orders/garnishee orders blocking payment.

4. Decision to Return Unpaid If any defect is found (e.g., insufficient funds, stop payment), the drawee bank: Flags the Cheque: Marks it for return in the clearing system. Assigns a Reason Code: Uses standardized codes (e.g., "Insufficient Funds" Code 101 under RBI India; "Stop Payment" = Code 108). Records the Decision: Logs details internally for audit trails.

5. Generating the Return Memo The drawee bank creates a Return Memo containing: Cheque details (number, amount, date). Account number of the issuer. Precise reason for return (with regulatory code). Timestamp of return decision. Deadline: Must be issued before the clearing cycle's return window (e.g., by 2 PM on T+1 day in India).

6. Notification & Settlement To Clearing House: Submits the Return Memo electronically via the clearing system (e.g., NACH/ECS in India). To Collecting Bank: Automatically notifies the presenting bank and reverses the provisional credit (if any). To Issuer: Sends an intimation to the account holder (optional but common). To Depositor: The collecting bank informs the depositor (cheque presenter) and may levy a penalty fee.

7. Physical Cheque Handling (if applicable) In non-CTS systems: The physical cheque is returned to the presenting bank with the Return Memo. In image-based systems (CTS): Only the electronic memo is sent. Key Regulatory Requirements

Timeliness: Return must occur within 24–48 hours of presentation (varies by country). Accuracy: Incorrect returns attract penalties (e.g., ₹1,000 per wrongful return in India under RBI guidelines). Transparency: Reason codes must be specific to guide the depositor. Common Return Reason Codes | Code | Reason | ||| | 101 | Insufficient Funds | | 108 | Stop Payment by Drawer | | 116 | Account Closed | | 132 | Stale Cheque (>3 months) | | 133 | Postdated Cheque | Outcome: The depositor's account is debited (if provisionally credited), and the cheque is returned unpaid. The issuer may face penalties from their bank, and repeated returns can impact their banking credibility. This process ensures accountability, speed, and regulatory compliance in cheque clearing ecosystems globally.

****

CHAPTER-10

CONVICTION AND SENTENCE

In cases where an accused is convicted in multiple cheque bounce cases (Section 138 of the Negotiable Instruments Act, 1881) filed by the same complainant, the general rule is that each dishonoured cheque constitutes a separate offence under Section 138 of the NI Act. Now the question arises: will a separate conviction run concurrently or consecutively? Several legal principles and procedural considerations come into play.

Below is a structured analysis:

1. Legal Position on Multiple Convictions General Rule: Each dishonoured cheque constitutes a separate offence under Section 138 NI Act. If the accused is convicted in multiple cases filed by the same complainant, separate sentences can be imposed for each conviction. Exception (Single Transaction Rule): If multiple cheques were issued as part of the same transaction (e.g., for repayment of a single loan), courts may consider it a single offence to avoid double punishment. Courts may order concurrent sentences (sentences run simultaneously) instead of consecutive ones.

2. Sentencing Guidelines (Section 138 NI Act) Punishment: Imprisonment: Up to 2 years. Fine: Up to twice the cheque amount. Multiple Convictions: If convicted in more than one case, the court may:

1. Impose separate sentences for each conviction (usually consecutive if cheques were for different liabilities).

2. Order concurrent sentences if cheques were part of the same transaction.

3. Key Judicial Precedents Single Transaction Test: K. Bhagya Lakshmi v. K.

N. Sunanda (2020): If multiple cheques were issued for one debt, courts may treat it as a single offence. R. Vijayan v. Baby (2012): If cheques represent separate transactions, separate convictions are valid. Concurrent vs. Consecutive Sentences: Sunil Kumar v. State of Haryana (2019): Courts have the discretion to order concurrent sentences to prevent excessive punishment.

4. Practical Considerations for Complainant Consolidation of Cases: If multiple cases arise from the same transaction, the complainant can request the court to club the cases for a joint trial. Recovery of Money: Even if the accused is convicted in multiple cases, the complainant must separately execute the sentence/compensation in each case.

5. For the Accused (Defense Strategies) Argue Single Liability: If cheques were issued for one debt, seek quashing of multiple complaints under Section 482 CrPC. Plea for Concurrent Sentences: Request the court to run sentences concurrently to reduce jail time. 6. Important Legal Provisions Section 138 NI Act (Cheque dishonour offence). Section 427 CrPC (Concurrent sentences). Section 482 CrPC (Quashing of complaints if abuse of process). Conclusion: If the accused is convicted in multiple cheque bounce cases by the same complainant, the court will assess whether the cheques were for separate transactions or a single liability. Separate transactions → Separate punishments (may be consecutive). Same transaction → Concurrent sentences likely.

SUPREME COURT ??

REVERSING CONCURRENT ACQUITTALS (TRIAL COURT + HIGH COURT)

by way of reversal by Supreme Court Here are the key Supreme Court judgments reversing concurrent acquittals (Trial Court + High Court) in cases under Sections 138/141 of the Negotiable Instruments Act, along with the legal principles applied: I. Landmark Judgments Reversing Acquittals

1. Dashrath Rupsingh Rathod v. State of Maharashtra (2014) 9 SCC 129 Issue: Acquittal based on wrong territorial jurisdiction (complaint filed at the drawer's bank instead of the payee's bank). SC Holding: Acquittal reversed; case remanded for trial at the correct jurisdictional court (payee's bank location). Legal

Principle: Jurisdictional defect is curable; it does not warrant acquittal if the offence is otherwise made out.

2. Kalamani Tex v. P. Balasubramanian (2021) 5 SCC 283 Issue: Acquittal despite cheque dishonour proof; lower courts held debt was "timebarred." SC Holding: Reversed acquittal; held that statutory presumption under Section 139 applies even for timebarred debts unless the accused rebuts it. Legal Principle: Presumption of liability exists irrespective of debt limitation; the burden to rebut lies on the accused.

3. Bir Singh v. Mukesh Kumar (2019) 4 SCC 197 Issue: Acquittal due to unsigned return memo. SC Holding: Defective memo not fatal; complainant allowed to cure defect via bank witness testimony. Legal Principle: Technical defects are curable under Section 146 NI Act; acquittal reversed for "hyper technical" approach.

4. Rajesh Jain v. Ajay Singh (2020) 16 SCC 581 Issue: Acquittal based on alleged "security cheque" defence without evidence. SC Holding: Accused failed to rebut Section 139 presumption; concurrent acquittals reversed. Legal Principle: Bare assertion of "security cheque" is insufficient without proof of no enforceable debt. II. Grounds for Reversing Concurrent Acquittals The Supreme Court intervenes where lower courts commit grave legal errors, such as:

1. Ignoring Statutory Presumptions: Failing to apply Sections 118(a) & 139 NI Act (presumption of consideration & liability).

2. Misapplying Jurisdiction: Acquitting due to jurisdictional defects instead of transferring the case (Dashrath Rupsingh).

3. Technical Defects Over Substance: Dismissing cases for curable irregularities (e.g., memo defects, notice particulars) (Bir Singh).

4. Shifting Burden Incorrectly: Requiring the complainant to disprove the accused's defence instead of placing the burden on the accused to rebut the presumption (Kalamani Tex).

III. Conditions for SC Intervention (CrPC Section 378) The Supreme Court reverses acquittals only if: The trial court & High Court's findings are "perverse" or legally untenable. There is a miscarriage of justice due to ignoring material evidence. Lower courts violated mandatory statutory provisions (e.g., Sections 138–142 NI Act). IV.

Recent Trends (Post2020) Strict Scrutiny of Acquittals: SC actively reverses acquittals where: Accused raises false defences (e.g., forged signatures without expert evidence). Lower courts ignored digital trails (bank statements, email correspondence). Directors' Liability: Acquittals of directors u/s 141 reversed if their role in the transaction is evident (P. J. Agro Tech Ltd. v. Water Base Ltd., 2023). Key Takeaways | Scenario | SC Action | ||| | Acquittal due to technical defects | Reversed; defects held curable | | Ignoring Section 139 presumption | Acquittal set aside; accused convicted | | Wrong jurisdictional reasoning | Case remanded to competent court.

****

CHAPTER-11

CROSS EXAMINATION

In a Negotiable Instruments (NI) Act, Section 138 case (cheque bounce case), when the accused (defendant) is deposing as a witness in his own defense, the complainant's advocate has the right to cross examine him. The scope of cross examination must be relevant to the issues in dispute. Relevant Areas for Cross Examination:

1. Defense Claims: If the accused claims the cheque was lost, stolen, or forged, he can be questioned on: When and how the cheque went missing. Whether an FIR was filed. Why he did not issue a stop payment instruction to the bank.

2. Financial Liability: If he denies liability, he can be asked: Why he issued the cheque if no debt existed. Whether he had sufficient funds in the account. Any previous transactions with the complainant.

3. Signature & Cheque Details: If he disputes the cheque's authenticity: Whether the
signature is his. Whether the account number and details belong to him.

4. Legal Notice Reply: If he did not reply to the legal notice under Section 138(b) NI Act, he can be questioned on: Why no reply was sent. Whether he received the notice.

5. Contradictions in Evidence: Any inconsistencies between his deposition in court and earlier statements (e.g., reply to legal notice, police complaint, etc.). What is NOT Relevant? Questions about unrelated transactions. Personal attacks or questions beyond the cheque bounce dispute. Key Legal Points: Section 145 NI Act allows the accused to give evidence (sworn statement). Section 138 presumption (that the cheque was for a debt) shifts the burden to the accused to rebut.

Cross examination must be confined to the accused's defense.

Cross to defense witness who is Proprietor, Developer.

Cross examination of DW1 (Builder/Developer) in a NI Act 138 case (By Complainant's advocate to discredit testimony & establish liability)

1. Introduction & Background Verification

Q: "You are the signatory of the cheque in question, correct?" (Confirm his role in issuing the cheque.)

Q: "This cheque was issued after the cancellation of the complainant's booking in your project, isn't it?"

(Establish the context of the transaction.)

2. Nature of the Cheque & Liability

Q: "Was this cheque issued as a refund or settlement for the cancelled booking?" (If he says yes, proceed to question intent.)

Q: "Then why was it dishonored? Was there insufficient funds in the account?" (Key for S. 138 – establishes default.)

Q: "Did you inform the complainant before issuing the cheque that it may bounce?" (Shows negligence/mala fide intent.)

3. Terms of Cancellation & Cheque Issuance

Q: "Was there any written agreement for the buyback at the time of cancellation?" (If no, question legitimacy; if yes, demand production.)

Q: "Does this agreement mention that payment would be made via cheque?" (If not, suggests justification.)

Q: "Were there any conditions attached to this cheque's encashment?"

(If yes, challenge why they weren't disclosed earlier.)

4. Financial Capacity & Intent

Q: "On the date of issuance, did you have sufficient funds to honor this cheque?" (If no, establishes culpability under S. 138.)

Q: "Have you issued similar cheques to other customers whose bookings were cancelled?"

(Pattern of behaviour – possible fraud.)

Q: "Did you ever attempt to settle this payment via RTGS/DD after the cheque bounced?"

(Shows wilful default if no effort was made.)

5. Contradictions in Testimony

Q: "In your affidavit, you stated [X], but today you say [Y]. Why this discrepancy?" (Highlights inconsistencies.)

Q: "You signed the cancellation agreement, but now claim the complainant breached terms. Why no mention earlier?"

(Exposes afterthoughts.)

6. Conclusion – Establishing Dishonest Intent

Q: "So you admit that: (1) You issued the cheque, (2) It bounced, (3) You took no steps to rectify it?"

(Summarizes liability under S. 138 NI Act.)

Key Objectives:

1. Prove cheque was for a legally enforceable debt (refund = liability).
2. Establish knowledge of insufficient funds (mens rea for S. 138).
3. Contradict DW1's testimony to weaken credibility.
4. Show no bona fide defense – cheque was not a 'gift' but a

discharge of liability.

Cross Examination of an Advocate by an Advocate for the Accused Side. In a Section 138 (NI Act) case where the complainant, PW1, is an advocate to whom a fee cheque was issued that was dishonored, the cross examination strategy should focus on discrediting his credibility, establishing possible ulterior motives, and challenging the validity of the complaint. Below is a structured cross-examination approach: Read 'The Practical Guide' NI Act.

Accused oriented cross examination strategy to dismantle the unpaid memo's credibility under Section 138 NI Act: 7 Deadly Questions for the Bank Manager (Accused Side)

1. Authentication Failure: "You admit this memo has no stamp, seal, or signature. Correct? Does RBI Circular DPSS.CO.CHD.No.1832/201819 not mandate authenticated return memos?" → Exposes violation of banking standards.
2. Evidence Tampering: "Without unique identifiers (URN), how can you rule out that this
memo was generated after the cheque return?" → Suggests fabrication.
3. Custody Chain Attack: "Prove the custody log showing who handled this memo from creation until court. If missing, could anyone have tampered with it?" → Highlights BSA 2023 Section 58 gaps (secondary evidence integrity).
4. System Integrity Doubt: "Where is the BSA Section 63(4) certificate for the software that generated this memo? Without it, isn't this 'article' legally worthless?" → Exploits inadmissibility.
5. Contradiction Trap: "In [Case XYZ], your bank insisted stamped memos are compulsory. Why is this exception being made only against my client?" → Alleges bias.
6. Procedural Void: "Show me the bank's internal policy approving unstamped memos. If none exists, isn't this memo ultra vires?" → Challenges authority.
7. Nuclear Option: "Given the missing seal, signature, URN, and custody logs—isn't the

truth that this memo was created only for this case?" → Forces denial or perjury risk.

Tactical Goals: Destroy evidentiary value: Prove the memo violates RBI norms + BSA rules. Invoke adverse inference: Argue the court should presume fabrication under BSA Section 167. Seek dismissal: File Application U/s 311 CrPC to discard the 'article' as inadmissible. Pro Tip: Follow with an affidavit demand—forcing the manager to commit answers on oath locks contradictions for appeal. "No stamp, no signature, no URN, no certificate = no case." Use these questions to convert procedural flaws into reasonable doubt.

FAQS Q NO. 80/81

Question No.80

Is the Court duty bound to allow cross-examination of witnesses whose examination in chief has already been recorded?

Answer:

Yes, because without allowing cross-examination of the witness, the chief examination cannot be read in evidence.

(Reference: Delhi High Court :

Venu Madhava K. Vs State (NCT of Delhi): 01-12-2017)

Question

Accused if despite several opportunities not cross the complainant effect?

Answer:

Conviction of Accused by Trial Court endorsed up to High Court. (Reference:. Karnataka High Court : Smt Deeparani Vs Rupesh Kumar : 01-02-2017)

VOLUNTARY DEPOSITIONS BY WITNESSES DURING CROSS-EXAMINATION

The voluntary deposition by a witness during cross-examination that the impugned cheques in a Section 138 Negotiable Instruments (NI) Act case were 'replaced ones' carries significant legal implications. Below is a structured analysis of the procedural, evidentiary, and strategic consequences:

1. Legal Presumptions and Burden of Proof Presumption under Section 139 NI Act: The law presumes that a cheque is issued for a legally enforceable debt unless disproved. If a witness (e.g., the accused or their associate) testifies that the cheques were 'replaced,' it attempts to rebut this presumption by arguing that the cheques were not issued for the debt claimed. Evidential Burden on Accused: The accused must prove via preponderance of probabilities that: The original debt was settled or altered, making the replaced cheques invalid. The replaced cheques were issued as security (not for immediate liability) and were presented prematurely. Failure to discharge this burden strengthens the presumption under Section 139.

2. Procedural Implications Admissibility of Testimony: Courts scrutinize such depositions for: Credibility: Whether the witness is independent or affiliated with the accused. Corroboration: If the claim lacks supporting evidence (e.g., bank records, communication), it may be dismissed. Timeliness: Raising this claim late (e.g., during cross examination) without prior disclosure may be viewed as an afterthought, inviting adverse inferences.

3. Impact on Case Outcome If the Testimony Is Accepted: The complaint may be quashed if the court concludes the cheques were not linked to a live debt. Example: In Dashrathbhai Trikambhai Patel v. Hitesh Mahendrabhai Patel, part repayment invalidated the cheque's enforceability. If Rejected: The presumption under Section 139 prevails, potentially leading to conviction. The accused may face penalties (up to 2 years imprisonment or twice the cheque amount).

4. Strategic Considerations for Parties For the Accused: Must file an application under Section 145(2) NI Act to summon witnesses supporting the 'replacement' claim. Provide documentary proof (e.g., settlement agreements, bank entries) to substantiate testimony. For the Complainant.

****

CHAPTER-12

DISMISSAL OF COMPLAINT

Dismissal at the Verification Stage

& DURING TRIAL

Reasons for Dismissal at the Verification Stage? Answer:

A case is typically dismissed at the verification stage for the following reasons:

1Non-Compliance with Mandatory Legal Conditions (The Most Common Cause)

☛Territorial Jurisdiction:

This is the primary reason following the Dashrath Rathod judgment.

The complaint must be filed only in a court within whose local jurisdiction the bank of the payee (the person who received the cheque) is located. If the complainant files it in a court where the drawer's bank is located or where they reside, but the payee's bank is elsewhere, the case will be dismissed for lack of jurisdiction.

The Rule: The cause of action arises only at the place where the payee's bank is situated, as that is where the cheque is presented for collection and where the dishonor occurs.

☛Failure to Send a Valid Demand Notice:

The complainant must have sent a legal demand notice to the drawer (the person who issued the cheque) within 30 days of receiving the dishonor memo from the bank.

☛Notice Sent Beyond 30 Days:

If the notice is sent after the 30-day window, the case is not maintainable.

☛Incorrect Address:

The notice must be sent to the correct address of the drawer as known to the complainant or as per the bank records.

☛If sent to the wrong address and it is returned, the court may deem the notice not served properly.

Insufficient Time for Compliance:

☛The notice must give the drawer 15 clear days from the date of its receipt to make the payment.

☛ If the complaint is filed before the expiry of this 15-day period, it is premature and will be dismissed.

☛Filing the Complaint Beyond the Limitation Period:

The complaint must be filed within thirty days from the date of expiry of the 15-day notice period. If there is even a day's delay, the magistrate has no power to take cognizance, and the case will be dismissed as time-barred.

☛The court can condone the delay only if a formal application is made and sufficient cause is shown, but this is not automatic.

2 Insufficient or Defective Evidence/Documents

The magistrate verifies the documents presented to see if they make out a prima facie case.

Missing Essential Documents: The complaint must be accompanied by:

- The original dishonoured cheque.
- The Deposit Slip
- The original dishonour memo (return memo) from the bank.
- Proof of sending the legal demand notice (postal receipts, tracking details).
- An affidavit of the complainant stating the facts.

If any of these are missing, the court may dismiss the complaint for being incomplete.

☛Defects in the Affidavit:

The affidavit must be sworn properly and must contain all the necessary facts constituting the offense.

Vague or incomplete affidavits can lead to dismissal.

☛No Cause of Action Disclosed:

If the documents, even if taken at face value, do not disclose the essential ingredients of the offense under Section 138 (e.g., the cheque was not drawn for a legally enforceable debt or liability), the magistrate will dismiss the case.

3 Lack of Prima Facie Case

The magistrate is not conducting a trial but is simply checking if the allegations, if presumed to be true, would constitute an offense.

Admission of Debt in Notice Not Denied:

While less common at the verification stage, if the demand notice was received but the accused did not reply at all, it can sometimes be used to strengthen the prima facie case. Conversely, a strong rebuttal in the reply might be considered, but usually, the merits are decided after summoning the accused.

DISMISSAL OF COMPLAINT (SECTION 138 NI ACT)

- GROUNDS FOR DISMISSAL OF COMPLAINT (SECTION 138 NI

ACT) Pre-Trial Scrutiny by Court C1[Jurisdictional Defects?] C2[Notice Defects?] C3[Limitation Lapse?] C4[Improper Accused?] C5[Documentary Deficiencies?] C6[Default by Complainant?] Jurisdictional Defects C1 |Yes| [Territorial/Pecuniary Jurisdiction Lacking] [Dismissed u/s 201 CrPC/Section 142(2) NI Act] Notice Defects C2 |Yes| [Notice Late/Incomplete/Non-Compliant] Limitation C3 |Yes| [Filed Beyond 30 Days from Notice Expiry] Accused Implementation C4 |Yes| [Company/Directors Not Properly

Named] Documents C5 |Yes| [No Bank Memo/Original Cheque/Postal Proof] Default by Complainant C6 |Yes| [Non-Appearance u/s 256 CrPC/No Process Fees] [Remedy: Revision Petition u/s 397 CrPC or Fresh Complaint] [Trial on Merits]

- Key Explanations
- 1. Jurisdictional Defects Dismissed if filed in the wrong court (territorial/pecuniary limits).
- 2. Notice Defects Invalid if sent via courier, late (30 days), or lacks 15-day payment demand.
- 3. Limitation Lapse Complaint must be filed within 30 days after the 15-day notice period expires.
- 4. Improper Accused It is mandatory to implead the company and responsible directors (Section 141).
- 5. Documentary Deficiencies Must file: Original cheque/bank memo. Postal receipts and tracking proof of notice.
- 6. Default by Complainant Dismissed under Section 256 CrPC for nonappearance/non-prosecution. Remedies Against Dismissal Revision Petition: File under Section 397 CrPC before the Sessions Court. Fresh Complaint: If defect is curable (e.g., proper notice sent later).

PROCEEDURAL DISMISSAL BEFORE DECISION

"Want of Prosecution" mean?

- It simply means the complainant's lack of action, negligence, or failure to pursue the case with due diligence. When a complainant is absent or unprepared on multiple hearings, the court can infer that they have lost interest in prosecuting the case.
- Grounds for Dismissal for Want of Prosecution
- A court may dismiss a complaint under Section 138/141 NI Act for the following reasons:
- 1. Non Appearance of the Complainant: This is the most common ground.
- If the complainant (or their counsel) is absent on a hearing date when their presence is necessary (e.g., for recording evidence), the court may dismiss the case.
- The Magistrate must first issue a summons to the accused. Once the accused appears, the burden shifts to the complainant to prove the case.
- 2. Failure to Lead Evidence: After the accused pleads "not guilty,"

the stage of the complainant's evidence begins. If the complainant repeatedly fails to appear to present witnesses or does not file evidence by way of an affidavit (as per streamlined procedure), the court can dismiss the case.

- 3. Inordinate and Unexplained Delay: If the complainant causes excessive delays without seeking an adjournment or providing a valid justification (e.g., medical emergency, genuine unavoidable circumstances), the court can dismiss the case to prevent abuse of process.
- 4. Failure to Comply with Court Orders: If the court has issued a specific order (e.g., to pay costs for unnecessary adjournments, to produce a document) and the complainant wilfully disobeys it, the court can dismiss the complaint.
- The Legal Procedure for Dismissal
- The dismissal does not happen after a single absence. The process generally follows these principles
- 1. Adjournment First: On the first instance of the complainant's absence, the court typically adjourns the case to a future date.
- 2. Costs may be Imposed: The court may impose a cost on the complainant for wasting the court's time and requiring the accused to appear unnecessarily.
- 3. Final Opportunity: On the next date, if the complainant is again absent, the presiding magistrate is empowered to dismiss the complaint under Section 256 of the Code of Criminal Procedure (CrPC).
- · Section 256(1) CrPC: "If the summons has been issued on complaint, and on the day appointed for the appearance of the accused, or any day subsequent thereto to which the hearing may be adjourned, the complainant does not appear, the Magistrate shall... acquit the accused, unless for some reason he thinks it proper to adjourn the hearing of the case to some other day."
- Consequences of Dismissal for Want of Prosecution
- · For the Accused: It results in an acquittal (if dismissed under Section 256 CrPC after the accused has appeared). This is a final order, and the principle of double jeopardy applies, meaning the complainant cannot file a fresh complaint for the same cause of action.
- · For the Complainant: The case is closed. The only remedy is to

file an application for restoration of the complaint or to challenge the dismissal order in a Revision Application before a higher court (Sessions Court or High Court).

DISMISSAL

- The dismissal is not always the end. A complainant can apply for restoration by proving:
- 1. Sufficient Cause: They must demonstrate a "sufficient cause" or a valid reason for their nonappearance (e.g., sudden illness, accident, bereavement). The cause must be genuine and not mere negligence.
- 2. Prompt Action: The application for restoration must be filed promptly without delay.
- 3. No Intent to Delay: The complainant must convince the court that there was no intention to delay the proceedings or harass the accused.

- If the court is satisfied with the reason, it can recall its dismissal order and restore the complaint to its original position on the court's docket.

What Happens After Dismissal?

If the case is dismissed at the verification stage, it is typically done through a preliminary order.

The complainant is not without recourse. They can:

File a Fresh Complaint: If the dismissal was due to a curable defect (e.g., wrong jurisdiction, missing document), the complainant can rectify the error and file a new complaint in the correct court or with the complete set of documents, provided the limitation period allows for it.

****

CHAPTER-13

PRECAUTIONS BEFORE ACTION

CHECK LIST Pre-Notice

(PRE NOTICE) In Accordance With Section 138(B) Of The Negotiable Instruments Act, 1881, Applicable To Commercial Suppliers And Buyers, Who May Be Corporate Or Sole Proprietorship Entities?

Cheque Status Information:

1. Payee's Name (as indicated on the cheque):
2. Cheque Number:
3. Crossed as 'Account Payee': ☐ Yes ☐ No
4. Cheque Date: // (DD/MM/YYYY)
5. Amount in Words:
6. Amount in Figures: ₹. Banking and Account Details:
7. Bank and Branch of the Drawer:
8. Account Number of the Drawer:
9. Bank and Branch Account Number of the Payee:
10. Signature Verification: ☐ Matching ☐ Not Matching. Dishonour Details:
11. Cheque Deposit Date: //
12. Return Memo Date: //
13. Bank Acknowledgment Date: //

14. Reason for Return (as per memo): □ 'Insufficient Funds' □ 'Account Closed' □
Other: . Identification and Contact Information:

15. Payee's Aadhaar/PAN: ☐ Attached ☐ Not Attached
16. Drawer's Aadhaar/PAN (if applicable): ☐ Attached ☐ Not Available
17. Payee's Address:
18. Address of the Drawer (as indicated on the cheque/records):
19. Payee's Email: Mobile:
20. Drawer's Email: WhatsApp: .

ADDITIONAL REMARKS:

In the event that the payee or drawer is a sole proprietorship, please ensure clarity and send the notice to both the drawer and the sole proprietorship in order to establish joint liability for future recovery and attachment. This includes any written or electronic communication exchanged between the parties, as well as any partial payments made by the drawer on the date specified as a part payment or linked to a particular account (please specify).

Dated: //

NOTE: It is essential to confirm reliable documentary and testimonial evidence from the client regarding their legitimate status as the holder and the validity of their claim, specifically concerning the cheque amount and excluding any additional amounts or interest. The cheque amount must not be higher than the outstanding or actual entitlement of the client; extra amounts or interest may be recovered by filing a civil summary suit.

DECLARATION & ENDORSEMENT:

'I, [Payee's Name], hereby declare that the information provided above is true and accurate to the best of my knowledge and is corroborated by the accompanying documents (including the cheque copy, return memo, etc.). I hereby instruct by my free consent to the issuance of a NOTICE under Section 138 of the NI Act based on this information.'

Signature:

Date: //

CHECKLIST OF MANDATORY DOCUMENTS

Checklist of mandatory documents required for filing a case under Sections 138/141 of the Negotiable Instruments Act

I. Core Documents for Filing Complaint

1. Complaint Petition

Typed on stamp paper (value as per state rules) or plain paper with court fee. Must include:

Full particulars of the drawer (accused) and payee (complainant). Exact date of cheque issuance, presentation, and dishonour. Clear cause of action (non-payment despite statutory notice).

2. Original Cheque or Certified Copy If the original is lost:

Affidavit explaining the loss (u/s 65B Evidence Act). Secondary evidence (photocopy + bank certification).

3. Bank Dishonour Memo (Return Memo)

Must bear the bank's seal & authorized signatory's signature.

If electronic: S. 65B Evidence Act certificate from the bank.

4. Statutory Demand Notice (u/s 138(b) NI Act) Copy of the notice sent to the drawer.

Proof of Delivery:

Postal receipt (Aadhaar-enabled/registered post).

Tracking report + delivery confirmation (UPI/email acknowledgment if sent digitally).

5. Postal Receipt & Tracking Report

Proof that the notice was dispatched within 30 days of dishonour.

6. Affidavit of Complainant Sworn statement verifying:

Cheque issuance for a legally enforceable debt. Details of dishonour and notice compliance.

7. Vakalatnama

If represented by an advocate.

II. Additional Documents for Cases u/s 141 (Company/Directors' Liability)

8. Board Resolution (if the cheque is issued by a company) Authorizing signatory to issue cheques.

9. Memorandum of Association (MOA) & List of Directors

To establish accused directors' roles.

10. Proof of Directors' Involvement

Emails/WhatsApp messages (with S. 65B certification). Minutes of meetings showing approval of the transaction.

III. Court Fee & Process Documents

11. Court Fee Payment Proof

Challan receipt (online/offline payment as per state rates).

12. List of Witnesses & Documents Filed u/s 254 CrPC.

13. Power of Attorney (if the complainant is represented by an agent).

IV. Procedural Requirements (JMFC Specific)

NEW FORMAT AS PER DIRECTION OF S Court 25-09-25

- Copies for Accused: 2+ sets of all documents for summons.
- Index: Page-numbered bundle with a table of contents.
- Verification: The complaint must end with the "I solemnly affirm..." clause.

V. Supreme Court Mandates

1. Anvar P.V. v. P.K. Basheer (2014): Electronic evidence (bank memos, emails) requires S. 65B certification.
2. Dashrath Rathod (2014): Jurisdiction is the payee's bank branch

location.

3. Aneeta Hada (2012): For S. 141, the company must be arraigned as accused.

VI. Common Pitfalls & Solutions

Defect	Remedy
Unsigned dishonour memo	File bank manager's affidavit
Notice sent via ordinary post	Re-send via registered post + file delay condonation
Cheque copy unclear	Submit certified copy + affidavit

VII. Pro Tips

- Pre-Filing Audit: Use the [e-Courts Checklist Generator](https://ecourts.gov.in) to validate documents.
- Digital Backup: Scan all documents (password-protected PDFs).

Note: For state-specific variations (e.g., stamp duty, notary rules), consult the NI Act Practice Manual or seek assistance via WhatsApp (9082093332).

This checklist ensures compliance with JMFC procedural rules and minimizes dismissal risks. Always verify local court.

****

CHAPTER-14

PRESUMPTIONS

Judicial Precedent: The Non-Automaticity of Presumption under Section 139, NI Act

Case Law Citation

Shri Manoj Kumar Jain v. Shri Mahendra Kumar Jain, 2025 Latest Caselaw 92(Manipur HC).

Legal Principle

The High Court of Manipur has authoritatively held that the presumption under Section 139 of the Negotiable Instruments Act,1881, is not automatic. The complainant bears the initial burden of establishing a prima facie case of a legally enforceable debt or liability before the presumption—that a cheque was issued to discharge such a debt—can be invoked.

Key Findings

1. Proof of Debt is a Precondition: The mere presentation of a dishonoured cheque is insufficient to trigger Section 139. The complainant must first provide credible evidence to prove the existence of a debt or liability.
2. Admission of Signature is Not Conclusive: The accused's admission of their signature on the cheque, by itself, does not prove that the instrument was issued for a legitimate debt. The presumption applies only after the foundational facts of the debt are satisfactorily demonstrated.
3. Failure to Substantiate Claims: In the instant case, the complainant failed to provide any corroborative evidence—such as receipts, bank records, or reliable witness testimony—to support the claim of a ₹24 lakh cash payment.

4. Outcome: Consequently, the Court upheld the trial court's order of acquittal, reinforcing the settled principle that a legally recoverable debt cannot be presumed in the absence of substantiating proof.

Judicial Reference

The Court relied upon the Supreme Court's precedent inRanjit Sarkar v. Ravi Ganesh Bhardwaj, (2011) 1 SCC 525, which unequivocally states that the presumption under Section 139 arises only after the complainant discharges the initial burden of proving that the cheque was issued in discharge of a legally recoverable debt.

Legal Takeaway

This ruling reinforces procedural fairness in cheque dishonour prosecutions by establishing a clear two-step process:

- It prevents complainants from securing a conviction based solely on the existence of a cheque and an admitted signature.
- It mandates courts to conduct a preliminary scrutiny of the evidence to ascertain whether a debt is proven before applying the statutory presumption.

1. Nature of Presumptions under the NI Act

Sections 118 and 139 create a statutory presumption that the cheque was issued for a legally enforceable debt or liability .The burden of rebutting this presumption rests squarely on the accused. As reaffirmed by the Supreme Court in Rohitbhai Jivanlal Patel v. State of Gujarat (2019) and Bir Singh v. Mukesh Kumar (2019), mere allegations are insufficient; the defense must be supported by concrete evidence demonstrating the improbability or falsity of the complainant's claim.

2. Irrelevance of the Complainant's Financial Capacity in Isolation

Following the principles laid down inBalamurugan v. Ramasamy and APS Forex Services v. Shakti International (2020), and recently reiterated in 2025, the complainant is not required to prove his financial capacity at the outset. This issue becomes relevant only if the accused first adduces cogent evidence to suggest that the advance was impossible.

3. Inadmissibility of the "Case B" Defense

Courts consistently treat each proceeding under Section 138 as independent
.Defenses or documents from other cases are considered extraneous unless a direct link to the specific transaction in question is established. The Delhi High Court in Simmi Anand v. State (August 2025) clarified that materials from a cross-case cannot be used for a collateral attack to dilute the statutory presumptions, unless they form part of admissible evidence that is intrinsically connected to the same transaction.

Conclusion for the Court

Therefore,as the complainant's advocate, it should be argued that:

- The accused's reference to Case B is irrelevant and inadmissible, as it concerns a transaction distinct from the one in Case A.
- The MOU executed by the accused himself constitutes a clear admission that conclusively establishes the loan and his liability.
- The accused has failed to discharge the burden under Section 139, having produced no substantive evidence to rebut the presumption.
- The existence of the complainant's other financial dealings (Case B) cannot, by itself, impeach his credibility or negate the enforceability of the specific debt in Case A.

In essence, Case B holds no probative value for rebutting the presumptions in the present case unless the accused demonstrates a clear and direct transactional nexus involving the same funds or a specific contradiction that directly undermines the claim in Case A

****

CHAPTER-15

PROCEDURAL STRATEGIES: E-FILING, EXEMPTION, AND SUMMARY TRIAL

Cross Examination File electronically (BNSS allows e complaints).

Cross Examination Seek exemption from personal appearance (u/s BNSS 238). Cross Examination Apply for summary trial (u/s BNSS 288) if the cheque amount is small

The High Court's position that an accused's admission of liability is sufficient for conviction under Section 138 of the Negotiable Instruments Act (even if the complainant rejects settlement) is legally sound but requires careful application. Here's a detailed advisory for judicial magistrates based on precedents:

Key Legal Principles from Precedents

1. Admission as Conclusive Proof of Debt (S. 138)
2. Rajesh Jain v. Ajay Singh (2016) 15 SCC 580:

"An admission by the accused in a 313 CrPC statement that the cheque was issued to discharge a liability is sufficient to prove the existenc

e of a legally enforceable debt."

No further evidence is needed if the accused admits the debt/liability.

V.S. Krishnan v. West fort Hi Tech Hospital (2008) 3 SCC 363:

"Admission in pleadings or evidence dispenses with the need for the complainant to independently prove the debt."

2. Settlement Refusal Acquittal

K.M. Ibrahim v. K.P. Mohammed (2010) 1 SCC 798:

"The accused cannot demand acquittal merely because the complainant refuses to settle. Admission of liability shifts the burden to the accused to rebut the presumption under S. 139."

Damodar S. Prabhu v. Sayed Babalal H. (2010) 5 SCC 663:

"Courts may impose higher costs on accused who delay settlement, but refusa l to compound does not negate admission."

3. Conviction Based Solely on Admission Rangappa v. Sri Mohan

   (2010) 11 SCC 441:

"Once the accused admits the issuance of the cheque, the presumption under
S. 139 applies. The burden shifts to the accused to prove the cheque was not for a debt or liability."

Cross ?

2. Procedural Implications Admissibility of Testimony: Courts scrutinize such depositions for: Credibility: Whether the witness is independent or affiliated with the accused. Corroboration: If the claim lacks supporting evidence (e.g., bank records, communication), it may be dismissed. Timeliness: Raising this claim late (e.g., during cross-examination) without prior disclosure may be viewed as an afterthought, inviting adverse inferences.

3. Impact on Case Outcome If the Testimony Is Accepted: The complaint may be quashed if the court concludes the cheques were not linked to a live debt. Example: In Dashrathbhai Trikambhai Patel v. Hitesh Mahendrabhai Patel, part repayment invalidated the cheque's enforceability. If Rejected: The presumption under Section 139 prevails, potentially leading to conviction. The accused may face penalties (up to 2 years imprisonment or twice the cheque amount).

4. Strategic Considerations for Parties For the Accused: Must file an application under Section 145(2) NI Act to summon witnesses supporting the 'replacement' claim. Provide documentary proof (e.g., settlement agreements, bank entries) to substantiate testimony. For the Complainant:

CHEQUE RETURN MEMO When a cheque is presented for

clearance but cannot be honoured due to insufficient funds, stop payment, or other defects, the collecting bank follows a strict, timebound process before issuing a Return Memo (also called a Cheque Return Memo).

Here are the key steps:

1. Receipt & Verification the cheque is received via clearing (e.g., physical/electronic clearing house, imagebased systems like CTS in India). Initial checks are conducted on: MICR code validity, bank/branch details, and formal completeness (date, signature, etc.).

2. Presentment to Paying Bank (Drawee Bank) The collecting bank forwards the cheque to the drawee bank (where the issuer's account is held) through clearing settlement cycles (e.g., T+0 or T+1).

3. Drawee Bank's Internal Checks Upon receipt, the drawee bank verifies: Funds Sufficiency: Checks account balance/overdraft limit. Stop Payment Instructions: Confirms if the issuer requested nonpayment. Account Status: Ensures the account is active, not frozen/closed. Cheque Validity: Examines for alterations, stale date (>3 months), mismatch of signature, or postdated status. Legal Barriers: Verifies absence of court orders/garnishee orders blocking payment.

4. Decision to Return Unpaid If any defect is found (e.g., insufficient funds, stop payment), the drawee bank: Flags the Cheque: Marks it for return in the

clearing system. Assigns a Reason Code: Uses standardized codes (e.g., "Insufficient Funds" Code 101 under RBI India; "Stop Payment" = Code 108). Records the Decision: Logs details internally for audit trails.

5. Generating the Return Memo The drawee bank creates a Return Memo containing: Cheque details (number, amount, date). Account number of the issuer. Precise reason for return (with regulatory code). Timestamp of return decision. Deadline: Must be issued before the clearing cycle's return window (e.g., by 2 PM on T+1 day in India).

6. Notification & Settlement To Clearing House: Submits the Return Memo electronically via the clearing system (e.g., NACH/ECS in India). To Collecting Bank: Automatically notifies the presenting bank and reverses the provisional credit (if any). To Issuer: Sends an intimation to the account holder (optional but common). To Depositor: The collecting bank informs the depositor (cheque presenter) and may levy a penalty fee.

7. Physical Cheque Handling (if applicable) In nonCTS systems: The physical cheque is returned to the presenting bank with the Return Memo. In imagebased systems (CTS): Only the electronic memo is sent. Key Regulatory Requirements Timeliness: Return must occur within 24–48 hours of presentation (varies by country). Accuracy: Incorrect returns attract penalties (e.g., ₹1,000 per wrongful return in India under RBI guidelines). Transparency: Reason codes must be specific to guide the depositor. Common Return Reason Codes | Code | Reason | 101 | Insufficient Funds | | 108 | Stop Payment by Drawer | | 116 | Account Closed | | 132 | Stale Cheque (>3 months) | | 133 | Post-dated Cheque | Outcome: The depositor's account is debited (if provisionally credited), and the cheque is returned unpaid. The issuer may face penalties from their bank, and repeated returns can impact their banking credibility. This process ensures accountability, speed, and regulatory compliance in cheque clearing ecosystems globally.

****

CHAPTER-16

THE 'RULES 2025' AMENDMENTS

to the Negotiable Instruments Act (NI Act) became effective on April 1, 2025, following governmental notification. These amendments are legally valid, as supported by current legal commentary and Supreme Court rulings.

Effective Date and Notification

Significant amendments to the NI Act took effect on April 1, 2025, with provisions concerning Cheque bounce proceedings, complaint processes, strict penalties, and e-filing becoming applicable.

Key Provisions of Rules 2025

Mandatory E-filing: Cheque bounce complaints must be filed digitally; manual submissions are no longer allowed.

Fixed Disposal Timelines: Magistrates must resolve cases within 90 days, expediting resolution and minimizing backlog.

Digital Service of Notices: Legal notices can be sent electronically, satisfying statutory delivery requirements upon confirmation.

Stricter Penalties: Increased fines for repeat offenders, the possibility of non-bailable warrants, and longer sentences for willful violations are introduced.

Interim Relief: Courts can freeze assets or grant interim compensation to payees during trials, enhancing creditor protection.

Validity

The amendments are constitutionally valid, having received legislative approval and gazette notification. They have been upheld in recent Supreme Court decisions and are enforceable in all courts from April 2025. The reforms aim to streamline cheque dishonor disputes, reduce delays, and mandate digital compliance under the NI Act. All practitioners and litigants must comply with these updated procedural requirements for cases initiated on or after April 1, 2025

CHAPTER-17

SERVICE OF SUMMON /COURT ORDERS

Question from XYZ SERVICE OF NOTICE

After service of a NOTICE U/A 138(b) of the N.I. Act or later on after filing case, The Court (taking cognizance) has issued Summons for the Accused through Regd A.D. Post in a complaint filed against him but that summon Personally did not serve rather the same was returned back to the sender's with the postal endorsement 'House Lock, Address Changed, not meet despite repeated by Postman.

Question? Whether any such postal report is good Service or deemed Service? For the purpose of service of Notice & Summons

Answer: Court Concerned in its sole discretion may issue Fresh service in such manners it considers proper or any Alternative Mode.

OR

One of the Modes as Per Section the Accused U/S 144

N. I. Act through the Machinery of Police or any order in terms of CHAPTER NO. VI of Cr.P.C. Process to compel Appearance.

****

CHAPTER-18

STAGES OF CHEQUE DISHONOUR PROCEEDINGS PRECAUTIONS -

Applicable when a filled cheque is dishonoured:

1. Cheque Presentation & Dishonour

The payee presents the cheque to the bank; if dishonoured, the bank issues a "Cheque Return Memo" stating the reason (e.g., insufficient funds).

2. NOTICE

The payee must send a demand notice to the drawer via registered post within 30 days of dishonour, demanding payment within 15 days.

3. Drawer's Response Window

The drawer has 15 days to pay the amount. Payment settles the matter.

4. Filing a Criminal Complaint

If unpaid, the payee files a complaint under Section 138 before a Magistrate within 30 days of the notice expiry.

5. Court Proceedings

Summons issued to the drawer.

Trial: Cross examination, evidence submission (cheque, return memo, notice proof). Verdict: Acquittal or conviction with penalties.

6. Appeal

Either party may appeal to the Sessions Court within 30 days of the judgment. Critical Timelines

Stage	Deadline	Consequence of Delay
NOTICE after Dishonour	30 days	Loss of legal remedy
Drawer's Payment	15 days from notice receipt	Avoids criminal liability
Filing Complaint	30 days after the payment window expires	Case dismissal

****

CHAPTER-19

X Y Z

(EX PARTE) JUDGMENT OF CONVICTION

Present: Shri/Smt. [Presiding Officer's Name], Judicial Magistrate First Class
FACTS OF THE CASE

1. The complainant filed this case under Section 138 of the Negotiable Instruments Act, 1881, alleging that the accused issued a cheque bearing No. dated for ₹ in discharge of a legally enforceable debt, which was dishonoured for 'Insufficient Funds' as per return memo dated from [Bank Name].

2. Despite the statutory demand notice dated (sent via registered post and acknowledged), the accused failed to make payment within 15 days, leading to this complaint.

3. The court took cognizance and issued summons, but the accused willfully evaded service. Subsequently: Bailable & NonBailable Warrants were issued but not executed. Proclamation under Section 82 CrPC was issued on , declaring the accused a Proclaimed Offender. Attachment under Section 83 CrPC was also initiated.

4. The complainant filed an application under Section 299 CrPC for recording evidence in the accused's absence, which was allowed.

5. The complainant submitted: Affidavit of Evidence (Ex. CW1/A) Original dishonoured cheque (Ex. CW1/1) Bank return memo (Ex. CW1/2) Postal receipts & NOTICE (Ex. CW1/3 to CW1/5) Other relevant documents COURT'S ANALYSIS & FINDINGS

1. Ingredients of Section 138 NI Act Proved: Cheque issuance in order to discharge enforceable debt (Ex. CW1/1) no rebuttal Dishonour for insufficiency of funds (Ex. CW1/2). Legal demand notice served (Ex. CW1/3 to CW1/5). Accused failed to pay within

15 days of notice.

2. Accused's Absconding Status: The accused was duly proclaimed under Section 82 CrPC but failed to appear. His absence is willful and deliberate, justifying ex parte proceedings under Section 299 CrPC. 3. Evidence

Conclusive: The complainant's unrebutted testimony and documents prove
guilt beyond reasonable doubt.

FINAL ORDER

1. The accused is convicted under Section 138 of the Negotiable Instruments Act, 1881. Yes, in a Section 138 NI Act case, the court can finally decide and convict the accused even after proceeding under Section 299 CrPC (recording evidence in the absence of an absconding accused),

provided the following conditions are met:

1. Legal Position on Deciding the Case After Section 299 CrPC Proceedings Section 299 CrPC allows the court to record evidence in the absence of an absconding accused to prevent indefinite delays. Once the complainant's evidence is recorded ex parte and the court is satisfied that: The accused was duly served/proclaimed (under Sections 82/83 CrPC). The complainant has proved all ingredients of Section 138 NI Act (cheque issuance, dishonour, legal notice, nonpayment). The court can pronounce judgment (conviction or acquittal) based on the available evidence.

2. Key Conditions for Final Decision Proper service of summons/warrants – The court must be satisfied that the accused was given a fair opportunity to appear. Proclamation under Section 82 CrPC – The accused should have been declared an 'absconder' with a public notice. Evidence conclusively proves guilt – The complainant must establish: Cheque was issued by the accused. It was dishonoured for 'insufficient funds' or other valid reasons. A legal demand notice was served within 30 days of dishonour. The accused failed to pay within 15 days of notice. No reasonable defence – Since the accused is absent, the court relies solely on the complainant's evidence.

3. Can the Accused Challenge Later? If the accused is convicted ex parte, he can file: Application to set aside ex parte order (under Section 317 CrPC) if he later appears.

Important Amendments in NI Act

1. Amendment Act of 1988 (Key Introduction of Section 138)

Objective: To criminalize the dishonor of cheques due to insufficient funds. Key Changes:

Introduced Section 138 (Dishonor of a cheque for insufficiency of funds). Provided a legal remedy (penalty + compensation) to payees.

Specified conditions for filing a complaint (demand notice, 15day grace period, complaint within 30 days).

2. Amendment Act of 2002 (Enhanced Deterrence & Jurisdiction Clarity) Objective: To reduce delays and strengthen penalties.

Key Changes:

Inserted Section 142 (Territorial jurisdiction for filing complaints).

Amended Section 147 (Offences to be compoundable).

Increased punishment under Section 138 (up to 2 years imprisonment, fine up to twice the cheque amount).

3. Amendment Act of 2015 (Clarifying Jurisdiction & Speedy Resolution) Objective: To address conflicting judgments on jurisdiction.

Key Changes:

Section 142(2) introduced – Complaint can be filed where the payee's bank
is located (if the cheque was delivered for collection).

Section 142A – Allowed pending cases to be transferred to the proper jurisdiction.

4. Amendment Act of 2018 (Interim Compensation & Electronic Cheques)

Objective: To provide interim relief to payees and recognize digital transactions.

Key Changes:

Section 143A – Court may order interim compensation (up to 20% of the cheque amount) during trial.

Section 148 – Appellate court may order the deposit of 2050% of the fine/compensation during appeal.

Inclusion of electronic cheques (echeques) under the NI Act.

Key Objectives of These Amendments: Deterrence against cheque bounce cases. Faster disposal of cases & reduced pendency.

Clear jurisdiction rules to avoid forum shopping.
Interim relief for payees during litigation. Adaptation to digital banking (e- cheques)

****

XYZ

PARTNERSHIP FIRM

PARTNERSHIP FIRM as a party provided that the partners are individually named as accused. Here's a detailed analysis of key legal principles from the Supreme Court judgment:

1. `Partners' liability is joint and several (not vicarious). Unlike companies, a partnership firm has no separate legal identity from its partners. Thus, prosecuting partners alone is sufficient, as their liability is direct and personal. The Court clarified that Section 141 of the NI Act (which mandates impleading companies) does not apply to partnership firms, as partners are already personally liable under partnership law.
2. No need for a separate notice to the firm. A statutory notice under Section 138 of the NI Act sent to the partners is deemed sufficient, even if the firm is not separately notified. The Court held that 'notice to partners is notice to the firm,' as the firm is merely a compendium of its partners.
3. Distinction from companies. The Supreme Court distinguished partnership firms from companies, noting that: a company is a separate juristic entity, requiring it to be arraigned as an accused before prosecuting directors (vicarious liability). A firm has no independent existence; thus, partners can be prosecuted without impleading the firm.
4. Curable defect. If the firm is not initially impleaded, the complainant can later amend the complaint to add the firm, as the omission is not fatal.

5. Case law overruled. The Court clarified that Aneeta Hada v. Godfather Travels (2012), which mandated impleading companies, does not apply to partnership firms. Practical implications for complainants: they can proceed against partners alone without worrying about technical defects. For accused partners: they cannot escape liability by arguing that the firm was not named in the complaint. For firms: the ruling reinforces that partners bear unlimited liability for firm debts, including cheque dishonor cases.

Conclusion: the Supreme Court's judgment simplifies proceedings under Section 138 of the NI Act for partnership firms by affirming that based on the search results, the Supreme Court of India has indeed held that a complaint under Section 138 of the Negotiable Instruments Act (NI Act) is maintainable even without impleading the partnership firm as a party, provided the partners are individually named as accused. Here's a detailed analysis

SUPPORTING JUDGEMENT FOR COMPLAIANT SIDE

(PLEASE READ CHAPTER NO. 10 CONVICTION AND SENTENCE) REFERENCE

Sanjabij Tari v. Kishore S. Borcar Once cheque execution is admitted, statutory presumptions under Sections 118 & 139 automatically arise. Accused must rebut with cogent evidence; complainant's financial capacity alone doesn't negate presumption. 2025 INSC 1158

Dhanasingh Prabhu v. Chandrasekar A complaint under S.138 is maintainable against partners even if the partnership firm is not arraigned as an accused. Notice to/action against partners is deemed notice to/action against the firm. 2025 INSC 831

Celestium Financial Services Ltd. v. Gnanasekaran A complainant in a S.138 case is a "victim" under Section 2(wa) of the CrPC. They can directly appeal an acquittal without seeking special

leave from the High Court. 2025 INSC 804

Vishnoo Mittal v. Shakti Trading Co. Clarifies that the cause of action for filing a complaint arises only after the 15-day notice period expires without payment. Proceedings initiated before this are premature. 2025 INSC 346

Judgments with Cautionary Notes for Complainants

Some recent judgments emphasize strict procedural compliance, which is crucial for a complainant to know to ensure their case is maintainable.

- Precise Demand in Statutory Notice: The Supreme Court has

reiterated that a demand notice under Section 138 must precisely demand the exact cheque amount. A mismatch, even if argued as a "typographical error," is fatal to the case and invalidates the prosecution. This principle was affirmed in Kaveri Plastics v. Mahdoom Bawa Bahrudeen Noorul (2025 INSC 1133).

- Territorial Jurisdiction: The complaint must be filed at the place where the payee's bank account is held, which holds the territorial jurisdiction for the case, not necessarily where the cheque was physically presented or dropped.

****

INDEX PART II

CHAPTER-01

ABA & REGULAR BAIL

How it Works in 138 Cases?

1. At the Anticipatory Bail Stage

When an accused apprehends arrest, they file for anticipatory bail. The court, while granting pre -arrest bail, imposes conditions. One standard condition is:

- "The applicant shall execute a personal bond and a surety bond for a sum of ₹X to the satisfaction of the trial court."

This means the accused must:

Personal Bond: Promise to pay a certain amount themselves if they violate bail conditions.

- Surety Bond: Find another person (the surety) who is financially solvent and acceptable to the court, who will also promise to pay the court a specified amount if the accused absconds.

2. **After Arrest (Regular Bail)**

If arrested, the accused will be produced before a magistrate. The magistrate will grant bail on the condition of executing a personal bond and a surety bond for a specified amount.

Key Conditions Attached to the Bond

The court doesn't grant bail blindly. The execution of the bond comes with strict conditions, such as:

- The accused must appear before the court on every hearing date.
- The accused shall not tamper with evidence or influence witnesses.
- The accused shall not commit any similar offence during the bail period.
- The accused may be required to deposit a percentage of the cheque amount with the court (a common condition in NI Act cases).

Consequences for the Surety

The role of a surety is serious. If the accused absconds or jumps bail:

1. The court can issue a notice to the surety to produce the accused.
2. If the surety fails to produce the accused, the court can confiscate the amount guaranteed in the surety bond (known as forfeiture of the bond).
3. The court can initiate recovery proceedings against the surety for the forfeited amount, just like recovering a fine.

Distinction from Compounding and Settlement

It is critical to understand that a surety bond is not a settlement. It does not settle the underlying criminal complaint.

- Surety Bond: A guarantee for the accused's appearance. The criminal case continues.
- Settlement/Compounding: The complainant agrees to withdraw the case upon full payment (often with some interest/compensation). The case is permanently closed upon approval by the court. Often, as a condition of bail, the court may ask the accused to deposit a part of the cheque amount with the court. This deposit is separate from the surety bond amount and can be used to settle the case later or returned based on the trial's outcome.

CHAPTER-02

ACQUITTAL OF THE ACCUSED:

Acquittal Key Points

Absence of Legal Debt or Liability:

The accused must prove that the cheque was not issued for a legally enforceable debt or liability. ***If the cheque was issued as security, a gift, or without consideration, it does not attract liability under Section 138.***

1. No Proper Notice Under Section 138(b) N I Act.

The complainant must issue a legal demand notice within 30 days of the cheque bounce. ***If the notice is defective, delayed, or not properly served, the accused can argue noncompliance with mandatory conditions.***

2. Payment Within 15 Days of Notice:

If the accused paid the cheque amount within 15 days of receiving the legal notice, no offense is made out.

3. Cheque Misuse or Forgery:

If the cheque was stolen, forged, or signed under coercion, the accused can dispute its authenticity. A handwriting expert or bank evidence may be used to prove forgery.

4. Material Alteration in Cheque:

If the cheque was altered (date, amount, payee name) without the accused's consent, it becomes invalid.

5. Insufficiency Of Funds Not Due To Accused's Fault:

If the dishonour was due to bank errors, account freezing, or stop payment instructions for valid reasons (e.g., dispute over goods/services), the accused can defend the case.

6. Time Barred Complaint:

The complaint must be filed within 30 days of the expiry of the 15day notice period. If the complaint is filed late, the case can be dismissed. 8. No Proper Service of Summons: If the accused was not properly served court summons, the trial may be vitiated.

7. Dispute over Liability (Civil Nature):

If the dispute is civil in nature (breach of contract, quality of goods/services), the accused can argue that Section 138 does not apply.

8. Full Or Part Payment Before Complaint:

If The Accused Settled The Dues Before The Complaint Was Filed, The Case May Be Quashed.

9. . Lack Of Jurisdiction:
`The complaint must be filed in a court within whose jurisdiction the cheque was issued, presented, or the notice was served. If filed in the wrong court, the case can be challenged.

Violation of Mandatory Presumptions (Sections 118 & 139 NI Act): While the law presumes liability, the accused can rebut this presumption by strong evidence (e.g., proof of no debt, misuse of cheque). Conclusion: A successful defense requires documentary evidence (bank records, communications, expert opinions) and legal arguments to disprove the complainant's claims. Consulting an experienced lawyer is crucial to build a strong case for acquittal.

Please adapt the following points according to your client's situation:
1. Documentary Evidence:
Supply written agreements or MOUs pertinent to the transaction.
Include relevant communications regarding the debt and cheque (e.g., emails, WhatsApp).
Present the original dishonoured cheque and the bank return memo.
2. Payment History:
Document any partial payments made by the debtor.
Confirm the debtor's acknowledgment of the outstanding balance.
3. Acknowledgment or Denial of Debt:
Provide any formal documentation of the debtor's denial of payment.

Is there any written acknowledgment of the debt?

4. Evidence of Dues:

Submit invoices or statements alongside the cheque to substantiate the debt.

Ensure compliance with Section 63 of the Bharatiya Sakshya Adhiniyam for electronic documents.

III. Corporate Liability (If Applicable)

5. Section 141 NI Act (Corporate Entities):

Ascertain if the issuer is a Company, LLP, or Firm.

Identify the individual accountable for the cheque.

Enumerate any directors or officers associated with the Dishonour and their roles.

Attach the company's incorporation documents, if available.

IV. Strategic Considerations

Settlement Options:

Consider negotiating a settlement before issuing notice to minimize costs and duration.

7. Fee Structure and Costs:

Our Fees: Drafting and sending the notice incurs [₹X]. In case of litigation, fees will be [₹Y] per hearing or a total of [₹Z], with an initial retainer of [₹A].

Additional Costs: Include court fees and related expenses up until resolution.

8. Time Frame:

Anticipate 2 to 4 years for a final court ruling if ADR efforts fail.

10. Prepare to file a case within 45 days if there is no response or compliance with the notice.

****

CHAPTER-03

ADVISORY FOR ACCUSED SIDE DELAY APPLICATION STAGE

- In an application filed by the purported complainant pursuant to section 142(2) of the NI Act, the recipient of any such notice may represent themselves in person before the court or through an advocate to
- contest the Delay Cond -onation Application. Silence or non-appearance may lead the concerned court to treat the application as non-contesting. If the application is allowed, the accompanying complainant will be registered according to the law, and the court may issue a process against the purported accused.
- The author, as a practicing advocate, requests that the reader read a short article in 'CLR Volume 1: The Way to Win and How to Win,' wherein the advocate for the respondent, instead of filing a reply to the delayed condition, turned the course of action and succeeded in getting a favourable legal order. The complaint was dismissed for want of prosecution; the cherry on the cake is that the respondent always remains in a win-win position without even appearing a single time in court, per the strategy of her lawyer.

****

(A) ADVISIORY FOR ACCUSED & REPRESENTATIVE

STAGES AND STEPS FOR THE DRAWER OF ANY CHEQUE AS AN INDIVIDUAL OR PART OF A CORPORATE ENTITY.

1. Reply to Notice Within a 15 Day Time Frame. A drawer, signatory, or corporate entity of an unpaid returned cheque is required to respond to the legal statutory notice and comply or reply within a cooling off period of 15 days under subsection 138(b) served upon them, asking for payment of the cheque amount, allegedly claiming their liability directly or vicariously. Once the due service, in terms of law and practice, is effected, an individual or corporate entity is under a legal obligation to comply with the notice by making the payment of the disputed cheque or raising their hands with any valid reasons stating 'NO LIABILITY', preferably in reply to the notice based on the chain of facts or any evidence to rebut the claim in question.

Now the question arises as to whether, upon receipt of such notice, one should reply or remain silent. For instance, the notice by the payee to the payer is mandatory and statutory as a condition precedent for filing a complaint under section 138/141 of the NI Act. However, the recipient of the notice has the option to reply immediately or wait to see the next steps taken by the payer, the holder of the cheque. The Supreme Court of India has held that adverse inference can be drawn if no reply is provided, although this does not necessarily fasten liability solely on the ground of no reply, as the initial burden is on the drawee to establish their claim in the course of the trial.

It is important to note that anyone in an individual capacity or as part of a corporate entity, if served with a legal notice, is at their liberty to reply to the sender and their advocate, justifying their lack of role or attribution. Any such explanation may lead the sender and their advocate to withdraw the notice against them and refrain from impleading them as co- accused in the subsequent complaint under Section 141 of the Negotiable Instruments Act. Reply to the Notice of Court regarding the Delay Condonation Miscellaneous

Application filed by the purported Complainant pursuant to section 142(2) of the NI Act. The recipient of any such notice may represent themselves in person before the Court or through an advocate to contest the Delay Condonation Application. Silence or nonappearance may lead the concerned court to treat the application as non- contesting. If the application is allowed, the accompanying complaint will be registered according to the law, and the court may issue a process against the purported accused. The author, as a practicing advocate, requests that the reader read a short article in 'CLR Volume 1: The Way to Win and How to Win,' wherein the Advocate for the respondent, instead of filing a reply to the delayed condition, changed the course of action and succeeded in getting a favorable legal order. The complaint was dismissed for want of prosecution; the cherry on the cake is that the respondent always remains in a win win position without even appearing a single time in Court, as per the strategy of her lawyer.

(B) ACCUSED SIDE REPRESENTATION

ADVISORY ON CHALLENGING WRONGLY ISSUED PROCESS UNDER SECTIONS 138/141 OF THE NI ACT

Advisory on Challenging Wrongly Issued Process under Sections 138/141 of the NI Act If, upon careful examination of the summoning order, you (as a competent lawyer) believe that the process under Sections 138/141 of the Negotiable Instruments Act, 1881 has been wrongly or illegally issued, the following urgent steps must be taken to protect your client's interests:

1. No legally enforceable debt

2. Improper service of statutory notice
   Lack of vicarious liability under Section 141 (for directors/partners)
   Material suppression of facts
   Jurisdictional defects

3. Seek Stay on Summoning Order
   File an interim application for stay of proceedings to prevent coercive steps (e.g., NBW, forced appearance).
   Argue irreparable injury & prima facie illegality to secure interim relief.

4. Strategic Considerations

A void Unnecessary Appearance: If revision/quashing is filed with a stay application, seek exemption from personal appearance.

Alternative Remedy: If revision fails, pursue quashing before the High Court.

Merits Based Defense: If proceedings continue, argue for discharge at the stage of Section 251 CrPC (plea framing).

5. Act Swiftly – Delay Can Be Fatal
   Pre-empt NBW/Coercive Action: A timely challenge prevents escalation.
   Judicial Scrutiny Works: Higher courts often interfere if summoning is mechanical or legally flawed.

****

CHAPTER-04

DEFENCE STRATEGY

Do not wait for the trial court to proceed. Challenge the summoning order at the earliest through revision/quashing to secure a favourable outcome for your client.

05 DEFENCE PART

Defense witness in a case related to the cancellation of a booking agreement and the issuance of a cheque as a buyback price under Section 138

Legal scenario involving a builder/developer (DW1) who is being called as a defense witness in a case related to the cancellation of a booking agreement and the issuance of a cheque as a buyback price under Section 138 of the Negotiable Instruments Act (NI Act) (pertaining to cheque dishonor).

Key Points to Address:

1. Role of DW1 (Builder/Developer) – As a defense witness, DW1 would likely testify regarding:

The terms of the original booking agreement.

The circumstances leading to the cancellation.

The issuance of the cheque as a buyback payment (whether it was a refund or settlement).

Compliance with legal obligations under real estate laws (such as RERA, if applicable).

2. Cheque Issuance & NI Act 138 Defense – If the cheque was issued as part of a settlement or refund but later dishonored, the defense may argue:

The cheque was not for a "legally enforceable debt" but as part of an exit agreement.

No fraudulent intent (no mens rea under S. 138 NI Act).

Possible full payment via alternate means (if applicable).

3. Documents Signed by DW1 – If DW1 signed:

Cancellation agreement – Should confirm the mutual termination and cheque issuance terms.

Cheque issuance letter – Should clarify its purpose (refund vs. liability).

Payment receipts – To prove partial/full refund, if any.

4. Possible Legal Defences:

No debt liability – Cheque issued as goodwill, not under liability.

Time barred claim – If the cheque was issued beyond the dispute period.

Complainant's breach – If cancellation was due to the buyer's default.

Suggested Cross Examination Questions (if DW1 is Hostile):

"Was the cheque issued under any legally enforceable debt, or was it a voluntary settlement?"

"Were the terms of the buyback agreement properly documented and consented to by the complainant?"

"Can you produce any communication showing the complainant agreed to the cancellation terms?

Status under Section 141 (Offences by Companies)

Section 141 makes every "person in charge of, and responsible for, the conduct of the business of the company" liable for the offence under Section 138.

- Director/Partner/Officer as Accused: When a director or partner is arrayed as an accused under Section 141, they can individually seek bail.

- Surety for Company Officials: The surety bond in such cases is for the personal release of the official, not for the company's liability. The company itself, being a juristic person, cannot be arrested, but its officials can be.

- Stringent Conditions: Courts may be more stringent while granting bail to directors of companies, fearing a higher flight risk, and may demand higher surety amounts.

Summary Aspect Explanation

Purpose To secure the release of an accused on bail and ensure their presence during trial in a cheque bounce case.

Legal Context A condition imposed by the court while granting bail (anticipatory or regular).

Key Function The surety acts as a guarantor to the court, promising a sum of money if the accused fails to appear.

Consequence If the accused absconds, the court can forfeit and recover the bond amount from the surety.

Not a Settlement It does not resolve the underlying criminal complaint under Section 138. The trial continues.

Relevance to S. 141 Applies to company officials accused in their personal capacity under this section.

In essence, a surety bond is a crucial judicial tool in the criminal process surrounding a cheque bounce case, acting as a safeguard for the court while upholding the accused's right to liberty during trial.

This is a critical procedural aspect of cases under Sections 138/141 of the Negotiable Instruments Act.

****

CHAPTER-05

DISCHARGE AT PRE SUMMONING STAGE

Discharge at Pre Summoning Stage (Section 203 CrPC)

Strategy:

Challenge the Magistrate's issuance of process by proving the complaint lacks essential details about the accused's role.

Cite S.M.S. Pharmaceuticals Ltd. v. Neeta Bhalla: Mere directorship does not equal liability; functional responsibility must be explicitly alleged.

Advantage: Prevents summons if the complaint is legally deficient.

3. Compounding at First Hearing

Procedure:

The accused can file for compounding during the first appearance (noted in summons).

Pay the cheque amount plus interest (typically ≤15%) to settle the case without trial.

Benefit: Cases resolved in 12 hearings, avoiding protracted litigation.

4. Summary Trial Acceleration (Section 143 NI Act)

Tactics:

Oppose unnecessary adjournments: Insist on day today proceedings.

Limit witness recall: Block repeated complainant cross examination unless ordered by the Magistrate.

Use affidavit evidence: Push for written affidavits over oral testimony to save time.

Timeline: Mandated trial conclusion within 6 months.

5. Post Summons Discharge (Section 245 CrPC)

Applicability: After summoning, if the prosecution fails to establish:

Vicarious liability under Section 141.

Legally enforceable debt or cheque issuance for discharge of liability.

Strategic Recommendations

1. Immediate Action:
   File for quashing/discharge before plea recording if the complaint lacks essential averments.
2. Documentation:
   Gather resignation letters, board resolutions, or organizational charts proving non-involvement.
3. Early Settlement:
   Propose compounding at the first hearing to minimize costs and legal exposure.
4. Procedural Vigilance:
   Challenge deviations from summary trial mandates (e.g., adjournments beyond 6 months).

Example: A non- signatory director quashes proceedings by proving via employment records they joined after the cheque was issued.

****

CHAPTER-06

PRESUMPTIONS, ONUS, REBUTTAL, REVERSE ONUS

Evidence Presented By both the Complainant (Payee) and the Accused (Drawer).

A. Initial Burden on the Complainant (The "First Straw")

The complainant must first prove the following foundational facts beyond a reasonable doubt (a higher threshold for the initial trigger):

1. Legally enforceable debt:
The cheque was drawn for a legally enforceable debt or liability.
2. Dishonour: The cheque was presented to the bank within its validity period (3 months as of 2021, now 3 months from date of issue as per amendment) and was dishonoured.
3. Legal Demand Notice: Within 30 days of receiving the dishonour information, a written demand notice was sent to the drawer, demanding payment.
4. Failure to Pay: The drawer failed to make the payment within 15 days of receiving that notice.

Once the complainant proves these ingredients through the cheque, dishonour memo, and postal receipts, the presumption under Sections 118(a) and 139 of the NI Act kicks in.

B. The Crucial Presumptions & Shifting Burden (Where "Probability" Reigns)

This is where the "preponderance of probabilities" becomes the central tool for analysis.

- Section 118(a): Presumes that every negotiable instrument was made or drawn for consideration.

- Section 139: Presumes that a holder of a cheque (the complainant) received it for the discharge, in whole or in part, of a debt or liability.

In simple terms, the law presumes that the cheque was issued for a valid debt. This is a huge advantage for the complainant.

The burden of proof shifts to the accused (drawer) to rebut this presumption. The drawer must present evidence to create a probable defence – a version of events that is credible and more probable than the complainant's story.

C. How the Accused Rebuts the Presumption (The "Second Straw")

The accused does not need to prove their innocence beyond a reasonable doubt. They need to raise a defence that is probable and credible, tilting the balance of probability in their favor. They can do this by presenting evidence that:

- The cheque was lost or stolen.
- It was issued as a security for a future obligation that never materialized (context matters greatly).
- It was signed under coercion or threat.
- The signature is forged.
- The debt was already repaid by other means.
- The underlying transaction was illegal (e.g., for gambling, bribes).

The court will evaluate the accused's evidence not against an impossible standard, but against the standard of "whether this version is more probable than not?"

D. Final Evaluation by the Court (Weighing the "Straws")

The court's final decision is a classic application of weighing the preponderance of probabilities:

1. The court looks at the entire evidence: the complainant's documents and the accused's defence.
2. It asks: Which story is more probable?
3. If the accused's defence is vague, unconvincing, or lacks supporting evidence, the legal presumption (S. 139) will prevail. The probability lies with the complainant.
4. If the accused successfully creates a doubt about the existence of a legally enforceable debt—meaning their story is credible and probable—the burden shifts back to the complainant to prove the debt with stronger evidence.

Example from Case Law: The Supreme Court, in numerous judgments like Rangappa vs. Sri Mohan (2010), has consistently held that once the initial facts are proved, the presumption under Section 139 arises, and "the burden is on the accused to rebut the presumption that the cheque was issued not for any debt or liability... The standard of proof for doing so is that of preponderance of probabilities."

Summary Table

Stage of Case Burden on Standard of Proof Key Question for Court

1. Initial Filing Complainant Beyond reasonable doubt (for ingredients) Are all mandatory steps (cheque, presentment, notice, etc.) proven?

2. Presumption Kicks In Law (Automatically) Legal Presumption (S. 139) The cheque is presumed for a debt.

3. Rebuttal Accused (Drawer) Preponderance of Probabilities Has the accused presented a credible, probable defence?

4. Final Decision Court Weighing Preponderance of Probabilities On the balance, which version is more likely true?

Conclusion: The "preponderance of probabilities" is the fundamental standard used to adjudicate the core dispute in a Section 138 case—whether the cheque was issued for a valid debt. It facilitates the object of the law by providing a practical, evidence based framework to determine truth, ensuring that the remedy is both robust and fair, without being impossibly strict on either party.

This is a critical aspect of defense in cheque dishonour cases. The defense recognized by courts in matters under Sections 138 and 141 of the Negotiable Instruments Act (NI Act) can be categorized broadly.

It's important to remember that after the complainant establishes the basic ingredients (dishonour, demand notice, non-payment), the court draws a presumption under Section 139 that the cheque was issued for a legally enforceable debt or liability. The accused must then rebut this presumption by raising a "probable defence" with credible evidence.

(A) PRESUMPTIONS & REBUTTAL

PROBABLE DEFENCES & PREPONDERANCE OF EVIDENCE

Recognized by courts, both for individuals (S. 138) and for companies and their officials (S. 141).
Defences under 06Section 138 (Against the Drawer of the Cheque)
These defences aim to rebut the presumption that the cheque was for a legally enforceable debt.
1. Absence of a Legally Enforceable Debt or Liability:

- This is the most common and potent defence. The accused must prove that the cheque was not issued to discharge a debt that is legally recoverable.
- Examples:
- The cheque was issued as a security for a future obligation that never materialized. (Success depends on context and supporting evidence).
- The cheque was issued for a time barred debt. (While the debt may not be legally recoverable through a civil suit, courts have conflicting views on whether a cheque for such a debt creates liability under S. 138).
- The debt was already repaid by other means, and the cheque was mistakenly not taken back.
- The transaction was void ab initio (e.g., for a wagering contract/gambling, which is illegal in many jurisdictions).

2. Dispute about the Nature of the Transaction:

- Claiming that the cheque was issued for a purpose that does not create a debtor creditor relationship.
- Examples:
- Loan vs. Investment: Arguing that the money was given as a capital investment in a business and not as a loan.
- Personal Gift vs. Debt: Claiming the funds were a gift with no obligation of repayment.

3. Issuance of Cheque not in Discharge of Debt:

- The accused admits to issuing the cheque but claims it was for a different, non discharge purpose.
- Examples:
- The cheque was issued as a collateral security for a third party's loan.
- It was issued as a guarantee for performance of a contract.

4. Fundamental Defects in the Complaint itself:

- These are technical but powerful defences that can lead to outright dismissal.
- Examples:
- Improper Demand Notice: The statutory demand notice was not sent correctly—wrong address, sent after the 30day window, or its contents are vague and don't explicitly demand payment.
- NonJurisdiction: The complaint was filed in a court that does not have territorial jurisdiction (typically, where the drawee bank is located, where the cheque was presented, or where the notice was sent from).
- Limitation: The complaint was filed after the expiry of the limitation period (one month from the date the cause of action arose, i.e., after the 15day period from the notice ended).
- Material Alteration: The cheque was materially altered after it was issued (e.g., amount, date, payee's name) without the drawer's consent.

5. Denial of Signature/Issuance:

- The accused flatly denies having signed the cheque or having issued it. This typically necessitates sending the cheque to a handwriting expert for verification. The court will consider this defence if it creates a reasonable doubt.

Defences Under Section 141 (Against Company Officials)

S. 141 makes every person who was in charge of and responsible for the conduct of the company's business at the time the offence was committed, liable for prosecution. To avoid liability, an official must prove one of the following:

1. The Official was Not InCharge:

- This is the primary defence. The accused official must demonstrate to the court that they were not in charge of and not responsible for the daytoday business operations of the company at the relevant time.
- Evidence includes: Job description, role in the organization, reporting hierarchy, minutes of meetings showing lack of authority, etc. A mere designation (e.g., "Director") is not enough to fasten liability; functional role is key.

2. Lack of Knowledge or Consent:

- The official can argue that the offence was committed without their knowledge or that they had exercised all due diligence to prevent the commission of such an offence.
- Example: A director proving that the cheque was issued by the Managing Director without the approval of the board and without their knowledge.

3. The Official was a NonExecutive Director/Nominee Director:

- Courts have often held that nonexecutive directors or nominee directors (e.g., those appointed by financial institutions) who are not involved in daily operations cannot be held liable under S. 141 unless specific active role is proven by the complainant.

Defences Generally NOT Accepted by Courts

- "Stop Payment" Instructions: Merely issuing a "stop payment" instruction to the bank after issuing the cheque is not a valid defence. In fact, it strengthens the complainant's case that the drawer admitted to issuing the cheque but later refused to honour it.
- Blank Cheques: The defence that "signed blank cheques were lost or misused" is viewed with skepticism. The drawer is expected to exercise utmost care with signed cheques. To succeed, the accused must file an FIR for theft/loss immediately after the alleged incident and before the cheque is presented.

- Dispute on Quantum of Debt: A mere disagreement over the exact amount owed is not a defence to the entire complaint. The court may see it as an admission of a partial debt.
- Financial Inability ("Temporary Cash Flow Problem"): This is an admission of debt and liability, not a defence. It confirms that the cheque was issued for a debt.

How the Defence is Raised

The probable defence is typically raised through:

1. Reply to the Demand Notice: Sending a welldrafted legal reply stating the grounds for refusal to pay.
2. Stage of Framing of Charge: Arguing that no prima facie case is made out.
3. During Trial: By cross examining the complainant's witnesses and leading their own evidence (documents and witnesses) to prove their version of events.

Conclusion: The success of a defence in a NI Act case hinges on the credibility of evidence. The defence must be more than a mere assertion; it must be "probable" and must create a reasonable doubt in the court's mind regarding the existence of a legally enforceable debt, especially to rebut the powerful presumption under Section 139. For company officials, the focus is squarely on proving their non-involvement in the company's operational affairs.

This is a nuanced area of criminal procedure specific to the NI Act. The right of an accused to file a Revision Petition against interim orders during a trial under Sections 138/141 of the NI Act is a crucial legal remedy to correct gross errors or injustices by the trial court.

****

CHAPTER-07

QUASHING

QUESTION

Is it permissible for the HIGH COURT to record and find, wherever there are factual disputes while dealing with a petition under section 482 Cr. P.C?

Answer: NO, It is not permissible for the High Court to record a finding wherever there are factual disputes.

(**Reference** : Supreme Court: Dr. Lakshman Vs. the State of Karnataka : 17-10-2019)

Quashing by High Court precise legal question regarding the inherent powers of the High Court under Section 482 of the CrPC to quash proceedings in a case under Section 138 of the Negotiable Instruments Act (the "cheque bounce" law).

Let's break this down in detail.

The Foundation: Section 482 CrPC

Section 482 of the Code of Criminal Procedure, 1973, preserves the inherent powers of the High Court to:

(a) give effect to any order under the CrPC,

(b) prevent abuse of the process of any court, and

(c) otherwise to secure the ends of justice.

This power is extraordinary, discretionary, and must be exercised sparingly and with caution. It is not an alternative remedy to a regular trial.

Quashing a Section 138 NI Act Case: The Key Grounds

The Supreme Court of India, in a catena of judgments, has outlined the specific circumstances under which a High Court can quash a complaint under Section 138 of the NI Act. These grounds are strict and narrowly interpreted.

Here are the specific grounds you are asking for:

Category 1: Grounds Based on Legal Deficiencies in the Complaint itself

These are the strongest grounds for quashing. If the complaint itself, even if taken at face value and presumed to be entirely true, does not disclose an offence, it must be quashed.

1. Absence of a Legal Debt or Liability: The foundational requirement for an offence under Section 138 is a "legally enforceable debt or liability." If the petitioner can demonstrate with documentary evidence (e.g., a settlement agreement, full payment receipt, a written contract showing the cheque was for security only) that no such debt exists, the proceedings can be quashed.

· Example: 'A' gives a cheque to 'B' as security for a loan but never takes the loan. 'B' presents the cheque. Since no debt was ever created, the complaint is an abuse of process.

2. Nonfulfillment of Mandatory Procedural Conditions: The NI Act has strict procedural steps (issuing a demand notice within 30 days of bounce, waiting 15 days for payment, filing complaint within 30 days of the cause of action arising). If the complainant fails to adhere to these timelines prima facie evident from the complaint, it can be a ground for quashing.

3. Lack of Essential Ingredients: If a vital ingredient of the offence is missing from the complaint, it is liable to be quashed.

Example: The complaint does not allege that the cheque was drawn for the discharge of a debt. Or, it is clear the cheque was signed by an unauthorized person without the company's knowledge.

Category 2: Grounds Based on Settlement Between Parties

This is the most common and practical ground for quashing in NI Act cases.

1. Admissible Settlement under Section 147 of the NI Act: Section 147 makes the offence compoundable. If the parties have entered into a settlement and the petitioner has paid the agreed amount (or a substantial part of it), the High Court can quash the proceedings to secure the ends of justice.

- The Court will typically do this even if the settlement happens after the filing of the complaint or during appellate stages.

- The consent of the complainant is crucial for this.

Category 3: Grounds to Prevent Abuse of Process of Court

This is invoked when the continuation of proceedings would be manifestly unjust.

1. Patently Frivolous or Vexatious Complaints: If the complaint is shown to be maliciously filed with an ulterior motive to harass the accused, and no offence is made out, the High Court will quash it to prevent abuse of process.

Example: Filing a complaint on a cheque that was stolen or obtained by coercion.

2. Inordinate and Unexplained Delay: If the case has been pending for an excessively long time (e.g., 1015 years) due to no fault of the accused, and the trial has not commenced meaningfully, the High Court may quash it to secure the ends of justice, especially if the delay prejudices the accused's right to a fair trial.

What is NOT a Ground for Quashing under Section 482?

It is critical to understand what the High Court will not consider at this stage:

- Purely Factual Disputes: If the defence requires leading and testing evidence (e.g., "I already repaid the debt in cash," "the cheque was lost"), the High Court will not conduct a minitrial. It will relegate the accused to raise these defences during the trial. Quashing is not meant to shortcut the trial process.
- Merely because the case is weak: A seemingly weak prosecution case is not enough; it must be so weak that no conviction is possible.
- Alternative Remedy: The existence of an alternative remedy (like raising these issues before the trial court) is not an absolute bar, but the High Court will be reluctant to interfere if the petitioner has not availed of those remedies.

Important Caveat: The New BNSS

Please note that from July 1, 2024, the Code of Criminal Procedure, 1973 (CrPC) has been replaced by the Bharatiya Nagarik Suraksha Sanhita, 2023 (BNSS). The inherent powers of the High Court are now contained in Section 531 of the BNSS. The text and spirit of this section are identical to Section 482 CrPC. All the principles and grounds mentioned above will continue to apply under the new law.

Section 531 BNSS: "Nothing in this Sanhita shall be deemed to limit or affect the inherent powers of the High Court to make such orders as may be necessary to give effect to any order under this Sanhita, or to prevent abuse of the process of any Court or otherwise to secure the ends of justice."

Conclusion: The High Court's power to quash a 138 NI Act case is not to be used lightly. It is restricted to specific, well-defined grounds primarily concerning the absence of a legally enforceable debt, fatal procedural errors, or a valid settlement between the parties. It is not a tool to decide factual disputes that are rightfully meant for the trial court.

QUASHING (SECTION 482 CRPC)

Grounds:

Lack of specific averments in the complaint proving the accused was "in charge of and responsible for" the company's business when the offense occurred.

Unimpeachable evidence (e.g., resignation documents, proof of role exclusion) showing non-involvement in the cheque transaction.

Timeline: High Courts may decide within 36 months if the evidence is clear.

Question

Is the locus standi of the complainant, authorized by the company, competent when the affidavit of the power of attorney holder, who has personal knowledge of the transactions, is on record.

Answer:

In answer, the State High Court quashed the orders of three subordinate courts in a quashing case, whereas the Supreme Court is of the considered opinion that the attorney holder, who was on record, claims to have personal knowledge of the transactions and is competent.

(Reference: Supreme Court: Mita India PVT. LTD. Vs Mahendra Jain

****

CHAPTER-08

SECURITY CHEQUE NO LIABILTY DEFENCE

Scenarios & Specific Repercussions

Scenario 1: Blank Signed Cheque Given as Security

Risk: The holder may fill in arbitrary details (amount, date) and present it.

Drawer's Liability:

If the cheque bounces, criminal liability under Section 138 applies unless fraud is proven.

Courts presume the cheque was issued for a valid debt; the drawer must prove otherwise.

Defence Strategies:

File a police complaint for misuse if threats are received.

Issue stoppayment instructions to the bank immediately (though this may still lead to a bounce).

Challenge in court by proving:

No legally enforceable debt existed (e.g., cheque was for a gift, not a loan).

Fraudulent alteration (e.g., amount filled without consent).

Scenario 2: Duly Signed Filled Cheque Bounced

Drawer's Options:

Pay within 15 days of notice to avoid prosecution.

Negotiate settlement out of court (e.g., via mediation).

Corporate Liability:

Directors can be held personally liable if the cheque was issued for company transactions.

Scenario 3: **Post Dated** or Stale Cheques

Post dated Cheques: Bounce treated similarly under Section 138.

Stale Cheques (>3 months old): Not enforceable; returnable by banks.

IV. Precautionary Measures for Drawers

1. Avoid Blank Cheques: Never issue signed blank cheques/stamp papers. Use formal agreements instead.

2. Stop Payment Orders: Valid for lost/stolen cheques but may not absolve liability if debt is proven.

3. Document Security:

Keep cheque records (dates, amounts).

Use secure methods (e.g., bank transfers).

- Blank cheque/Cheque not filled by accused

Dishonour of cheque - Blank cheque - Can be filled up by the Holder thereof. which will be a valid instrument in the eye of law. (MADRAS HIGH COURT. M.VENUGOPAL, J., Date of Decision/21.11.2012). (A.dhinakar Vs L.Kezhson).

- Blank cheque/Cheque not filled by accused

SC Dishonour of cheque - Blank cheque - If a signed blank cheque is voluntarily presented to a payee, towards some payment, payee may fill up the amount and other particulars - This in itself does not invalidate the cheque - Onus will still be on accused to prove that cheque was not in discharge of debt or liability by adducing evidence. (SUPREME COURT OF INDIA, R.BANUMATHI AND INDIRA BANERJEE, JJ., Date of Decision/06.02.2019). (Bir Singh Vs Mukesh Kumar)

BLANK CHEQUE VS. PRE- FILLED CHEQUE

Question

Whether The Complaint Be Dismissed If The Fill-Up Cheque Is Filled With Different Ink And The Witness Cannot Explain It?

Answer:

Yes, It Was Held That The Trial Court Had Taken A Reasonable And Probable View While Dismissing The Complaint.

(Reference: Punnjab And Haryana High Court:

Subhash Chander Sharma Vs Ravinder alias Babli : 16-01-

The "**Security Cheque**" is one of the most common and contentious issues in cases under Sections 138/141 of the Negotiable Instruments Act. It sits at the intersection of commercial practice and legal defense, often creating a "my word against yours" scenario.

Whether it is a truthful transaction or a tool for defense depends entirely on the context and the evidence led by both parties.

Here's a breakdown of both sides:

1. The "Truth": When a Security Cheque is a Legitimate Transaction

In commercial dealings, it is standard practice to provide post-dated cheques (PDCs) or undated cheques as security for a loan, advance, or fulfilment of an obligation.

Characteristics of a Legitimate Security Cheque:

- Existence of a Underlying Liability: There is a legally enforceable debt or liability. This could be a loan agreement, a contract for goods/services, an advance payment, or a rental agreement.
- Contemporaneous Documentation: The issuance of the cheque is supported by other documents executed at the same time. This is crucial evidence.
- Examples: A loan agreement mentioning the cheque details, a receipt acknowledging the amount, an email trail discussing the

terms and the security, or a promissory note.

- Clear Purpose: The cheque is meant to be presented only upon a specific default (e.g., failure to repay an instalment by a due date, failure to deliver goods).
- Presentation upon Default: The complainant presents the cheque only after the agreed upon default condition has been triggered.

In this scenario, the cheque is a "truth" – it represents a real, contingent liability. Its dishonor upon presentment (after the default) validly invokes the provisions of Section 138.

2. The "Tool for Defense": When the Accused Claims it was a Security Cheque

This is where the accused uses the "security cheque" claim as a shield against the presumption under Section 139. The strategy is to rebut the presumption that the cheque was for the "discharge of a debt or liability."

Common Defense Narratives:

1. Security for an Obligation that Never Materialized:

- Story: The accused claims the cheque was given as security for a future contract, deal, or joint venture that never took off. Since the main transaction didn't happen, there was no debt, and the cheque should never have been presented.
- Example: "I gave this cheque as security for our proposed joint venture to build a property. The JV agreement was never signed, so the deal fell through. The complainant encashed the cheque fraudulently."

2. Blank Signed Cheque given as Security:

- Story: The accused admits to handing over a signed blank cheque but claims the amount, date, or payee name was filled by the complainant without their consent or beyond the agreed terms.
- Example: "I gave a blank cheque as security for a loan of ₹5 Lakhs. The complainant has fraudulently filled it for ₹20 Lakhs and presented it."

3. Security for a Third Party:

- Story: The cheque was issued as a guarantee for the debt of another person/company. The accused argues that their liability was only secondary and contingent on the main debtor's default, and the complainant did not first exhaust remedies against the main debtor.
- (Note: This defense is often weak. If the cheque is signed by you, you are primarily liable as a drawer under the NI Act, regardless of the internal arrangement).

4. The Cheque was Misused/Stolen:

- While not strictly a "security" defense, it's related. The accused claims the cheque was meant for a specific security purpose but was lost, stolen, and misused by the complainant or someone else.

3. How Courts Evaluate the "Security Cheque" Defense

The outcome hinges on the "preponderance of probabilities". The court weighs the evidence from both sides to see whose story is more credible.

SECURITY CHEQUE

The "**security cheque**" is one of the most common and contentious issues in cases under Sections 138/141 of the Negotiable Instruments Act. It sits at the intersection of commercial practice and legal defense, often creating a "my word against yours" scenario.

Whether it is a truthful transaction or a tool for defense depends entirely on the context and the evidence led by both parties.

Here's a breakdown of both sides:

1. The "Truth": When a Security Cheque is a Legitimate Transaction

In commercial dealings, it is standard practice to provide post-dated cheques (PDCs) or undated cheques as security for a loan, advance, or fulfilment of an obligation.

Characteristics of a Legitimate Security Cheque:

- Existence of a Underlying Liability: There is a legally enforceable debt or liability. This could be a loan agreement, a contract for goods/services, an advance payment, or a rental agreement.
- Contemporaneous Documentation: The issuance of the cheque is supported by other documents executed at the same time. This is crucial evidence.
- Examples: A loan agreement mentioning the cheque details, a receipt acknowledging the amount, an email trail discussing the terms and the security, or a promissory note.
- Clear Purpose: The cheque is meant to be presented only upon a specific default (e.g., failure to repay an instalment by a due date, failure to deliver goods).
- Presentation upon Default: The complainant presents the cheque only after the agreed upon default condition has been triggered.

In this scenario, the cheque is a "truth" – it represents a real, contingent liability. Its dishonor upon presentment (after the default) validly invokes the provisions of Section 138.

2. The "Tool for Defense": When the Accused Claims it was a Security Cheque

This is where the accused uses the "security cheque" claim as a shield against the presumption under Section 139. The strategy is to rebut the presumption that the cheque was for the "discharge of a debt or liability."

Common Defense Narratives:

1. Security for an Obligation that Never Materialized:

- Story: The accused claims the cheque was given as security for a future contract, deal, or joint venture that never took off. Since the main transaction didn't happen, there was no debt, and the cheque should never have been presented.

- Example: "I gave this cheque as security for our proposed joint venture to build a property. The JV agreement was never signed, so the deal fell through. The complainant encashed the cheque fraudulently."

2. Blank Signed Cheque given as Security:

- Story: The accused admits to handing over a signed blank cheque but claims the amount, date, or payee name was filled by the complainant without their consent or beyond the agreed terms.

- Example: "I gave a blank cheque as security for a loan of ₹5 Lakhs. The complainant has fraudulently filled it for ₹20 Lakhs and presented it."

3. Security for a Third Party:

- Story: The cheque was issued as a guarantee for the debt of another person/company. The accused argues that their liability was only secondary and contingent on the main debtor's default, and the complainant did not first exhaust remedies against the main debtor.

- (Note: This defense is often weak. If the cheque is signed by you, you are primarily liable as a drawer under the NI Act, regardless of the internal arrangement).

4. The Cheque was Misused/Stolen:

- While not strictly a "security" defense, it's related. The accused claims the cheque was meant for a specific security purpose but was lost, stolen, and misused by the complainant or someone else.

3. How Courts Evaluate the "Security Cheque" Defense

The outcome hinges on the "preponderance of probabilities". The court weighs the evidence from both sides to see whose story is more credible.

What Works in Favour of the Complainant (Holder of the Cheque)?

- The Legal Presumption (Section 139): This is the complainant's biggest weapon. The law presumes the cheque was received for a debt or liability. The burden is on the accused to rebut this.

- Supporting Documentation: The complainant produces a loan agreement, a receipt, an email, or a ledger entry showing the transaction and the purpose of the cheque.

- Admission by Accused: If the accused, in their reply to the statutory notice or in their deposition, admits to taking the money but disputes the amount or terms, it strengthens the complainant's case that a debt exists.

****

CHAPTER-09

XYZ

Important questions for accused side .

Question

Whether to place a heavy burden on the accused to prove the debt

The Hon'ble Supreme Court held that the trial court committed an error in placing a heavy burden on the complainant to prove the debt.

(Reference: Supreme Court: Pavan Dilprao Dike Vs Vishal Narendrabhai Parmar: 12-07-2019)

PROBABLE DEFENCE

Question

Is the lack of capability of the complainant to pay money a probable or a good defense for the accused in the case of Section 138 NI Act.

Answer :

The Calcutta State High Court held no.

(Reference: Calcutta High Court: Subrata Bose Vs Mithu Ghosh:07-11-2022)

PREPONDERANCE OF PROBABILITIES

The term "preponderance of probabilities" is not a standard legal phrase but is correctly understood as a reference to the "preponderance of probabilities", which is the standard of proof applied in civil cases, including those under Section 138 of the NI Act.

Let's break this down in terms of its scope, object, and application.

1. The Standard of Proof: "Preponderance of Probabilities"

- Meaning: This standard means that a fact is considered proven if it is more likely than not to be true. It is a balance of probabilities. If the evidence presented by one side is more convincing and has greater weight than the evidence presented by the other side, the court will rule in favor of the side with
- the superior evidence.
- Contrast with Criminal Standard: This is distinct from the criminal standard of "proof beyond a reasonable doubt," which requires a much higher degree of certainty. A cheque bounce case is a quasi criminal offence. While the proceedings are criminal in nature (as they can lead to imprisonment), the standard of proof for establishing the core liability is civil, i.e., preponderance of probabilities.

2. Object of Section 138 of the NI Act

The primary object of introducing Section 138 was to:

- Enhance the credibility of negotiable instruments, especially cheques, which are the backbone of commercial transactions.
- Prevent dishonesty on the part of the drawer of a cheque from sustaining liability.
- Promote financial discipline and ensure trust in the banking system.

- Provide a speedy and effective remedy to the payee for the loss suffered due to the dishonour of a cheque.

The standard of "preponderance of probabilities" aligns perfectly with this object. It allows the courts to decide cases based on a commonsense assessment of the evidence (like the existence of a debt, the issuance of the cheque, and its subsequent dishonour) without requiring the draconian level of proof needed in a murder or theft case. This makes the remedy effective and accessible.

3. Scope & Application of "Preponderance of Probabilities" in a Section 138 Case

PREPONDENCE OF PROBABILITIES

Question

How can the term Preponderance of Probabilities be defined and how can the accused establish it in the record of the Court during the Trial?

Answer:

The preponderance of probabilities means the facts and circumstances that may lead the court to conclude either that the consideration did not exist or that its non-existence was so probable that a prudent man would, under the circumstances of the case, act upon the plea that the consideration did not exist. (**Reference**: Coaching Part)

Question

The complainant contended that the cheque in question was for the purchase of a certain article; however, no evidence was produced?

Answer:

The accused is acquitted as the defense is more than sufficiently demonstrated based on the preponderance of probabilities. (**Reference**:.Bombay High Court : Ghanshyamdas lalchand Vs Sheikh hamid Sheikh Gulab & others

:09-01-2018)

PROCLAIMED OFFENDER

Question

Whether the Trial Court was required to invoke the provisions of Section 82 Cr. P.C. when the warrant of arrest was received back unexecuted with the report that the accused had left the given address?

Answer:

The Court is duty-bound to ask the complainant

to furnish a fresh address of the accused and ensure that the accused is duly served before commencing with the coercive process. Therefore, the Trial Court was not required to invoke the provisions of Section 82 Cr.P.C. The order of declaring the accused a proclaimed offender and consequent registration of FIR cannot be sustained.

(**Reference**:. Punjab And Haryana High Court : Surender Singh Vs State Of Haryana & Anr: 12-01-2021)

QUASHING U/S 482 DISMISSED

QUESTION

Is it permissible for the HIGH COURT to record and find, wherever there are factual disputes while dealing with a petition under section 482 Cr.P.C.??

Answer :

NO, It is not permissible for the High Court to record a finding wherever there are factual disputes.

(**Reference** : Supreme Court: Dr. Lakshman Vs. the State of Karnataka : 17-10-2019)

Quashing by High Court

question regarding the inherent powers of the High Court under Section 482 of the CrPC to quash proceedings in a case under Section 138 of the Negotiable Instruments Act (the "cheque bounce" law).

Specific Grounds on which the High Court can exercise this power.

Let's break this down in detail.

The Foundation: Section 482 CrPC

Section 482 of the Code of Criminal Procedure, 1973, preserves the inherent powers of the High Court to:

(a) give effect to any order under the CrPC,

(b) prevent abuse of the process of any court, and

· (c) otherwise to secure the ends of justice.

This power is extraordinary, discretionary, and must be exercised sparingly and with caution. It is not an alternative remedy to a regular trial.

Quashing a Section 138 NI Act Case: The Key Grounds

The Supreme Court of India, in a catena of judgments, has outlined the specific circumstances under which a High Court can quash a complaint under Section 138 of the NI Act. These grounds are strict and narrowly interpreted.

Here are the specific grounds you are asking for:

Category 1: Grounds Based on Legal Deficiencies in the Complaint itself

These are the strongest grounds for quashing. If the complaint itself, even if taken at face value and presumed to be entirely true, does not disclose an offence, it must be quashed.

1. Absence of a Legal Debt or Liability: The foundational requirement for an offence under Section 138 is a "legally enforceable debt or liability." If the petitioner can demonstrate with documentary evidence (e.g., a settlement agreement, full payment receipt, a written contract showing the cheque was for security only) that no such debt exists, the proceedings can be quashed.

· Example: 'A' gives a cheque to 'B' as security for a loan but never takes the loan. 'B' presents the cheque. Since no debt was ever created, the complaint is an abuse of process.

2. Nonfulfillment of Mandatory Procedural Conditions: The NI Act has strict procedural steps (issuing a demand notice within 30 days of

bounce, waiting 15 days for payment, filing complaint within 30 days of the cause of action arising). If the complainant fails to adhere to these timelines prima facie evident from the complaint, it can be a ground for quashing.

3. Lack of Essential Ingredients: If a vital ingredient of the offence is missing from the complaint, it is liable to be quashed.

· Example: The complaint does not allege that the cheque was drawn for the discharge of a debt. Or, it is clear the cheque was signed by an unauthorized person without the company's knowledge.

Category 2: Grounds Based on Settlement Between Parties

This is the most common and practical ground for quashing in NI Act cases.

1. Amissible Settlement under Section 147 of the NI Act: Section 147 makes the offence compoundable. If the parties have entered into a settlement and the petitioner has paid the agreed amount (or a substantial part of it), the High Court can quash the proceedings to secure the ends of justice.

· The Court will typically do this even if the settlement happens after the filing of the complaint or during appellate stages.

· The consent of the complainant is crucial for this.

Category 3: Grounds to Prevent Abuse of Process of Court

This is invoked when the continuation of proceedings would be manifestly unjust.

1. Patently Frivolous or Vexatious Complaints: If the complaint is shown to be maliciously filed with an ulterior motive to harass the accused, and no offence is made out, the High Court will quash it to

prevent abuse of process.

· Example: Filing a complaint on a cheque that was stolen or obtained by coercion.

2. Inordinate and Unexplained Delay: If the case has been pending for an excessively long time (e.g., 1015 years) due to no fault of the accused, and the trial has not commenced meaningfully, the High Court may quash it to secure the ends of justice, especially if the delay prejudices the accused's right to a fair trial.

What is NOT a Ground for Quashing under Section 482?

It is critical to understand what the High Court will not consider at this stage:

· Purely Factual Disputes: If the defence requires leading and testing evidence (e.g., "I already repaid the debt in cash," "the cheque was lost"), the High Court will not conduct a minitrial. It will relegate the accused to raise these defences during the trial. Quashing is not meant to shortcut the trial process.

· Merely because the case is weak: A seemingly weak prosecution case is not enough; it must be so weak that no conviction is possible.

· Alternative Remedy: The existence of an alternative remedy (like raising these issues before the trial court) is not an absolute bar, but the High Court will be reluctant to interfere if the petitioner has not availed of those remedies.

Important Caveat: The New BNSS

Please note that from July 1, 2024, the Code of Criminal Procedure, 1973 (CrPC) has been replaced by the Bharatiya Nagarik Suraksha Sanhita, 2023 (BNSS). The inherent powers of the High Court are now contained in Section 531 of the BNSS. The text and spirit of this section are identical to Section 482 CrPC. All the principles and grounds mentioned above will continue to apply under the new law.

Section 531 BNSS: "Nothing in this Sanhita shall be deemed to limit or affect the inherent powers of the High Court to make such orders as may be necessary to give effect to any order under this Sanhita, or to prevent abuse of the process of any Court or otherwise to secure the ends of justice."

Conclusion: The High Court's power to quash a 138 NI Act case is not to be used lightly. It is restricted to specific, welldefined grounds primarily concerning the absence of a legally enforceable debt, fatal procedural errors, or a valid settlement between the parties. It is not a tool to decide factual disputes that are rightfully meant for the trial court.

Question

Does any post-dated cheque issued as collateral security attract Section 138 of the NI Act.

Answer:

When a Post dated cheque is issued as collateral security and the point of time, is on the date of issuance of the Cheque No subsisting liability, No 138 attracts.

(**Reference**: Gauhati High Court : Sri Don Ayengia Vs State of Assam : 02-04- 2014)

Stages and Steps of the Drawer of Any Cheque as an Individual or Part of a Corporate Entity.

4. Reply to Notice Within a 15Day Time Frame. A drawer, signatory, or corporate entity of an unpaid returned cheque is required to respond to the legal statutory notice and comply or reply within a coolingoff period of 15 days under subsection 138(b) served upon them, asking for payment of the cheque amount, allegedly claiming their liability directly or vicariously. Once the due service, in terms of law and practice, is effected, an individual or corporate entity is under a legal obligation to comply with the notice by making the payment of the disputed cheque or raising their hands with any valid reasons stating 'NO LIABILITY', preferably in reply to the notice based on the chain of facts or any evidence to rebut the claim in question.

Now the question arises as to whether, upon receipt of such notice, one should reply or remain silent. For instance, the notice by the payee to the payer is mandatory and statutory as a condition precedent for filing a complaint under section 138/141 of the NI Act. However, the recipient of the notice has the option to reply immediately or wait to see the next steps taken by the payer, the holder of the cheque. The Supreme Court of India has held that adverse inference can be drawn if no reply is provided, although this does not necessarily fasten liability solely on the ground of no reply, as the initial burden is on the drawee to establish their claim in the course of the trial.

It is important to note that anyone in an individual capacity or as part of a corporate entity, if served with a legal notice, is at their liberty to reply to the sender and their advocate, justifying their lack of role or attribution. Any such explanation may lead the sender and their advocate to withdraw the notice against them and refrain from impleading them as co- accused in the subsequent complaint under Section 141 of the Negotiable Instruments Act. Reply to the Notice of Court regarding the Delay Condonation Miscellaneous Application filed by the purported Complainant pursuant to section 142(2) of the NI Act. The recipient of any such notice may represent themselves in person before the Court or through an advocate to contest the Delay Condonation Application. Silence or nonappearance may lead the concerned court to treat the application as non- contesting. If the application is allowed, the accompanying complaint will be registered according to the law, and the court may issue a process against the purported accused. The author, as a practicing advocate, requests that the reader read a short article in

'CLR Volume 1: The Way to Win and How to Win,' wherein the Advocate for the respondent, instead of filing a reply to the delayed condition, changed the course of action and succeeded in getting a favorable legal order. The complaint was dismissed for want of prosecution; the cherry on the cake is that the respondent always remains in a winwin position without even appearing a single time in Court, as per the strategy of her lawyer. The Practical Guide Updates Dated 26.07.2025

VAKALATNAMA

Vakalatnama Specifically Authorizing An Advocate To Plead "Not Guilty" and Vicariously LIABILITY defend your case under Sections 138/141 of the NI Act, while retaining all essential safeguards:

VAKALATNAMA WITH SPECIFIC POWER

"NOT GUILTY" PLEA AUTHORIZATION

IN THE COURT OF JMFC, [CITY/STATE]

Case Title: [X] v. [Your Name]

Case No.: [__] of 202

I, [Your Full Name], accused in the above case, hereby appoint [Advocate's Name] as my counsel with special emphasis on:

1. NOT GUILTY PLEA & DEFENSE STRATEGY

To enter a formal plea of "Not Guilty" on my behalf at the first hearing

To vigorously challenge all allegations through:

Technical Defenses:

Jurisdictional objections

Invalid statutory notice (u/s 138(b))

Cheque alterations (u/s 87 NI Act)

Substantive Defenses:

Rebutting presumption u/s 139 (no legally enforceable debt)

Proving the cheque was issued as security/without consideration

Establishing the complainant's unclean hands

2. EVIDENTIARY PROTECTION

To object to inadmissible evidence:

Uncertified electronic records (noncompliant with S.65B Evidence Act)

Improperly served notices

Hearsay testimony

To crossexamine the complainant/witnesses on:

Debt validity

Cheque handling chain

Notice delivery

3. LIMITED SETTLEMENT POWERS

Any settlement/compounding requires my prior written consent

May explore ADR only after consulting me

4. TRIAL MANAGEMENT

To seek exemption from personal appearance (where permissible)

To demand strict proof of all allegations

Special Instruction: My advocate SHALL NOT make any admission of liability without my express written authorization.

[Rest of the Vakalatnama remains unchanged regarding signatures, declarations, etc.]

Why This Matters?

1. Preserves Your Defense: Prevents inadvertent admissions by counsel

2. Strategic Focus: Targets both technical and substantive weaknesses in the complainant's case

3. Control Retained: Ensures you decide on settlements

*******THE END *******

INDEX PART III

CHAPTER-01

ARTICLE QUA HANDWRITING EXPERT

Shivani Gupta LLb. LLm. DFS, Phd(Sh)(Criminal and forensic Science) HOD Law Department at RMCL, Mumbai. Under Mumbai university.

Question Document Expert

Forgery on Cheques — A Forensic and Legal Perspective

1. Introduction

In recent decades, the increase in economic and digital literacy, along with globalized banking practices, has contributed to a surge in non-violent, financially motivated crimes, commonly referred to as white-collar crimes.

These offenses are often committed by individuals with access to financial

instruments and are characterized by planning, sophistication, and

concealment. Cheque forgery falls squarely within this category. It often goes unnoticed until the funds have been withdrawn or damage has been done.

As

such, early detection, investigation, and prosecution are vital to maintaining

the integrity of financial transactions.

forgery is a critical financial crime that undermines the integrity of monetary

transactions. It involves the manipulation, alteration, or fabrication of cheques to commit fraud. Given the surge in white-collar crimes, the detection and prosecution of cheque forgery demand the application of scientific methods—

particularly through the specialized forensic science discipline of Questioned Document Examination (QDE)—as well as the support of a robust legal framework under the Bharatiya Nyaya Sanhita (BNS), 2023.

2.What is a Questioned Document?

A questioned document is any document whose authenticity, origin, or

alterations are in dispute in a legal context. In the context of cheque forgery,

this often includes disputed signatures, altered entries, or counterfeit cheques.

3.Role of QDE in Cheque Forgery

- Authentication of signatures and handwriting
- Detection of material alterations
- Analysis of ink, paper, and printing mechanisms
- Establishing chronological sequence of writings
- Detection of erasures, additions, or overwriting

4.Tools & Techniques Used

- Video Spectral Comparator (VSC)- A VSC is a highly specialized imaging system that uses various light sources and filters to examine the properties of inks, papers, and security features in documents. It combines video imaging, spectral analysis, and digital enhancement to reveal hidden details not visible to the naked eye. Ink Differentiation
- Compares inks that appear similar under normal light but differ under UV, IR,

or narrowband lighting.

- Helps determine if multiple pens were used (e.g., in forgeries or alterations).
- Infrared (IR) Luminescence & Absorption

- Reveals writing that's been erased, obliterated, or altered.
- Some inks luminesce under IR light, while others absorb it—this contrast

helps identify tampering.

- UV and IR Imaging
- Detects invisible inks, watermarks, security threads, and fibers embedded in

paper.

- Useful for verifying the authenticity of passports, ID cards, banknotes, and

cheques.

- Document Dating and Sequence of Entries
- Through ink comparison and overlay techniques, VSC can help determine

which text was written first.

- Magnification and Microscopy
- High-resolution zoom to examine microprinting, edge defects, or printer

characteristics.

- Digital Image Capture and Analysis
- Stores, enhances, and compares document images using software tools.
- Provides documentation for reports and courtroom presentations.

This scientific branch delivers conclusive expert reports admissible in courts under the Indian Evidence Act (now Bharatiya Sakshya Adhiniyam, 2023).

- Legal Provisions Applicable in Questioned Document Examination In the forensic analysis of questioned documents—especially in cases involving forgery, cheque manipulation, and handwriting disputes—several legal provisions under Indian law are applicable. These provisions ensure that the findings from devices like the Video Spectral Comparator (VSC) are legally admissible and used effectively in judicial proceedings. Under Bharatiya Nyaya Sanhita (BNS), 2023

• The Bharatiya Nyaya Sanhita (BNS), 2023, which replaced the Indian Penal

Code (IPC), provides detailed sections related to forgery and cheating. These

offenses are often encountered in document fraud cases:

• Section 334 defines forgery as the creation of false documents with intent to

deceive.

• Section 335 addresses simple forgery, which involves making or signing a

false document knowingly.

• Section 336 deals specifically with the forgery of cheques or valuable

securities, a serious offense punishable with imprisonment that may extend

to life.

• Section 337 covers forgery for the purpose of cheating, wherein forged

documents are created to deceive someone.

• Section 338 penalizes the act of using a forged document as genuine,

knowing it to be false.

• Section 316 addresses cheating, which involves dishonestly inducing a

person to deliver property based on deceit.

• These sections form the backbone of legal action in forgery and documentrelated

criminal cases.

5.Under the Negotiable Instruments Act, 1881

- When the questioned document involves negotiable instruments like

cheques, the Negotiable Instruments Act, 1881, becomes applicable:

- Section 138 deals with the dishonour of cheques due to insufficient funds or

similar reasons, which is a criminal offense.

- Section 139 creates a presumption in favour of the holder of the cheque,

unless rebutted by the drawer.

- Section 142 outlines the procedural aspects for taking cognizance of

offences under this Act, including the filing of complaints.

- These sections are particularly relevant in cases involving forged or bounced

cheques, where forensic tools help prove alterations or identify the writer.

6. Forensic Examination Process of Forged Cheques, covering each phase under

appropriate subheadings:

(a) Signature & Handwriting Examination

The first and most fundamental step in examining a forged cheque is the analysis of the signature and handwriting. Forensic document examiners use both macro-level and micro-level techniques to scrutinize various characteristics of the handwriting. At the macro level, the examiner observes overall handwriting features such as slant, alignment, baseline consistency, and spacing between letters and words. At the micro level, they focus on pen pressure, hesitation marks, tremors, speed of writing, and stroke formation, which can indicate forgery or unnatural writing.

To authenticate a signature or detect forgery, a comparison is made with admitted or known genuine signatures. This is done using tools like a comparison microscope or a Video Spectral Comparator (VSC), which allows side-by-side examination of fine writing details.

Any unnatural variations—such as inconsistent stroke movement or interrupted flow—can suggest that the signature was forged, traced, or written under duress.

b.Ink & Paper Analysis

Beyond handwriting, the ink and paper used on a cheque can provide critical forensic evidence. One of the most widely used techniques is Thin Layer Chromatography (TLC), which helps separate the different components of ink. By comparing the chemical makeup of inks, experts can determine whether different pens or inks were used in different sections of the cheque—an indicator of tampering. In some cases, forensic labs attempt to estimate the age of ink to determine when the writing was made. This is done using chemical degradation analysis and optical techniques, such as measuring the solvent evaporation or pigment fading rate.

Additionally, paper examination includes analysis of Fiber content, thickness, optical brighteners, and security features. Watermark verification under transmitted light helps confirm the authenticity of the cheque paper and detect any substitutions or fabrications.

c.Erasure & Tampering Detection

One of the most common forms of cheque fraud involves erasing or altering original information—such as the payee name, amount, or date. This is where erasure and tampering detection becomes crucial. A key tool used is Electrostatic Detection Apparatus (ESDA), which can reveal indented writing—the impressions left on the paper by a pen, even if the ink has been removed. This technique is especially useful in identifying erased content or overwritten text. Further, infrared and ultraviolet imaging plays a vital role in detecting chemical alterations, such as ink removal using solvents or overwriting with a different pen. Under UV or IR light, original and tampered areas may reflect or absorb light differently, making it possible to visually isolate altered sections. This allows the examiner to detect forgeries that are invisible under normal lighting.

7. The Role of Handwriting Expert Reports in Disputed Cheque Cases

When dealing with a disputed cheque, particularly in cases involving suspected signature forgery or alterations to the document, the handwriting expert report becomes a crucial piece of forensic evidence. Courts and investigating authorities rely heavily on the scientific findings and opinions of forensic document examiners because the authenticity of signatures and the integrity of cheque details often determine the outcome of litigation. The analysis process undertaken by handwriting experts is methodical and involves several key stages, from identifying the core dispute to presenting the findings in a structured report.

1. Core Dispute Scenarios in Cheque Forgery Cases

Cheque-related disputes generally arise in two primary contexts.

The first is a signature dispute, where the signatory of the cheque denies having signed the instrument, alleging that the signature was forged. This scenario is common when unauthorized parties gain access to a cheque book or when blank signed cheques are misused. The second context involves alterations, where it is suspected that critical details of the cheque—such as the amount, the payee's name, or the date— have been tampered with after the cheque's original issuance. Alterations may be carried out using chemical erasure, overwriting, or substitution, which can be subtle and difficult to detect without forensic analysis.

2. Handwriting Expert Analysis Process

The analysis conducted by handwriting experts is comprehensive and divided into multiple stages, each of which is aimed at isolating and evaluating features indicative of forgery or alteration.

a) Examination of Questioned Features

The expert begins by thoroughly examining the questioned signature or suspected

alteration using magnification tools. In the case of a signature, the focus is on the

line quality (whether the strokes are smooth or shaky), pen pressure (variation in ink deposition), slant, letter formation, spacing between characters, pen lifts, and the natural flow of writing. Forgers often fail to reproduce the fluidity of genuine signatures, resulting in tremors or unnatural hesitation marks. For suspected alterations, the examiner looks for evidence of ink mismatches, erasures, paper fiber disturbances, or inconsistent handwriting in the modified portions. Alterations often disturb the surface fibers of the paper, which can be detected under oblique lighting or with the help of chemical reagents.

b) Comparison with Known Samples

Once the questioned features have been documented, they are compared against known samples. Experts obtain requested specimens—signatures and handwriting samples contemporaneous with the disputed cheque—from the account holder or bank records. In some cases, collected standards are obtained under controlled conditions to ensure authenticity. These samples provide a benchmark for comparison. The analysis is supported by sophisticated tools such as microscopes, Video Spectral Comparators (VSC) for ink and security feature analysis, and Electrostatic Detection Apparatus (ESDA) for revealing indentations from prior writings.

c) Key Indicators of Forgery or Alteration

Through this process, handwriting experts look for specific indicators that point

toward forgery or tampering. These include:

- Tremors or hesitations in signature lines, often resulting from slow and

deliberate tracing.

- Unnatural pen lifts and retouching at letter junctions.
- Inconsistencies in ink color or absorption, which may reveal additions made

at different times.

- Misaligned text, overwriting, or spacing irregularities that disturb the baseline

of writing.

- Discrepancies in slant or letter proportions that are inconsistent with genuine

samples.

Components of a Credible Expert Report

A credible handwriting expert report must be methodical and transparent. It typically includes:

- Methodology: A detailed description of the techniques and equipment used,

such as VSC, microscopy, or ESDA.

- Side-by-Side Comparisons: Enlarged photographic exhibits highlighting

similarities and differences between questioned and known samples. These

visual aids are vital for judges and lawyers to understand the basis of the

findings

Admissibility and Acceptance of Expert Opinion in Courts

1. Legal Basis: Section 45 of Bharatiya Sakshya Adhiniyam, 2023 Under Section 45, the opinion of persons specially skilled in areas such as handwriting, signatures, document examination, ink analysis, and related scientific disciplines is treated as admissible evidence. This provision ensures that matters requiring specialized knowledge are evaluated by individuals trained in forensic science, particularly those attached to State Forensic Science Laboratories (SFSLs) or Central Forensic Science Laboratory (CFSL). Experts in Questioned Document Examination (QDE), handwriting analysis, and forensic chemistry are considered competent witnesses.Their opinions are considered evidence, not mere suggestions, because they are based on scientific analysis.

Judicial Approach towards Expert Evidence in Cheque Forgery Cases

In India, courts place significant reliance on expert evidence in cheque forgery cases because such crimes typically involve technical and specialized questions about handwriting, signatures, and alterations. However, the judiciary treats expert testimony with caution, ensuring that conclusions are drawn only after corroborating and scrutinizing the scientific opinion.

Nature of Expert Evidence

Expert evidence is opinion evidence, not direct evidence. Unlike eyewitnesses who testify to facts they have directly perceived; experts provide their inference based on scientific or technical analysis. This distinction forms the basis of the cautious approach adopted by courts. Courts recognize that experts can make mistakes or their opinions can differ. Judges, who are laypersons in scientific disciplines, cannot accept expert testimony blindly.This multi-layered approach ensures that expert reports are considered within the entire body of evidence, not in isolation.

Section 73 of Bharatiya Sakshya Adhiniyam: Judicial Comparison When doubts remain, Section 73 empowers the court to compare the disputed handwriting or signature with admitted samples available on record. This provision enables judges to personally examine the questioned cheque alongside known specimens. However, the Supreme Court has repeatedly held that this power must be exercised with caution because judges are not forensic experts.Judicial comparison is intended to supplement, not replace, expert evidence.

Case Reference: Murari Lal v. State of Madhya Pradesh (AIR 1980 SC 531) – The Supreme Court held that while judges may compare signatures, their decision should be based on expert guidance wherever possible.

Greater Weight to Government Forensic Reports

Courts give higher evidentiary weight to reports from State or Central Forensic

Science Laboratories (FSLs) because:

- These laboratories follow standardized protocols and maintain a strict chain

of custody.

- Experts working in these institutions are neutral and not hired by any

litigating party.

- Reports are often admissible without summoning the expert unless

challenged by the opposing party.

However, even government reports are not binding; the court may reject them if found inconsistent with other evidence.

Judicial Observations from Landmark Cases

1. S. Gopal Reddy v. State of Andhra Pradesh (AIR 1996 SC 2184)

Expert evidence is advisory but can form the sole basis of conviction if reliable and corroborated.

2. State Bank of India v. P. Soupramaniane (2007 (1) MLJ (Crl) 1151)

Court relied heavily on a detailed forensic handwriting report with

photographic enlargements to convict the accused.

3. Kisan Trimbak Kothule v. State of Maharashtra (2013 CriLJ 4424)

Prosecution's failure to obtain expert opinion weakened the case and led

to acquittal.

These cases demonstrate that expert evidence is often decisive in cheque forgery

cases but must meet strict reliability standards.

Case Law on Judicial Interpretation

Indian judiciary has consistently addressed the scope and limitations of expert

opinion:

1. Murari Lal v. State of Madhya Pradesh (AIR 1980 SC 531) – The Supreme

Court held that expert opinion must always be tested by the court and

preferably corroborated by other evidence.

2. S. Gopal Reddy v. State of Andhra Pradesh (AIR 1996 SC 2184) – Expert

evidence is advisory in nature but can form the basis of conviction if found

reliable and corroborated.

3. Kisan Trimbak Kothule v. State of Maharashtra (2013 CriLJ 4424) – The

absence of expert opinion in a cheque forgery case weakened the prosecution, highlighting its necessity.

4. State Bank of India v. P. Soupramaniane (2007 (1) MLJ (Crl) 1151) – Court

upheld conviction on the strength of a well-reasoned handwriting expert

report, supported by visual aids.

Conclusion

Expert opinions play a decisive role in cheque forgery cases because the crime often leaves little direct evidence. The Bharatiya Sakshya Adhiniyam, 2023, by recognizing forensic experts as competent witnesses, strengthens the justice delivery system. However, judicial prudence dictates that such opinions should be scrutinized, corroborated, and supplemented by other evidence before being relied upon for conviction or acquittal.

Question

Whether the examination by handwriting expert is justified when no grievance in respect of signature of cheque rather grievances about handwriting of cheque?

Answer: FAQS PART A

The Bombay High court held no justification for examination by handwriting expert in view of section 20 of the NI Act drawer of the cheque can issue blank cheque and by his act give authority to the person to fill up it's contents.

(Reference:. Bombay High Court: Simratmal Hiralal Gandhi Vs Kedarnath Badrinarayan Bang & Ors. : 01-08-2011)

Articles 02

AMENDMENT IN CHEQUE BOUNCE CASES: INTERIM COMPENSATION According to the newly inserted Section 143A in the Negotiable Instrument Act, which empowers the Trial Court to take cognizance of a complaint under Section 138 of the Act, the court concerned may order the accused to pay the complainant interim compensation to the extent of 20% of the check amount. Such an order can be passed in a summary or summons trial where the accused does not plead guilty in terms of the statutory provisions of Section 251 of the Criminal Procedure code, consequently, the trial commences.

After the date of the order of the Trial Court, a period of 60 days is stipulated by the legislature. However, an additional 30 days may be extended at the sole discretion of the court if a sufficient reason is assigned by the accused. Overall, the accused must comply with the order within a time frame of 60+30 days with no further provision or discretion of extension. Otherwise, they may face consequences. The consequences of attachment and sale of moveable and immovable property, as well as Section 421 and 431 of the Cr.P.C., would come into play in terms of sub-section 5 of 143A. However, it's crystal clear in the light of sub-section 6 of Section 143A that the amount of fine imposed or compensation awarded under Section 357 of the Cr.P.C. shall be ***reduced by the amount paid or recovered as interim compensation***. Sub-clause 4 of 143A further reflects very clearly that if the accused drawer of the cheque is acquitted, the court shall direct the complainant to repay the recovered sum along with interest at the bank rate as published by the RBI prevalent at the beginning of the relevant financial year.

As per the personal view of the authors of this article and as a practicing lawyer, the complainant will be under no legal obligation to return

or repay the 20% amount until and unless the order of acquittal passed by the trial court attains finality or no further statutory remedy is availed by the complainant to safeguard and avail. His right to appeal, revision, and statutory appeal, whichever is available to him. An appeal against acquittal is a part of the trial. So, the complainant will hold the recovered sum until final adjudication and until all statutory remedies are exhausted. If the quantum of interim compensation received by him is a substantial and huge amount, the accused will have to wait for a number of years to get back his payout. The steps of the complainant will obviously invite multiple, long-lasting litigations, blocking the High judiciary. Somehow, the object of the legislature might be turned defeated to some extent.

Additionally, Section 148 A empowers the Appellate Court to order payment of a minimum of 20% of the fine or compensation awarded by the trial court, pending appeal against conviction. The amount payable under this section shall be in addition to any interim compensation already paid by the accused under Section 143 A. This means that the complainant will get an additional 20%, not just of the cheque amount, but also of 20% of the aggregate compensation. For instance, if a compensation of double the amount, i.e., ten lakh, is awarded against a five lakh cheque, the accused has to pay 20% of the ten lakh, not against five lakh. However, Section 148 A is silent as to whether the 20% deposit will be a condition precedent for filing the statutory appeal or if it would be the discretion of the Appellate Court to exercise their acumen in the prevailing scenario in each and every matter before the Appellate Court.

However, if the appeal of the accused is allowed, then the complainant will be directed to repay the accused with interest (the recovered sum) as per the provisions of section 143A, subclause 4, and section 148.

Another question arises: if the accused possesses no movable or immovable property and raises their hands, how will the complainant be compensated qua interim relief? What will be the role and power of the court to react and proceed in that situation? Because section 143A or 148A nowhere provides to award a sentence in default of the fine imposed under the above

provisions. Additionally, the order to interim compensation cannot be defined as a fine until the final adjudication of the trial. Only if the accused are held guilty, does section 357 of the Cr.P.C. attract for imposing compensation. Section 5 of 143A of N.I. Act only prescribes how the interim compensation may be recovered.

"An important question is whether an interim order can only be passed in cases where plea U/S 251 is yet to be recorded, or even in those cases reflecting afterwards captions, which means the implementation of the doctrine of retrospective and prospective for the enforcement of amended and inserted sections.

Before the Hon'ble Supreme Court of India, in the case of SEBI versus Classic Credit Limited in Para No 11 (in Hitendra Vishnu Thakur Vs State of Maharashtra), referring to the ***question whether the amendment in question affects the substantive right or the amendment supra is procedural amending statute.***

A statute which affects substantive rights is presumed to be prospective in operation unless made retrospective, either expressly or by necessary intendment, whereas a statute which merely affects procedure, unless such a construction is textually impossible, is presumed to be retrospective.

A statute which not only changes the procedure but also creates new rights and liabilities shall be construed to be prospective in operation, unless otherwise provided either expressly or by necessary implication. Thus, in the light of the discussion by the Apex Authority of law, newly amended provisions prime-facie don't attract Law of Retrospective effect.

The step and object of the amendment is to provide relief to payees to some extent and to discourage frivolous and unnecessary litigation. According to the statement of object, the amendment will strengthen the credibility of Cheques.

SO, LET US SEE "HOW THE CAMEL GOT HIS HUMP".

Author

Advocate Vinod Kumar Chhabra

Disclaimer: ALL concerned subscribers and readers of this article are very humbly requested to please verify very minutely before taking any steps or knocking the door of any court for any relief based on the information contained herein. This article is just a personal opinion and does not amount to any assurance of its absolute correctness and application before any court of law.

CITATION TITLE AND CRUX OF JUDGEMENTS OF SUPREME COURT AND STATE HIGH COURT :

Interim Compensation Section 143A NI Act.

Supreme Court

(1)

G.J.Raja v. Tejraj Surana Supreme Court of India Section 143A is prospective in application and cannot be applied retrospectively to complaints filed before its introduction on September 1, 2018.

2

Surinder Singh Deswal@ Col.S.S Deswal & Ors. vs. Virender Gandhi & Anr. (2019)

Crux:Section 143A applies only prospectively, i.e., to offences committed after the 2018 amendment to the NI Act. Interim compensation mechanism is not retrospective, safeguarding accused's rights in pre-amendment cases.

3

Rakesh Ranjan Shrivastava vs.State of Jharkhand (2023)

Crux:The power to grant interim compensation under Section 143A is discretionary and not mandatory. Courts must assess the merits of the complainant's case and accused's defense, financial condition of the accused, and other relevant factors before ordering interim compensation.Crl. Appeal No. 741 of 2024 (Supreme Court)

Crux:The use of "may" in Section 143A(1) means the power is directory, not mandatory. Awarding interim compensation before determination of guilt is a drastic measure and must be exercised judiciously with recorded reasons. The court must prima facie evaluate the case and defense and consider financial distress before ordering compensation, including the quantum of interim compensation. These rulings collectively establish that Section 143A enables courts to order interim compensation up to 20% of the cheque amount to aid complainants in cheque dishonor cases but with judicial discretion and safeguards protecting accused persons until guilt is proved. These citations and crux provide concise guidance on the judicial interpretation and application of Section 143A from 2019 to date.

4Gurudatta Sugars Marketing Pvt.Ltd. v. Prithviraj Sayajirao Deshmukh & Ors. Supreme Court of India (July 24, 2024) Liability to pay interim compensation u/S. 143A is only on the "drawer" of the cheque (the company); it does not extend to directors or authorized signatories of the company, who are not the "drawer".

......See FAQs Book

To read more on FAQs Part "A" questions No. 121 to 137 related to Interim Compensation during trial and at the appellate stage, OR please wait for the second volume of The Practical Guide.

NOTE: PLEASE READ CHAPTER 6 OFTHIS BOOK NAMELY INTERIM COMPENSATION 20% FOR BOTH SIDE REPRENTATION

ARTICLE 03

✍Vinod Kumar Chhabra...

Law of Presumptions under Section 118/139 of the N.I. Act.

VERSUS

Law of Rebuttal

&

Standard of proof

Plain & Opening bare language of **Section 118 Of The Negotiable Instrument Act** reflect the certain Presumptions in favour of the Payee until the contrary is proved that every such instrument **If Accepted, Endorsed Negotiated Or Transferred For Consideration** and as to the date bearing and was accepted within a reasonable time after its date and before its maturity, order of endorsement, that holder is a holder in due course **provided that where the instrument has been obtained from its lawful owner** or lawful custody ***not amounting to be obtained by playing fraud or by unlawful consideration***, the burden of proving that the holder is a holder in due course lies upon him, ***Whereas Section 139 of the act supra reveals that presumption is in favour of the holder, unless the contrary is proved*** that the holder of a cheque received the cheque of the nature referred to in section 138 for the discharge, in whole or in part, or any other debt or other liability.

The Hon'ble Supreme Court of India in the case of Kumar Exports vs. Sharma Carpet held that "***there is a presumption that every negotiable instrument duly executed is for discharge of a debt or liability, but the presumption is rebuttable by proving the contrary.***

In the facts and circumstances of the case, it was found that the cheque in question was in advance for the purchase of carpets, which were in fact not sold by the payee of the cheque to the drawer, as proved from the deposition of an official of the Sales Tax Department, who stated that the payee had admitted that he had not sold the carpets.

In the matter of Hiten P. Dalal vs. Bratindranath Banerjee, the Hon'ble Supreme Court held that both Sections 138 and 139 require that the Court presume the liability of the drawer of the cheques for the amounts for which the cheques are drawn.

Whereas in State of Madras vs. Vaidyanatha Iyer, the Hon'ble Supreme Court held "***that it was obligatory on the Court to raise this presumption***."

Presumption of innocence is undoubtedly a human right, **as contended on behalf of the respondent-accused, relying on the judgments of the Hon'ble Supreme Court in Ranjitsing Brahmajeetsing Sharma vs. State of Maharashtra and Anr and Rajesh Ranjan Yada @ Pappu Yadav vs. CBI through its Director.** However, guilt may be established by recourse to presumptions in law and presumptions in facts, as observed above.

The Hon'ble Supreme in the Case Titled Laxmi Dyechem vs. State of Gujarat & Ors., this Court reiterated "***that in view of Section 139, it has to be presumed that a cheque was issued in discharge of a debt or other liability, but the presumption could be rebutted by adducing evidence. The burden of proof was, however, on the person who wanted to rebut the presumption.*** This Court held, "However, this presumption coupled with the *object of Chapter XVII of the Act leads to the conlusion that by countermanding payment of a post-dated cheque, a party should not be allowed to get away from the penal provision of Section 138 of the Act."*.

In K.N. Beena vs. Muniyappan and Another, the Hon'ble Supreme Court held that in view of the provisions of Section 139 of the Negotiable Instruments Act read with Section 118 thereof, the Court had to presume that the cheque had been issued for discharging a debt or liability. The said presumption was rebuttable and could be rebutted by the accused by proving the contrary.

But mere denial or rebuttal by the accused was not enough. The accused had to prove with cogent evidence that there was no debt or liability. This Court clearly held that the High Court had erroneously set aside the conviction by proceeding on the basis that denials or averments in the reply of the accused were sufficient to shift the burden of proof on the complainant to prove that the cheque had been issued for the discharge of a debt or a liability. This was an entirely erroneous approach. The accused had to prove in the trial by leading cogent evidence that there was no debt or liability.

The Hon'ble Apex Court in the Matter of Raj Kumar Khurana vs. State of (NCT of Delhi) & Anr. was rendered in the particular facts of the case **where the drawer of the cheque had reported to the police and the bank that two unfilled cheques signed by him had been stolen.**

Peculiar facts and circumstances of the case indicate that several civil suits between the parties were pending.

The Hon'ble Apex Court of India, in the case Krishna Janardhan Bhat vs. Dattatraya G. Hegde, cited on behalf of the respondent-accused, reaffirmed that Section 139 of the Act raises a presumption that a cheque duly drawn was towards a debt or liability. However, keeping in view the peculiar facts and circumstances of the case, this Court was of the opinion that the courts below had approached the case from a wholly different angle through the wrong application of legal principles.

In the light of the chain of the above-referred Judgement the Hon'ble Supreme Court of India, in a very recent Judgement dated 06/02/2019 in the Cross Criminal Revisions, categorically held that, in the considered opinion of their lordships, the Punjab and Haryana High Court, patently erred in holding that burden was on the appellant or complainant to prove that he had advanced (A Charted account) had advanced the loan and the blank signed cheque was given to him in repayment of the same.

To be continued ……………..

PLEASE READ CHAPTER 6 NAMELY PRESUMPTIONA AND REBUTELL IN PART II OF THIS GUIDE

TO BE CONTINUED _____IN NEXT VOLUME

ARTICLE 04

INDIAN EVIDENCE ACT

Admissibility Of Document & Mode Of Proof

The Author's positivism and purpose, to scribe the Article in question Titled cited above, is in order to enable and enlightened in a better way to the neophyte entrants Law students and readers.

Its crystal clear that Certain Parts Sections provisions and Portions of Indian Evidence Act, Particularly CHAPTER NO. V if read or analysis in conjunction instead reading in isolating may be for better and much easier way and mode to understand the scope, object and thrust of the law makers and interpreter thereof.

Document How to be proved or can be said to be proved, disproved or unproved are defined in the Interpretation clause 3 of the Indian Evidence Act, 1872 And defined the words and expressions used in the Act unless a contrary intentions appears from the context so in terms of the Act, the Document means any matter expressed or described upon any substance by means of letters, figures or marks, or by more than one of those means, intended to be used, or which may be used, forthe purpose of recording that matter.

Whereas Evidence" means and includes

1. All statements which the Court permits or requires to be made before it by witnesses, in relation to matters offact under inquiry; such statements are called **Oral Evidence**;

2. All document including electronic records produced for the inspection of the Court, such statements are called

Documentary Evidence;

"Proved" – A fact is said to be proved when, after consideringthe matters before it, the Court either believes it to exist, or considers its existence so probable that a prudent man ought, under the circumstances of the particular case, to act upon the supposition that it exists.

"Disproved"– A fact is said to be disproved when, after considering the matters before it, the Court either believes that it does not exist, or considers its non-existence so probable that a prudent man ought, under the circumstances of the particular case, to act upon the supposition that it does not exist.

"Not proved"– A fact is said not to be proved when it is neither proved nor disproved.

Accordingly, Any such document if produced or taken on record by the courts of law in a accordance with the law takes the place of Document Evidence- CHAPTER NO. V of the Indian Evidence Act is concerned and connected and the context of document may be proved either by primary or secondary evidence.

S.56.that the facts of which the court will take the judicialnotice need not to be proved and certain facts which court shall take judicial notice are as under.

S.57. Facts of which Court must take judicial notice: The Court shall take judicial notice of the following facts:-

1) All laws in force in the territory of India.
2) All public Acts passed or hereafter to be passed by Parliament, and all local and personal Acts directed by Parliament to be judicially noticed.

(1) Articles of War for [the Indian] Army [Navy or Air Force].

(2) The course of proceeding of Parliament of the United Kingdom, of the Constituent Assembly of India, of Parliament and of the legislatures established under any laws for thetime being in force in a Province or in the States.

(3) The accession and the sign manual of the Sovereign for thetime being of the United Kingdom of Great Britain and Ireland.

(4) All seals of which English Courts take judicial notice:the seals of all the [Courts in India] and of all Courts outof India established by the authority of the seals of Courtsof Admiralty and Maritime Jurisdiction and of Notaries Public,and all seals which any person is authorized to use by Act or Regulation having the force of law in.

(5) The accession to office, names, titles, functions and signatures of the persons filling for the time being any public office in any State, if the fact of their appointmentto such office is notified in any Official Gazette.

(6) The existence, title and national flag of every State or Sovereign recognized by the Government of India.

(7) The divisions of time, the geographical divisions of the world, and public festivals, fasts and holidays notified in the Official Gazette;

(8) The territories under the dominion of the Government of India.

(9) The commencement, continuance,and termination of hostilities between the Government of India and any otherState or body of persons.

(10) The names of the members and officers of the Court and oftheir

deputies and subordinate officers and assistants, and also of all officers acting in execution of its process, andof or all advocates, attorneys, proctors, vakils, pleaders and other persons authorized by law to appear or act before it.

(11) The rule of the road on land or at sea.

In all these cases, and also on all matters of public history, literature, science or art, the Court may resort for its aidto appropriate books or documents of reference.

If the Court is called upon by any person to take judicial notice of any fact, it may refuse to do so unless and until such person produces any such book or document as it may consider necessary to enable it to do so.

S.58. says that facts admitted need not to be proved, failure to prove a defence does not amount to an admission and nordoes it reserve discharge the burden of proof as held bHon'ble Supreme Court in case Manager, RBI v. S. Mani.

Consent by a party to exhibit a document.- Defending party has right to put every piece of evidence before the courtwhich would include the circumstances that may ultimately effect the appreciation of evidence in the trail. The purpose of the cross examination is to place all the factors before the court so as to enable it to come to just decision on the completing cases and to enable the party to take out material which will help or otherwise show the probability in laying down its defence as held by Hon'ble Bombay High Court in case Sanjay Cotton Co. v. Om Prakash.

According to S.59. all facts except the contents ofdocuments records may be proved by oral evidence whereas S.60.clearly says that all evidence must be direct. An hearsay evidence is not admissible. In case Munir Ahmad v. State of Rajasthan the Hon'ble Supreme Court

says that when a person isliving his evidence must be recorded by tendering him in courtand not by affidavit.

Section 294 of Criminal Procedure Court is very attractive and helpful and a shortest mode,in the event of any documentif is 0filed in the Court either by the prosecution or the Accused,the particular of document in question shall beincluded in a List and the Prosecution or the accused or the pleader of the respective party shall be called upon to admit or deny the genuineness of each such document and where the genuineness is not disputed such document may be read in the evidence without proof of the signature of the person to whom it purports to be signed, provided that the concerned courtmay in its discretion required such signature to be proved.

S.61. Proof of contents of documents

The contents of document may be proved either by primary orby secondary evidence. It also means that what the document states and not the truth of what the document says. As held Hon'ble Bombay High Court in case Omprakash Berlia v. Unit Trust Of India.

Meanings thereby veracity of the document is rebuttable if not proved as per thrust of law & thus document itself is not admissible in evidence until and unless duly proved by way of adopting legal Mode Of Proof And Contents Of The Documents Are Duly Proved. Mere Marking Of EXHIBITS Cannot Be The Proof Of Document as held by Hon'ble Supreme Court of India in caseSait Tarajee Khimchand v. Yelamarti Satyam.

In the case of Byramjee Jeejeebhoy Private Limited v. Govindabhai Appaji Bhatte, it is held by Hon'ble Bombay High Court that as soon as execution of a document is proved, document stands proof and proving of contents not necessary. It was further held that document and evidentiary value are two distinct and different factors. In case of Ramji Dayawala& Sons, the Hon'ble Supreme Court held that mere proof of handwriting of a document would not amount to proof of all thecontents or the fact stated in the document. Whereas the Hon'ble Bombay High Court is of the view that a document is required to be proved under the provision of the act.

Primary evidence means the document in question produced for the inspection of the court. Whereas **Secondary evidence** means certificate copies given under the provision including copies made from the original by mechanical processes that ensure theaccuracy of the copy and copies compared with such copies and copies made from of compared with the original and counterparts of documents. As against the parties who did not execute them and or the accounts of the document given contexts of a documents given by some person who has listed and are within the definitions of secondary evidence.

Presumptive Value of a Document if delivered through post Section 27 comes into play and thus an integral part of the law of presumption however qua a specific part of service through of a document posting by register post,a lettercontaining the document and Disclaimer: Readers are hereby sincerely advised to corroborate the correctness of aforesaid Factum of Article, by any other Recognized modes and sources to arrive at definite conclusion in the prevailing scenario Author in no case will be answerable qua the applicability of the above.

Photographs: The Hon'ble Bombay High Court has held in one of the case that the copy of the Photographs is not admissible and the negative thereof is required there to be produced and proved.

Photostat copies: If the records have been tampered and fictitious document were produced in court then it certainly vitiates
the finding. The certified copies should be accepted in evidence after examining the original records .Secondary Evidence When comes into play?

Loss of original Document: Permissibility of allowing secondary evidence- Proper reading of the various provisions of CHAPTER NO. V of the Indian Evidence Act therefore disclosed that whenever an original document is lost and the party informs the court that the document has been lost and craves leave to produce secondary evidence in relation to such document, the court has to consider the matter in the facts and circumstances of each case based on the case put forth before the Court and accordingly decide whether the case isfit for allowing the party to lead secondary evidence in respect of a document which is said to be proved to have been lost to the satisfaction of the court.

The Hon'ble Delhi High Court had held in case Shalu v. Sandeep Soni that," Party In Possession Of The Best EvidenceIs Bound To Produce The Same On Record Irrespective Of Onus OrBurden Of Proof, and an adverse inference can be done if withheld important document which can throw light on the factsas issued.

In trial of section 138 read with section 146 of the Negotiable instrument Act or memo having thereon the official mark denoting that the cheque has been dishonoured of such cheque, unless and until such fact is disapproved.

Proof of Document.- A Document can only be proved by primary evidence and not by secondary evidence unless it is covered under S. 65 of the Indian Evidence Act.

Public Document: are Admissible in Evidence, Judicial and official acts-

Presumption.- In respect of public document which form the acts of the sovereign authority official bodies and Tribunals,and of public officers, legislative, judicial and executive, the presumption can be and is in fact invariably drawn that the judicial and official acts have been regularly performed. It is necessary however to appreciate that the source of presumption is S. 114.

S.67. Proof of signature and handwriting of person alleged tohave signed or written document produced.- if a document is alleged to be signed or to have been written wholly or in partby any person, the signature or the handwriting of so much of the document as is alleged to be in that person's handwriting must be proved to be in his handwriting. Truth of contents of document. If by mere production of the original document for the inspection of the Court the truth of its contents was proved prima facie, the requirement of proof of the handwriting and of the signature upon it would be almost superfluous.

Proof of documentary evidence-

Expert evidence.- wherein there was no testimony of a person able to identify the handwriting hence the document cannot be proved by testimony of a person who was not is a position to be familiar with the handwriting. Proof of handwriting,- it has been held that conclusion based on clear comparison of handwriting must at best be indecisive and yield to positive evidence.

Proof of execution.- Certificate of registration is not enough proof of execution.

S.68.- Proof of execution of document required by law to be attested.- If a document is required by law to be attested, its hall not be used as evidence until one attesting witness at least has been called for the purpose of proving its execution, if there be attesting witness alive, and subject to the process of the court and capable of giving evidence. Mere registration of document does not dispense with the need of proving registration of document does not dispense with the need of proving the execution and attestation of a document inthe manner as provided in S. 68 of Indian Evidence Act.

S.70.- Admission of execution by party to attested document.- The Admission Of A Party To An Attested Document Of Its Execution By Himself Shall Be Sufficient Proof Of Its Execution As Against Him, Though It Be Document Required ByLaw To Be Attested.

S.71.- Proof when attesting witness denies the execution.- It the attesting witness denies or does not recollect the execution of the document, its execution may be proved by other evidence.

S.73.- Comparison of signature, writing or seal with others admitted or proved.- in order to ascertain whether a signature, writing or seal is that of the person by whom it purports to have been written or made, any signature writing or seal admitted or proved to the satisfaction of the court tohave been writing or made by that person may be compared with the one which is to be proved, although that signature, writing, or seal has not been produced or proved for any otherpurpose.

The court may direct any person present in court to write any words or figures for the purpose of enabling the court to compare the words or figures so written with any words or figures alleged to have been written by such person.

S.73A. Proof as to verification of digital signature.- inorder to ascertain whether a digital signature is that of the person by whom it purports to have been affixed, the Court maydirect,-

(a) that person or the controller of the Certifying Authority to produce the Digital Signature Certificate;

(b) any other person to apply the public key listed in the Digital Signature Certificate and verify the digital signaturepurported to have been affixed by that person.

Certified copies-

Proof of contents.- Even though the copy of return was certified by registrar to be true under S.610 of the CompaniesAct, 1956 did not establish, even prima facie, the truth or accuracy or correctness of the contents of the original. It proved only what the contents of the original were.

As per CHAPTER NO. 3 of the act certain facts which need not to beproved

S.74. Public Documents.- the, following document are public document :-

1. Document forming the acts, or records of the acts-

a) Of the sovereign authority;

b) Of official bodies and tribunals, and

c) Of public officers, legislative, judicial and executive

2. Public records kept of private document.

S.114. Court may presume existence of certain acts

The court may presume the existence of any fact which it thinks likely to have happened, regard being had to the common course of natural events, human conduct and public and private business, in their relation to the facts of the particular case.

Illustrations

The Court may presume—

(a) That a man who is in possession of stolen goods soon after the theft is either the thief or has received the goods knowing them to be stolen, unless he can accounts for his possession.

(b) That an accomplice is unworthy of credit, unless he is corroborated in material particulars;

(c) That a bill of exchange, accepted or endorsed, was accepted or endorsed for good consideration.

(d) That a thing or state of things which has been shown to be in existence within a period shorter than that withinwhich such things or states of things usually cease to exist,is still in existence;

(e) That judicial and official acts have been regularly performed;

(f) That the common course of business has been followed in particular cases;

(g) That evidence which could be and is not produced would, if produced, be unfavourable to the person withholds it.

(h) That if a man refuses to answer a question which he is not compelled to answer by law, the answer, if given would be unfavourable to him;

(i) That when a document creating and obligation is in the hands of the obligor, the obligation has been discharged

Disclaimer:

Readers are hereby sincerely advised to corroborate the correctness of aforesaid Factum of Article, by any other Recognized modes and sources to arrive at definite conclusion in the prevailing scenario Author in no case will be answerable qua the applicability of the above.

Art

CHAPTER-02

A D R

Alternative Disputes Redressed

Settlement and Compounding Options

1. Explore Compounding:

If the accused surfaces for settlement, file a joint compounding application under Section 147 of the NI Act to quash the proceedings. The court will require full payment of the cheque amount plus interest before cancelling the NBW. Caution: Post settlement, the original complaint cannot be revived if the accused defaults on new cheques (Gimpex v. Manoj Goel, SC 2021).

Critical Implications for BOTH Sides:

1. Statutory Notice (S.138): Payee MUST send a written demand notice to the drawer within 30 days of receiving the "return memo" from the bank. The drawer MUST pay the amount within 15 days of receiving this notice to avoid criminal prosecution.

2. Burden of Proof: Under S.138, once dishonour is proven, the legal presumption is against the drawer. They must actively prove their defense (e.g., bank closed account, valid stop reason, genuine signature, freeze external).

3. Civil Liability is Separate: Criminal proceedings under S.138 do not negate the underlying civil debt. The payee can pursue both avenues simultaneously.

4. Documentation is Crucial:

Payee: Keep Return Memo, Proof of Notice Delivery, Original Cheque.

Drawer: Keep Bank Closure/Frozen Account notices, Proof of valid stop payment reason (emails, contracts), Evidence of fraud (FIR), Proof of payment within 15 days of notice.

5. Bank's Role: Primarily follows instructions/legal orders. Charges fees. Not liable under S.138 unless proven gross negligence/fraud.

Exceptions Table

No "Lawfully Enforceable Debt": S.138 does not apply if the cheque was for an illegal purpose (gambling debt), gift, or donation without consideration.

Material Alteration: If the payee altered the cheque (amount, name, date) without the drawer's consent, it voids the cheque and S.138 liability.

Merger: If the payee accepts alternative payment after notice but before filing a complaint, the S.138 case may not proceed.

Bank Error (Signature/Freeze): If the bank admits fault (e.g., wrongly reported signature mismatch, froze account in error), this is a strong defense for the drawer.

Action Steps:

Drawer: Upon dishonour, IMMEDIATELY contact the payee to explain if there is a valid defense. If the payee sends a S.138 notice, CLIENT SHOULD CONSULT A LAWYER. TO Pay CHEQUE AMOUNT within 15 days or prepare strong defense evidence.

Payee: Upon dishonour, get the Return Memo. Send S.138 notice via Registered AD within 30 days. If no payment in 15 days, FILE COMPLAINT in Magistrate Court within 3CLIENT 0 days of the notice expiry.

This structure clarifies the distinct risks and required actions for both parties under each common return reason. Legal advice is essential in all cases.

02 A D R

Alternative Disputes Redressed

Settlement and Compounding Options

1. Explore Compounding:

If the accused surfaces for settlement, file a joint compounding application under Section 147 of the NI Act to quash the proceedings.

The court will require full payment of the cheque amount plus interest before cancelling the NBW. Caution: Post settlement, the original complaint cannot be revived if the accused defaults on new cheques (Gimpex v. Manoj Goel, SC 2021).

Procedural Best Practices

Document Everything: Maintain records of police correspondence, court applications, and investigation reports.

Leverage Technology: Request the court to serve hearing notices via email or WhatsApp under amended NI Act procedures.

Avoid Delays: File all applications within 30 days of discovering police inaction to prevent dismissal on laches grounds.

Key Precedent: The Supreme Court in Inder Mohan Goswami v. State of Uttaranchal (2007) emphasized that NBWs should be a last resort, but once issued, courts must ensure execution to uphold judicial authority.

Conclusion

Complainants must aggressively use court monitored enforcement and evidence backed applications to break police inaction. Simultaneously, remain open to compounding if the accused cooperates. Proactive engagement with the judiciary is crucial to prevent Section 138 cases from stagnating due to procedural lapses.

A- Application for Referring the Matter to Mediation Centre

IN THE COURT OF THE JUDICIAL MAGISTRATE FIRST CLASS (JMFC), [CITY/DISTRICT]

Application u/s 89 CPC / Section 320 CrPC (if criminal) for Referral to Mediation

Case No.: _

Title: [Your Name] vs. [Opposite Party Name]

Respectfully Showeth:

1. That the present case is pending before this Hon'ble Court between the parties.

2. That the applicant/defendant believes that the dispute is of a nature that can be resolved amicably through mediation, without further burdening the court.

3. That both parties are willing to explore a settlement through mediation in the interest of harmony and mutual benefit.

4. That mediation is a recognized mode of alternative dispute resolution under Section 89 of the CPC (for civil cases) or Section 320 CrPC (for compoundable criminal cases).

Prayer:

In light of the above, it is humbly prayed that this Hon'ble Court may kindly:

Refer the matter to the court annexed mediation centre or a certified mediator.

Stay proceedings for a period of [X weeks/months] to allow mediation.

Pass any other order deemed fit in the interest of justice.

Place: [City]

Date: [DD/MM/YYYY]

Signature of Applicant/Advocate

Name: [Your Name]

Address: [Your Address]

Contact No.: [Your Phone Number]

Key Points:

1. Mention the correct legal provision (CPC for civil cases, CrPC for criminal cases).

2. Attach a joint request if the opposite party consents to mediation (strengthens your application).

3. Specify the duration for mediation (usually 30–90 days).

****

CHAPTER-03

COMPOUNDING OF OFFENCES

Here are the key Supreme Court verdicts on compounding of offences under Sections 138/141 of the Negotiable Instruments Act, outlining the legal principles, conditions, and judicial approach:

I. Foundational Principles

1. Damodar S. Prabhu v. Sayed Babalal H. (2010) 5 SCC 663

Key Holdings:

Compounding is encouraged at any stage (trial, appeal, Supreme Court) to reduce case burden.

Graded costs imposed for belated compounding:

15% of cheque amount if compounded during trial.

20% if compounded during appeal.

Consent of complainant is mandatory; courts cannot compel settlement.

3. Kaushalya Devi Massand v. Roopkishore Khore (2011) 4 SCC 593

Key Holding:

Courts must facilitate compounding even after conviction, but cannot override complainant's consent.

No automatic acquittal: Accused must deposit costs (per Damodar Prabhu) for compounding.

II. Conditions for Compounding

3. Vijay Shekhar v. State of NCT Delhi (2024) SCC OnLine SC 521

Requirements:

Joint application by accused + complainant.

Full payment of cheque amount + costs (as per Damodar Prabhu).

Court satisfaction that settlement is voluntary.

4. JIK Industries Ltd. v. Amarlal V. Jumani (2022) 3 SCC 458

PostConviction Compounding:

Allowed even after conviction, but accused must:

Pay undisputed cheque amount + interest + litigation costs.

Prove complainant's consent via affidavit.

III. Exceptions & Limitations

5. Meters and Instruments (P) Ltd. v. Kanchan Mehta (2017) 14 SCC 560

Cannot compound if:

Accused absconds or avoids trial.

Complainant proves settlement was secured via coercion/fraud.

6. R. Vijayan v. Baby (2012) 1 SCC 260

No compounding for partial payments:

Full payment of cheque amount is mandatory.

Settlement for "lesser amount" voids compounding.

IV. Vicarious Liability (S. 141)

7. Aneeta Hada v. Godfather Travels & Tours (P) Ltd. (2012) 5 SCC 661

Compounding for Directors/Officers:

Company must be impleaded as accused.

Compounding by company does not absolve directors; separate consent needed.

V. Procedural Guidelines

8. Gian Singh v. State of Punjab (2012) 10 SCC 303

Role of Courts:

Criminal courts can close proceedings postcompounding under Section 147 NI Act (nonobstante CrPC).

No need for separate quashing petition under Section 482 CrPC.

9. P. Mohanraj v. Shah Brothers Ispat (P) Ltd. (2021) 6 SCC 258

Insolvency Barrier:

Compounding not allowed if accused company is in CIRP/liquidation (IBC overrides NI Act).

Summary: Legal Conditions for Compounding

Stage	Costs/Payment	Consent Required
During Trial	15% of cheque value + full amount	Complainant + Accused
During Appeal	20% of cheque value + full amount	Complainant + Accused
Post Conviction	Full amount + interest + litigation costs	Affidavit from complainant

Strategic Considerations

1. Early Compounding: Minimizes costs (15% vs. 20%) and avoids trial.
2. Director Liability: Ensure specific compounding applications for each accused under S. 141.
3. Fraud Defense: Complainants can oppose compounding if accused acted maliciously.
4. IBC Impact: Compounding barred if company is insolvent (P. Mohanraj).

Note: The Supreme Court consistently prioritizes amicable resolution in NI Act cases but mandates strict compliance with payment conditions and voluntary consent to prevent abuse.

****

CHAPTER-04

DEATH OF PARTIES TO THE COMPLAINT

If the original complainant dies during the pendency of the proceedings, his legal heirs can continue the case. Below are the answers to your queries based on legal provisions and judicial precedents.

1. Procedure for Legal Heirs to Come on Record: File an Application under Section 256(2) CrPC: The legal heirs must file an application before the trial court seeking substitution in place of the deceased complainant. The application should include: The death certificate of the original complainant. Proof of legal heir ship (succession certificate, will, or affidavit declaring heirs). An affidavit stating their intention to continue the case. Court's Order: The court will examine the documents and, if satisfied, will pass an order allowing the legal heirs to be substituted as complainants. The case then continues with the heirs as the new complainants. Relevant Law: Section 256(2) CrPC permits the continuation of a complaint by legal heirs in case of the complainant's death. Judicial Precedent: Ashwin Nanubhai Vyas v. State of Maharashtra (AIR 1967 SC 983) supports the principle that legal heirs can pursue a complaint under Section 138 NI Act.

2. Can Both Legal Heirs Proceed Together? Yes, if both heirs are entitled to the cheque amount (e.g., as co- legal heirs under succession laws), they can jointly continue the complaint. The court may allow both to be complainants if: They file a joint substitution application. There is no dispute between them regarding the claim. Note: If the cheque was issued to the deceased complainant (not jointly to heirs), the court may still permit joint prosecution if the debt is inherited by both.

3. If Only One Legal Heir Wants to Proceed: No Objection Certificate (NOC) from Other Heir: The heir wishing to proceed should obtain a written NOC from the other legal heir(s) stating they have no objection to the case continuing. The NOC should be filed with the substitution application. Power of Attorney (POA) Not Required: A POA is unnecessary since the heir is acting in their own capacity as a legal representative, not as an agent. However, if one heir wants to authorize the other to represent them, a specific POA for court proceedings can be executed. Exception: If the other heir opposes the continuation, the court may require evidence (e.g., a succession certificate) to determine who has the legal right to proceed.

Key Takeaways:

1. File a sub situation application with proof of heir ship and the death certificate.
2. Both heirs can jointly proceed if they agree.
3. A single heir can continue with an NOC from others (or the court's permission if disputed).

Important questions

Question

Whether the complaint is abated in case of death of the accused under section 138 of the Negotiable Instrument Act affect?

Answer :

In the event of the death of an accused in a Complaint 138 NI Act, the complaint dies (abated) in totality. However, the Complainant is at his liberty to file a civil suit against the legal heirs of the deceased accused. But no 138 Complaint further survives against Legal heirs (Reference: Authors opinion without dictum & from reliable sources).

Question

Do legal heirs have the right to challenge the conviction of their predecessor?

Answer :

Yes, legal heirs have the right to challenge the conviction of their predecessor only on the grounds that he was not guilty of any offense. However, in such cases, they are neither liable to pay the fine nor to undergo imprisonment.

(Reference : Supreme Court: M. Abbas Haji Vs T.N. Channakeshava : 19-09- 2019)

****

CHAPTER-05

INTERIM COMPENSATION 20%

Short Note:

MAINTAINABILITY OF REVISION ?

Section 143A NI Act is not an 'interlocutory order.' Is interim compensation revision maintainable before the Sessions Court?

Yes: An order for interim compensation passed under Section 143A of the Negotiable Instruments Act, 1881, is not considered an 'interlocutory order' for the purpose of Section 397(2) of the Code of Criminal Procedure, 1973. Consequently, a revision petition under Section 397(1) of the Cr.P.C. is maintainable before the Sessions Court against such an order. Multiple High Courts have affirmed this position. Notably, the Karnataka High Court in Sanjay P.S. v. Abhishek M. (Criminal Petition No. 5944 of 2023, decided on July 28, 2023) held that an order on an application under Section 143A is an 'intermediate order.' This is because it conclusively determines the rights and liabilities of the parties concerning the specific application for interim compensation, as opposed to being merely procedural or step-by-step. Therefore, the bar under Section 397(2) of the Cr.P.C. on revising interlocutory orders does not apply.

Key Judgment Extract: Karnataka High Court in Sanjay P.S. v. Abhishek M.: 'An order passed on an application filed under Section 143A ... is not an interlocutory order but an intermediate order ... determining the rights and liabilities of the parties regarding the application. A revision petition before the Court of Sessions ... would be maintainable, and it is open to the aggrieved party, whether the complainant or the accused, to approach the Court.' The court relied on the Supreme Court's ruling in Madhu Limaye v. State of Maharashtra (1977), which clarified that orders that affect substantive rights are not interlocutory. This principle has been reiterated by other High Courts, including the Bombay High Court

(2025), which emphasized that when substantive rights are affected, the order is intermediate, and a revision is maintainable. Practical Position: A revision petition under Section 397 of the Cr.P.C. is maintainable against orders passed under Section 143A of the N.I. Act. The restriction under Section 397(2) does not apply because such orders are classified as intermediate, not interlocutory. **How to Avoid Liability or Seek Dismissal of an Application under Section 143A NI ACT (INTERIM COMPENSATION)**

Interim 20% landmark judgments from various State High Courts interpreting Section 143A

Section 143A of the Negotiable Instruments Act, 1881, covers both pro complainant and pro accused perspectives:

The Supreme Court judgments interpreting Section 143A

Various High Courts are interpreting Section 143A through divergent lenses

****

CHAPTER-06

PROCLAIMED OFFENDER (OP)

When an accused is declared a Proclaimed Offender (P.O.) under Section 82 CrPC and the trial court proceeds to record evidence in their absence under Section 299 CrPC, the following legal course is adopted by the trial court:

1. Declaration as Proclaimed Offender (P.O.) – Section 82 CrPC

If the accused absconds and evades trial, the court issues a proclamation requiring their appearance.

If the accused fails to comply, the court declares them a Proclaimed Offender (P.O.).

2. Recording of Evidence in Absence – Section 299 CrPC

Once the accused is declared a P.O., the trial court can:

Record evidence of prosecution witnesses in the accused's absence (if the court is satisfied that the accused is absconding and there is no immediate prospect of arrest).

Such evidence can be used later if the accused is arrested/reappears, subject to crossexamination.

3. Trial Court's Course of Action After Section 299 Evidence

(A) If Accused is Apprehended Later

The trial resumes, and the accused is allowed to:

Cross Examination witnesses whose statements were recorded under Section 299 CrPC.

Present their own defense evidence.

The court then proceeds to judgment based on complete evidence.

(B) If Accused Remains Absent

The court may:

Continue exparte proceedings (if sufficient evidence exists).

Pronounce judgment if the prosecution proves its case beyond reasonable doubt.

Issue a conviction warrant (if accused is convicted).

(C) If Accused Surrenders/Appears Voluntarily

They can file an application to set aside the P.O. order (under Section 70 CrPC).

The court may:

Recall the P.O. status.

Allow the accused to Cross Examination witnesses (if their earlier evidence was recorded).

Restart trial from the appropriate stage.

Key Legal Considerations

Evidence under Section 299 CrPC is admissible but not conclusive until the accused gets a chance to Cross Examination .

No final conviction can be based solely on Section 299 evidence if the accused reappears and disputes it.

Warrant remains active until the accused appears before the court.

Suggested Steps for Accused (If Arrested/Appearing Later)

1. File an application to recall the P.O. order.

2. Seek permission to Cross Examination witnesses (if evidence was recorded in absence).

3. Present defense evidence (if required).

4. Challenge conviction (if judgment was passed exparte) by filing an appeal/revision.

Under Section 138(b) safeguards against misconduct or oversight:

Critical Steps for Issuing a Statutory Demand Notice

(Payee to Drawer)

Objective: Ensure legal compliance, prevent procedural flaws, and create defensible evidence.

1. Trigger Event Confirmation:

Verify the cheque was dishonored (return memo from the bank stating "insufficient funds," "account closed," etc.).

Obtain the original cheque return memo from your bank immediately.

2. Strict Adherence to Timeline (NonNegotiable):

30Day Window: The notice must be sent within 30 calendar days from the date the payee receives the cheque return memo.

Calculate Precisely: Exclude the day of receiving the memo; count 30 days thereafter. Use a calendar tool to avoid miscalculation.

3. Drafting the Notice (Content Safeguards):

Cross Examination Mandatory Elements:

Full name & address of both Drawer (debtor) and Payee (creditor).

Specifics of the dishonored cheque (No., date, bank, branch, amount).

Explicit mention of dishonor (quote reason from memo).

Cross Examination Demand: Clearly state the demand for payment of the cheque amount.

15Day Ultimatum: Specify the drawer has 15 days from receipt to pay.

Cross Examination Consequence: State that failure to pay within 15 days will result in legal action under S. 138 NI Act.

Cross Examination Safeguards:

Cross Examination Accuracy: Crosscheck all details (names, addresses, cheque details, amount) against original documents (cheque, agreement, memo).

Cross Examination Clarity: Use unambiguous language. Avoid

threats beyond legal consequences.

Cross Examination Professional Tone: Maintain a formal, non abusive tone.

Cross Examination Attach Copy: Include a photocopy of the dishonored cheque and the bank return memo.

Legal Review: Highly recommended: Have a lawyer specializing in NI Act matters review the draft notice.

4. Dispatch & Delivery (Evidence Safeguards):

Cross Examination Authorized Modes Only (Crucial): Registered Post with Acknowledgement Due (RPAD): Primary & safest method.

Cross Examination Speed Post: An acceptable alternative under India Post.

Cross Examination Certificate of Posting (COP): Use only as a secondary precaution, never as the sole method. Notoriously weak evidence.

Cross Examination Safeguards: Simultaneous Dual Mailing: Send one notice via RPAD and another via Speed Post to the drawer's correct, known address (usually the address on the cheque or as per agreement). This mitigates risk if one service fails.

Cross Examination Accurate Addressing: Use the drawer's address meticulously as known. Avoid typos.

Cross Examination Post Office Protocol: Obtain dated postal receipts for RPAD/Speed Post/ immediately upon dispatch.

Cross Examination Preserve Originals: Safeguard all postal receipts.

Cross Examination Track Diligently: Track the RPAD/Speed Post consignment online daily.

Cross Examination Acknowledgement Due (RPAD): Ensure the AD card is returned. This is the best evidence of receipt.

Cross Examination Refusal Handling: If the notice is "refused" or "unclaimed," preserve the returned envelope unopened. This is deemed valid service by courts.

5. Post Dispatch Documentation & Preservation:

Cross Examination File Creation: Create a dedicated file for this specific cheque/default.

Cross Examination Store Securely: File originals/true copies of:

The signed statutory demand notice.

The dishonored cheque (copy).

The bank return memo.

All postal receipts (RPAD, Speed Post,

The returned RPAD Acknowledgement Due card (if received).

Proclamation & Attachment in Cheque Dishonor Cases (S.138/141 NI Act)

(Old CrPC: Sections 82/85 | New BNSS: Sections 84/88)

In cases under Sections 138 (cheque bounce) & 141 (liability of directors) of the Negotiable Instruments Act, if the accused absconds or avoids court appearances, the court may resort to proclamation (public notice) and attachment of property under BNSS Sections 8488 (previously CrPC 8285)

1. When & Why Apply These Provisions?

Situations Where Proclamation & Attachment Are Used:

Accused is evading summons/warrants (S.138 cases).

Directors of a company (S.141 NI Act) avoid court despite multiple notices.

Accused is untraceable, and police cannot execute warrants.

PURPOSE:

To compel the accused's appearance by threatening property attachment.

To prevent misuse of delaying tactics in cheque dishonour cases.

2. How to Apply? (Step by step Process)

Step 1:

Issue Warrant First (BNSS S.72/73 / CrPC S.70/71) Court must first issue a bailable/nonbailable warrant. If warrant remains unexecuted (accused not found), proceed to proclamation.

Step 2:

Proclamation (BNSS S.84 / Cr.P.C S.82)

Court orders a public notice (newspaper, police station, residence). Accused is given 30 days (as per BNSS) to appear.

Essential Contents of Proclamation:

Name, address of accused.

Offence (e.g., S.138 NI Act).

Warning: "Appear within 30 days, or property will be attached."

Step 3:

Attachment of Property (BNSS S.85 / CrPC S.83) If accused still doesn't appear, court can attach property (movable/immovable).

· Property can be sold after 6 months if accused remains absconding.

Step 4:

Restoration of Attached Property (BNSS S.88 / CrPC S.85) If accused surrenders later, they can claim back property by appearing in court.

3. Special Considerations for S.141 NI Act (Company Directors)

Proclamation & attachment can be issued against directors if they are avoiding trial.

Courts must verify if the director was actually in charge of the company's affairs (as per K.K. Ahuja vs V.K. Bhargava, 2009).

Merely being a director does not make one liable—active role in cheque issuance must be proven.

Question

Whether the Trial Court was required to invoke the provisions of Section 82 Cr. P.C. when the warrant of arrest was received back unexecuted with the report that the accused had left the given address?

Answer:

The Court is duty-bound to ask the complainant to furnish a fresh address of the accused and ensure that the accused is duly served before commencing with the coercive process. Therefore, the Trial Court was not required to invoke the provisions of Section 82 Cr.p.c. The order of declaring the accused a proclaimed offender and consequent registration of FIR cannot be sustained.

(**Reference**:. Punjab And Haryana High Court : Surender Singh Vs State Of Haryana & Anr: 12-01-2021)

****

CHAPTER-07

TRANSFER OF COMPLAINTS

TRANSFER OF CASE FROM ONE COURT TO ANOTHER COURT

In India, if there is a reasonable apprehension of not receiving fair justice in a Negotiable Instruments Act, 1881 (NI Act) case pending in Court No. A, you can seek a transfer under Section 407 of the Code of Criminal Procedure (CrPC) (for criminal complaints under Section 138 NI Act) or Section 24 of the Code of Civil Procedure (CPC) (for civil proceedings, if applicable).

Steps to Seek Transfer of an NI Act Case:

1. Grounds for Transfer:

Bias or reasonable apprehension of bias by the presiding officer.

Convenience of parties (e.g., undue hardship in attending Court No. A).

Fair trial concerns (e.g., undue influence, hostility, or procedural irregularities).

2. Jurisdiction for Transfer:

High Court (under Section 407 CrPC for criminal cases).

District & Sessions Judge (for lower court transfers under Section 408 CrPC).

3. Procedure:

File a Transfer Petition before the appropriate court.

Submit affidavits & evidence supporting the apprehension of unfair justice.

Cite relevant judgments (e.g., Maneka Sanjay Gandhi v. Rani

Jethmalani, AIR 1979 SC 468).

4. Interim Relief (if needed):

Seek a stay on proceedings in Court No. A until the transfer petition is decided.

Key Considerations:

Mere dissatisfaction with court proceedings is insufficient; substantial grounds must be shown.

The alternative court (where transfer is sought) must have jurisdiction.

Delay in filing may weaken the case.

Legal Precedents:

The Supreme Court in Nahar Industrial Enterprises Ltd. v. Hong Kong & Shanghai Banking Corp. (2009) held that transfer can be granted if a fair trial is jeopardized.

The High Court may transfer a case if justice demands (State of Punjab v. Dharam Singh, AIR 1968 SC 1210).

Legal Information

Here's a consolidated update on the latest RBI circulars, judicial developments, and landmark Supreme Court judgments related to cheque dishonour cases as of July 2025:

I. Latest RBI Circulars (2025)

1. Master Circular on Prudential Norms (April 2025)

Ref No.: DOR.STR.REC.9/21.04.048/2025 26

Key Focus: Updates on income recognition, asset classification, and provisioning for bank advances. Though not directly on cheque dishonour, it impacts banks' handling of NPAs linked to unpaid cheques.

2. KYC/AML Updates (June 2025)

Ref No.: RBI/2025 2026/53 (DOR.AML.REC.31/14.01.001/2025

26)

Relevance: Stricter KYC norms may affect account operations for frequent cheque defaulters.

3. Digital Lending Directions (May 2025)

Ref No.: RBI/2025 2026/36 (DOR.STR.REC.19/21.07.001/2025 26)

Implication: Encourages digital transactions, reducing reliance on cheques.

II. Judicial Developments

1. Madras HC Simplifies Appeals (July 2025)

Ruling: Victims of cheque bounce cases can now file appeals against acquittals directly in district courts (instead of HC), effective from July 7, 2025.

2. Procedural Fairness Mandate (SC, March 2025)

Case: Rekha Sharad Ushir v. Saptashrungi Sahakari Bank

Holding: Complainants must disclose all material facts (e.g., prior correspondence) in cheque bounce cases. Suppression can lead to quashing of complaints.

III. Landmark Supreme Court Judgments

1. Presumption of Cheque Genuineness (2024)

Case: Ajitsinh Rathod v. State of Gujarat

Key Ruling:

Accused must actively rebut the presumption of cheque validity (Section 118, NI Act).

Courts won't assist the accused in gathering evidence (e.g., handwriting analysis) if requests are dilatory.

2. Jurisdiction Clarity (Overruling Bhaskaran)

Trend: Recent judgments emphasize territorial jurisdiction based on:

Place of cheque issuance, presentation, or dishonour

IV. Practical Takeaways

1. For Complainants:

File separate complaints for each dishonoured cheque to avoid procedural dismissal.

Ensure full disclosure of facts in complaints to prevent quashing.

2. For Accused:

Submit timely replies to demand notices with documented evidence to counter presumptions.

3. Legal Strategy:

Leverage district courts for appeals post acquittal (post July 7, 2025).

V. Pending Reforms

The RBI's Digital Lending Directions (2025) may reduce cheque frauds by promoting traceable transactions.

For detailed circulars/judgments, refer to [RBI's portal] (https://www.rbi.org.in) or [Supreme Court archives] (https://main.sci.gov.in). Let me know if you need help drafting legal notices or analysing specific cases!

Kerala High Court's ruling in Saju v Shalimar Hardware & Anr regarding the service of notice under Section 138(b) of the Negotiable Instruments Act, 1881 (NI Act):

Key Points from the Judgment

1. Strict Compliance with Notice Requirements

The Court emphasized that Section 138(b) NI Act mandates personal service of the statutory notice on the drawer of the cheque (the accused). Serving the notice on a relative without proof that the accused was aware of it does not constitute valid service.

2. Invalid Service Vitiated Proceedings

The complainant had sent the notice to the accused's relative but failed to prove that the accused had actual or constructive knowledge of the notice.

Citing the Supreme Court's precedent in Thomas MD v PS Jaleel (2009), the Court held that service on a spouse/relative is insufficient unless the accused's awareness is established.

3. Legal Consequences

The conviction and sentence (initially 3 months' imprisonment) were set aside due to noncompliance with Section 138(b).

The Court directed the refund of any amount deposited by the accused during proceedings.

1. Accelerated Trial Mechanisms: Mandatory Summary Trials: Cases must be resolved via summary procedures (not regular summons trials) unless imprisonment > 1 year is anticipated. Magistrates must record detailed reasons for conversion to summons trials. Strict Timelines: Trials should conclude within 6 months of filing. Courts must minimize adjournments and prioritize daytoday hearings. Joint Trials for Multiple Cheques: Complaints arising from the same transaction can be consolidated, bypassing CrPC limits of 3 offenses per trial.

2. Digital Integration & Paperless Litigation EFiling Mandate: Complaints, evidence, and legal notices can be filed/submitted electronically (email/WhatsApp with delivery proof). Virtual Hearings: Courts to permit video conferencing for appearances, reducing logistical delays. ESummons: Service of summons via SMS/email alongside physical copies.

3. Strengthened Evidence & Affidavit Protocols AffidavitBased Testimony: Witness examination via written affidavits (not oral

testimony) under Section 145 NI Act, except when crossexamination is essential. Presumption of Liability: Drawers claiming "signature mismatch" or "blank cheque misuse" must provide conclusive proof (e.g., bank audits, digital trails). Mere denial is insufficient (Ajitsinh Rathod v. Gujarat, 2024). Complainants must prove financial capacity (Shri Datta Rai v. Nappa, 2024) via ITR/bank records.

4. Penalties & Deterrence Measures Harsher Punishment for Repeat Offenders: Enhanced fines and imprisonment for habitual defaulters. Interim Compensation: Courts may award up to 20% of cheque amount as interim relief but must assess: Prima facie case strength Accused's financial capacity Nature of transaction. Appeal Curbs: Appellate courts can demand a minimum of 20% deposit of cheque amount before hearing appeals (Section 148).

5. Mediation & Settlement Promotion PreLitigation ADR: Courts must refer disputes to mediation centers before trial. Settlements avoid criminal prosecution. Compounding at Any Stage: Cases can be settled by paying cheque amount + interest (≤ 15%), even after conviction. 6. Director Liability & Corporate Safeguards Moratorium Protection (IBC Conflict) | Scenario | Director Liability | | | | | Moratorium imposed BEFORE cause of action | No liability (Vishnoo Mittal v. Shakti Trading, 2025) | | Moratorium imposed AFTER cause of action | Personal liability applies | NonExecutive Directors: Immune unless proven involved in financial decisions (K.S. Mehta v. Morgan Securities, 2025). Critical Compliance Deadlines

1. Legal Notice: Payee must notify drawer within 30 days of bounce.

2. Drawer Payment Window: 15 days postnotice to avoid prosecution.

3. Complaint Filing: Within 30 days after the 15day period expires. Strategic Implications For Complainants: Use enotices with delivery tracking. Consolidate multiple bounced cheques in one complaint. For Accused: Rebut presumption of debt via transaction inconsistencies (e.g., changing complainant statements). Seek pretrial quashing if complaint lacks specific averments (S.M.S. Pharmaceuticals standard). The guidelines restore trust in cheque transactions while unclogging courts.

Success hinges on digital adoption, strict judicial compliance, and stakeholder awareness. For full judgments, refer to: Vishnoo Mittal v. Shakti Trading (INSC 346/2025) Ajitsinh Rathod v. Gujarat (2024). The guidelines restore trust in cheque transaction… The Supreme Court's advisory guidelines in cheque dishonor cases (under Section 138 of the Negotiable Instruments Act, 1881) aim to tackle India's massive backlog (over 43 lakh pending cases) through procedural reforms.

****

CHAPTER-08

X Y Z

Admission in 313 CrPC Statement:

If the accused admits liability during examination, it constitutes evidence under S. 313(4) CrPC and can form the basis for conviction.

Magistrate's Action Plan

1. Verify the Admission

Ensure the admission is clear, unambiguous, and covers:

(a) Issuance of the cheque,

(b) Existence of a legally enforceable debt,

(c) Liability for the amount.

Example: Accused stating, "I issued the cheque for a loan of ₹5 lakhs which remains Forming part of FAQS CONCEPT PART "A"

Question No 3 and 4

Question No.3

Does the account being blocked or not being used have an effect in the case of Section 138 of the NI Act?

Answer:

There is no rescue for the accused, even if the check is returned unpaid due to the account being closed or not in use.

(Reference: Bombay High Court :Dilip Vs Nishant Sahakari Gramin:09-12- 2011)

Unpaid" suffices.

2. Check Rebuttal of S. 139 Presumption

Even with admission, the accused can rebut S. 139 by proving:

Cheque was stolen/forged,

Issued as security without liability,

Debt was time barred.

If no rebuttal: Conviction is mandatory.

3. Address Complainant's Refusal to Settle

Record the complainant's refusal to accept instalments.

Sentencing Options:

Order compensation under S. 357 CrPC (directing accused to pay the cheque amount + interest).

Impose symbolic imprisonment (e.g., 1 day) if compensation is paid.

For non payment: Apply S. 64 IPC (sentence till payment).

4. Judgment Drafting

Explicitly state:

"Accused admitted liability in [pleading/evidence/313 statement]. Despite the complainant's refusal to settle, the admission proves the debt under S. 138. The presumption under S. 139 remains unrebutted."

Reference High Court Ruling: Cite the binding precedent in your jurisdiction.

Pitfalls to Avoid

Assuming settlement refusal vitiates admission.

Ignoring the limited scope of admission (e.g., if the accused admits cheque issuance but disputes the debt).

Overlooking S. 141 liability (admission by one accused ≠ guilt of all directors).

B- <u>BLANK SIGNED CHEQUES</u>

Analysis of the repercussions and stages involved in cheque issuance cases, covering both <u>BLANK SIGNED CHEQUES</u> and duly signed filled cheques:

I. Legal Framework & Key Concepts

1. Cheque Bounce as a Criminal Offence

Under Section 138 of the Negotiable Instruments Act (NI Act), a dishonoured cheque due to insufficient funds, signature mismatch, account closure, or expired validity (beyond 3 months) is a criminal offence.

Penalties: Imprisonment for up to 2 years, a fine of up to twice the cheque amount, or both.

2. Blank Cheques

Legally treated as voluntary authorisation to fill in details. Misuse attracts liability unless coercion is proven.

Courts presume such cheques were issued to discharge a legally enforceable debt (Section 139, NI Act).

SIGNATORY OF CHEQUE ?

Even if it is held that specific averments are necessary, whether in the absence of such averments, can the signatory of the cheque and/or the Managing Directors of Joint Managing Director, who admittedly would be in charge of the company and responsible to the company for the conduct of its business, be proceeded against **?**

Answer:

The answer to the question has to be in the affirmative. The question notes that the Managing Director or Joint Managing Director would be admittedly in charge of the company and responsible to the company for the conduct of its business. When that is so, holders of such positions in a company become liable under Section 141 of the Act. By virtue of the office they hold as Managing Director or Joint Managing Director, these persons are in charge of and responsible for the conduct of the business of the company. Therefore, they are covered under Section 141. As far as the signatory of a dishonored cheque is concerned, he is responsible for the incriminating act and will be covered under sub-section (2) of Section 141.

(Reference: Supreme Court : S.M.S Pharmaceuticals Ltd vs Neeta Bhalla And Anr:20-09-2005: Part of CLR Volume 2 page no. 177-198.)

Question

Whether a complaint under section 138 Negotiable Instruments Act would be maintainable against the company if the statutory notice under section 138 Negotiable Instruments Act is issued only to its Managing Director and is not issued to the company which is maintaining the account from which the subject cheque is issued.

Answer :

Yes, Maintainable.

(Reference: Delhi High Court : DSC Ltd.Vs Dada Jeetu Buildcon Pvt. Ltd.,:16-11-2018: Part of CLR Volume 2 page no. 365-378.)

Question

The entire amount of compensation, if deposited by the appellant, for the register of the Supreme Court, will have what effect?

Answer:

All proceedings emanating from the complaint are quashed. (Reference:. Supreme Court: Vikas Jalan Vs M/s Shreya Pet Pvt . Ltd. & Ors.: 07-03-2011)

Question

After the closing of the defense side witness, the accused wanted to examine at the Argument Stage, whether permissible at such a belated stage.

Answer :

Section 315 of Cr.P.C. does not prescribe any time limit, so there is no legal bar expressly available to reject on the belated ground. Such an opportunity would normally not be denied. (Reference: Madras High Court :E.Vanitha Vs Smt.S.Lakshmi : 30-08-2017)

Q QUANTUM OF COMPENSATION

Enhancement of Compensation by way of modification of the order of the Judicial Magistrate, the accused shall pay the compensation to the complainant the cheque amount with interest at the rate of 9% per annum from the date of dishonour of the cheque till its realization and in default to undergo rigorous imprisonment for 6 months > Bombay High Court Prashant S/o Chhaganrao Gadekar Versus The State of Maharashtra

INDEX OF DRAFT LIBRARY PART IV PAGES

MISC. APPLICATIONS: *BUNCH OF 20 TWENTY*

Synopsis & Scrutiny

CHAPTER-01

APPLICATIONS FROM COMPLAINANT SIDE PART OF TRIAL.

---

1. APPLICATION PRAYING FOR CONDONATION OF DELAY IN FILING COMPLAINT.
2. APPLICATION FOR SUBSTITUTION OF LEGAL HEIRS OF THE DECEASED COMPLAINANT
3. APPLICATION FOR SUMMONING THE BANK WITNESS (MANAGER) AND RELATED DOCUMENTS
4. APPLICATION FOR WITHDRAWAL OF A COMPLAINT AGAINST ALL OR SPECIFIC ACCUSED PERSONS, WITH SUFFICIENT REASONS:
5. APPLICATION TO DISPENSE WITH THE PERSONAL ATTENDANCE OF THE COMPLAINANT UNDER SECTION(S): 256 CR. PC
6. APPLICATION SECTION 65 OF THE INDIAN EVIDENCE ACT, 1872, TO LEAD SECONDARY EVIDENCE.
7. APPLICATION UNDER SECTION 65B(4) OF THE INDIAN EVIDENCE ACT FOR FILING CERTIFIED AFFIDAVIT FOR DIGITAL DOCUMENTS
8. APPLICATION UNDER SECTION 65B OF THE INDIAN EVIDENCE ACT FOR PLACING AFFIDAVIT ON RECORD
9. APPLICATION UNDER SECTION 311 CR. PC FOR PRODUCTION OF ADDITIONAL EVIDENCE

APPLICATION FOR EARLY HEARING & EXPEDITIOUS TRIAL INTER-ALIA ON THE FOLLOWING GROUNDS

10. APPLICATION FOR PASSING AN ORDER ON AN APPLICATION DATED
11. APPLICATION FOR ISSUANCE OF NBW/ OR

ALTERNATIVE COERCIVE MODE WHERE THE OPPOSITE

12. PARTY HAS FAILED TO FILE THEIR SAY:
13. APPLICATION FOR EX PARTE PROCEEDINGS DUE TO ABSCONDING OF ACCUSED
14. APPLICATION UNDER SECTION 299 CRPC FOR RECORDING EVIDENCE IN THE ABSENCE OF AN ABSCONDING ACCUSE
15. APPLICATION PRAYING TO CLOSE THE RIGHT TO CROSS EXAMINATION DUE TO DELAY TACTICS.
16. APPLICATION UNDER SECTION 319 CR.P.C. FOR IMPLEADING ADDITIONAL ACCUSED
17. APPLICATION UNDER SECTION 143(3) OF N.I. ACT READ WITH SECTION 260(2) CR. PC FOR CONVERSION OF SUMMARY TRIAL TO REGULAR TRIAL
18. APPLICATION

UNDER SECTION 313(B) CR. PC FOR DISPENSING WITH THE STATEMENT OF THE ACCUSED

19. APPLICATION FOR ISSUANCE OF A WARRANT TO THE COLLECTOR UNDER SECTION 461B NS 2023 FOR RECOVERY OF UNPAID FINE.
20. Application u/s 330 BNSS 2023,

****

Application No.1

PRAYING FOR CONDO -NATION- OF DELAY IN FILING COMPLAINT.

IN THE COURT OF THE JUDICIAL MAGISTRATE FIRST CLASS (JMFC),

Misc. Application No.: of 2025

In the matter of:

ABC

(Applicant/Complainant)

Vs.

XYZ

(Proposed Accused)

APPLICATION PRAYING FOR CONDONATION OF DELAY IN FILING COMPLAINT. ....days... inter alia on the following grounds.

Respectfully Showeth:

1. Introduction:

The applicant/complainant could not file the complaint within the prescribed limitation period due to severe health issues, family crises, and financial difficulties.

The delay was unintentional, bona fide, and beyond the applicant's control.

2. Reasons for Delay:

Health Issues: The applicant suffered from [mention illness, e.g., prolonged hospitalization, medical treatment] from [dates], supported by medical certificates/reports (Annexure1).

Family Issues: [Explain family problems, e.g., death of a family member, legal disputes, caregiving responsibilities] (supported by affidavit and documents, if any).

Financial Crisis: The applicant faced extreme financial hardship, preventing timely legal action (provide proof of financial distress, if available).

3. Bona Fide Intentions:

The applicant always intended to pursue legal remedies but was physically, emotionally, and financially incapacitated.

The delay was not deliberate and deserves con donation in the interest of justice.

4. Legal Grounds:

NI Act allows courts to condone delay if sufficient cause is shown.

Judicial Precedents: Cite relevant case laws (e.g., Collector, Land Acquisition v. MST Katiji (AIR 1987 SC 1353), where courts upheld a liberal approach in condo nati on for genuine hardship).

5. Prayer for Relief:

The Hon'ble Court may kindly:

Condone the delay in filing the complaint.

Allow the complaint to be registered and proceed as per law.

Grant any other relief deemed fit.

Place: [City]
Date: [DD/MM/YYYY]

Applicant/Complainant
AFFIDAVIT IN SUPPORT OF APPLICATIONS
I, [Your Name], aged , residing at [Your Address], do solemnly affirm and state as follows:
1. That I am the applicant in the above matter and am fully conversant with the facts.
2. That the contents of the accompanying application are true and correct to my knowledge.
3. That I could not file the complaint in time due to reasons stated above, which were beyond my control.
4. That I am submitting supporting documents (medical reports, death certificate, bank statements, etc.) as proof.

APPLICANT

Application No.2

IN THE COURT OF THE JUDICIAL MAGISTRATE FIRST CLASS (JMFC),

Criminal Misc. Application No.: of 2024

In the matter of:

[Original Complaint Case No. /2021]

(Under Section 138 of the Negotiable Instruments Act, 1881)

Between:

[Name of Legal Heir 1],

S/o [Father's Name],

Aged [Age],

Residing at [Address]

AND

[Name of Legal Heir 2],

S/o [Father's Name],

Aged [Age],

Residing at [Address]

(Legal Heirs of the deceased complainant, [Original Complainant's Name])

... Applicants

Versus

[Accused Name],

S/o [Father's Name],

Aged [Age],

Residing at [Address]

... Respondent

Application for Substitution of Legal Heirs of the Deceased Complainant

Respected Sir/Madam,

1. Introduction:

The original complainant, [Name of Deceased Complainant], filed the abovementioned case under Section 138 of the Negotiable Instruments Act, 1881, against the accused for dishonour of cheque(s).

The complainant unfortunately passed away on [Date of Death], as per the attached death certificate (Annexure 1).

2. Legal Heirship:

The applicants are the sole legal heirs of the deceased complainant, being his sons (or other relation, as applicable).

Proof of heir ship is attached:

Succession Certificate / Legal Heir Certificate / Affidavit (Annexure

2). Copy of Will (if any) (Annexure 3).

3. Request for Substitution:

Under Section 256(2) of CrPC, legal heirs are entitled to continue the proceedings initiated by the deceased complainant.

The applicants wish to jointly pursue the case (or individually, if only one heir is applying).

4. No Objection (if applicable):

In case only one heir is prosecuting, a No Objection Certificate (NOC) from the other heir(s) is attached (Annexure 4).

5. Prayer:

The applicants humbly pray that this Hon'ble Court may:

Allow this application for substitution.

Permit the applicants to continue the complaint case as legal heirs of the deceased complainant.

Grant any other relief deemed fit.

Place: [City]

Date: [DD/MM/YYYY]

Signature of Applicant 1

(Name)

Signature of Applicant 2

(Name)

Verification:

I, [Name], solemnly affirm that the contents of this application are true to my knowledge and belief.

Place: [City]

Date: [DD/MM/YYYY]

Signature of Applicant(s)

List of Annexures (Attachments):

1. Death Certificate of the original complainant.
2. Legal Heir Certificate / Succession Certificate / Affidavit of Heirship.
3. Copy of Will (if applicable).
4. No Objection Certificate (NOC) from other heirs (if only one heir is prosecuting).
5. Copy of the original complaint and relevant court orders.

Key Notes:

File in Duplicate: Submit one copy to the court and keep one for your records.

Court Fees: Check local rules for applicable fees (usually nominal).

Serve Notice: A copy may need to be served to the accused (varies by jurisdiction).

Application No.3

Application for summoning the bank witness (Manager) and related documents IN THE COURT OF THE LEARNED METROPOLITAN MAGISTRATE / JUDICIAL MAGISTRATE, [CITY/STATE]

Case No.: __ of 20_
Complainant: ___
Accused: ___

APPLICATION SUMMONING BANK WITNESS AND DOCUMENTS

To,
The Hon'ble Court,

Respectfully Showeth:

1. That the present complaint has been filed by the Complainant under Section 138 of the Negotiable Instruments Act, 1881, for dishonour of cheque No. _ dated _ drawn on _ Bank (Branch: _) for an amount of ₹__.

2. That the accused has raised a defence disputing the authenticity of the cheque and the transaction in question. The testimony of the Bank Manager (or authorized official) along with the original cheque, bank statement, and a certificate under Section 65B of the Indian Evidence Act (for electronic evidence, if any) is essential to prove:
The cheque was issued from the accused's account.
The cheque was dishonoured for reasons of "insufficient funds" or "account closed."
The authenticity of the bank's records.

3. That Section 254(2) of the Cr.P.C. empowers this Hon'ble Court to summon and examine any person as a witness or direct the production of any document if it appears essential for a just decision in the case.

PRAYER

In view of the above, it is most respectfully prayed that this Hon'ble Court may:

a) Summon the Manager/Authorized Officer of _ Bank (Branch: _) to appear as a witness and produce:

The original cheque No. __ (bearing the bank's endorsement of dishonour).

The account statement of the accused for the relevant period.

Certificate under Section 65B of the Indian Evidence Act (if electronic records are relied upon).

b) Pass any other order(s) as this Hon'ble Court deems fit in the interest of justice.

Place: __

Date: __

Deponent/Complainant

Through:

[Advocate's Name]

[Bar Council No.]

[Lawyer's Address]

[Contact No.]

Key Points to Note:

1. Section 254(2) Cr.P.C. allows the Magistrate to summon witnesses/documents at any stage of the trial if necessary for a just decision.

2. Bank witness is crucial to prove:

Cheque issuance from the accused's account.

Dishonour memo (return memo) with reasons.

Account details (if disputed).

3. Section 65B Certificate is mandatory if relying on electronic records (e.g., scanned bank statements).

Application 4
Application for withdrawal of a complaint against all or specific accused persons, with sufficient reasons:

IN THE COURT OF THE JUDICIAL MAGISTRATE FIRST CLASS (JMFC) AT

Criminal Case No.: [Case Number]

Under Section(s): [e.g., 138 NI Act, 420 IPC, etc.]

Title: [Complainant Name] vs. [Accused Name(s)]

Application Under Section 280 BNSS 2023 For Withdrawal Of Complaint

(Against All/Specific Accused: [Name(s)])

Respectfully Sheweth:

1. That the applicant, [Complainant's Full Name], is the original complainant in the abovereferenced case filed against the accused persons:

Accused 1: [Full Name]

Accused 2: [Full Name] (if applicable)

(List all accused)

2. That the present complaint was lodged on [Date of Filing] alleging offences under Section(s) [Relevant Sections] of [Act Name, e.g., NI Act, IPC]. A copy of the complaint is annexed as Annexure A.

3. That the applicant now seeks to withdraw the complaint against [Specify: "All Accused" OR "Accused [Name(s)] only"] under Section 280 of the BNSS 2023, for the following sufficient and bona fide reasons:

Amicable Settlement: The parties have mutually resolved the dispute through mediation/compromise dated [Date]. A copy of the settlement agreement is annexed as Annexure B.

OR

Financial Settlement: The accused has paid the outstanding dues of ₹[Amount] via receipt dated [Date] (copy annexed as Annexure B).

OR

Lack of Intent to Prosecute: The complainant has no further grievance against the accused due to [Explain: e.g., family reconciliation, business resolution, lack of evidence, etc.].

(Customize reasons based on facts)

4. That the withdrawal is:

Voluntary: Without coercion, threat, or undue influence.

In Good Faith: Not detrimental to public interest or justice.

Legally Permissible: The offence(s) are compoundable/noncompoundable, but the reasons justify withdrawal in the interest of justice (cite precedents if known).

5. That Section 280 BNSS 2023 permits withdrawal of prosecution by the complainant with the consent of the Court for sufficient grounds. The stated reasons satisfy this requirement.

PRAYER:

In light of the above, it is most respectfully prayed that this Hon'ble Court may:

a) Permit the withdrawal of the complaint against [Specify: All Accused OR Accused [Name(s)]] in Criminal Case No. [Case Number] under Section 280 BNSS 2023;

b) Discharge the said accused from the proceedings;

c) Pass any other relief(s) deemed fit in the interest of justice.

Place: [City]

Date: [Date of Filing]

DEPONENT/APPLICANT:

[Signature]

[Complainant's Full Name]

S/o, D/o, W/o [Parent/Spouse Name]

Address: [Complete Address]

Contact: [Phone/Email]

THROUGH ADVOCATE:

[Signature of Advocate]

[Advocate's Name]

[Bar Council No.]

[Chamber Address]

VERIFICATION

I, [Complainant's Full Name], solemnly affirm that the contents of this application are true to my knowledge and belief. I seek withdrawal voluntarily for the reasons stated herein.

Verified at [City] on this [Date].

[Complainant's Signature]

Key Legal & Procedural Notes:

1. Section 280 BNSS 2023:

Allows a complainant to withdraw prosecution against all or any accused with the court's consent.

Requires sufficient grounds (e.g., settlement, lack of evidence, reconciliation).

2. Essential Attachments:

Annexure A: Certified copy of the original complaint.

Annexure B: Proof of settlement/payment (e.g., agreement, receipt, affidavit).

Affidavit: Sworn statement supporting voluntariness (if required by court).

3. Critical Considerations:

Compoundable Offences (e.g., Section 138 NI Act): Courts readily permit withdrawal on settlement.

NonCompoundable Offences (e.g., IPC 420): Court must ensure withdrawal serves "ends of justice" and isn't against public policy.

Application 5

Application to dispense with the personal attendance of the Complainant Under Section(s): 256 CR. PC

IN THE COURT OF THE JUDICIAL MAGISTRATE FIRST CLASS (JMFC) 43RD COURT, BORIVALI

Criminal Case No.: / Year

Complainant:

Accused:

Person(s)

Application to dispense with the personal attendance of the Complainant Under Section(s): 256 CR. PC

Respectfully Showeth:

1. That the Complainant is the above named person in the present case.

2. That today is the date of hearing in the above case.

3. That the Complainant is currently out of town due to a personal issue and finds it extremely difficult to appear personally before this Honourable Court today.

4. That the Complainant has duly appointed Advocate Mr VK Chhabra on Record, who is fully conversant with the facts and circumstances of the case and is duly authorized to represent the Complainant.

5. That the Complainant's Advocate on Record will be present before this Honourable Court on the next date of hearing and all subsequent dates to conduct the case on behalf of the Complainant.

Therefore, the Complainant most respectfully prays that this Honourable Court may be pleased to:

Grant exemption from personal appearance to the Complainant for the hearing scheduled on 29.07.2025

and permit the Complainant's Advocate on Record to appear and represent the Complainant.

AND FOR THIS ACT OF KINDNESS, THE COMPLAINANT SHALL AS IN DUTY BOUND, EVER PRAY.

Place:

Date:

Applicant/Complainant

[Your Full Name & Signature]

Through:

Advocate for Complainant

[Advocate's Full Name]

[Advocate's Address/Chamber Details]

Application No.6

Application Section 65 of the Indian Evidence Act, 1872, to lead Secondary Evidence.

IN THE COURT OF THE JUDICIAL MAGISTRATE FIRST CLASS, [CITY]

Complaint Case No. / 2024

Misc. Application No. of 2025

BETWEEN:

XYZ S/o ABC

Residing at [Address]

... COMPLAINANT/APPLICANT

VERSUS:

DEF S/o GHI

Residing at [Address]

... ACCUSED

Application Under Section 65 Of The Indian Evidence Act, 1872 Seeking Permission To Lead Secondary Evidence

Respectfully Showeth:

1. Introductory Facts:

The applicant issued a cheque bearing No. dated for ₹ (Cheque) drawn on Bank to the accused. The said Cheque was dishonoured, as per the Return Memo dated for "Insufficient Funds" (Return Memo).

2. Loss of Originals:

The original Cheque and Return Memo were dispatched to the applicant via Courier (Tracking ID) but were lost in transit, as confirmed by:

(i) Courier Company's Loss Report dated (Annexure A)

(ii) FIR No. dated (Annexure B)

(iii) Bank Manager's Affidavit (Annexure C)

3. Statutory Notice:

A NOTICE dated was sent to the accused under Section 138(b) NI Act. The accused refused delivery, as per Postal Proof (Annexure), but the applicant's office copy was destroyed in an office flood (Insurance Report, Annexure).

4. Grounds for Secondary Evidence:

(i) Loss of Documents – Originals lost beyond the applicant's control [S. 65(c) Evidence Act].

(ii) Refusal by Addressee – Service of notice presumed under Section 27 General Clauses Act.

(iii) Certified Copies Available – The bank has issued certified copies of:

Cheque image (Annexure F)

Return Memo (Annexure G)

Notice draft (Annexure H)

5. Legal Precedents:

(i) Kishan Rao v. Shankargouda (2018 SCC OnLine SC 2434): Secondary evidence admissible if loss is proved.

(ii) MSR Leathers v. Palaniappan (2013) 1 SCC 177: Technical defects not to defeat NI Act remedy.

PRAYER

It is therefore prayed that this Hon'ble Court may:

(a) Allow the applicant to lead secondary evidence of:

Cheque (through certified copy, AnnexureF)

Return Memo (through certified copy, AnnexureG)

Statutory Notice (through office draft, AnnexureH and postal proof, AnnexureD)

(b) Permit such evidence to be read in the main complaint under Section 138 NI Act.

VERIFICATION

I, , do hereby solemnly affirm that the contents of this application are true to my knowledge and belief.

Place:

Date:

SIGNATURE OF APPLICANT

(Through Advocate)

ADVOCATE'S CERTIFICATE

Certified that the co

ntents are duly verified from original records.

Advocate for Applicant

Enrollment No.

[Stamp & Signature]

ANNEXURES

A: Courier Loss Report

B: FIR

C: Bank Manager’s Affidavit

D: Postal Proof (Refused Notice)

E: Insurance Report (Flood Damage)

F: Certified Cheque Copy

G: Certified Return Memo

H: Notice Draft (Computer Logs Printout)

KEY PRACTICAL ADVICE

1. File Early: Submit this application before leading evidence in the main complaint.

2. Notarize Affidavits: Ensure Annexures C (Bank Manager) and the applicant’s verification are notarized.

3. Serve Copy: Provide an advance copy to the accused with acknowledgment (Order to expedite hearing).

4. Cite Procedural Law: Mention Order XIII Rule 10 CPC (certified copies) by analogy.

"The law permits secondary evidence where the party has done his utmost to produce the original but cannot do so through no fault of his own."

– U. Sree v. U. Srinivas (2013) 2 SCC 114

Application No.7

Section 65B INDIAN EVIDENCE ACT.

IN THE COURT OF THE JUDICIAL MAGISTRATE FIRST CLASS,

(Criminal Jurisdiction)

C.C. No.: of 20

Complainant: [Your Name]

Vs.

Accused: [Accused Name]

Application Under Section 65b(4) Of The Indian Evidence Act For Filing Certified Affidavit For Digital Documents

Respectfully Showeth:

1. That the present complaint under Section 138 of the Negotiable Instruments Act, 1881 is pending before this Hon'ble Court.

2. That the complainant relies upon certain digital documents including:

Bank return memo (computer generated)

Invoices/digital transaction records

Email communications with the accused

Other electronic evidence

3. That as per Section 65B of the Indian Evidence Act, such electronic records require:

Certification by a responsible person

An affidavit explaining the manner of creation/storage

Compliance with conditions under Section 65B(2)

4. That the complainant has obtained:

An affidavit from [Bank Manager's Name], Branch Manager of [Bank Name], certifying:

Authenticity of the bank return memo

Details of the computer system used

Confirmation of the regular course of business

An affidavit from [Your Name] regarding other digital documents

Prayer:

It is therefore most respectfully prayed that this Hon'ble Court may:

1. Take the affidavits under Section 65B(4) on record

2. Permit the complainant to rely on certified digital documents

3. Grant leave to file additional certificates if required

4. Pass such other orders as deemed fit

Place: [City]

Date: [Date]

VERIFICATION:

I, [Your Name], the Complainant, do hereby solemnly affirm that the contents of this application are true to my knowledge and that the digital documents are genuine.

Signature of Complainant/Advocate

Name: [Your Name]

Address: [Your Address]

Contact No.: [Your Number]

Advocate (if any): [Advocate Name]

Enclosures:

1. Affidavit of the bank manager under Section 65B(4)
2. Affidavit of the complainant
3. Copies of digital documents (with hash value, if available)
4. List of dates/particulars of electronic evidence

Key Features of Proper 65B Affidavit:

Bank Manager's Affidavit Must State:

He/she is the competent person to issue the certificate

The computer system was operating properly

Information was created in the regular course of business

Details of the system used to generate records

Technical Details to Include:

Device identification (servers/computers used)

Time/date of creation

Storage/maintenance protocol

Any hash values/electronic signatures

Application 8

IN THE COURT OF THE JUDICIAL MAGISTRATE FIRST CLASS (JMFC)

Case No.: of 20

MISC. Application No. of 2025

Complainant:

Accused:

Under: Section 138/141 of the Negotiable Instruments Act, 1881

APPLICATION UNDER SECTION 65B OF THE INDIAN EVIDENCE ACT FOR PLACING AFFIDAVIT ON RECORD

Respectfully Showeth:

1. That the present complaint has been filed by the applicant/complainant under Sections 138/141 of the Negotiable Instruments Act, 1881, for dishonor of a cheque issued by the accused.

2. That in support of the complaint, the complainant relies upon certain electronic evidence (such as bank statements, emails, digital records, or CCTV footage), which is crucial for proving the case.

3. That as per Section 65B of the Indian Evidence Act, 1872, any electronic record must be accompanied by a certificate verifying its authenticity, issued by a person responsible for managing the electronic device/system.

4. That the complainant has obtained the necessary affidavit under Section 65B IEA from the concerned authority (e.g., bank manager, IT officer, or record custodian) certifying the authenticity of the electronic evidence.

5. That the said affidavit is essential for the proper adjudication of the case, as it validates the electronic evidence relied upon by the complainant.

6. That the complainant could not file the affidavit earlier due to [mention reason, if any, e.g., delay in obtaining the certificate from the bank/authority].

PRAYER

In view of the above facts and circumstances, it is most respectfully prayed that this Hon'ble Court may be pleased to:

Allow the present application;

Permit the complainant to place on record the affidavit under Section 65B of the Indian Evidence Act; and

Grant any other relief(s) as this Hon'ble Court deems fit in the interest of justice.

Place: [City]

Date: [DD/MM/YYYY]

Deponent/Complainant

[Name]

[Address]

[Contact Details]

Verification

I, [Name of Complainant], do hereby solemnly affirm and declare that the contents of this application are true and correct to the best of my knowledge and belief, and no part of it is false or misleading.

Place: [City]

Date: [DD/MM/YYYY]

Solemnly affirmed before me

Advocate/Complainant

[Signature]

Key Points to Remember:

1. Affidavit Must Comply with Section 65B IEA:

It should be signed by the person responsible for the electronic record (e.g., bank official, IT expert).

Must contain details of the device used, manner of record creation, and integrity of data.

2. Court's Permission is Mandatory:

If the affidavit was not filed earlier, a proper explanation (e.g., delay from the bank) should be provided.

3. Cross Examination Rights:

The accused may demand cross examination of the person who issued the affidavit.

4. Supporting Judgments:

Cite Anvar P.V. v. P.K. Basheer (2014) and Arjun Panditrao v. Kailash Kushanrao (2020), which mandate strict compliance with Section 65B.

Next Steps:

File the application along with the affidavit and electronic evidence.

Serve a copy to the opposite party (accused).

Be prepared for objections from the accused side.

Application 9

For Production Of Additional Evidence

IN THE COURT OF THE JUDICIAL MAGISTRATE FIRST CLASS (JMFC), [CITY]

(Criminal Misc. Application No. of 2024)

In the matter of:

[Your Name]

Vs.

[Accused Name]

(Complaint Case No. /2024 u/s 138/141 NI Act)

Application Under Section 311 CR. PC For Production Of Additional Evidence

Respectfully Showeth:

1. Case Background:

The complainant filed the present case u/s 138/141 NI Act for dishonour of cheque No. dated .

The matter is presently at the [evidence/arguments] stage.

2. Grounds for Seeking Additional Evidence:

Newly Discovered Bank Statements:

The complainant recently obtained supplementary bank statements (Annexure1) revealing:

Additional transactions proving the accused's liability.

Proof of funds being diverted postcheque issuance.

Expert Opinion:

A handwriting expert's report (Annexure2) confirms the accused's signature on disputed documents.

(OR) A forensic audit report proving financial fraud.

3. Legal Justification (Section 311 CrPC):

The evidence is crucial to establish the accused's guilt and was unavailable earlier despite due diligence.

Judicial Precedents:

Rajaram Prasad Yadav v. State of Bihar (2013) – Courts must allow evidence essential for justice.

Zahira Habibulla Sheikh v. State of Gujarat (2004) – Right to fair trial includes summoning material witnesses.

4. Prayer:

Allow production of supplementary bank statements and expert report as additional evidence.

Summon the bank manager/expert witness for examination.

For expert opinion, cite Section 45 of the Evidence Act.

Pass any other order deemed fit.

Place: [City]

Date: [DD/MM/YYYY]

Applicant/Complainant

AFFIDAVIT IN SUPPORT

I, [Your Name], aged , residing at [Address], solemnly affirm:

1. I am the complainant in the above case.
2. The facts in the application are true to my knowledge.
3. The bank statements/expert opinion were not earlier available as [explain reason, e.g., "bank delayed providing statements"].
4. This evidence is vital to prove the accused's liability.

Deponent: [Your Name]

Verification: Verified at [Place] on [Date].

Key Points:

1. Annexures:

   Annexure1: Certified bank statements with transaction highlights.

   Annexure2: Expert report (if procured).

2. Procedure:

   File in duplicate with court fee.

   Serve copy to the accused's advocate.

   Mention the next hearing date for arguments.

3. Legal Strategy:

   Argue that the evidence will not cause prejudice but aid in a just decision (State of H.P. v. Rattan Singh).

Application 10

For Early Hearing & Expeditious Trial

IN THE COURT OF THE JUDICIAL MAGISTRATE FIRST CLASS (JMFC), [CITY]

(Misc. Application No. of 2024)

In the matter of:

[Your Name] (Complainant)

Vs.

[Accused Name] (Accused)

(Complaint Case No. /2024 u/s 138/141 NI Act)

Application For Early Hearing & Expeditious Trial inter-alia on the following grounds

Respectfully Showeth:

1.Case Background:

The complainant filed the present case u/s138/141 of the Negotiable Instruments Act, 1881 for dishonour of cheque No. dated .

The matter is presently at the stage of[mention current stage: evidence/arguments/final hearing].

2. Grounds for Urgency (Choose Applicable Reasons):

Medical Emergency: The complainant is suffering from a serious illness (Annexure1: Medical Certificate) and requires immediate funds for treatment.

Financial Hardship: The complainant is facing severe financial distress due to nonrecovery of the cheque amount (Annexure2: Bank Statement/Loan Documents).

Age/Health of Key Witness: A crucial witness (e.g., bank official) is elderly/terminally ill and may not be available if trial is delayed.

Legal Precedent: The Supreme Court in P. Ramachandra Rao v. State of Karnataka (2002) emphasized theright to speedy trial underArticle 21 of the Constitution.

3.Prayer:

Expedite the trial and fix early/daily hearings.

Advance the next hearing date to the earliest available slot.

Pass any other order in the interest of justice.

Place: [City]

Date: [DD/MM/YYYY]

Applicant/Complainant

AFFIDAVIT IN SUPPORT

I, [Your Name], aged , residing at [Address], solemnly affirm:

1. I am the complainant in the above case.

2. The facts stated in this application aretrue to my knowledge.

3. The urgency is genuine and bona fide (explain briefly).

4. I am submitting supporting documents (medical reports/bank statements) as proof.

Deponent: [Your Name]

Verification: Verified at [Place] on [Date].

Key Points:

1.Supporting Documents:

Medical certificates (if health related urgency).

Bank statements/loan documents (if financial hardship).

Affidavit of witness (if witness availability is an issue).

2.Legal Provisions:

Section 309 CrPC: Court has power to postpone or expedite hearings.

Article 21 of Constitution: Right to speedy trial (cite Hussainara Khatoon v. State of Bihar).

3. Procedure:

File induplicate with court fee.

Serve copy to the accused's advocate.

Mention urgency in the prayer for early listing.

Application 11

APPLICATION For Passing An Order On An Application Dated

Where The Opposite Party Has Failed To File Their Say:

IN THE COURT OF THE JUDICIAL MAGISTRATE FIRST CLASS, [Court Name]

Criminal Case No.: of 20

[Complainant/Accused Name] vs. [Opposite Party Name]

ORDER

1. The application dated //20 filed by the Complainant/Accused seeks relief of [mention relief sought, e.g., "quashing of proceedings"/"exemption from appearance"/"interim protection"].

2. A copy of the said application was duly served upon the Opposite Party/Respondent, and this Court had directed them to file their reply/say by //20. The matter was listed for hearing today (//20).

3. Despite sufficient opportunity, the Opposite Party has not filed any reply/say, for reasons best known to them.

4. In view of the above, this Court is left with no option but to proceed in the matter exparte under [relevant provision, if applicable, e.g., Section 126 of CrPC or any other applicable law].

5. Accordingly, the application dated //20 is allowed/disposed of in terms of the prayers made therein.

6. Let necessary orders be issued accordingly.

Pronounced in open Court on this day of , 20.

(Judge's Name)

Judicial Magistrate First Class

[Court Name]

Notes:

Fill in the blanks with relevant dates, names, and sections as applicable.

Modify the relief sought based on the actual prayer in the application.

If the order is exparte, mention the legal provision allowing such a decision.

Application 12

Application No. for requesting coercive measures to secure the presence of the accused

IN THE COURT OF THE JUDICIAL MAGISTRATE FIRST CLASS (58TH COURT), BANDRA, MUMBAI

Criminal Misc. Application No.: of 2025

In the matter of:

[Case Title, e.g., State vs. XYZ]

Police Station: [Name of PS]

Case No.: [Number]

Under Section:

[Relevant IPC/CrPC sections]

Application For Issuance Of Non Bailable Warrant/Coercive Measures To Secure Presence Of Accused

Respectfully Showeth:

1. Facts of the Case: The applicant/complainant filed a case under [mention sections] against the accused, [Name], for [briefly state the offense, e.g., "cheating under Section 420 IPC"]. The court issued summons to the accused vide order dated [date], directing them to appear before this Hon'ble Court.

2. Return of Summons: The summons were sent to the last known address of the accused, [full address], via postal service. The

summons were returned undelivered with the postal endorsement: "Address left premises" (copy annexed as Annexure A).

3. Grounds for Coercive Measures: The accused is evading service of process and avoiding judicial proceedings, which hampers the administration of justice. Despite diligent efforts, the applicant cannot locate the accused's current address. Under Sections 70–72 of the CrPC, the court may issue a nonbailable warrant (NBW) or other coercive measures (e.g., attachment of property under Section 83 CrPC) to secure the accused's presence.

4. Prayer: In light of the above, the applicant humbly prays that this Hon'ble Court may: Issue a non bailable warrant (NBW) against the accused to en sure their presence. OR direct the local police to trace the accused under Section 73 CrPC. OR initiate proclamation and attachment proceedings under Sections 82–83 CrPC if the accused remains untraceable.

Verification:

I, [Applicant's Name], solemnly declare that the contents of this application are true to my knowledge and belief. Place: Mumbai Date: [Date] Signature of Applicant/Advocate Name: [Full Name] Address: [Your Address] Contact No.: [Your Number] Advocate for the Applicant (if applicable)

Key Legal Provisions: Supporting Documents to Annex:

1. Copy of returned summons with postal endorsement.

2. Copy of earlier court order issuing summons. Dated 23.07.2025

Application 13

Application For Ex Parte Proceedings Due To Absconding Of Accused

IN THE COURT OF THE JUDICIAL MAGISTRATE FIRST CLASS (JMFC),

Criminal Case No.: of 20

Under Section 138 of the Negotiable Instruments Act, 1881

Between:

XYZ ...(Complainant)

Address: [Your Address]

...V/s...

ABC ....(Accused)

Address: [Last Known Address]

Application For Ex Parte Proceedings Due To Absconding Of Accused

Most Respectfully Showeth:

1. That the present complaint under Section 138 of the Negotiable Instruments Act, 1881 was filed by the complainant against the accused for dishonour of a cheque bearing No. dated for an amount of ₹.

2. That this Hon'ble Court took cognizance of the offence and issued summons to the accused, but despite repeated attempts, the accused could not be served due to his deliberate evasion and absconding.

3. That subsequently, this Hon'ble Court issued bailable and nonbailable warrants, but the accused could not be apprehended as he has concealed himself and is untraceable.

4. That the complainant has made all possible efforts to serve the accused, including through process servers and police authorities, but

the accused is deliberately avoiding court proceedings.

5. That in view of the above, the complainant has also filed an application for declaring the accused as an absconder under Section 82/83 CrPC, and necessary proclamation and attachment proceedings have been initiated.

6. That despite all efforts, the accused has failed to appear before this Hon'ble Court, and his absence is wilful, deliberate, and without any lawful excuse.

PRAYER

In light of the above facts and circumstances, it is most respectfully prayed that this Hon'ble Court may:

a) Declare the accused as an absconder under Section 82 CrPC (if not already done);

b) Allow the complainant to proceed his Part of Submissions in the prevailing scenario and to go ahead in accordance with practice, procedure and law .

c) Permit the recording of evidence in the absence of the accused;

d) Pass any other order(s) as this Hon'ble Court deems fit in the interest of justice.

Place: [Your City]

Date: [Date of Filing]

Deponent/Complainant

(Name & Signature)

[Your Contact Details]

VERIFICATION

I, [Your Name], the complainant in the above matter, do hereby solemnly affirm and declare that the contents of this application are true and correct to the best of my knowledge, information, and belief.

Verified at [Place] on [Date].

Signature of Complainant

Supporting Documents to be Attached:

1. Copy of complaint u/s 138 NI Act.

2. Copies of summons/non bailable warrants issued.

3. Affidavit of process server/police regarding non service.

4. Application u/s 82 CrPC (if filed separately).

5. Any other relevant proof of accused's evasion.

In the case of an application to proceed ex parte under Section 138 of the Negotiable Instruments Act, 1881, where the accused has absconded, the Judicial Magistrate First Class (JMFC) Court may pass an order allowing the complainant to proceed with the case in the absence of the accused.

Typical Order of JMFC Court in Such Cases:

1. Recording of Absence of Accused – The court will verify whether the accused has been duly served but is intentionally evading trial or cannot be found despite reasonable efforts.

2. Satisfaction of Due Process – The court must ensure that summons/warrants were issued properly and that the accused's absence is willful.

3. Hearing the Complainant – The court may hear the complainant's arguments and examine evidence to determine if a prima facie case exists.

4. Ex Parte Proceedings – If satisfied, the court may order the case to proceed ex parte under Section 126 of the Criminal Procedure Code (CrPC).

5. Recording Ex Parte Evidence – The complainant will be allowed to lead evidence (witnesses, documents, etc.) in the absence of the accused.

6. Judgment – Based on the evidence, the court may convict or acquit the accused.

Key Legal Provisions:

Section 138 NI Act – Dishonour of cheque.

Sections 82, 83 CrPC – Proclamation and attachment if accused is absconding.

Section 126 CrPC – Power to proceed ex parte if accused fails to appear.

Conditions for Ex Parte Order:

Proper service of summons (Proved by process server's affidavit).

No reasonable explanation for absence (Court must be convinced of willful evasion).

No prejudice to accused (Accused can later apply to set aside ex parte order under Section 317 CrPC).

Application 14

Application Under Section 299 Crpc For Recording Evidence In The Absence Of An Absconding Accused In A Section 138 NI Act Case:

IN THE COURT OF THE JUDICIAL MAGISTRATE FIRST CLASS

(OR: CHIEF JUDICIAL MAGISTRATE, AS APPLICABLE)

Criminal Case No.: of 20

Under Section 138 of the Negotiable Instruments Act, 1881

Between:

[Your Name], Complainant

Address: [Your Full Address]

...Versus...

[Accused Name], Accused

[Last Known Address]

APPLICATION UNDER SECTION 299 CrPC FOR RECORDING EVIDENCE IN ABSENCE OF ABSCONDING ACCUSED

Respectfully Showeth:

1. That the present complaint under Section 138 of the Negotiable Instruments Act was filed against the accused for dishonour of cheque No. dated for ₹ issued by [Bank Name].

2. That this Hon'ble Court has taken cognizance and issued:

Summons on (date)

Bailable warrant on (date)

Non bailable warrant on (date)

3. That despite diligent efforts by:

Process server (Affidavit attached as Annexure)

Local police (Report attached as Annexure)

the accused could not be served/apprehended as he is deliberately evading process.

4. That this Hon'ble Court has already:

Issued proclamation under Section 82 CrPC on (date)

Ordered attachment under Section 83 CrPC on (date)

(OR: That application for such proclamation is pending)

5. That the accused has been declared absconder/proclaimed offender vide order dated (copy attached).

6. That Section 299 CrPC permits recording of evidence in the absence of an absconding accused to prevent undue delay in justice.

Prayer:

It is therefore most respectfully prayed that this Hon'ble Court may:

a) Permit recording of complainant's evidence and witness testimony under Section 299 CrPC;

b) Direct the prosecution to produce all relevant documents;

c) Fix dates for ex parte evidence recording;

d) Pass such other orders as this Hon'ble Court deems fit.

Place:

Date:

Deponent/Complainant

[Your Signature]

[Your Name]

[Your Contact Details]

VERIFICATION

I, [Your Name], solemnly affirm that the contents above are true to my knowledge and belief.

Verified at [Place] on [Date].

Signature of Complainant

Key Supporting Documents to Annex:

1. Copy of complaint u/s 138 NI Act
2. Copies of all process reports (summons/warrants)
3. Proclamation order u/s 82 CrPC (if any)
4. Police report on accused's no availability
5. Affidavit of process server
6. Previous court orders in the case

Important Notes:

1. Section 299 CrPC applies when:

   Accused is absconding

   There's no immediate prospect of arresting him

   Court has initiated proceedings under Sections 82/83 CrPC

2. The recorded evidence remains admissible if the accused is later tried.

3. Ensure all previous steps (proper service, warrants, proclamation) are duly executed.

Yes, in a Section 138 NI Act case, the court can finally decide and convict the accused even after proceeding under Section 299 CrPC (recording evidence in the absence of an absconding accused), provided the following conditions are met:

1. Legal Position on Deciding the Case After Section 299 CrPC

Proceedings

Section 299 CrPC allows the court to record evidence in the absence of an absconding accused to prevent indefinite delays.

Once the complainant's evidence is recorded ex parte and the court is satisfied that:

The accused was duly served/proclaimed (under Sections 82/83 CrPC).

The complainant has proved all ingredients of Section 138 NI Act (cheque issuance, dishonour, legal notice, nonpayment).

The court can pronounce judgment (conviction or acquittal) based on the available evidence.

2. Key Conditions for Final Decision

✔ Proper service of summons/warrants – The court must be satisfied that the accused was given a fair opportunity to appear.

✔ Proclamation under Section 82 CrPC – The accused should have been declared an "absconder" with a public notice.

✔ Evidence conclusively proves guilt – The complainant must establish:

Cheque was issued by the accused.

It was dishonoured for "insufficient funds" or other valid reasons.

A legal demand notice was served within 30 days of dishonour.

The accused failed to pay within 15 days of notice.

✔ No reasonable defence – Since the accused is absent, the court relies solely on the complainant's evidence.

3. Can the Accused Challenge Later?

If the accused is convicted ex parte, he can file:

Application to set aside ex parte order (under Section 317 CrPC) if he later appears with a valid reason for absence.

Appeal under Section 374 CrPC (but must explain his absence).

However, if the court has followed due process (proper summons, proclamation, and evidence), the conviction will likely stand.

4. Final Judgment Possible?

Yes, the court can:

Convict the accused (if evidence is sufficient) and issue:

Sentence (jail up to 2 years / fine up to twice the cheque amount).

Compensation under Section 357 CrPC.

Acquit the accused if evidence is insufficient.

5. Practical Consideration

Some courts may wait longer before final judgment to see if the accused appears.

Others may proceed straight to judgment after recording evidence under Section 299 CrPC if the accused's absence is clearly willful.

Conclusion

If the court is satisfied that:

1. The accused is wilfully absconding, and

2. The complainant's evidence proves guilt beyond doubt,

then the case can be finally decided even in the accused's absence.

Application 15

Application Praying To Close the Right To Cross Examination Due To Delay Tactics.

IN THE COURT OF THE JUDICIAL MAGISTRATE FIRST CLASS (JMFC),

Application Praying For Closing

The Right To Cross Examination Due To Delay Tactics.

Respectfully Showeth:

1. That the present case is pending before this Hon'ble Court under Section 138 of the Negotiable Instruments Act, 1881, wherein the accused has been deliberately delaying the trial.

2. That the complainant's evidence was recorded, and the accused

was granted multiple opportunities to cross-examine the complainant, but despite several adjournments, the accused has failed to conduct cross examination without any valid reason.

3. That the conduct of the accused clearly indicates an intention to prolong the trial unnecessarily, causing prejudice to the complainant.

4. That the Hon'ble Supreme Court and various High Courts have held that if an accused misuses the liberty of adjournments to delay cross examination, the Court has the power to close the right to cross examine in the interest of justice.

Prayer: In view of the above, it is most respectfully prayed that this Hon'ble Court may be pleased to:

Close the right of the accused to cross examine the complainant;

Proceed with the trial in accordance with the law; Pass any other order(s) as this Hon'ble Court deems fit in the interest of justice.

]

Key Legal Points to Argue:

1. Section 311 CrPC – Gives the court the power to summon or recall witnesses but also implies the authority to restrict cross-examination if misused.

2. Section 254(2) CrPC (if applicable in summons trial) – Allows the court to proceed if the accused fails to cross-examine despite opportunities.

3. Judicial Precedents:

Courts have held that if an accused unreasonably delays cross examination, the right can be forfeited (K.K. Velusamy v. N. Palanisamy, (2011) 11 SCC 275). Delaying tactics should not be allowed to defeat justice (Vadiraj Naggappa Vernekar v. Sharadchandra Prabhakar Gogate, (2009) 4 SCC 410).

Application 16

APPLICATION UNDER SECTION 319 Cr.P.C. For Impleading Additional Accused

IN THE COURT OF JUDICIAL MAGISTRATE FIRST CLASS (JMFC),

Criminal Misc. Application No. of 2024

In the matter of:

[Your Name] (Complainant)

Vs.

[Existing Accused Name] (Accused)

Under:

Complaint Case No. /2024 u/s 138/141 of Negotiable Instruments Act, 1881

APPLICATION UNDER SECTION 319 CR.P.C. FOR IMPLEADING ADDITIONAL ACCUSED

Respectfully Showeth:

1. That the present complaint was filed under Section 138/141 of the Negotiable Instruments Act against [Existing Accused Name] for dishonour of cheque No. dated .

2. That during the course of proceedings/evidence, it has emerged that:

[Name of Proposed Additional Accused] was actively involved in the transaction

As [designation, e.g., Director/Partner/Authorized Signatory] of [Company Name]

Was responsible for issuance/management of the dishonoured cheque

Had direct knowledge and control over the transaction

3. That the evidence on record shows:

[Specific evidence e.g., bank records showing their signature]

[Witness testimony implicating them]

[Documentary proof of their role]

4. That under Section 319 Cr.P.C., this Hon'ble Court has the power to proceed against any person not already accused if it appears from evidence that such person has committed the offence.

5. That in the interest of justice, it is necessary to implead [Proposed Additional Accused Name] as an accused in the present case.

Prayer:

It is therefore most respectfully prayed that this Hon'ble Court may be pleased to:

a) Issue notice to [Proposed Additional Accused Name] under Section 319 Cr.P.C.;

b) Summon them to face trial in the present case;

c) Pass such other orders as this Hon'ble Court may deem fit.

Place: [City]

Date: [DD/MM/YYYY]

Applicant/Complainant

VERIFICATION

I, [Your Name], the applicant abovenamed, do hereby solemnly affirm and declare that the contents of this application are true to my knowledge and belief, and no part of it is false or misleading.

Deponent

[Your Signature]

ENCLOSURES:

1. Affidavit in support

2. Relevant documents/evidence

3. Copy of complaint

4. Proof of proposed accused's involvement

Important Notes:

1. File with proper court fee

2. Serve copy to existing accused

3. Mention specific evidence showing proposed accused's involvement

4. Refer to any witness statements implicating the proposed accused

5. Cite relevant precedents if available (e.g., Hardeep Singh v. State of Punjab)

Legal Basis:

Section 319 CR.P.C. allows adding accused during trial if evidence emerges

Court must be satisfied about their involvement from evidence

Opportunity must be given to proposed accused to be heard

Standard of proof is "appears to have committed offence" (lower than conviction standard)

Application 17

Application Under Section 143(3) Of N.I. Act Read With Section 260(2) CR. PC For Conversion Of Summary Trial To Regular Trial

IN THE COURT OF JUDICIAL MAGISTRATE FIRST CLASS (JMFC), [CITY]

Criminal Misc. Application No. of 2024

In the matter of:

[Your Name] (Complainant)

Vs.

[Accused Name] (Accused)

Under:

Complaint Case No. /2024 u/s 138/141 of Negotiable Instruments Act, 1881

Application Under Section 143(3) Of N.I. Act Read With Section 260(2) Crpc For Conversion Of Summary Trial To Regular Trial

Respectfully Showeth:

1. That the present complaint was filed under Section 138 of the Negotiable Instruments Act, which is ordinarily tri able as a summary case under Section 143 of the Act.

2. That during the course of proceedings, the following circumstances have emerged which necessitate conversion to regular

trial:

The case involves complex questions of fact and law regarding the liability of directors under Section 141 of NI Act

Multiple accused persons are involved requiring detailed examination

Voluminous documentary evidence needs to be considered

Several witnesses are required to be examined at length

The defence has raised complicated legal issues regarding transactions

3. That under Section 143(3) of NI Act read with Section 260(2) CrPC, this Hon'ble Court has the discretion to convert the summary trial to regular trial if the case warrants more elaborate inquiry.

4. That in the interest of justice and fair trial, it would be appropriate to convert the present proceedings to regular trial to enable:

Proper examination of all witnesses

Detailed consideration of documentary evidence

Complete adjudication of all legal issues raised

Prayer:

It is therefore most respectfully prayed that this Hon'ble Court may be pleased to:

a) Convert the present summary trial to regular trial;

b) Pass such other and further orders as this Hon'ble Court may deem fit in the interest of justice.

Place: [City]

Date: [DD/MM/YYYY]

Applicant/Complainant

[Your Name]

[Your Address]

[Contact Details]

VERIFICATION

I, [Your Name], the applicant abovenamed, do hereby solemnly affirm and declare that the contents of this application are true to my knowledge and belief, and no part of it is false or misleading.

Deponent

[Your Signature]

Notes:

1. File with supporting affidavit
2. Attach copy of complaint and relevant documents
3. Serve copy to opposite party
4. Mention existing case number and next hearing date

Key Legal Points:

Section 143(3) NI Act specifically provides for conversion to regular trial

Judicial discretion to be exercised based on complexity of case

Precedents support conversion where detailed inquiry needed Opportunity should be given to both parties to be heard

Application 18

Under Section 313(B) CR. PC For Dispensing With The Statement Of The Accused

IN THE COURT OF THE JUDICIAL MAGISTRATE FIRST CLASS, 28TH ESPLANADE, MUMBAI

C.C. No.: of 2017

Nitian

Complainant

Vs

Accused

Application Under Section 313(B) CR. PC For Dispensing With The Statement Of The Accused

Respectfully Showeth:

1. That the present matter is fixed today for recording the statement of the accused under Section 313 CrPC, but neither the accused nor his advocate is present despite due notice.

2. That this Hon'ble Court has already passed a "no cross" order (as the accused failed to crossexamine witnesses), and a recalling application filed by the accused was also dismissed/turned down.

3. That the case pertains to the year 2017 and has been lingering solely due to the accused's deliberate delaying tactics, including: Nonappearance for the Section 313 statement, Earlier absence during witness cross examination, Frivolous adjournment requests.

4. That under Section 313(b) CrPC, this Hon'ble Court has the discretion to dispense with the accused's statement if his examination is deemed unnecessary or if he evades the process.

5. That in the interest of justice and to prevent further delay, it is just and necessary to: Dispense with the accused's statement under Section 313 CrPC, Fix the matter for final arguments at the earliest.

Prayer:

In view of the above, it is most respectfully prayed that this

Hon'ble Court may:

a) Dispense with the accused's statement under Section 313(b) CrPC due to his nonappearance.

b) Fix the matter for final arguments on the next date.

Place:

Mumbai Date:

Vinod K Chhabra

on record through holding lawyer.

Advocate Divya Joshi

Application 19

Application for Issuance of a Warrant to the Collector under Section 461B NS 2023 for Recovery of Unpaid Fine.

IN THE COURT OF THE JUDICIAL MAGISTRATE FIRST CLASS (JMFC) AT [PLACE] CASE NO.: [Case Number, e.g., CC No. 123/2024]

STATE

vs.

[Name of Accused Respondent(s)]

U/S: [Relevant Sections of Law under which convicted/sentenced]

Application Under Section 461bns 2023 For Issuance Of Warrant To The Collector For Recovery Of Unpaid Fine

Respectfully Showeth:

1. That in the abovementioned case, this Hon'ble Court was pleased

to pass a Judgment and Order dated [Date of Conviction/Order Imposing Fine], whereby the Accused Respondent(s), [Name(s) of Accused Respondent(s)], was/were: Convicted for the offence(s) under Section(s) [Relevant Sections] of [Name of Act, e.g., IPC, NDPS Act, etc.]. Sentenced to undergo [State Sentence if any, e.g., Simple Imprisonment for X months]. Fined a sum of Rs. [Amount of Fine in Figures] (Rupees [Amount in Words]). Directed that in default of payment of the said fine, the Accused Respondent(s) shall undergo [State Default Sentence, e.g., Simple Imprisonment for Y months].

2. That a certified copy of the said Order dated [Date of Conviction/Order Imposing Fine] is annexed herewith and marked as Annexure A.

3. That as per the said Order, the fine amount of Rs. [Amount of Fine] was to be paid by the Accused Respondent(s) on or before [Due Date for Payment, if specified, otherwise state "within the time stipulated by law/court"].

4. That despite the lapse of the stipulated time and the passing of the said Order, the Accused Respondent(s), [Name(s) of Accused Respondent(s)], has/have wilfully failed, neglected, and refused to pay the imposed fine amount of Rs. [Amount of Fine].

5. That recovery proceedings for the said fine amount through the ordinary process of warrant for levy of fine (Section 421 CrPC) have either been attempted unsuccessfully or are deemed inappropriate/ineffective due to [Briefly state reason e.g., inability to locate sufficient movable property, Accused absconding, etc.]. Therefore, recovery as arrears of land revenue under Section 461B NS 2023 is the appropriate recourse.

6. That Section 461B NS 2023 empowers this Hon'ble Court to issue a warrant to the Collector of the District, authorizing him to realize the amount as if it were an arrear of land revenue.

PRAYER:

In view of the facts stated above, it is most respectfully prayed that this Hon'ble Court may be pleased to: a) Issue a Warrant under Section 461B NS 2023 addressed to the Collector, [Name of District] District, directing the said Collector to recover the unpaid fine amount of Rs. [Amount of Fine] from the Accused Respondent(s), [Name(s) of Accused Respondent(s)], as if it were an arrear of land revenue; and b) Pass such other and further orders as this Hon'ble Court deems fit and proper in the interest of justice.

Place: [Place]

Date: [Date of Application]

APPLICANT / DEPONENT:

[Signature]

[Name and

VERIFICATION

I, [Name of Applicant/Deponent], the [Designation], do hereby solemnly verify and declare that the contents of paragraphs 1 to 6 of the above application are true and correct to the best of my knowledge and belief, derived from the official record of the case, and that nothing material has been concealed therefrom. Verified at [Place] on this [Date] [Signature of Deponent]

Designation of Applicant] (Public Prosecutor / Assistant Public Prosecutor / [Specify if other authorized person]) For the State

20 APPLICATION

U/S 330 OF THE BNSS, 2023

for Presumption Of Genuineness of Documents

IN THE COURT OF THE JUDICIAL MAGISTRATE FIRST CLASS AT , [STATE]

Criminal Complaint Case No.: ____ of 2024
(To be filled after filing)

In the matter of:
Complainant: ABC
Vs.
Accused: XYZ

Application under Section 330 of (BNSS), 2023, for Presumption Of Genuineness of Documents Filed Along with The Complaint

Respected Sir/Madam,

The Complainant above-named most respectfully submits as under:

1. That the Complainant has filed the present complaint under Section 138 of the Negotiable Instruments Act, 1881, against the Accused, which is pending for taking cognizance before this Hon'ble Court.

2. That along with the said Complaint, the Complainant has filed the following documents, which are crucial for establishing a prima facie case for taking cognizance:

Annexure A: The original dishonoured cheque No. [Cheque Number], dated [Date], drawn on [Bank Name, Branch].

Annexure B: The Cheque Return Memo (also known as the Dishonour Memo) dated [Date] issued by the Complainant's bank.

Annexure C: A copy of the Statutory Demand Notice dated [Date], sent to the Accused under Section 138(b) & (c) of the N.I. Act.

Annexure D: The original postal receipts (UPC/Speed Post/Registered AD) and the tracking details evidencing the dispatch of the said statutory notice.

Annexure E: The affidavit of the Complainant sworn in support of the complaint.

3. That the aforementioned documents have been duly signed by the Complainant and filed as an integral part of the complaint.

4. That Section 330(1)(c) of The Bharatiya Nagarik Suraksha Sanhita (BNSS), 2023, which has replaced the Code of Criminal Procedure, 1973, explicitly states:

"330. No formal proof of certain documents.-- (1) The Court shall presume the genuineness of every document purporting to be... (c) a document signed by the complainant or the accused, as the case may be, and filed along with the complaint or the first information report, as the case may be, before the Court."

5. That in light of the mandatory language of the statute ("the Court shall presume"), this Hon'ble Court is obligated to presume the genuineness of the documents listed at Para 2 above for the purpose of taking cognizance and issuing process against the Accused.

6. That the purpose of this provision is to expedite the early stages of the trial and to prevent unnecessary delay in the administration of justice by doing away with the requirement of formal proof of these foundational documents at the pre-summoning stage.

PRAYER

In view of the facts and grounds stated hereinabove, it is most respectfully prayed that this Hon'ble Court may be pleased to:

a) Take judicial notice of the provisions of Section 330 of the BNSS, 2023;

b)Presume the genuineness of the documents filed along with the complaint (Annexures A to E);

c)Take cognizance of the offense under Section 138 of the Negotiable Instruments Act; and

d)Issue process/summons against the Accused for the said offense.

And for this act of kindness, the Complainant shall, as in duty bound, ever pray.

Place: [City]

Date:[Date]

Through:

[Signature of Advocate/Complainant]

ADVOCATE FOR THE COMPLAINANT

[Name of Advocate]

—

20 No. Important Practical Notes for Filing:

1. Filing with Complaint: This application should be filed along with

your main complaint under Section 138 of the NI Act or immediately thereafter, before the court considers the complaint for cognizance.

2. Cause Title: Ensure the cause title (the heading with court name, parties, case number) is correctly filled. If the complaint is not yet numbered, write "Criminal Complaint Case No. .... of 20....".

3. Annexure List: The list of annexures (A, B, C, etc.) must exactly match the documents you have filed and paginated with your complaint.

4. Local Rules: Always check if your specific court has any additional formatting requirements or a preferred cover page for applications.

5. Serve a Copy: A copy of this application must be served to the opposite party (the Accused) only after the court has taken cognizance and summoned them. At this pre-cognizance stage, it is an ex-parte application meant only for the court's consideration.A

Applications ANNEXED In Next Volume Applications 21 Onward
To Be Continued +

****

CHAPTER-02

BUNCH OF APPLICATIONS FROM ACCUSED SIDE

---

1. UNDER SECTION 204 CR. PC READ WITH SECTION 482 CR. PC FOR RECALL OF SUMMONING ORDER
2. DISCHARGE APPLICATION (SEEKING DISMISSAL BEFORE TRIAL)
3. APPLICATION TO DISCARD AFFIDAVIT OF EVIDENCE DUE TO LACK OF DE FACTO VERIFICATION
4. APPLICATION UNDER SECTION 65 OF THE INDIAN EVIDENCE ACT TO DE-EXHIBIT/EXCLUDE UNSTAMPED AND UNSIGNED BANK RETURN MEMO
5. APPLICATION UNDER SECTION 272 BNSS 2023 (NON-APPEARANCE OF COMPLAINANT) FOR DISMISSAL OF COMPLAINT AND ACQUITTAL OF ACCUSED
6. APPLICATION UNDER SECTION 248(8) BNSS 2023 (DEATH OF ACCUSED) FOR DISMISSAL OF
7. APP FOR PERMANENT EXEMPTION
8. APP FOR RECALLING OF NO CROSS ORDER
9. APP FOR CHANGING CAPTION DISMISSAL TRIAL
10. APP FOR RECALLING OF COERCIVE ORDER OF WARRANT/ PO
11. APP FOR DISCHARGE ATTACHMENT OF PO
12. APP FOR COMPOUNDING OF OFFENCE BY MUTUAL CONSENT

13. APPLICATION FOR ALLOWING CASH DEPOSIT IN LIEU OF SURETY

To Be Continued NUIMBER 14 ONWARDS IN NEXT VOLUME

Application No.1

Under Section 204 CrPC Read With Section 482 CrPC for Recall of Summoning Order
IN THE COURT OF THE JUDICIAL MAGISTRATE FIRST CLASS
Criminal Misc. Application No. 2025
[Your Name]
(Applicant/Accused No. _)
Versus
[Complainant's Name] (Respondent/Complainant)
Application for Recall Of Summoning Order
Dated [Date] Passed by the Concerned Competent Court, inter-alia on the following grounds :
Respectfully Showeth:

Preliminary Submissions:

1. The Applicant is Accused No. _ in Complaint Case No. of 2025 under Section 138/141 of the Negotiable Instruments Act, 1881. The Concerned Competent Court was pleased to issue summons vide order dated [Date], which is legally untenable as against the Applicant.
2. Grounds for Recall:
A. No Offence Made Out Against Applicant: The Applicant was not the signatory of the dishonoured cheque no. _ dated _. The Complaint fails to show any role of the Applicant in the alleged transaction. Essential ingredients of Section 138 NI Act (legally enforceable debt, liability, etc.) are not satisfied against the Applicant.
B. No Vicarious Liability under Section 141 NI Act: The Applicant is not a Director/Partner of the accused company/firm. Even if associated, the Complaint does not allege the Applicant's active role

in day-to-day affairs. Reliance: K.K. Ahuja v. V.K. Vora Summons Issued without Application of Mind: The Ld. Magistrate did not scrutinize whether the Complaint disclosed a prima facie case against the Applicant. Reliance: Adalat Prasad v. Rooplal Jindal (2004)

3. Prayer:

In view of the above, it is most respectfully prayed that this Hon'ble Court may: Recall/Set Aside the summoning order dated [Date] qua the Applicant.

Drop proceedings against the Applicant. Pass any other relief(s) deemed fit.

Verification:

I, [Your Name], solemnly affirm that the contents of this application are true to my knowledge.

Place: _ Date: __

APPLICANT/ACCUSED

[Your Name]

[Your Address]

[Your Contact]

Application No.2

Discharge Application And Grounds... This is a critical stage in a case under Section 138 of the Negotiable Instruments Act (NI Act). A discharge application is the accused's primary tool to seek dismissal of the case before the trial begins, avoiding the lengthy and arduous trial process.

Here is a detailed explanation of the provisions, grounds, and strategy for a discharge application in a 138 NI Act case.

1. The Legal Provision: Section 239 of the CrPC / Section 262 of the BNSS

The right to seek discharge is not found in the NI Act itself but in the procedural criminal code.

Under the Old Law (CrPC): The provision is Section 239 of the Code of Criminal Procedure, 1973. It empowers a Magistrate to discharge the accused if, upon considering the police report (in a police case) or the complaint and documents (in a complaint case), the Magistrate finds that "no sufficient ground exists for proceeding against the accused."

Under the New Law (BNSS): With effect from July 1, 2024, the CrPC is replaced by the Bharatiya Nagarik Suraksha Sanhita, 2023 (BNSS). The corresponding provision is now Section 262 of the BNSS. The language and intent remain virtually identical.

2. The Objective & Stage of Filing

Objective: To convince the Magistrate that even if all the allegations made by the complainant are taken at face value and presumed to be true, they do not make out a legally enforceable case against the accused. The goal is to stop the case at the threshold.

Stage: It is filed after the cognizance of the offence has been taken by the court and the summons has been issued to the accused, but before the recording of evidence (i.e., before the trial begins in earnest). This is typically at the first hearing or soon after.

3. Key Grounds for Seeking Discharge in a 138 NI Act Case

The grounds for discharge are specific and legalistic. The accused must demonstrate a fatal flaw in the complainant's case based on the complaint, pre summoning evidence, and documents.

Here are the most common and successful grounds:

Ground 1:

Absence of a Legally Enforceable Debt or Liability This is the most potent ground. The accused must provide strong, incontrovertible evidence that the cheque was not issued for the discharge of a legally enforceable debt.

Examples:

The cheque was issued as a security for a future obligation that never materialized.

The debt was a time barred debt under the Limitation Act, and there was no fresh acknowledgment to revive it.

The debt was for an illegal or unlawful purpose (e.g., gambling, bribing).

Full and final settlement had already been reached, and the complainant is misusing the cheque.

Ground 2:

Noncompliance with Mandatory Procedural Conditions The NI Act has strict procedural requirements. Failure to meet them is a valid ground for discharge.

Examples:

Invalid Demand Notice: The statutory demand notice under Section 138(b) was not sent to the correct address as known to the drawer, or it was sent beyond the 30day period from the date of the cheque return memo.

Premature Filing: The complaint was filed before the expiry of 15 days from the date of serving the demand notice. The cause of action arises only after this period if payment is not made.

Delay in Filing: The complaint was filed after 30 days from the date the cause of action arose (i.e., after the 15day notice period ended).

Ground 3: Fundamental Defect in the Complaint or Evidence The complaint itself ,even if entirely true, does not disclose an offence.

Examples:

The complaint or the preliminary evidence does not specifically state that the cheque was issued for the "discharge, in whole or in part, of any debt or other liability."

There is a material discrepancy in the date of the transaction, the amount, or the purpose, which goes to the root of the matter.

The accused was not a signatory to the cheque or was not responsible for the company's conduct at the relevant time (e.g., a director who resigned before the cheque was issued).

Ground 4:

Lack of Prima Facie Case The accused can demonstrate through documents that the complainant's story is so inherently improbable that no reasonable court could convict based on it.

Example: The accused provides bank statements showing the full amount was repaid via bank transfer, making the subsequent presentation of the cheque malicious.

4. **What is NOT a Ground for Discharge?**

It is crucial to understand what arguments will likely fail at the discharge stage:

· Purely Factual Disputes: "I already repaid the money in cash," "the quality of goods was poor," "the cheque was lost and misused." These are defences that require a trial where evidence is led and cross-examination takes place. The discharge stage is not a ministerial.

· Merely a Denial: Simply filing an application denying the allegations without providing strong supporting documentary evidence will not suffice

5. Process and Evidence

1. Filing the Application: A formal application is drafted citing Section 239 CrPC / Section 262 BNSS, outlining the specific grounds with legal arguments.

2. Supporting Affidavit: The accused must file a detailed affidavit swearing to the facts.

3. Documentary Evidence: This is the key to success. The application must be supported by documents such as:

- Bank statements showing repayment.
- Resignation letter from a directorship.
- Email/SMS records showing the cheque was for security.
- Legal opinion on a time barred debt.
- The demand notice and proof of delivery with dates.

4. Hearing: The court will hear arguments from both sides. The court's job is to sift through the evidence to see if there is enough to proceed, not to decide on the truth of the allegations.

Summary Table

Aspect Details

Governing Law Section 239 of CrPC (until June 30, 2024) / Section 262 of BNSS (from July 1, 2024)

When to File After summons are issued, but before the recording of evidence begins.

Test Applied by Court

"Whether the material presented, if taken at face value without rebuttal, makes out a case against the accused?"

Strong Grounds 1. No Legal Debt: (Security, time barred, illegal purpose). 2. Procedural Lapse: (Faulty notice, premature complaint). 3. Fundamental Defect: (Missing essential allegation in complaint).

Weak Grounds 1. Factual debateable Disputes requiring trial (e.g., repayment in cash). 2. Mere denial of allegations.

Key Notes:

1. Attach Supporting Documents: Copy of the cheque (showing Applicant is not a signatory). Bank records/KYC proving non-involvement. Copy of the Complaint & Summoning Order.

2. File Immediately: Delay may weaken the case.

3. Follow-Up: If rejected, file a Quashing Petition u/s 482 CrPC before the High Court Typical Order of JMFC Court in Such Cases:

Application No.3

Application to Discard Affidavit of Evidence Due to Lack of De Facto Verification

APPLICATION FOR DISCARDING AFFIDAVIT OF EVIDENCE DUE TO LACK OF DE FACTO VERIFICATION

IN THE COURT OF THE JUDICIAL MAGISTRATE FIRST CLASS (JMFC) AT
Criminal Case No.: __
Applicant/Accused: ____ Vs. Complainant/Prosecution:

APPLICATION UNDER SECTION PRAYING TO DISCARD AFFIDAVIT OF EVIDENCE FOR LACK OF DE FACTO VERIFICATION

RESPECTFULLY SHOWETH:

1. Preliminary Facts:

The deponent [Deponent's Name], acting on behalf of the complainant/prosecution, filed an Affidavit of Evidence dated [Date] (Annexure A1) in the present proceedings.

The aforementioned affidavit purports to serve as evidence but is legally invalid due to the absence of de facto verification (i.e., verification of facts based on personal knowledge).

GROUNDS FOR DISCARDING THE AFFIDAVIT

A. ABSENCE OF DE FACTO VERIFICATION

2. The affidavit lacks compliance with mandatory legal requirements:

It fails to clearly distinguish between:

(i) Statements based on the deponent's personal knowledge (de facto), and

(ii) Statements based on information, belief, or hearsay.

It violates Section 297(1) CrPC, which mandates that affidavits must explicitly state which parts are true to the deponent's knowledge and which are based on information/belief.

The deponent has not declared the source of information for hearsay assertions, rendering the affidavit inadmissible (Ref: K. Veeraswami v. Union of India, AIR 1991 SC 739).

B. DEFECTIVE VERIFICATION CLAUSE 3. The verification clause (if any) is vague, boilerplate, and noncompliant:

It does not specify:

"True to my personal knowledge" for factual assertions, or

"Based on information received and believed to be true" for secondary information.

It contravenes Rule 3 of the Affidavits Rules, 2020, read with Form No. 25 of Appendix I, CrPC.

C. PREJUDICE TO FAIR TRIAL 4. The affidavit attempts to introduce unverified, speculative, or irrelevant content that:

Prejudices the applicant's right to a fair trial under Article 21 of the Constitution.

Burdens the court with inadmissible evidence (Ref: State of U.P. v. Sheo Lal, AIR 2014 SC 3098).

PRAYER It is therefore prayed that this Hon'ble Court may:

1. Discard the Affidavit of Evidence dated [Date] filed by [Deponent's Name] for lack of de facto verification.

2. Exclude the contents of the said affidavit from the trial record.

3. Pass any other relief(s) deemed fit in the interest of justice.

VERIFICATION

I, [Applicant's Name], the applicant herein, do solemnly affirm that:

The contents of this application are true to my personal knowledge (de facto).

I have not concealed any material facts.

Place: __ Date: __

SIGNATURE OF APPLICANT

[Applicant's Name]

KEY LEGAL PROVISIONS & SUPPORT

1. Section 297 CrPC:

Affidavits must specify whether statements are based on knowledge, information, or belief.

2. Section 3, Oaths Act, 1969:

Mandates sworn verification before an oath commissioning authority.

3. Precedents:

Mehta Teja Singh & Co. v. FAIT, AIR 1977 Del 231: Affidavits without sourcebased verification are void.

Virendra Kumar v. State of U.P., 2021 SCC OnLine All 432: Boilerplate verification invalidates affidavits.

ANNEXURES

1. Annexure

A1: Copy of the defective Affidavit of Evidence.

2. Annexure

A2: Proof of service to the opposite party.

Application 4

To De exhibit/Exclude Unstamped & Unsigned Bank Return Memo

IN THE COURT OF THE JUDICIAL MAGISTRATE FIRST CLASS (Criminal Jurisdiction)

Case No.: _ of 20__

Complainant: [Name]

Vs.

Accused: [Your Name]

APPLICATION UNDER SECTION 65 INDIAN EVIDENCE ACT TO DEEXHIBIT/EXCLUDE UNSTAMPED & UNSIGNED BANK RETURN MEMO

Most Respectfully Showeth:

1. That the complainant has relied upon a Bank Return Memo (Exhibit No. _) allegedly showing dishonour of the cheque in question.

2. That the said memo lacks: Official seal/stamp of the bank Signature of any authorized bank official Any certification under Section 2A of the Bankers' Books Evidence Act, 1891

3. That such document is inadmissible in evidence as per: Section 61 of the Indian Evidence Act (Proof of contents of documents) Section 65B(4) (Requirement of certificate for electronic records) Apex

Court judgment in Anvar P.V. v. P.K. Basheer (2014) 10 SCC 473

4. That the complainant has failed to: Produce any affidavit from a bank official Examine any witness to prove authenticity Submit a certified copy as required by law

Prayer:

It is therefore most respectfully prayed that this Hon'ble Court may be pleased to:

1. De=exhibit/Exclude the purported Bank Return Memo (Exhibit No.) from evidence

2. Declare the same as inadmissible for consideration 3. Pass such other orders as deemed fit in the interest of justice Place: [City] Date: [Date]

VERIFICATION:

I, [Your Name], the Accused in the above case, do hereby solemnly affirm that the contents of this application are true and correct to the best of my knowledge and belief. Signature of the Accused/Advocate Name: [Your Name] Address: [Your Address] Contact No.: [Your Number] Advocate (if any): [Advocate Name]

Application No 5

Application for dismissal of a Section 138 NI Act complaint for want of Prosecution .

IN THE COURT OF THE JUDICIAL MAGISTRATE FIRST CLASS (JMFC) AT [CITY]

Criminal Case No.: [Number]

Under Section: 138 of the Negotiable Instruments Act, 1881

Title: [Complainant Name] vs. [Accused/Applicant Name]

APPLICATION UNDER SECTION 272 BNSS 2023 (NONAPPEARANCE) / SECTION 248(8) BNSS 2023 (DEATH) FOR DISMISSAL OF COMPLAINT AND ACQUITTAL OF ACCUSED

RESPECTFULLY SHEWETH:

1. Case Background:

That the complainant [Complainant Name] filed this case under Section 138 NI Act against the applicant/accused on [Filing Date], alleging dishonour of cheque No. [Number] dated [Date] for ₹[Amount].

2. Grounds for Dismissal:

(Choose ONE scenario below and delete the other)

A. NONAPPEARANCE OF COMPLAINANT (Section 272 BNSS 2023)

That on the last hearing dated [Date]:

The complainant was absent without justification.

The complainant's counsel was absent.

No adjournment application was filed.

This is the [Number]th consecutive absence.

The accused was present/represented and ready for trial.

(Attach Order Sheet copy as Annexure A)

OR

B. DEATH OF COMPLAINANT (Section 248(8) BNSS 2023)

That the complainant expired on [Date of Death] (Death Certificate attached as Annexure B).

No legal heir has applied to continue prosecution within [Number] days/months.

Notice issued to legal heirs vide order dated [Date] remains uncompleted with.

Prosecution cannot continue without a complainant.

3. Legal Provisions:

Section 272 BNSS 2023: Mandates acquittal if the complainant is absent without lawful excuse.

Section 248(8) BNSS 2023: Requires acquittal if the complainant dies and no legal representative appears.

4. Prayer Grounds:

The complainant's nonappearance demonstrates abandonment of prosecution.

Continuation would abuse judicial process and prejudice the accused.

No reasonable prospect of conviction.

PRAYER:

It is most respectfully prayed that this Hon'ble Court may:

(a) Dismiss the complaint and acquit the accused under Section 272/248(8) BNSS 2023;

(b) Release the accused from bail bonds (if any);

(c) Grant costs of litigation;

(d) Pass any other relief(s) deemed fit.

Place: [City]

Date: [Date]

APPLICANT/ACCUSED:

[Signature]

[Accused Full Name]

S/o [Father's Name]

Address: [Complete Address]

Mobile: [Number]

THROUGH ADVOCATE:

[Advocate Signature]

[Advocate Name]

[Bar Council ID]

[Law Firm Address]

VERIFICATION

I, [Accused Name], solemnly affirm that:

Contents of paras 1–4 are true to my knowledge.

Annexures are genuine.

No material facts concealed.

Verified at [City] on [Date].

[Accused Signature]

ANNEXURES:

1. Annexure A: Court order sheet showing absence (for nonappearance)
2. Annexure B: Death Certificate (for death)
3. Annexure C: Affidavit supporting the application

<u>KEY LEGAL POINTS:</u>

1. For Nonappearance (S.272 BNSS):

The court must acquit the accused unless the adjournment is justified.

The first absence may warrant an adjournment; repeated absences compel acquittal.

2. For Death (S.248(8) BNSS):

Legal heirs have 30 days (or a reasonable time) to seek impleadment.

If no heir appears, mandatory acquittal.

3. Procedure:

File in duplicate with court fee.

Serve a copy to the complainant's heirs/counsel.

The court may hear the Public Prosecutor /other side if representing before the order.

Note

The death certificate must be issued by a competent authority.

For company complainants: The death of the signatory requires a board resolution for a new representative.

Disclaimer: Consult an advocate to address case specific nuances and local court practices.

Application 6

Application for dismissal of a Section 138 NI Act complaint due to the nonappearance of the complainant -or the death of the complainant, filed by the accused under relevanrovisions of BNSS 2023:

IN THE COURT OF THE JUDICIAL MAGISTRATE FIRST CLASS (JMFC) AT [CITY]

Criminal Case No.: [Number]

Under Section: 138 of the Negotiable Instruments Act, 1881

Title: [Complainant Name] vs. [Accused/Applicant Name]

APPLICATION UNDER SECTION 272 BNSS 2023 (NONAPPEARANCE) / SECTION 248(8) BNSS 2023 (DEATH) FOR DISMISSAL OF COMPLAINT AND ACQUITTAL OF ACCUSED

RESPECTFULLY SHEWETH:

1. Case Background:

That the complainant [Complainant Name] filed this case under Section 138 NI Act against the applicant/accused on [Filing Date], alleging dishonor of cheque No. [Number] dated [Date] for ₹[Amount].

2. Grounds for Dismissal:

(Choose ONE scenario below and delete the other)

A. NONAPPEARANCE OF COMPLAINANT (Section 272 BNSS 2023)

That on the last hearing dated [Date]:

The complainant was absent without justification.

The complainant’s counsel was absent.

No adjournment application was filed.

This is the [Number]th consecutive absence.

The accused was present/represented and ready for trial.

(Attach Order Sheet copy as Annexure A)

OR

B. DEATH OF COMPLAINANT (Section 248(8) BNSS 2023)

That the complainant expired on [Date of Death] (Death Certificate attached as Annexure B).

No legal heir has applied to continue prosecution within [Number] days/months.

Notice issued to legal heirs vide order dated [Date] remains uncompleted with.

Prosecution cannot continue without a complainant.

3. Legal Provisions:

Section 272 BNSS 2023: Mandates acquittal if the complainant is absent without lawful excuse.

Section 248(8) BNSS 2023: Requires acquittal if the complainant dies and no legal representative appears.

4. Prayer Grounds:

The complainant's nonappearance demonstrates abandonment of prosecution.

Continuation would abuse judicial process and prejudice the accused.

No reasonable prospect of conviction.

PRAYER:

It is most respectfully prayed that this Hon'ble Court may:

(a) Dismiss the complaint and acquit the accused under Section 272/248(8) BNSS 2023;

(b) Release the accused from bail bonds (if any);

(c) Grant costs of litigation;

(d) Pass any other relief(s) deemed fit.

Place: [City]

Date: [Date]

APPLICANT/ACCUSED:

[Signature]

[Accused Full Name]

S/o [Father's Name]

Address: [Complete Address]

Mobile: [Number]

THROUGH ADVOCATE:

[Advocate Signature]

[Advocate Name]

[Bar Council ID]

[Law Firm Address]

VERIFICATION

I, [Accused Name], solemnly affirm that:

Contents of paras 1–4 are true to my knowledge.

Annexures are genuine.

No material facts concealed.

Verified at [City] on [Date].

[Accused Signature]

ANNEXURES:

1. Annexure A: Court order sheet showing absence (for nonappearance)
2. Annexure B: Death Certificate (for death)
3. Annexure C: Affidavit supporting the application

KEY LEGAL POINTS:

1. For Nonappearance (S.272 BNSS):

The court must acquit the accused unless the adjournment is justified.

The first absence may warrant an adjournment; repeated absences compel acquittal.

2. For Death (S.248(8) BNSS):

Legal heirs have 30 days (or a reasonable time) to seek

impleadment.

If no heir appears, mandatory acquittal.

3. Procedure:

File in duplicate with court fee.

Serve a copy to the complainant's heirs/counsel.

The court may hear the Public Prosecutor before the order.

Note:

BNSS 2023 replaces CrPC sections:

S.272 BNSS ≈ Old S.256 CrPC.

S.248(8) BNSS ≈ Old S.256(2) CrPC.

The death certificate must be issued by a competent authority.

For company complainants: The death of the signatory requires a board resolution for a new representative.

Applications

CHECKLIST FOR FINANCIAL LOAN

Cheque Dishonour Cases Under Sections 138/141 Of The NI Act, Covering All Borrower Types (Individuals, Sole Proprietorships, And Companies):

FINANCIAL LOAN CHEQUE DISHONOUR PRE-NOTICE CHECKLIST

(For Complaints under Sections 138/141, NI Act)

I. ESSENTIAL ELEMENTS TO PROVE

1. Legally Enforceable Debt

Loan agreement with repayment terms

Sanction letter/disbursement proof

Acknowledgment of debt (promissory note, ledger confirmation)

2. Valid Cheque Issuance

Cheque signed by authorized person

For companies: Issued for the company's benefit (not personal debt)

3. Proper Dishonour

Return memo states "insufficient funds" or "account closed"

No material alterations on the cheque

4. Timely Action

Notice sent within 30 days of dishonour

Complaint filed within 30 days after the 15-day notice period

II. DOCUMENTARY REQUIREMENTS

| Category| Individual Borrower | Sole Proprietorship | Company Borrower|| Loan Documents Loan agreement Disbursement proof (bank transfer) Payment demand notices | same as individual + Business license/GST | same as individual + Board resolution authorizing loan MCA records |

| Cheque Records| Original cheque/copy Return memo Deposit slip |

same as individual | Same as individual + List of authorized signatories |

| Borrower ID Proof | PAN/Aadhaar Address proof | Proprietor's PAN Shop Act license | CIN PAN Director's KYC |

| NOTICE | Draft notice Postal/email delivery proof | Same as individual | Must name the company AND directors |

III. SPECIAL CONSIDERATIONS FOR SECTION 141 (COMPANIES)

1. Director Liability

Cheque must be issued for the company's business

Directors must be actively involved in day-to-day operations

2. Defences Available

Director was not in charge of financial affairs

Cheque issued without company authorization

IV. CRITICAL ACTION POINTS

1. Pre-Notice Verification

Confirm cheque was issued towards loan repayment (not as security)

Verify borrower's current address for notice delivery

2. Notice Contents

Loan account number & outstanding

Cheque details & dishonour date

Clear 15-day payment demand

Warning of prosecution under S.138/141

3. Post-Notice Steps

Track payment for partial settlements

Prepare complaint with an affidavit of documents

V. COMMON PITFALLS TO AVOID

- Missing 30-day notice deadline
- Failing to mention the company name as Accused No.1 and all

directors in company cases having vicarious liability

- Not preserving the original cheque/dishonour memo
- Claiming incorrect amounts (stick to cheque value)

VI. PENALTIES & RECOVERY

Criminal Case: Up to 2 years jail + 2x cheque amount fine

Civil Suit: For principal + interest (if cheque covers partial amount)

Director Liability: Personal assets may be attached for company cheques

Pro Tip: For company borrowers, attach:

- Latest MCA 21 form (list of directors)
- Board resolution authorizing loan
- Bank mandate for signatories

Bombay High Court

CHAPTER NO 19
SPECIAL POWER OF ATTORNEY

ACTUAL DRAFT

Know All Men by These Presents: I, Mr. Nitian Led, S/o [Father's Name], residing at [Full Address], do hereby appoint, constitute, and authorize: Name of Attorney Holder: [Full Name of Common Friend], Son/Wife/Daughter of: [Details], Residing at: [Full Address], as my true and lawful attorney to act on my behalf in Complaint Case No. 138 NI/CC pending before [Court/Forum Name] for the following purposes:

1. To appear, represent, and plead on my behalf before the concerned court/forum.

2. To sign, verify, and submit all necessary documents, affidavits, and pleadings.

3. To file and receive papers, applications, and orders.

4. To negotiate, settle, or compromise (if required) in the best interest of the case.

5. To take all necessary steps from the date of this authorization until the final decision, execution of the award, and full conclusion of the matter. This Special Power of Attorney is given voluntarily, with full understanding, and shall remain in force until the final disposal of the case or until revoked in writing.

IN WITNESS WHEREOF, I set my hand on this day of , 20 at [Location]. Executant (Principal):

Mr. Nitian Led

(Signature)

Witnesses:

1. Name:

Signature:

Address:

2. Name:

Signature:

Address:

Note: Require Attestation from Notary Public

CONVERSATION FORM

Conversations before Issuance of Statutory Notice and Subsequently to File Complaint/138/141 NI Act.

Introduction:

Key Principles for Section 138/141 NI Act Complaints

Before the conversations, remember the strict sequence (Cause of Action Chain) for a Section 138 case:

1. Cheque Issued (for a legally enforceable debt/liability).
2. Cheque Presented to the bank within 3 months of issue or validity period.
3. Cheque Dishonoured (Returned unpaid by the bank).
4. Demand Notice issued to the drawer within 30 days of dishonour, demanding payment.
5. Drawer fails to pay the amount within 15 days of receiving the notice.
6. Complaint Filed within 30 days of the expiry of the above 15-day period.

All conversations must help gather facts that satisfy this chain.

Templates for Advocate-Client Interaction

Template 1: Advocate-Client Consultation Prior to Sending Demand Notice (S. 138(b)

Participants: Mr./Ms. [Advocate Name] (Advocate) & Mr./Ms. [Client Name] (Client) Matter:Dishonour of Cheque(s) issued by [Name of Drawer]

Advocate: "Thank you for coming in, Mr./Ms. [Client Name]. I understand a cheque issued to you has been dishonoured. To proceed with a legal demand notice, I need to ask you some specific questions. Please have your documents ready."

Client: "Yes, I have everything here."

Advocate: "Perfect. Let's begin:

1. The Parties: What is the full name and complete address of the person/company who gave you the cheque?"

2. The Liability: What was this cheque for? Please describe the underlying transaction (e.g., loan repayment, fee for services, goods supplied, etc.). Do you have a contract, invoice, or agreement supporting this?"

3. The Instrument: Do you have the original dishonoured cheque? May I see it? What was the date on the cheque? What was the amount?"

4. Presentation & Dishonour: When did you deposit or present the cheque to your bank? (Client provides date). When did you receive the dishonour memo from your bank? (Client provides date). What was the reason for dishonour mentioned on the memo? ('Insufficient Funds' is crucial)."

5. Current Status: Have you contacted the drawer after the dishonour? Have they made any promises or part payments?"

6. Entity Cheque: If the drawer is a company, what is your role in it? Are you a director? Shareholder? Or are you an external party?"

Client: "The cheque was from [Drawer's Name] for [Purpose, e.g., outstanding consultancy fees]. The date was [Date], and it was for ₹[Amount]. I presented it on [Presentation Date] and got the memo back on [Dishonour Date] stating 'Insufficient Funds'. I am not related to the company; I am an external vendor."

Advocate: "Based on this, the 30-day period to send the demand notice started on [Dishonour Date]. We must act quickly. I will draft a statutory demand notice under Section 138 of the NI Act. We will send it via registered AD post and courier to their official address. They will have 15 days from receipt to pay. If they fail, we can file a criminal complaint."

Template 2: Conversation Format - Law Firm (Advocate) & Client (Actor/Director)

Participants: [Senior Advocate] (Law Firm) & [Mr. ABC] (Film

Director/Producer) Matter: Dishonour of Cheque from Production House against Acting Services.

Client (Mr. ABC): "My production house, [Production House Name], issued a cheque to [Actor Name] for his last film. It has bounced. The bank says 'Account Closed'. The actor is now threatening legal action."

Advocate: "I see. We need to strategize. First, confirm: was the cheque issued from the company's account or your personal account?"

Client: "It was from the company's account. I am the managing director."

Advocate: "Under Section 141 of the NI Act, every director in charge of the company's conduct at the time of the offence can be held liable. Were you actively involved in the day-to-day operations?"

Client: "Yes, completely."

Advocate: "We need to assess the defence. Was the cheque issued as an advance? Was there a breach of contract by the actor? Do you have a clause in the agreement about payments being subject to the film's completion?"

Client: "The cheque was for the final payment. The actor has completed all his work. We are facing a cash flow crisis."

Advocate: "A 'cash flow crisis' is not a legal defence to a S. 138 complaint. Our best course is to settle before a notice is sent or immediately upon receipt. If a complaint is filed, we will have to plead for compounding under Section 147 at the earliest stage to avoid a criminal record. I advise you to negotiate a settlement and issue a new cheque from a functional account immediately."

Template 3: Consultation - Director (Client) vs. Production House (Accused)

Participants: Advocate & Director (Client who received the cheque) Matter:Seeking recovery of dues from a production house.

Director (Client): "I directed a web series for [Production House Pvt. Ltd.]. My final payment cheque of ₹[Amount] has bounced. The reason is 'Payment Stopped by Drawer'."

Advocate: "'Payment Stopped' is a clear dishonour and falls under S. 138. This is a deliberate act. Do you have the agreement and the delivery acceptance email proving you fulfilled your obligations?"

Client: "Yes, I have both. I also have emails where they acknowledge the debt but ask for more time."

Advocate: "Excellent. Those emails are crucial evidence. We will send a strong demand notice. Since it's a company, we will send it to the company's registered office and to every director as per the MCA records. This will personalise the liability and force them to respond. Given their conduct, we should also immediately apply for attachment of their bank accounts after filing the complaint to pressure them for a quick settlement."

Templates for Professional Consultations

Template 4: Banking Official & Advocate regarding dishonoured ECS

Participants: [Mr. Sharma] (Bank Manager) & [Advocate Mehta] Matter:Recurring ECS Mandate dishonoured for a client.

Bank Manager: "Advocate Mehta, our client, [Lender Name], has an ECS mandate from [Borrower Name] for their loan EMI. The last two ECS presentations have failed due to 'Exceeds Arrangement'."

Advocate Mehta: "Thank you for informing me. An ECS dishonour is treated similarly to a cheque dishonour under the NI Act. Please ensure you send the official ECS return memo to our client immediately. This memo is equivalent to the cheque return memo. Our client will then need to issue a demand notice within 30 days of receiving that memo from you."

Bank Manager: "Understood. We will dispatch the memo today. Should we attempt the presentation again?"

Advocate Mehta: "You may, but from a legal standpoint, the cause of action has already accrued on the first dishonour. Please provide a statement of account reflecting the failed transactions as well."

Template 5: Conversation between a CA and an Advocate

Participants: [CA Ananya] (Chartered Accountant) & [Advocate Roy] Matter:Financial analysis of a company that issued bounced cheques.

CA Ananya: "Advocate Roy, as per your request, I've analysed the financials of [Accused Company]. Their net worth is negative, and the bank account from which the cheque was issued has been inactive for months."

Advocate Roy: "This is helpful. Does it appear to be a case of intentional cheating, or just insolvency?"

CA Ananya: "The directors have siphoned off funds through related party transactions. Look at these ledger entries. The insolvency is likely fraudulent. I can prepare a report tracing the funds to show that the debt was legally enforceable and the dishonour was wilful."

Advocate Roy: "Please do. This forensic report will be vital for opposing any bail application and to show the court that this is not a simple case of business failure but one of fraud."

Template 6: Multispecialty Hospital vs. Supplier/Patient

Participants: [Hospital Administrator] & [Advocate] Matter:Bounced cheque from a medical equipment supplier.

Hospital Admin: "We purchased equipment from [Supplier Pvt. Ltd.] and issued a post-dated cheque. They delivered faulty equipment. We stopped the cheque and now they are threatening us with a 138 case!"

Advocate: "A 'stop payment' instruction is a dishonour. However, a legally enforceable debt is a prerequisite. If you can prove the equipment was faulty and not as per the agreed specifications, the debt is disputed and may not be 'legally enforceable'. We have a defence."

Hospital Admin: "We have inspection reports from two independent engineers."

Advocate: "Perfect. If they send a demand notice, we will send a detailed reply refuting the liability and enclosing those reports. If they still file a complaint, we will use this to seek acquittal. Do not ignore their notice; a cogent reply is essential."

Template 7: Flat Owner (Defaulter), Housing Society Executive & Society's Advocate

Participants: Mr. Kapoor (Defaulter Owner), Ms. Desai (Society Secretary), Mr. Iyer (Society's Advocate) Matter:Recovery of outstanding maintenance via dishonoured cheque.

Ms. Desai (Secretary): "Mr. Kapoor, your cheque for maintenance dues has bounced. This is the second time."

Mr. Kapoor (Owner): "I know, I'm facing financial difficulties. The society can't file a criminal case for this!"

Mr. Iyer (Advocate): "Mr. Kapoor, I must correct you. Maintenance dues are a legally enforceable debt as per the Society bylaws and the Ownership Act. The dishonoured cheque creates a criminal liability under S. 138. The society is within its rights to file a complaint."

Mr. Kapoor: "What are my options?"

Mr. Iyer: "You have 15 days from receiving our NOTICE to pay the entire outstanding amount along with the bank charges and our legal fees. If you do that, the matter ends. If you cannot pay the lump sum, propose a written settlement with post-dated cheques from a confirmed account. If you do nothing, we will be compelled to file a criminal case, and the court can impose a fine double the cheque amount and even a prison sentence."

Ms. Desai: "We prefer to avoid litigation. Please give us a written proposal for settlement within a week."

CONVERATION FORM BUNCH

1. **ADVOCATE CLIENT CONSULTATION.**
2. **BETWEEN A LAW FIRM (ADVOCATE) AND A CLIENT (ACTOR/DIRECTOR).**
3. **CONSULTATION: DIRECTOR VS. PRODUCTION HOUSE.**
4. **CONVERSATION FORMAT BETWEEN A BANKING OFFICIAL AND AN ADVOCATE REGARDING DISHONORED ECS (ELECTRONIC CLEARING SERVICE).**
5. **CONVERSATION BETWEEN CA AND ADVOCATE.**
6. **A MULTISPECIALTY HOSPITAL LODGED A COMPLAINT AGAINST Y.**
7. **BETWEEN THE FLAT OWNER (DEFAULTER),**

HOUSING SOCIETY EXECUTIVE, SOCIETY'S ADVOCATE.

Conversation Form No.1 ADVOCATE-CLIENT CONSULTATION

1. Advocate Client Consultation Prior to Section 138(b) NI Act Demand Notice

Please adjust the following points based on your client's specific circumstances:

1. Documentary Evidence:

Provide written agreements or MOUs related to the transaction.

Include relevant communications (emails, WhatsApp) about the debt and cheque.

Submit the original dishonoured cheque and bank return memo.

2. Payment History:

Record any partial payments made by the debtor.

Confirm acknowledgment of the outstanding balance by the debtor.

3. Acknowledgment or Denial of Debt:

Present documentation of any formal denial of payment by the debtor.

Is there a written acknowledgment of the debt?

4. Evidence of Dues:

Along with the cheque, submit invoices or statements verifying the debt.

Ensure compliance with Section 63 of the Bharatiya Sakshya Adhiniyam concerning electronic documents.

III. Corporate Liability (If Applicable)

5. Section 141 NI Act (Corporate Entities):

Verify if the issuer is a Company, LLP, or Firm.

Identify the individual responsible for the cheque.

List any directors or officers involved in the dishonour and their roles.

Attach the company's incorporation documents if available.

IV. Strategic Considerations

6. Settlement Options:

Consider negotiating a settlement prior to issuing notice to reduce costs and duration.

7. Fee Structure and Costs:

Our Fees: Drafting and sending the notice costs [₹X]. In the event of litigation, fees will be [₹Y] per hearing or a total of [₹Z], with an initial retainer of [₹A].

Additional Costs: Include court fees and related expenses until resolution.

8. Time Frame:

Expect a minimum of 2 to 4 years for a final court ruling if ADR efforts are unsuccessful.

9. Be prepared to file a case within 45 days if there is no response or compliance with the notice.

Conversation Form No ,2 LAW FIRM AND CLIENT (ACTOR/DIRECTOR) CONSULTATION

Conversation Format No. Between A Law Firm (Advocate) And A Client (Actor/Director) to collect critical facts before issuing a NOTICE under Sections 138 & 141 of the Negotiable Instruments Act.

I. Core Cheque Details

1. A: When was the cheque issued? (Date) C: [Date]

2. A: Exact amount? (₹) C: ₹[Amount]

3. A: Cheque number & issuing bank? C: No. [XXXX], [Bank Name, Branch]

4. A: Whose name is printed on the cheque? (Production house name) C: [Full Name of Production House] II. Dishonor Evidence

5. A: When did your bank notify you of dishonor? (Date) C: [Date]

6. A: Reason for return? (e.g., 'Insufficient Funds,' 'Account Closed') C: 'Insufficient Funds' (as per bank memo)

7. A: Do you have the original cheque and bank return memo? C: Yes, here they are. (Hands over documents) III. Underlying Transaction

8. A: What was this cheque for? (Fee/contractual payment?) C: My acting/directing fee for the project '[Project Name].'

9. A: Is there a written agreement/invoice? C: Yes, here's the contract/email trail confirming the amount. IV. Debtor Entity & Signatory

10. A: Full address of the production house? (Registered office) C: [Full Address]

11. A: Who signed the cheque? C: [Name], Designation: [e.g., 'Managing Director']

12. A: Is the signatory a director/partner? (Crucial for Section 141 liability) C: Yes, as per their website/MCA records. V. Post Dishonor Actions

13. A: Did you demand repayment after dishonor? (Verbally/written?) C: Yes, I sent an email on [Date] – no response.

14. A: Any partial payments/promises to pay? C: None. VI. Corporate Structure (Section 141)

15. A: Is the production house a Pvt Ltd/LLP/Partnership? C: Pvt Ltd Company.

16. A: Names of all directors/partners? (For notice liability) C: [Names] – I can share their website/MCA extract. VII. Critical Compliance Check

17. A: Today is [Current Date]. Your bank notified you on [Dishonor Date]. We have 30 days from that date to issue notice. We're within the limit.

C: Understood. A: Based on this, we'll draft a notice: Demand ₹[Amount] within 15 days of receipt. Cite Sections 138 (dishonor) + 141 (director liability). Send to BOTH the company AND every director. C: What next if they ignore? A: We file a criminal complaint within 30 days after their 15day window ends. Directors can face jail (up to 2 years) + double cheque fine. Fact Summary Checklist for Notice Drafting | Item | Client's Input | | | | Cheque Date | [Date] | | Cheque Amount (₹) | ₹[Amount] | | Cheque No. & Bank |

[No.], [Bank] | | Debtor (Company Name) | [Production House Name] | | Signatory (Name/Designation) | [Name], [Designation] | | Directors/Partners | [List Names] | | Registered Address | [Full Address] | | Dishonor Date | [Date] | | Dishonor Reason | 'Insufficient'

Conversation Form.3

Consultation: Director vs. Production House

Participants:

1. Mr. X (Director)

2. Adv. Y (Entertainment Law Specialist)

Setting: Advocate's Office / Virtual Consultation

1. Opening: Director Explains the Situation

Mr. X: "Advocate, I directed a film titled '[Movie Name]' for [Production House]. My contract stipulated a fee of ₹1.2 crore, payable in 3 instalments. They issued a cheque for the final ₹40 lakh, but it bounced due to 'insufficient funds'. I've emailed them thrice, but they're avoiding me. What can I do?"

Adv. Y: "Mr. X, let's methodically assess your case. First, confirm:

Do you have the original bounced cheque and the bank return memo?

Is there a written contract specifying payment terms?

Did you issue any formal payment reminder before this meeting?"

2. Document Verification & Legal Grounds

Mr. X: "Yes, I have:

1. The dishonoured cheque (No. 456, dated 15/03/2024, drawn on XYZ Bank).

2. Bank memo stating 'insufficient funds' (dated 20/03/2024).

3. Signed contract (Clause 7 mentions instalments).

4. Email reminders (attached)."

Adv. Menon: "Good. This is a clear case under Section 138 of the NI Act. However, before sending a legal notice, let's explore:

Option 1: A stern lawyer's letter demanding payment within 7 days (nonlegal notice).

Option 2: A statutory Section 138 notice – triggers criminal liability if unpaid in 15 days.

Which approach aligns with your goal – quick recovery or legal deterrence?"

3. Strategy Discussion

Mr. Kapoor: "I want my money, but I also want to set an example. The producer has a history of cheating artists. However, if they pay promptly, I'll avoid court."

Adv. Menon: "Understood. Here's the plan:

1. Step 1: We'll issue a hybrid notice – a stern letter (nonstatutory) giving 7 days to pay, mentioning our intent to file under Section 138. Often, this speeds up settlement.

2. Step 2: If they ignore it, we escalate to a formal 138 notice (attaching all proofs).

3. Step 3: Simultaneously, we'll draft a complaint for JMFC Court to file immediately after notice expiry."

4. Cost & Timeline Clarity

Mr. Kapoor: "How long will this take? And what are your fees?"

Adv. Menon: "Timeline:

Settlement: 2–4 weeks (if they respond to the hybrid notice).

Court case: 8–18 months (but we'll seek interim attachment of their assets).

Fees:

Notice drafting: ₹5,000–10,000.

Court case: ₹25,000 (lump sum) + 10% of recovered amount.

We'll also add 18% interest and litigation costs to your claim."

5. Director's Authorization & Next Steps

Adv. Menon: "To proceed, I need:

1. Your signed vakalatnama (to represent you).

2. Original documents for notarization.

3. A brief affidavit of facts.

Shall I draft the hybrid notice today?"

Mr. Kapoor: "Yes, please proceed. I'll also share the producer's other contact details – they've changed offices to avoid notices."

Adv. Menon: "Noted. We'll serve notices to all known addresses and publish in a newspaper if needed. Rest assured."

Key Takeaways from the Conversation:

1. Documents Reviewed: Contract, cheque, bank memo, communication trail.
2. Options Offered: Negotiation (hybrid notice) vs. legal action (Section 138).
3. Strategy: Graded escalation to maximize recovery chances.
4. Transparency: Clear timelines, fees, and risks explained.

Next Steps Template:

Draft hybrid notice → Send via email/registered post → Wait 7 days → Escalate to Section 138 notice if unpaid.

Question and Proposition: With regard to one cheque, whether it was lost, misplaced, or lost along with a bank return memo, legal notice, etc., if it was misplaced by the holder (payee), what practical advice can you provide? Before proceeding with the answer or advising on appropriate steps, please specify at which stage and in which scenario the cheque in question was misplaced or lost:

1. The cheque was originally misplaced by an individual who is the payee before presentation to the bank.
2. The cheque was misplaced from the corporate office before its presentation.
3. The cheque and bank return memo were lost before issuing a notice.
4. The cheque, memo, and notice copy were lost before filing the case.
5. The cheque return memo, notice, dispatch postal receipt, and postal tracking report in the original were lost before the court took cognizance, meaning before verification and issuance of process.

6. All originals were misplaced before filing the affidavit of evidence and tendering the originals in court, meaning before marking exhibits.

7. Lost in any other way

Conversation Form 4 BANKING OFFICIAL AND ADVOCATE REGARDING DISHONORED ECS

Conversation Format Between A Banking Official And An Advocate Regarding Dishonored ECS (Electronic Clearing Service) cheques issued as security (PDCs) under the Payment and Settlement Systems Act, 2007:

Conversation: Banking Official (Mr. Sharma) & Advocate (MS Desai)

Subject: Legal Action for Dishonored ECS Cheques (Security PDCs)

Mode: Phone Call / Office Meeting

Date: [DD/MM/YYYY]

1. Initial Context (Banking Official)

Mr. Sharma (Bank Manager):

"Advocate, we have a corporate client, 'XYZ Ltd', who issued 12 ECS cheques as Security PDCs against a credit facility. These were to cover future EMIs, but 3 cheques were dishonored due to 'insufficient funds'. The loan agreement clearly mentions these PDCs are for 'prospective liability'. What's our legal recourse under the Payment and Settlement Act?"

2. Advocate's Clarification

Adv. Desai:

"Mr. Sharma, let's break this down:

1. Nature of Cheques: Were these ECS mandates explicitly labeled as 'Security PDCs' in the loan arrangement?

2. Dishonor Reason: Confirm if the bounce memos cite 'Insufficient Funds' or 'Account Closed'.

3. Agreement Clause: Does the contract state that PDC dishonor constitutes a default event?"

Mr Sharma:

"Yes, the agreement's Clause 8 specifies PDCs as security for future EMIs. The bounce memos show 'Insufficient Funds'. We've already issued a recall notice but want to escalate legally."

3. Legal Strategy Discussion

Adv. Desai:

"Here's the actionable plan:

Step 1: Immediate Notice

Issue a demand notice under Section 25 of the Payment and Settlement Act, 2007 (for ECS dishonor) + Section 138 NI Act (since cheques are involved).

Highlight that PDCs were for 'discharge of liability' as per ICICI Bank v. Prakash Kaur (2007).

Step 2: Dual Action

Civil Suit: File for summary judgment under Order XXXVII CPC to recover the amount.

Criminal Complaint: Under Section 138 NI Act against the company and its directors.

Step 3: RBI Complaint

Notify the RBI's Banking Ombudsman for ECS mandate violation under RBI Circular No. DPSS.CO.CHD.No.1832/04.07.05/2018 19."

4. Banking Official's Queries

Mr. Sharma:

"Can we invoke SARFAESI Act simultaneously? The loan is secured by property."

Adv. Desai:

"Absolutely. Since PDC dishonor is a default event:

1. SARFAESI Action: Issue a Section 13(2) notice to take possession of collateral.

2. Parallel Proceedings: NI Act complaint won't affect SARFAESI proceedings (M.D. Frozen Foods v. Axis Bank, 2016)."

5. Documentation & Timeline

Adv. Desai:

"To proceed, I'll need:

1. Original loan agreement + PDC copies.
2. ECS dishonor memos from NPCI.
3. Board resolution authorizing legal action.

Timeline:

Notice can be sent within 30 days of dishonor.

Complaint must be filed within 1 month after notice expiry."

Mr. Sharma:

"We'll share the documents today. Draft the notice with a 15day payment window."

Key Legal Points Covered

1. ECS Cheques as PDCs:

Treated as 'security' but still attract Section 138 NI Act liability if dishonored (Sampelly Satyanarayana Rao v. Indian Renewable Energy, 2016).

2. Payment and Settlement Act:

Section 25: Penalizes unauthorized debit/ECS dishonor with fines up to ₹1 lakh per instance.

3. Dual Remedies:

Criminal action (NI Act) + Civil recovery (SARFAESI/Order XXXVII CPC).

4. RBI Compliance:

Mandatory reporting of ECS defaults to RBI under DPSS Circulars.

Next Steps Template

1. Draft Notice: Combine Section 138 NI Act + Section 25 Payment Act demands.

2. File Complaint: Before JMFC Court + Debt Recovery Tribunal (if SARFAESI invoked).

3. RBI Reporting: Submit ECS default details via the RBI's Complaint Management System.

Conversation Form .5 CONVERSATION BETWEEN CA AND ADVOCATE

Conversation between CA and Advocate: The Chartered Accountant A, whose cheque for twentyfive lakhs was returned unpaid, issued it against the rendering of professional services for the entire financial year to Company X. A conversation is needed between the CA, who is a client, and an esteemed advocate firm during this dialogue. CA (Client) and an Advocate from a reputed law firm regarding the dishonored cheque of ₹25 lakhs issued for professional services rendered to Company X. The conversation covers legal options, procedural steps, and strategic advice under the Negotiable Instruments Act, 1881: Dialogue: CA (Client) vs. Advocate Setting: Advocate's Office | Virtual Consultation

1. Initial Explanation by the CA (Client): CA: "Good morning. I'm a Chartered Accountant, and I provided yearlong financial advisory services to Company X. They issued a cheque for ₹25 lakhs as payment, but it was dishonored due to 'insufficient funds.' I've already sent a legal demand notice under Section 138 of the NI Act, but they haven't responded. What are my options now?"

2. Advocate's Clarification Questions: Advocate: "Thank you for the details. To proceed, I need to confirm a few points:

1. Do you have the original cheque, bank return memo (with dishonor reason), and proof of service of the demand notice (postal receipts/Aadharlinked tracking)?

2. Was the cheque issued for a legally enforceable debt? (i.e., Is there a contract/invoice for your services?) 3. Did you issue the demand notice within 30 days of dishonor?" CA: "Yes, I have all documents—the cheque, bank memo, and postal receipts. The services were under a signed contract (attached here). The notice was sent within 25 days of dishonor."

3. Advocate's Legal Strategy Breakdown: Advocate: "Understood.

Here's the roadmap:

Step 1: File a Complaint – We'll draft a criminal complaint under Section 138 NI Act before the JMFC Court within 1 month of your notice expiry. Penalty: Up to 2 years imprisonment or a fine of twice the cheque amount.

Step 2: Parallel Recovery – We can initiate a summary suit under Order XXXVII CPC for speedy recovery without a lengthy trial.

Step 3: Negotiation Leverage – The legal threat often pushes defaulters to settle. Would you consider a onetime settlement if Company X offers?"

4. CA's Concerns & Advocate's Reassurance: CA: "How long will the case take? And what if Company X disputes the liability?" Advocate: "Timeline: Typically 6–18 months for resolution. However: Evidence Strength: Your contract, invoices, and bank memo make this a strong case. Dispute Handling: If they claim 'service deficiency,' we'll counter with your service delivery proofs (emails, approvals). Interim Relief: We can also seek attachment of Company X's assets during the case."

5. Fee Structure & Next Steps: Advocate: "Our fee for the 138 complaint is(depending on court location). For the recovery suit, it's 8–10% of the recovered amount. We'll need: 1. Your authorization letter. 2. Original documents for filing. Shall we proceed?" CA: "Agreed. Let's file the complaint immediately and explore settlement talks in parallel."

Key Legal Points Highlighted:

1. Documentation is Critical: Cheque + Return Memo + Demand Notice + Contract = Strong Prima Facie Case.

2. Dual Strategy: Criminal prosecution (Section 138) + Civil recovery (Order XXXVII CPC).

3. Settlement Window: Negotiation can be pursued even after filing the complaint. Suggested Next Steps: Draft the complaint, file in the jurisdictional court (where the cheque was issued/presented). Let me know if you'd like to refine any part of this dialogue or need help with drafting the actual complaint.

Conversation Form No.6 MULTISPECIALTY HOSPITAL V/S PATIENT

A multispecialty hospital lodged a complaint against Y, the patient's father, following discharge and a cheque issuance for outstanding payments related to services, equipment, and medicine, which later bounced. A senior attorney reviewed the details and discussions before proceeding with the legal demand notice.

A multispecialty hospital lodged a complaint against Y, the patient's father, following discharge and a cheque issuance for outstanding payments related to services, equipment, and medicine, which later bounced.

Conversation Form 7 FLAT OWNER (DEFAULTER), HOUSING SOCIETY EXECUTIVE, AND SOCIETY'S ADVOCATE

between the Flat Owner (Defaulter), Housing Society Executive, Society's Advocate, and Society Matters Expert to address potential cheque dishonor and legal action:

1. Initial Notice from Society to Flat Owner (Official Letter/Email)

Subject: Urgent: Clear Outstanding Dues of ₹[Amount] to Avoid Legal Action

Content:

"Dear [Owner's Name],

Outstanding: Maintenance (₹) + Fines (₹) + Interest (₹) = Total ₹[X] as of [Date].

Cheque No. for ₹[X] (issued on) is likely to bounce due to insufficient clearance.

Immediate Options:

1. Clear dues in full by [Date] via NEFT/DD (Account: [Society's Bank Details]).

2. Submit a written settlement proposal to the Managing Committee.

Consequences of Non Payment:

NOTICE u/s 138 NI Act + complaint to Registrar Cooperative Societies.

Restriction on property transactions (if applicable under state laws).

Contact: [Secretary/Manager] at [Phone] or visit society office by [Date]."

2. Flat Owner's Discussion with Society Executive

Key Points to Address:

Clarify Dues:

"Can I get a detailed breakdown of fines and maintenance arrears?"

"Is there flexibility to waive penalties or pay in instalments?"

Negotiation:

"I propose to pay ₹[X] now and clear the balance by [Date]."

"Can the society accept a post dated cheque for the remaining amount?"

Warning:

Executive: "If the issued cheque bounces, we must initiate legal action per society bylaws."

3. Society's Internal Discussion (Executive + Advocate + Expert)

Checklist:

1. Verify Legal Standing:

Advocate: "Confirm if the byelaws allow recovery via 138 NI Act for maintenance dues."

Expert: "Check state cooperative society rules for additional remedies (e.g., lien on property)."

2. Documentation Review:

Ensure demand letters, meeting minutes, and cheque issuance proof are recorded.

3. Next Steps:

If dues are unpaid, issue a 15day NOTICE u/s 138 NI Act (via advocate).

File a complaint with the Registrar of Cooperative Societies simultaneously.

4. Advocate's Direct Communication with Flat Owner

Formal Notice/Phone Call:

"This is to inform you that the cheque issued for society dues was returned unpaid.

You have 15 days from [Date] to pay ₹[X] or face:

JMFC complaint (criminal case).

Attachment of property (if state laws permit).

Submit your reply in writing to avoid escalation."

5. Flat Owner's Last Chance Response

Suggested Reply (If Seeking Time):

"I acknowledge the dues and request 3 months to pay in instalments ([Proposed Plan]).

I will provide post-dated cheques as security.

Kindly confirm if the society accepts this to avoid legal action."

Critical Documents to Exchange

| Party | Documents to Provide

| Society |

1. Dues breakdown

2. Cheque return memo

3. Copy of byelaws (highlighting recovery clauses)

| Flat Owner

1. Payment proposal

2. Proof of financial hardship (if any)

3. Alternate security (if offering)

Key Legal Considerations

1. For Society:

Ensure bylaws authorize cheque payments for dues (to qualify u/s 138 NI Act).

Maharashtra Societies Act: Allows property attachment for dues (Section 101).

2. For Owner:

Negotiate before cheque bounce to avoid criminal liability.

Seek expert help if dues are disputed.

Next Steps if Deadlock Continues:

Society files JMFC complaint + Registrar complaint.

Owner may explore mediation through cooperative authorities.

Would you like templates for:

1. Settlement agreement?

2. NOTICE u/s 138?

3. Complaint to Registrar?

(This structured approach balances legal compliance with negotiation scope.

****

BUNCH OF STATUORY NOTICE/ S ISSUED TO THE FOLLOWING DRAWER/ CORPORATES

1. **FROM A CONSUMER** TO AN REAL ESTATE DEVELOPMENT COMPANY CHEQUE BUYBACK CONSIDERATION
2. **FROM A FINANCIAL INSTITUTION TO A BORROWER**
3. **FROM AN ADVOCATE**, NAMELY X, (MACT SIDE), WHOSE CHEQUE WAS RETURNED UNPAID BY HIS CLIENT DUE TO THE PROFESSIONAL FEE AGREED UPON WITH ONE PERSON,
4. **FROM DIRECTOR'S** TO PRODUCER FOR UNPAID DIRECTOR'S FEES
5. **FROM BANK:** UNDER SECTION 25 OF THE PAYMENT AND SETTLEMENT SYSTEMS ACT, 2007 (PSS ACT) FOR DISHONOR OF ECS (ELECTRONIC CLEARING SERVICE)
6. **FROM FLAT BUYER TO BUILDER** WHOSE BUYBACK CONSIDERATION IS DISHONOURED.
7. **FROM COOPERATIVE HOUSING SOCIETY TO A FLAT OWNER** WHOSE CHEQUE IS DISHONEST ISSUED BY THE COOPERATIVE HOUSING SOCIETY FOR OUTSTANDING MAINTENANCE CHARGES, ETC.
8. **FROM CA (CHARTED ACCOUNTANT TO A COMPANY** his Client
9. **FROM A SUPPLIERE TO A BUYER OF PRODUCTES BUISNESS**

TRANSACTION (latest and actual draft) SURYANSHI

Advisory Note:

Under Section 138(b) Safeguards against Misconduct Or Oversight:

Critical Steps for Issuing a Statutory Demand Notice

(Payee to Drawer)

Objective: Ensure legal compliance, prevent procedural flaws, and create defensible evidence.

1. Trigger Event Confirmation:

Verify the cheque was dishonored (return memo from the bank stating "insufficient funds," "account closed," etc.).

Obtain the original cheque return memo from your bank immediately.

2. Strict Adherence to Timeline (NonNegotiable):

30Day Window: The notice must be sent within 30 calendar days from the date the payee receives the cheque return memo.

Calculate Precisely: Exclude the day of receiving the memo; count 30 days thereafter. Use a calendar tool to avoid miscalculation.

3. Drafting the Notice (Content Safeguards):

Cross Examination Mandatory Elements:

Full name & address of both Drawer (debtor) and Payee (creditor).

Specifics of the dishonored cheque (No., date, bank, branch, amount).

Explicit mention of dishonor (quote reason from memo).

Cross Examination Demand: Clearly state the demand for payment of the cheque amount.

15Day Ultimatum: Specify the drawer has 15 days from receipt to pay.

Cross Examination Consequence: State that failure to pay within 15 days will result in legal action under S. 138 NI Act.

Cross Examination Safeguards:

Cross Examination Accuracy: Crosscheck all details (names, addresses, cheque details, and amount) against original documents (cheque, agreement, memo).

Cross Examination Clarity: Use unambiguous language. Avoid threats beyond legal consequences.

Cross Examination Professional Tone: Maintain a formal, non abusive tone.

Cross Examination Attach Copy: Include a photocopy of the dishonored cheque and the bank return memo.

Legal Review: Highly recommended: Have a lawyer specializing in NI Act matters review the draft notice.

4. Dispatch & Delivery (Evidence Safeguards):

Cross Examination Authorized Modes Only (Crucial): Registered Post with Acknowledgement Due (RPAD): Primary & safest method.

Cross Examination Speed Post: An acceptable alternative under India Post.

Cross Examination Certificate of Posting (COP): Use only as a secondary precaution, never as the sole method. Notoriously weak evidence.

Cross Examination Safeguards: Simultaneous Dual Mailing: Send one notice via RPAD and another via Speed Post to the drawer's correct, known address (usually the address on the cheque or as per agreement). This mitigates risk if one service fails.

Cross Examination Accurate Addressing: Use the drawer's address meticulously as known. Avoid typos.

Cross Examination Post Office Protocol: Obtain dated postal receipts for RPAD/Speed Post/ immediately upon dispatch.

Cross Examination Preserve Originals: Safeguard all postal receipts.

Cross Examination Track Diligently: Track the RPAD/Speed Post consignment online daily.

Cross Examination Acknowledgement Due (RPAD): Ensure the AD card is returned. This is the best evidence of receipt.

Cross Examination Refusal Handling: If the notice is "refused" or "unclaimed," preserve the returned envelope unopened. This is deemed valid service by courts.

5. Post Dispatch Documentation & Preservation:

Cross Examination File Creation: Create a dedicated file for this specific cheque/default.

Cross Examination Store Securely: File originals/true copies of:

The signed statutory demand notice.

The dishonored cheque (copy).

The bank return memo.

All postal receipts (RPAD, Speed Post,

The returned RPAD Acknowledgement Due card (if received).

AD <u>USUAL /FORMAT IN ORDINARY COURSE OF PRACTICE</u>

To, M/s. ABC Pvt. Ltd. **(Registered Office Address**)

FROM: ADVOCATE/LAW FIRM OR THE PAYEE HIMSELF

Registered A.D. NOTICE

Subject: NOTICE under Section 138 of the Negotiable Instruments Act, 1881

Dear Sir/Madam,

1. This notice is issued on behalf of Mr. X (the Complainant) concerning the dishonor of Cheque No. _, dated _, for ₹_ drawn on _ Bank (Branch).

2. The said cheque was dishonored due to "Insufficient Funds" (or another reason) as per the Return Memo dated __.

3. You are hereby called upon to pay the said amount within 15 days from the receipt of this notice, failing which legal action under Section 138 shall be initiated.

4. Please treat this as a formal notice under the law. Legal Implications: If the notice is not properly addressed to the company, it may be considered defective, and the complaint may be dismissed. The directors/officers in charge can also be made liable if they were responsible for the company's affairs when the cheque was issued. Conclusion: The notice must be issued in the name of the company, but it can also include responsible individuals (if applicable). Proper service and compliance with statutory timelines are crucial for a valid case under Section 138/141 of the NI Act.

FINAL ADVICE : Statuary Notice is a foundation of the upcoming complaint 138/141 NI act, that requires a proper legal, factual covering valid Notice, instead an omnibus or defect-o notice ,New Advocates are genuinely requested to must take the help of a Senior Advocate ,Particularly whe huge amount or Vicarious liability involved.

STATUTORY NOTICE FROM A FINANCIAL INSTITUTION TO A BORROWER

NOTICE NO.1

STATUTORY NOTICE UNDER SECTION 138 OF THE NEGOTIABLE INSTRUMENTS ACT, 1881 (From a Financial Institution to Borrower/Drawer for Dishonored Cheque) '

NOTICE HEADER On Official Letterhead of

[Financial Institution Name]

Date: [Date]

Ref: [Loan Account No./File Reference]

To: Mr./Ms. [Drawer's Full Name]

[Drawer's Address]

Via: Registered AD/Speed Post with Acknowledgement From:

[Financial Institution Name],

through its Authorized Signatory

SUBJECT Notice under Section 138 of the Negotiable Instruments Act, 1881 for the dishonor of Cheque No. [Number] dated [Date] for ₹[Amount] **towards part repayment of Loan Account No. [Account Number].**

KEY FACTS

1. Loan Disbursement: On [Date], you availed a loan of ₹[Total Loan Amount] under Loan Account No. [Account Number] from our institution. As per the agreement dated [Date], repayment was due in [EMIs/lumpsum] by [Due Date].

2. Cheque Issuance: Towards part payment of outstanding dues, you issued Cheque No. [Number] dated [Date] for ₹[Amount] drawn on [Bank Name], [Branch].

3. Dishonor Event: Upon presentation on [Date], the cheque was dishonored vide [Bank Name]'s Return Memo dated [Date] (Ref: [Memo ID]) with the remarks: "[Reason: Insufficient Funds/Account Closed/Exceeds Arrangement]"

4. Statutory Compliance: This notice is issued within 30 days of dishonor (intimation received on [Date]). LEGAL DEMAND You are required to pay within 15 days of receiving this notice: | Component | Amount | | Dishonored Cheque Amount | ₹[Cheque Amount] | | Penal Interest (@ [Rate]% p.m. from cheque date) | ₹[Calculated Interest] | | NOTICE Costs | ₹[Amount] | | TOTAL | ₹[Total] | Payment Mode: Demand Draft/RTGS to:Cross Examination Account Name: [Financial Institution Name]Cross Examination Account No.: [Account Number]Cross Examination IFSC: [IFSC Code]Cross Examination Branch: [Branch Address] CONSEQUENCES OF NON

COMPLIANCE Failure to pay within 15 days will compel us to:

1. Initiate criminal proceedings under Section 138 NI Act (punishable with imprisonment of up to 2 years/fine of up to twice

the cheque amount/both).

2. File a summary civil suit under Order XXXVII CPC for recovery of the total outstanding loan (₹[Total Dues]) + interest + costs.

3. Initiate proceedings under SARFAESI Act, 2002 (if applicable) for asset seizure.

4. Report default to credit bureaus (CIBIL/Experian), impacting your credit score.

ATTACHMENTS

1. Copy of dishonored Cheque No. [Number]

2. Bank Return Memo (Ref: [Memo ID])

3. Loan Statement (outstanding dues as of [Date]) SIGNATURE For [Financial Institution Name] [Authorized Signatory Name] [Designation] [Seal/Stamp] Contact: [Phone/Email] Copy to: Legal Department, [Financial Institution Name]

CRITICAL NOTES FOR FINANCIAL INSTITUTION

1. Dispatch Proof: Send notice via Registered AD and retain the postal receipt/Acknowledgment Due.

2. Timeline Compliance: File a criminal complaint within 30 days after the 15day notice period expires.

3. Documentation: Attach certified copies of: Loan agreement clauses confirming cheque issuance for debt discharge. Cheque return memo (original retained for court). Loan account statement reflecting cheque amounts as part payment.

4. Legal Strategy: Simultaneously initiate SARFAESI proceedings

(if a secured loan) for parallel recovery. Submit the board resolution authorizing the signatory (for the institution's validity).

Discussion Format

Between:

Advocate (for Multispecialty Hospital)

&

Hospital Management/Billing Team

1. Introduction & Purpose

Advocate:

"We are initiating legal action under Section 138 of the Negotiable Instruments Act, 1881, for the dishonored cheque issued by Mr. Y (father of the patient). Before drafting the demand notice, let's clarify the facts, documents, and legal strategy."

2. Factual Discussion

A. Patient Admission & Discharge Details

Hospital Representative:

Patient Name:

Admission Date: | Discharge Date:

Treating Doctor: | Department:

Nature of Treatment: (e.g., Surgery/ICU/Therapy)

B. Outstanding Dues Breakdown

(Verify each component with supporting bills/receipts)

1. Hospital Services: ₹ (Room charges, nursing, doctor's fees)
2. Medical Equipment: ₹ (Ventilator, monitors, etc.)
3. Medicines/Consumables: ₹ (Pharmacy bills)
4. Other Charges: ₹ (Diagnostics, ambulance, etc.)

Total Outstanding: ₹

C. Cheque Details & Dishonor

Cheque No.: | Date: | Amount: ₹

Bank: | Account No.:

Dishonor Reason: "Insufficient Funds"/"Account Closed"

Return Memo Date: (Attach copy)

D. Prior Communication

Any written reminders/emails sent? (Attach copies)

Any verbal promises by Mr. Y to repay?

3. Legal Strategy Discussion

A. Grounds for Legal Notice

The cheque was issued for a legally enforceable debt (hospital services).

No dispute on liability (the patient was treated & discharged).

Dishonor confirmed by bank memo.

B. Demand Notice Drafting Points

Mention breakup of dues (hospital bills attached).

Give 15 days to repay (as per Section 138(b)).

Warn of criminal complaint + recovery suit if unpaid.

C. Additional Legal Options

1. Civil Suit for Recovery: If the cheque amount < total dues.
2. Consumer Court Complaint: Deficiency in service (if applicable).

4. Document Checklist

Hospital Must Provide:

Copy of dishonored cheque + return memo

Detailed final bill (signed by patient/relative at discharge)

Admission form/agreement (terms of payment)

All receipts/acknowledgments (if partial payment was made)

Email/SMS reminders (if any)

5. Next Steps

1. Advocate drafts NOTICE u/s 138 NI Act (sample format shared).
2. Hospital reviews & approves notice content.
3. Notice sent via Registered AD + Courier (tracking proof kept).
4. If no payment in 15 days, file complaint before JMFC.

Sample Key Sentences for Notice

"The cheque was issued in discharge of a legally enforceable debt for medical services availed by [Patient Name]. Despite repeated reminders, you failed to clear the dues, and the cheque was dishonored. Pay ₹ within 15 days, failing which criminal proceedings will be initiated."

Special Considerations for Hospitals

Medico legal angle: Ensure no patient care dispute (pure payment issue).

Ethical tone: Avoid aggressive language (maintain hospital reputation).

Tax compliance: Ensure bills are GST compliant for legal validity.

NOTICE UNDER SECTION 138(B) FOR DISHONOUR OF CHEQUE NO [XXX]

Notice Number.2

An advocate, namely X, by profession (MACT side), whose cheque was returned unpaid by his client due to the professional fee agreed upon with one person,

To:

Mr. Y (Client/Drawer)

[Full Address]

Date: [DD/MM/YYYY]

Subject: NOTICE u/s 138(b) of the Negotiable Instruments Act, 1881 for Dishonour of Cheque No. dated for ₹

1. INTRODUCTION

I, Advocate Z, am duly appointed by my client, Advocate X (hereinafter referred to as "the Payee"), to issue this NOTICE to you, Mr. Y (hereinafter referred to as "the Drawer"), under Section 138(b) of the Negotiable Instruments Act, 1881, for the dishonour of a cheque issued towards unpaid professional fees.

2. FACTUAL MATRIX

a) You, Mr. Y, had engaged the professional services of Advocate X for [briefly mention the nature of work, e.g., "a Motor Accident Claim Tribunal (MACT) case"].

b) In discharge of your liability towards unpaid professional fees, you issued a cheque bearing:

Cheque No.:

Date: [DD/MM/YYYY]

Amount: ₹

Bank: [Bank Name & Branch]

Account No.:

c) The said cheque was presented for encashment on [DD/MM/YYYY] but was dishonoured by your bank with the return memo dated [DD/MM/YYYY] citing the reason: "Insufficient Funds"/"Account Closed"/[Other Reason]. A copy of the dishonoured cheque and return memo are enclosed.

d) The liability arises out of a fee agreement/[oral understanding] dated [DD/MM/YYYY] between you and Advocate X.

3. LEGAL DEMAND u/s 138(b)

a) Through this notice, you are legally demanded to pay the cheque amount of ₹ (Rupees only) within 15 days from the receipt of this notice.

b) Consequences of Non Payment:

Failure to pay will compel Advocate X to initiate criminal proceedings under:

Section 138 of the N.I. Act (Punishable with imprisonment of up to 2 years and/or fine).

Section 420 IPC (Cheating), if applicable.

You will also be liable for litigation costs and interest.

4. MODE OF PAYMENT

Pay via Demand Draft/Online Transfer to:

Account Name: Advocate X

Bank Details: [Account No., IFSC, Bank & Branch]

5. ENCLOSURES

1. Copy of the dishonoured cheque.
2. Copy of the bank return memo.
3. Copy of the fee agreement (if available).

6. CC

The Branch Manager, [Bank Name], [Branch Address] (for record).

NOTE: This notice is without prejudice to any other legal remedies available to my client.

Sincerely,

Advocate Z

[Stamp & Signature]

Key Points for Compliance:

1. Timeline:

Notice must be sent within 30 days of dishonour.

Complaint must be filed within 30 days after the 15day notice period expires.

2. Service:

Send via Registered AD/Speed Post with tracking. Retain proof of delivery.

3. Tone:

Professional and unambiguous. Avoid extraneous threats.

NOTICE FOR DISHONOUR OF CHEQUE ISSUED TOWARDS REPAYMENT OF FRIENDLY LOAN

NOTICE NO.3

NOTICE Regarding Cheque Dishonour for a Friendly Loan

LEGAL NOTICE

UNDER SECTION 138 OF THE NEGOTIABLE INSTRUMENTS ACT, 1881

Via Registered AD with Acknowledgement Due

Date: 5th July 2025

To:

Mr. [Full Name of Drawer],

S/o [Father's Name],

[Full Address].

From:

[Your Full Name],

S/o [Your Father's Name],

[Your Full Address].

(Through Advocate: [Advocate's Name], [Bar Council No.], [Law Firm/Address])

Subject: NOTICE Under Section 138 of the Negotiable Instruments Act, 1881, for Dishonour of Cheque No. for ₹10,00,000 (Ten Lakh) Issued Towards Repayment of Friendly Loan.

KEY DEMANDS & CONSEQUENCES

Demand	Deadline	Legal Consequence of NonCompliance
Payment of ₹10,00,000 (Principal)	15 Days from Receipt	Criminal Complaint U/S 138 NI Act
Interest @ 2% P.M. (From Cheque Date Till Payment)	15 Days from Receipt	Civil Recovery Suit U/Order XXXVII CPC
₹5,000 (NOTICE Cost)	15 Days from Receipt	Liability for Litigation Costs

DETAILED FACTUAL BACKGROUND

1. Friendly Loan Agreement:

On [Date], you requested a friendly loan of ₹10,00,000 from me to address urgent personal needs, promising repayment on demand with monthly interest @ 2%.

Given our longstanding acquaintance (since [Year]), I disbursed the amount in cash/transfer on [Date] without formal documentation, trusting your integrity.

2. Issuance of Cheque:

Towards liability discharge, you issued Cheque No. dated [Date] for ₹10,00,000 drawn on [Bank Name], [Branch].

The cheque was expressly handed over as repayment security for the loan.

3. Dishonour Event:

Upon presentation on [Date], the cheque was dishonoured via Return Memo dated [Date] with remarks: "Insufficient Funds" (copy enclosed).

Bank intimation received on [Date], triggering my 30day statutory notice period.

4. Failure to Rectify:

Despite telephonic reminders on [Dates] and a personal meeting on [Date], you neglected repayment.

LEGAL VIOLATIONS

Section 138 NI Act: Dishonour constitutes a criminal offence punishable with imprisonment for up to 2 years or a fine of up to twice the cheque amount.

Breach of Trust: Issuing a cheque without ensuring the sufficiency of funds reflects dishonest intent, inviting liability under Section 420 IPC (Cheating).

Civil Liability: You remain liable for principal + interest (@ 2% p.m. since [Cheque Date]) + costs.

REMEDIAL DEMAND

Within 15 days of receiving this notice:

1. Pay ₹10,00,000 (Principal) + accrued interest (@ 2% p.m. from [Cheque Date]) + ₹5,000 (notice costs) via demand draft/RTGS to my account.
2. Provide written confirmation of payment to my advocate.

Failure to comply will compel me to:

File a criminal complaint U/S 138 NI Act before the competent Magistrate;

Initiate summary civil suit U/Order XXXVII CPC for recovery;

Seek costs and punitive damages.

ATTACHMENTS

1. Copy of dishonoured cheque.
2. Bank Return Memo (Reason: "Insufficient Funds").
3. Loan disbursement proof (if available).

Note: This notice is without prejudice to my other legal rights. A copy is retained for court proceedings.

Advocate's Signature

[Advocate's Name]

[Enrollment No.]

[Law Firm Address]

[Contact Details]

CRITICAL NEXT STEPS FOR YOU

1. Send via Registered AD: Ensure proof of delivery.
2. Preserve Evidence: Original cheque, return memo, loan

transaction proofs (e.g., bank statements, witness details).

3. Timeline Compliance:

File complaint within 30 days after the 15day notice period expires.

4. Legal Consultation: If the drawer disputes the loan, strengthen your case with:

Witness affidavits confirming the transaction;

Documentary trail (messages/emails acknowledging debt).

NOTICE FOR DISHONOUR OF CHEQUE FOR UNPAID DIRECTOR'S FEES

LEGAL NOTICE: 4 To Producer for Unpaid Director's Fees

Under Section 138 Of The Negotiable Instruments Act, 1881

From:

[Director's Name]

[Director's Address]

[City, State, PIN Code]

[Contact Number]

[Email ID]

To,

[Producer's Name]

[Production House Name]

[Registered Office Address]

[City, State, PIN Code]

Date: [DD/MM/YYYY]

Subject: NOTICE under Section 138 of the Negotiable Instruments

Act, 1881 for Dishonor of Cheque No. [XXX] for Unpaid Director's Fees

Through: Registered AD/Speed Post with Acknowledgment

Dear Sir/Madam,

1. INTRODUCTION

I, [Director's Name], hereby serve this NOTICE upon you in my capacity as the director of the film [Film Name], for which I was engaged by your production house, [Production House Name], under an agreement dated [Agreement Date].

2. BACKGROUND OF THE LIABILITY

As per the terms of our agreement, you were liable to pay me a total fee of ₹[Total Fee Amount] for my services as the director of the aforementioned film. The payment was to be made in [Number of Instalments] instalments, out of which you have failed to pay the final instalment of ₹[Unpaid Amount].

In discharge of this legally enforceable debt, you issued:

Cheque No.: [XXX]

Dated: [DD/MM/YYYY]

Amount: ₹[Unpaid Amount] (Rupees [Amount in Words] only)

Drawn on: [Bank Name], [Branch Name].

3. DISHONOR OF THE CHEQUE

Upon presentation, the aforementioned cheque was dishonored on [Date of Dishonor] due to "Insufficient Funds" (as per the Bank Return Memo dated [Date of Return Memo]). A copy of the dishonored cheque and the bank return memo are enclosed herewith for your reference.

4. STATUTORY DEMAND

Under Section 138(b) of the Negotiable Instruments Act, 1881, you are hereby called upon to:

Pay the cheque amount of ₹[Unpaid Amount] within 15 days from the receipt of this notice.

5.CONSEQUENCESOF NONCOMPLIANCE

Failure to comply with this demand will compel me to initiate legal proceedings against you under Section 138 of the Negotiable Instruments Act, 1881, which may result in:

Criminal prosecution punishable with imprisonment up to 2 years and/or a fine up to twice the cheque amount.

Civil recovery suit for the unpaid amount along with interest @ 18% p.a. from the date of dishonor until realization.

Costs of legal proceedings.

6. DOCUMENTS ENCLOSED

1. Copy of the dishonored cheque.
2. Copy of the bank return memo.
3. Copy of the agreement (if applicable).
4. Copy of payment reminders (if any).

7. FINAL NOTE

This notice is issued without prejudice to any other legal remedies available to me under any other law for the time being in force.

Yours faithfully,

[Director's Name]

[Contact Details]

Copy to:

1. [Advocate's Name], [Law Firm Name], [Address] – for records

and further action.

Key Points to Remember:

1. Service of Notice: Ensure the notice is sent via registered post/speed post with acknowledgment due to maintain proof of delivery.

2. Timeline: The recipient has 15 days from the date of receipt to make the payment.

3. Next Steps: If the payment is not made within the stipulated time, file a complaint under Section 138 before the appropriate court within 30 days from the expiry of the 15day notice period.

NOTICE UNDER PSS ACT, 2007 FOR DISHONOUR OF ECS CHEQUES

NOTICE 05

under Section 25 of the Payment and Settlement Systems Act, 2007 (PSS Act) for dishonor of ECS (Electronic Clearing Service) cheques issued as security PDCs (Post Dated Cheques) by an accused enterprise to discharge prospective liability:

[Law Firm's Letterhead]

ADVOCATES & LEGAL CONSULTANTS

[Address] |

[Contact] |

[Email] |

[GSTIN/UIN]

Date: [DD/MM/YYYY]

To, The Managing Director,
[Accused Enterprise Name],
[Registered Office Address].

SUBJECT: NOTICE under section 25 of the payment and settlement systems act, 2007 for DISHONOR OF ECS cheques (security PDCS)

DATED [DATE(S)]
Through:

Registered AD/Speed Post with Acknowledgment Dear Sir/Madam,

1. Background of Liability Our client, [Creditor's Name], entered into an agreement dated [Agreement Date] with your enterprise for [Purpose of Transaction, e.g., supply of goods/loan facility]. As security for prospective liabilities, your enterprise issued: ECS Cheques (Security PDCs): Cheque No. [XXX], Dated [DD/MM/YYYY], Amount: ₹[X] Cheque No. [XXX], Dated [DD/MM/YYYY], Amount: ₹[X] (List all dishonored cheques) Drawn on: [Bank Name], [Branch].
2. Dishonor of ECS Cheques The above cheques were presented for encashment on [Date(s)] but were dishonored due to: "Insufficient Funds" (Bank Return Memo(s) dated [Date(s)] enclosed). Or "Account Closed" (if applicable).
3. Statutory Demand under Section 25, PSS Act Under Section 25(1) of the PSS Act, read with CHAPTER NO. XVII of the Negotiable

Instruments Act (NI Act), you are liable for: Criminal Offense: Dishonor of electronic funds transfer (ECS cheques) for discharge of debt/liability. Penalty: Imprisonment of up to 2 years or a fine of up to twice the cheque amount, or both. You are hereby demanded to:

1. Pay the total dishonored amount of ₹[Total Amount] within 15 days of receiving this notice.
2. Submit written confirmation of payment to our office.
4. Consequences of Non Compliance Failure to comply will compel our client to: File a criminal complaint under Section 25 PSS Act + Section 138 NI Act. Initiate civil recovery proceedings with 18% interest from the date of dishonour. Seek attachment of your enterprise's assets under interim relief provisions.
5. Documents Enclosed

1. Copy of dishonored cheques + Bank Return Memos.
2. Copy of Agreement (highlighting the PDC clause).
3. Proof of prior reminders (if any). Note: This notice is issued without prejudice to other legal remedies.

[Contact Details]

Copy to:

1. [Creditor's Name] – for records.

Key Legal Points:

1. Applicability of Section 25 PSS Act: Covers ECS cheques issued as security PDCs for prospective liability (if linked to a legally enforceable debt). Presumption of Liability: Under Section 25(2), the transfer is presumed for debt discharge unless disproven.

2. Notice Requirements: Must be sent within 30 days of dishonor. Payer gets 15 days to rectify post receipt.

3. Dual Liability: Criminal: Prosecution under PSS Act + NI Act (via Section 25(5)). Civil: Summary suit for recovery under Order XXXVII CPC.

4. Enterprise Liability: Directors/officers in charge are vicariously liable under Section 141 NI Act (applied via Section 25(5) PSS Act).

1. Defences Invalid: Lack of knowledge about insufficient funds is not a defense. Next Steps: File Complaint: Within 1 month after notice expiry (JMFC Court). RBI Reporting: Notify RBI's Banking Ombudsman for ECS default. For templates, refer to:

Draft NOTICE From Flat Buyer To Builder For Dishonoured Buyback Cheque

NOTICE 6

From Flat Buyer to Builder Whose Buyback Consideration is Dishonoured.

From: [Your Name]

Advocate for Mr./Ms. A

[Your Law Firm's Name]

[Your Office Address]

[City, State, PIN Code]

[Email Address]

[Contact Number]

[Date]

To: Builder X

[Designation, if applicable]

[Builder's Company Name]

[Registered Office Address]

[City, State, PIN Code]

Subject: NOTICE NUMBER

for Dishonour of Cheque Issued Towards Buyback Consideration

Demand for Immediate Payment. Dear Sir/Madam, Under instructions from and on behalf of our client, Mr./Ms. A (hereinafter referred to as 'Our Client'), we serve upon you this NOTICE regarding the dishonour of the cheque issued by you towards the buyback consideration under the Housing Project [Project Name] at [Project Location], pursuant to the mutual cancellation of the flat allotment. Background & Facts:4

1. Our Client had booked Flat No. [X], Tower [Y], in [Project Name] under an Allotment Letter/Buyer's Agreement dated [Agreement Date].
2. Due to prolonged delays in construction and legal issues concerning the project, the parties mutually agreed to cancel the allotment via the Cancellation Agreement/Mutual Termination Letter dated [Cancellation Date].
3. As per the terms of cancellation, you agreed to refund the buyback consideration and issued a cheque bearing No. [Cheque No.], dated [Cheque Date], drawn on [Bank Name & Branch], for an amount of ₹[Amount in Figures & Words].

4. Upon presentation, the said cheque was dishonoured with the remarks '[Return Reason, e.g., "Insufficient Funds"/"Account Closed"]' via return memo dated [Return Memo Date].

5. Despite our Client's repeated requests, you have failed to make the payment, thereby violating the terms of the mutual cancellation agreement. Legal Violations: Your actions constitute: Breach of the Cancellation Agreement under the Indian Contract Act, 1872. An offence under Section 138 of the Negotiable Instruments Act, 1881 (Dishonour of Cheque). Deficiency in service and unfair trade practice under the Consumer Protection Act, 2019 (if applicable).

Demands: In view of the above, we call upon you to:

1. Immediately pay the due amount of ₹[Amount] along with interest @ [X]% p.a. from the due date till realization.

2. Compensate our Client for the financial loss, mental harassment, and legal costs incurred, quantified at ₹[Amount]. Notice Period & Consequences: You are granted 15 days from the receipt of this notice to comply with the demands. Failure to do so will compel our Client to initiate legal action, including but not limited to: Filing a criminal complaint under Section 138 of the Negotiable Instruments Act. Initiating a civil suit for recovery and breach of contract. Lodging a complaint before the Consumer Forum for deficiency in service. All costs and consequences shall be borne by you. Copy retained for future legal recourse.

Yours faithfully,

[Your Name] Advocate for Mr./Ms. A

[Enclosures:

1. Copy of Dishonoured Cheque & Return Memo
2. Copy of Cancellation Agreement/Mutual Termination Letter
3. Copy of Allotment Letter/Buyer's Agreement (if applicable)]

Note: This is a draft for reference. Kindly consult your legal counsel for modifications based on specific facts and jurisdictional laws

NOTICE FOR DISHONOUR OF CHEQUE FOR OUTSTANDING DUES (VIA REGISTERED POST)

NOTICE 07

to a flat owner whose cheque is dishonest issued by the cooperative housing society for outstanding maintenance charges, etc.

To: [Flat Owner's Name]

[Flat No. and Address]

[Cooperative Housing Society Name]

[Society Address] Date: [DD/MM/YYYY]

Subject: NOTICE for Dishonor of Cheque No. [XXX] dated [DD/MM/YYYY] for Outstanding Dues Via Registered Post/Speed Post Dear Sir/Madam,

1. Reference to Cheque and Liability You issued Cheque No. [XXX] dated [DD/MM/YYYY] for ₹[Amount] drawn on [Bank Name, Branch] in favor of [Society Name] towards: Outstanding maintenance charges: ₹[X] Fines/penalties: ₹[X] (specify reasons, e.g., late payment, rule violations).

2. Dishonor and Statutory Demand The cheque was presented for encashment on [DD/MM/YYYY] but was dishonored due to "[Reason: Insufficient Funds/Account Closed/etc.]" as per the bank's return memo dated [DD/MM/YYYY]. Under Section 138(b) of the NI Act, you are hereby demanded to pay: "The said amount" (cheque value): ₹[X] within 15 days of receiving this notice. Note: Additional claims (interest/costs) may be specified separately but cannot overshadow the cheque amount demand.

3. Consequences of NonPayment Failure to comply will compel the society to initiate legal proceedings under Section 138 of the NI Act, punishable with imprisonment of up to 2 years and/or a fine of up to twice the cheque amount.

4. Proof of Service This notice is sent to your registered address. Service on relatives/third parties without proof of your awareness is invalid. Authorized Signatory [Name] [Designation] [Cooperative Housing Society Name] [Contact Details]

<u>Key Legal Points to Include</u>

1. Clarity of Demand: The notice must explicitly demand the cheque amount ("the said amount") as per Supreme Court rulings. Other dues (interest/fines) should be listed separately to avoid invalidation.
2. Timeline: The 15day window for payment starts from the date of receipt (not issuance) of the notice.
3. Service Validity: Ensure the notice is delivered to the drawer's official address. Service on relatives without proof of acknowledgment is insufficient.
4. Attachments: Include copies of the dishonored cheque, return memo, and ledger of dues for transparency.

NOTICE FOR DISHONOUR OF CHEQUE NO [XXX] FOR ₹25,00,000/-

NOTICE NO.08

ON BEHALF OF THE CHARTERED ACCOUNTANT (CLIENT) TO COMPANY

[Law Firm's Letterhead]

ADVOCATE & LEGAL CONSULTANTS

[Address] | [Contact] | [Email] | [GSTIN/UIN]

Date: [DD/MM/YYYY]

To,

The Managing Director,

Company X,

[Registered Office Address].

SUBJECT:

LEGAL DEMAND NOTICE NUMBER

UNDER SECTION 138(b) OF THE NEGOTIABLE INSTRUMENTS ACT, 1881 FOR DISHONOR OF CHEQUE NO. [XXX] FOR ₹25,00,000/

From CA to Client

Through: Registered AD/Speed Post with Acknowledgment

Dear Sir/Madam,

1. Background of Liability

Our client, CA [Name], provided professional accounting/advisory services to your company for the financial year [YYYY YY] as per the agreement dated [DD/MM/YYYY]. In discharge of this legally enforceable debt, your company issued:

Cheque No. [XXX]

Dated: [DD/MM/YYYY]

Amount: ₹25,00,000/ (Twenty Five Lakhs)

Drawn on: [Bank Name], [Branch].

2. Dishonor of Cheque

Upon presentation, the cheque was dishonored on [DD/MM/YYYY] due to 'Insufficient Funds' (Bank Return Memo attached).

3. Statutory Demand

Under Section 138(b) of the NI Act, you are hereby called upon to:

Pay the cheque amount of ₹25,00,000/ within 15 days from receipt of this notice.

Failure to comply will compel our client to initiate:

Criminal proceedings (punishable with imprisonment up to 2 years/fine up to twice the cheque amount).

Civil recovery suit with interest (@18% p.a.) and costs.

4. Documents Enclosed

1. Copy of dishonored cheque.
2. Bank return memo.
3. Copy of service agreement/invoices.

5. Consequences of Nonpayment

Legal action will be initiated without further intimation.

Liability for additional costs (legal fees, interest, etc.).

Note: This notice is issued without prejudice to our client's other rights.

Yours faithfully,
[Advocate's Name]
Enrollment No.: [XXX]
For [Law Firm Name]
[Contact Details]
Copy to:
1. CA [Client Name] – for records.

Key Legal Requirements Addressed

1. Mandatory 15Day Notice: As per Section 138(c), NI Act.
2. Specific Demand: Only the cheque amount is demanded (other claims like interest can be pursued separately).
3. Proof of Service: Send via registered post (acknowledgment receipt is crucial evidence).
4. Annexures: Attach cheque copy, return memo, and proof of debt (agreement/invoices).

Next Steps if Unpaid:

File a complaint under Section 138 before the JMFC Court within 30 days after notice expiry.

Consider a parallel civil suit for recovery.

NOTICE FOR DISHONOUR OF CHEQUE NO [XXX] FOR ₹[AMOUNT]

NOTICE:09

Addressed To A Real Estate Development Company For A Bounced Cheque Issued As Part Of A Buyback Agreement:

[On Advocate's Letterhead] Date

To,

The Director,

[Developer Company Name],

[Registered Office Address].

SUBJECT: NOTICE UNDER SECTION 138 OF THE NEGOTIABLE INSTRUMENTS ACT, 1881 FOR DISHONOUR OF CHEQUE NO. [XXX] FOR ₹[AMOUNT]

Dear Sir/Madam,

1. Introduction:

I act as the duly appointed advocate for my client, Mr./Ms. [Complainant's Name], residing at [Address] ("Complainant"), and address you on their behalf.

2. Background:

On [Booking Date], the Complainant booked [Flat/Plot No.] in your project "[Project Name]" under a Booking Agreement.

Due to [reason: delay/failure to deliver/other breach], a Buyback

Agreement was executed on [Cancellation Date], whereby your company agreed to refund ₹[Amount] and issued:

Cheque No. [XXX], dated [Cheque Date], for ₹[Amount], drawn on [Bank Name, Branch].

3. Dishonour of Cheque:

The cheque was presented for encashment on [Presentation Date] but was dishonoured with the remark "Insufficient Funds" (copy of return memo enclosed).

4. Legal Demand:

Under Section 138 of the Negotiable Instruments Act, 1881, and Section 141 (for company liability), you are hereby:

Notified of the dishonour.

Called upon to pay the cheque amount of ₹[Amount] within 15 days from the receipt of this notice.

5. Consequences of Nonpayment:

If payment is not made within 15 days, my client will:

Initiate criminal proceedings under Section 138 NI Act.

Seek punishment (imprisonment of up to 2 years and/or fine of up to twice the cheque amount).

Claim costs and interest under applicable laws.

6. Copy to:

Bank Manager, [Bank Name], [Branch] – for record.

Yours faithfully,

[Advocate's Name]

Encl.:

1. Copy of dishonoured cheque and return memo.
2. Copy of Buyback Agreement.
3. Postal tracking receipt (to be attached after sending).

Key Points to Include in the Notice:

1. Specific Details:

   Cheque number, date, amount, and bank.

   Clear reference to the buyback agreement (attach copy).

2. Legal Compliance:

   Sent within 30 days of dishonour (Section 138 proviso).

   Explicit 15day payment deadline.

3. Mode of Service:

   Send via Registered AD/Speed Post + Courier + Email (for proof).

   Retain postal receipts and tracking reports.

4. Section 141 NI Act (Liability of Directors):

   Name the Director(s) responsible for company operations to ensure personal liability.

IMPORTANT NOTE

As An usual Practice, and in terms of the implied authority vested with the Advocates to issue Notice as per the instance of Client/s Still it's advisable that All pages of the Notice preferably be signed both by Client/s and Advocate to avoid facing any finger qua the issue of Admissibility in due course of law.

Next Steps if No Reply:

1. File A Complaint Under Section 138/141 NI Act After 15 Days OF RECEIPT OF NOTICE AS PER POSTAL RECCORD.

2. Attach:

Original cheque and return memo.

Proof of notice delivery.

Buyback agreement. Or other supporting document .

****

COMPLAINANT: BUNCH:

1. Hospitals Versus Father Of Patient
2. In Between Advocate & Former Client
3. Between A Banking Official And An Advocate

Regarding Dishonored ECS Cheques Issued As Security PDC

4. Supplier And Buyer
5. In Between Co-Operative Housing Society Flat Owner
6. Advocated Complaint Versus Client
7. Director Versus Producer

COMPLAINT NO. 1 TO ___

HOSPITALS VERSUS THE FATHER OF THE PATIENT

IN BETWEEN Hospitals versus Father of Patient [Patient's Name] Whose CHEQUE RETURNED UNPAID

IN THE COURT OF THE JUDICIAL MAGISTRATE FIRST CLASS (JMFC) AT

Criminal Complaint Number

Case No.: of 2024

Under: Section 138 of the Negotiable Instruments Act, 1881

Between:

[Name of Multispecialty Hospital]

Through its Authorized Signatory [Name]

[Hospital Address]

(Complainant)

Versus

Mr. Y (Father of Patient)

[Full Address]

(Accused)

COMPLAINT UNDER SECTION **138 OF THE NEGOTIABLE INSTRUMENTS ACT, 1881**

Respected Sir/Madam,

1. INTRODUCTION

The Complainant is a reputed multispecialty hospital. The Accused is the father of patient [Patient's Name] who was admitted and treated at the Complainant hospital. This complaint is filed for dishonour of cheque issued by the Accused towards outstanding hospital bills.

2. FACTS OF THE CASE

a) Patient [Name] was admitted on [Date] for treatment of [Condition] and discharged on [Date]

b) Total outstanding amount: ₹ (Breakup attached as Annexure 1)

c) The Accused issued Cheque No. dated for ₹ drawn on [Bank Name]

d)The cheque was dishonoured on [Date] for reason: "Insufficient Funds"/"Account Closed"

e) NOTICE dated was duly served but the Accused failed to:

Make payment within 15 days

Send any reply to the notice

Offer any explanation

3. CAUSE OF ACTION

The cause of action arose on:

(Date of cheque dishonour)

(Date of notice expiry)

(Date of final payment default)

4. DOCUMENTARY EVIDENCE

(Attach as annexures):

Original dishonoured cheque + return memo

Copy of NOTICE + postal receipts

Detailed hospital bill with breakup

Patient admission/discharge records

Authorisation letter from hospital

Affidavit verifying complaint

5. PRAYER

The Complainant prays:

a) To take cognizance of offence u/s 138 NI Act

b) To summon the Accused

c) To punish the Accused as per law

d) To direct payment of:

- Cheque amount ₹
- Interest @ 18% p.a.
- Litigation costs

6. VERIFICATION

"I, [Name], authorized signatory of [Hospital Name], solemnly affirm that the contents are true to my knowledge and belief."

Place: [City]

Date: [DD/MM/YYYY]

Signature of Complainant

[Name & Designation]

[Hospital Stamp]

Through:

Advocate [Name]

[Enrollment No.]

[Address]

[Mobile No.]

ENCLOSURES:

1. List of documents
2. Court fee
3. Vakalatnama
4. Copies for accused/Court

IMPORTANT NOTES:

1. File within 30 days of notice expiry
2. Ensure all annexures are properly notarized
3. Include calculation of interest
4. Mention exact dates of:

    Cheque presentation

    Dishonour

    Notice issuance

    Notice expiry

Would you like me to include:

1. Sample affidavit format?
2. Interest calculation sheet?
3. Any specific state specific requirement

COMPLAINT NO.2 In Between Advocate & Former Client

IN THE COURT OF THE JUDICIAL MAGISTRATE FIRST CLASS (JMFC),

Criminal Complaint Case No.: of 2024

Under: Section 138 of the Negotiable Instruments Act, 1881 IN THE MATTER OF:

Advocate X [Address]

(Complainant)

Vs.

Mr. Y (Client/Drawer)

[Address] ... (Accused)

COMPLAINT UNDER SECTION 138 OF THE NEGOTIABLE INSTRUMENTS ACT, 1881

Advocate

Versus

Client Respected Sir/Madam,

1. INTRODUCTION The complainant, Advocate X, is a practicing advocate specializing in Motor Accident Claims Tribunal (MACT) cases. The accused, Mr. Y, was the complainant's client and issued a cheque towards unpaid professional fees, which was dishonoured. Despite a NOTICE under Section 138(b) of the N.I. Act, the accused failed to make the payment. Hence, this complaint is filed.

2. FACTUAL MATRIX

a) Professional Engagement: The accused engaged the

complainant's services for [briefly describe the case, e.g., "MACT Case No. of 2023"]. The agreed professional fee was ₹, payable as per [written agreement/oral understanding].

b) Issuance of Cheque: In discharge of this liability, the accused issued a cheque: Cheque No.: Date: [DD/MM/YYYY] Amount: ₹ Bank: [Bank Name & Branch] Account No.:

c) Dishonour of Cheque: The cheque was presented for encashment on [DD/MM/YYYY] but was dishonoured due to "Insufficient Funds"/"Account Closed" (Return Memo dated [DD/MM/YYYY] enclosed).

d) Legal Notice: A demand notice under Section 138(b) N.I. Act was sent via Registered AD/Speed Post on [DD/MM/YYYY] (Postal Receipt No.:). The accused failed to reply or pay within 15 days.

3. CAUSE OF ACTION The cause of action arose on: First Dishonour Date: [DD/MM/YYYY] (when the cheque was returned unpaid). Notice Period Expiry: [DD/MM/YYYY] (15 days after notice receipt). Complaint Filing Date: Within 30 days of notice expiry (as mandated u/s 142).

4. PRAYER FOR RELIEF The complainant prays for:

1. Punishment u/s 138 N.I. Act (imprisonment up to 2 years and/or fine).
2. Compensation u/s 357 CrPC for the cheque amount (₹) + interest.
3. Litigation costs.

5. LIST OF DOCUMENTS (Annexed)

1. Original dishonoured cheque + return memo.
2. Copy of NOTICE + postal receipts.

3. Fee agreement (if any).

4.Affidavit of the complainant.

5. Vakalatnama (if filed through an advocate).

6. VERIFICATION

"I, Advocate X, solemnly affirm that the contents of this complaint are true to my knowledge and belief." Place: [City] Date: [DD/MM/YYYY] Signature of Complainant (Advocate X) Through: Advocate Z [Enrollment No.] [Address] [Mobile No.]

Key Notes for Filing:

1. Jurisdiction: File in the JMFC Court where the cheque was presented for encashment.
2. Limitation: The complaint must be filed within 30 days after the 15day notice period expires.
3. Process: Submit 23 copies of the complaint + annexures. Pay court fees (varies by state). The court will issue summons to the accused.

COMPLAINT No.3

BETWEEN A BANKING OFFICIAL AND AN ADVOCATE REGARDING DISHONORED ECS CHEQUES ISSUED AS SECURITY PDCS:

COMPLAINT FORMAT UNDER THE PAYMENT AND SETTLEMENT SYSTEMS ACT, 2007

IN THE COURT OF THE JUDICIAL MAGISTRATE FIRST CLASS [CITY]

Complaint Case No: of 2024

Under: Section 25 of the PSS Act, 2007, read with Section 138 of the NI Act, 1881.

Between:

[Bank Name], through its Manager [Name]

Branch Address

...Complainant

Versus

1. [Company Name]
2. [Director/Authorized Signatory Name]

...Accused

Subject: Dishonor of ECS cheques issued as security PDCs

Facts:

1. The accused availed themselves of a credit facility of ₹ vide an agreement dated .
2. Issued ECS cheques as security PDCs (list cheque numbers, dates,

amounts).

3. Cheques were dishonored on due to 'Insufficient Funds.'

4. A statutory notice dated was served, but no payment was received.

Prayer:

Punishment under Section 25 of the PSS Act.

Compensation under Section 357 of the CrPC.

Costs of proceedings.

Enclosures:

1. Original cheques and return memos.
2. Loan agreement copy.
3. Notice proof and tracking.
4. Board resolution authorizing the complaint.

Application No. Seeking No Cross Order

COMPLAINT No.4

SUPPLIER AND BUYER

IN THE COURT OF THE METROPOLITAN MAGISTRATE

[CITY NAME]

COMPLAINT CASE NO. OF 2024

Under:

Section 138 of the Negotiable Instruments Act, 1881

Section 141 of the Negotiable Instruments Act, 1881

Section 420 of the Indian Penal Code, 1860 (if applicable)

IN THE MATTER OF:

M/s. [Complainant Company Name]

(A registered company incorporated under the Companies Act, [Year])

Having its registered office at: [Address]

Through its Authorized Signatory: [Name]

...COMPLAINANT

VERSUS

1. M/s. X Company
   (A registered distributor company)
   Having its office at: [Address]
2. Mr. Y
   (Director of M/s. X Company)
   Resident of: [Address]

3. Mr. Z

(Authorized Signatory of M/s. X Company)

Resident of: [Address]

...ACCUSED

UNDER SECTION 138 READ WITH SECTION 141 OF THE NEGOTIABLE INSTRUMENTS ACT, 1881

The Complainant most respectfully submits:

1. INTRODUCTION

The Complainant is a registered manufacturer and supplier of digital devices and electronic goods.

Accused No. 1 is a distributor company, and Accused Nos. 2 & 3 are its directors/signatories responsible for daytoday affairs.

2. MATERIAL FACTS

Business Transaction:

Accused No. 1 purchased goods worth ₹2,00,00,000/ (Two Crores Only) from the Complainant as per:

Invoice No. Dated

Delivery Challan No. Dated

GST Paid Receipts (attached as Annexure 1)

Payment Terms:

Accused paid ₹50,00,000/ (Fifty Lakhs Only) as part payment (proof attached as Annexure 2).

For the balance ₹1,50,00,000/ (One Crore Fifty Lakhs Only), Accused No. 1 issued:

Cheque No. Dated drawn on [Bank Name], [Branch] (Annexure

3). Dishonour of Cheque:

Upon presentation on , the cheque was returned unpaid with remarks: "Funds Insufficient" (Return Memo attached as Annexure 4).

A NOTICE dated was duly served (Annexure 5), but the Accused failed to pay.

3. LEGAL GROUNDS

The dishonour constitutes an offence under Section 138 of the NI Act.

Accused Nos. 2 & 3 are liable under Section 141 of the NI Act as they were in charge of the company's affairs.

Section 420 IPC is invoked if fraudulent intent is established.

4. PRAYER

The Complainant prays that the Hon'ble Court may be pleased to:

1. Take cognizance of the offence under Sections 138 & 141 NI Act.
2. Issue summons against all Accused.
3. Punish the Accused as per law.
4. Direct the Accused to pay:

   ₹1,50,00,000/ (cheque amount)

   Interest @ 24% p.a. from the date of dishonour.

   Litigation costs.

5. LIST OF DOCUMENTS

1. Annexure 1: Invoice, Delivery Challan, GST Receipts
2. Annexure 2: Proof of part payment (₹50,00,000/)
3. Annexure 3: Copy of dishonoured cheque
4. Annexure 4: Return Memo

5. Annexure 5: NOTICE & Postal Receipt

6. VERIFICATION

I, [Name], Authorized Signatory of the Complainant, solemnly affirm that the contents of this complaint are true to my knowledge.

Place: [City]

Date: [Date]

DEPONENT

[Name]

[Designation]

M/s. [Complainant Company Name]

VERIFICATION

Verified at [Place] on this [Date] that the contents are true and correct.

ADVOCATE FOR COMPLAINANT

[Your Name]

[Enrollment No.]

[Law Firm Name]

[Address]

[Mobile No.]

KEY NOTES:

1. Ensure all annexures are properly stamped and attested.
2. The affidavit of the authorized signatory must be notarized.
3. Court fees must be paid as per local rules.
4. Section 420 IPC can be added if fraudulent intent is evident.

COMPLAINT No.5

IN BETWEEN CO-OPERATIVE HOUSING SOCIETY FLAT OWNER

THE COURT OF THE JUDICIAL MAGISTRATE FIRST CLASS (JMFC), Complaint Case No.: of 2024

Under: Section 138 of the Negotiable Instruments Act, 1881 Between:

[Cooperative Housing Society Name],

Through its Authorized Signatory [Name],
Registered Office:
[Society Address] …Complainant
And
[Flat Owner's Name],
[Flat No. and Address] …Accused

COMPLAINT UNDER SECTION 138 OF THE NI ACT

Respected Sir/Madam,

1. Introduction The Complainant is a registered cooperative housing society, and the Accused is a member/flat owner liable to pay maintenance charges, fines, and other dues as per society bylaws.
2. Facts of the Case The Accused issued Cheque No. [XXX] dated [DD/MM/YYYY] for ₹[Amount] drawn on [Bank Name, Branch] in favor of the Complainant towards: Outstanding maintenance charges:

₹[X] Fines/penalties: ₹[X] (specify reasons, e.g., late payment, rule violations). The cheque was presented for encashment on [DD/MM/YYYY] but was dishonored due to "[Reason: Insufficient Funds/Account Closed/Stop Payment]" (Bank Return Memo dated [DD/MM/YYYY] attached as Annexure A).

3. Statutory Demand Notice A legal demand notice under Section 138(b) of the NI Act was duly served to the Accused via Registered Post/Speed Post on [DD/MM/YYYY] (Postal Receipt and Acknowledgment attached as Annexure B). The notice demanded payment of the cheque amount within 15 days, but the Accused failed to comply (No reply/payment received as of [Current Date]).

4. Cause of Action The cause of action arose on: Date of Dishonor: [DD/MM/YYYY] Date of Notice Service: [DD/MM/YYYY] Date of Non Compliance: [DD/MM/YYYY] (after 15 days from notice receipt).

5. Prayer for Relief The Complainant prays for: Conviction of the Accused under Section 138 of the NI Act. Payment of the cheque amount: ₹[X] + interest @ 12% p.a. from the date of dishonor. Compensation under Section 357 of CrPC (up to twice the cheque amount). Costs of legal proceedings. 6. List of Annexures Annexure A: Dishonored cheque + Bank Return Memo. Annexure B: Copy of Demand Notice + Postal Proof. Annexure C: Society's ledger/certificate of outstanding dues. Annexure D: Society's Resolution authorizing the complaint. Verification I, [Name], authorized signatory of the society, solemnly affirm that the contents of this complaint are true to my knowledge. Place: [City] Date: [DD/MM/YYYY] Signature of Complainant [Name] [Designation]

[Cooperative Housing Society Name] [Contact Details]

Key Legal Considerations

1. Jurisdiction: File the complaint in the JMFC Court within 30 days from the date the cause of action arises (i.e., after 15 days from notice expiry).
2. Evidence: Ensure all documents (cheque, return memo, demand notice, postal receipts, ledger of dues) are notarized/attested.
3. Authorized Signatory: The complaint must be filed by a person authorized via society resolution (Annexure D).
4. Limitation: The complaint must be filed within 1 month of the notice expiry date (Section 142, NI Act).

COMPLAINT No.6

ADVOCATED COMPLAINT VERSUS CLIENT

IN THE COURT OF THE JUDICIAL MAGISTRATE FIRST CLASS AT

Criminal Complaint Case No.: of 2025

Under Section 138 of the Negotiable Instruments Act, 1881

Advocate X Practicing Advocate, Enrolment No. [Number],
Year Residing/Office at [Full Address], ...COMPLAINANT

VERSUS Y [Accused's Full Name],
S/o [Father's Name], Aged [Age],
Residing at [Full Address],
[Occupation] , ACCUSED

Complaint Under Section 138 Of The Negotiable Instruments Act, 1881 Most Respectfully Showeth:

1. INTRODUCTION OF THE COMPLAINANT The complainant is a practicing advocate enrolled with the [State Bar Council] (Enrolment No. [Number], Year) and is legally competent to file this complaint.

2. INTRODUCTION OF THE ACCUSED The accused is the drawer of the dishonoured cheque and was the complainant's client in a previous matter involving a dishonoured cheque of ₹50,00,000 (Fifty

Lakh). As per the agreed fee arrangement, the accused was liable to pay the complainant 10% of the decree amount (₹5,00,000) for professional services rendered.

3. NATURE OF RELATIONSHIP & FEE AGREEMENT The complainant successfully represented the accused in the earlier cheque dishonour case, which resulted in a conviction order, and the cheque amount of 50 lakhs was directed to be paid to the complainant by the accused. The accused later filed an appeal against the conviction and settled the matter clandestinely with the opposing party without informing the complainant, thereby defrauding the complainant of his legitimate fee.

4. ISSUANCE OF CHEQUE & DISHONOR In discharge of the legally enforceable liability of ₹5,00,000 (professional fees), the accused issued: Cheque No. [Number], dated [Date], Drawn on [Bank Name], Branch [Branch Name], For ₹5,00,000 (Five Lakh). Upon presentation, the cheque was dishonored on [Date] with the memo: “Insufficient Funds” (or “Account Closed”). Annexure C1: Copy of the dishonoured cheque + bank return memo.

5. NOTICE & NONCOMPLIANCE A statutory NOTICE was sent via Registered AD/Speed Post on [Date] (within 30 days of dishonour), demanding payment within 15 days. The accused received the notice (proof: Postal Receipt & Tracking Report – Annexure N1) but failed to pay, and there was no reply to the notice.

6. CAUSE OF ACTION The cause of action arose on: [Date]: Cheque dishonored. [Date]: NOTICE served. [Date + 15 Days]: Accused failed to pay. Complaint filed within 30 days of the expiry of the 15day notice period (Section 142(b) NI Act).

PRAYER The complainant humbly prays:

1. Take cognizance under Section 138 NI Act and summon the accused.
2. Punish the accused with: Imprisonment (up to 2 years), Fine (up to twice the cheque amount), and Compensation (under Section 357 Cr.p.c.)
3. Grant costs and any other relief deemed fit. 4. Pray for penal interest retrospectively from the date of cause of action. Place: [City] Date: [DD/MM/YYYY]

VERIFICATION

I, [Your Name], solemnly affirm that the contents of this complaint are true and correct to my knowledge. Signature of Complainant [Your Name]

LIST OF ANNEXURES

1. Annexure C1: Dishonored cheque + bank return memo.
2. Annexure N1: NOTICE copy + postal receipts + tracking report.
3. Annexure ID: Complainant's Bar Council enrolment certificate.
4. Annexure: Included previous court order as evidence.
5. Annexure: Fee Agreement (if any written agreement exists).

Key Legal Points to Highlight

1. Legally Enforceable Debt: The cheque was issued for professional fees, which constitutes a legally recoverable debt under the NI Act.
2. Fraudulent Settlement: The accused's clandestine settlement during the appeal demonstrates mala fide intent to evade payment.
3. Jurisdiction: File in the court where: The cheque was presented/dishonored.

COMPLAINT NO.7

DIRECTOR VERSUS PRODUCER

IN THE COURT OF THE JUDICIAL MAGISTRATE FIRST CLASS (JMFC),

Complaint Case No.: of 2025

Under: Sections 138 & 141 of the Negotiable Instruments Act, 1881

Between:

[Director's Name],

[Address], [Contact Details]

...Complainant

And

1. [Film Production X],
   [Registered Office Address]
2. [Producer Y], (Managing Director/Partner)
   [Address]
3. [Signatory's Name], (Cheque Signatory)
   [Address]

...Accused

****

CHAPTER-03

COMPLAINT UNDER SECTIONS 138 & 141 OF THE NI ACT

Respected Sir/Madam,

1. Introduction

The Complainant is a film director engaged by Accused No. 1 (Film Production X) under an agreement dated [Agreement Date] for directing the film [Film Name]. As per the agreement, a fee of ₹[Amount] was payable, of which ₹[Unpaid Amount] remains unpaid.

2. Dishonor of Cheque

Accused No. 1 issued Cheque No. [XXX] dated [DD/MM/YYYY] for ₹[Amount], drawn on [Bank Name], signed by Accused No. 3.

The cheque was dishonored on [DD/MM/YYYY] due to "Insufficient Funds" (Bank Return Memo attached as Annexure A).

3. Statutory Compliance

A NOTICE under Section 138(b) of the NI Act was sent via Registered Post on [Notice Date] (Postal Receipt & Acknowledgment at Annexure B).

The accused failed to reply or pay within 15 days of notice receipt.

4. Liability of Accused

Accused No. 1 (Company): Liable as the issuer of the cheque for a legally enforceable debt (director's fees).

Accused No. 2 (Producer Y): As the Managing Director/Person in

Charge, responsible for the company's conduct under Section 141(1).

Accused No. 3 (Signatory): Liable under Section 141(2) for signing the cheque and participating in the offence.

5. Prayer for Relief

The Complainant prays for:

Conviction of all accused under Sections 138/141 of the NI Act.

Payment of ₹[Amount] + 18% interest from the date of dishonor.

Compensation under Section 357 of the CrPC (up to twice the cheque amount).

Costs of litigation.

6. Annexures

1. Annexure A: Dishonored cheque + Bank Return Memo.
2. Annexure B: Statutory Notice + Postal Proof.
3. Annexure C: Director's Agreement + Payment Invoices.
4. Annexure D: Resolution authorizing the complaint (if applicable).

Verification

I, [Director's Name], solemnly affirm that the contents are true to my knowledge.

Place: [City]

Date: [DD/MM/YYYY]

Signature of Complainant

[Name]

[Contact Details]

Key Legal Points :

1. Jurisdiction: File within 30 days of the notice expiry date (from

the 16th day after notice receipt).

2. Evidence: Ensure all documents (cheque, return memo, notice proof, agreement) are notarized.

3. Liability under Section 141:

Producer Y (Accused No. 2) is liable as the "person in charge" of the company's operations.

Signatory (Accused No. 3) is liable for signing the cheque, irrespective of their role in the company.

4. Company Liability: Even if the production house dissolves, its directors remain liable.

Next Steps:

1. File the Complaint in the court where the cheque was presented.

2. Seek Interim Relief: Apply for attachment of the accused's assets under Section 145 of the NI Act.

3. Parallel Civil Suit: For faster recovery, file a summary suit under Order XXXVII of the CPC.

Say reply/objection by the Accused opposing the Complainant's application seeking a "No Cross Order" in a cheque dishonor case (Section 138, NI Act) before the JMFC Court:

Draft library

18PRACTICE & PROCEDURE

CHECK LIST Pre-Notice

(PRE NOTICE) In Accordance With Section 138(B) Of The Negotiable Instruments Act, 1881, Applicable To Commercial Suppliers And Buyers, Who May Be Corporate Or Sole Proprietorship Entities?

Cheque Status Information:

1. Payee's Name (as indicated on the cheque):
2. Cheque Number:
3. Crossed as 'Account Payee': ☐ Yes ☐ No
4. Cheque Date: // (DD/MM/YYYY)
5. Amount in Words:
6. Amount in Figures: ₹. Banking and Account Details:
7. Bank and Branch of the Drawer:
8. Account Number of the Drawer:
9. Bank and Branch Account Number of the Payee:
10. Signature Verification: ☐ Matching ☐ Not Matching. Dishonour Details:
11. Cheque Deposit Date: //
12. Return Memo Date: //
13. Bank Acknowledgment Date: //
14. Reason for Return (as per memo): ☐ 'Insufficient Funds' ☐ 'Account Closed' ☐ Other: . Identification and Contact Information:
15. Payee's Aadhaar/PAN: ☐ Attached ☐ Not Attached
16. Drawer's Aadhaar/PAN (if applicable): ☐ Attached ☐ Not Available
17. Payee's Address:
18. Address of the Drawer (as indicated on the cheque/records):
19. Payee's Email: Mobile:
20. Drawer's Email: WhatsApp: .

ADDITIONAL REMARKS:

In the event that the payee or drawer is a sole proprietorship, please ensure clarity and send the notice to both the drawer and the sole proprietorship in order to establish joint liability for future recovery and attachment. This includes any written or electronic communication exchanged between the parties, as well as any partial payments made by the drawer on the date specified as a part payment or linked to a particular account (please specify).

Dated: //

NOTE: It is essential to confirm reliable documentary and testimonial evidence from the client regarding their legitimate status as the holder and the validity of their claim, specifically concerning the cheque amount and excluding any additional amounts or interest. The cheque amount must not be higher than the outstanding or actual entitlement of the client; extra amounts or interest may be recovered by filing a civil summary suit.

DECLARATION & ENDORSEMENT:

'I, [Payee's Name], hereby declare that the information provided above is true and accurate to the best of my knowledge and is corroborated by the accompanying documents (including the cheque copy, return memo, etc.). I hereby instruct by my free consent to the issuance of a NOTICE under Section 138 of the NI Act based on this information.'

Signature:

Date: //

CHECKLIST OF MANDATORY DOCUMENTS

Checklist of mandatory documents required for filing a case under Sections 138/141 of the Negotiable Instruments Act

I. Core Documents for Filing Complaint

1. Complaint Petition

Typed on stamp paper (value as per state rules) or plain paper with court fee.

Must include:

Full particulars of the drawer (accused) and payee (complainant).

Exact date of cheque issuance, presentation, and dishonour.

Clear cause of action (non-payment despite statutory notice).

2. Original Cheque or Certified Copy

If the original is lost:

Affidavit explaining the loss (u/s 65B Evidence Act).

Secondary evidence (photocopy + bank certification).

3. Bank Dishonour Memo (Return Memo)

Must bear the bank's seal & authorized signatory's signature.

If electronic: S. 65B Evidence Act certificate from the bank.

4. Statutory Demand Notice (u/s 138(b) NI Act)
Copy of the notice sent to the drawer.
Proof of Delivery:
 Postal receipt (Aadhaar-enabled/registered post).
 Tracking report + delivery confirmation (UPI/email acknowledgment if sent digitally).
5. Postal Receipt & Tracking Report
Proof that the notice was dispatched within 30 days of dishonour.
6. Affidavit of Complainant
Sworn statement verifying:
 Cheque issuance for a legally enforceable debt.
 Details of dishonour and notice compliance.
7. Vakalatnama
If represented by an advocate.
II. Additional Documents for Cases u/s 141 (Company/Directors' Liability)
8. Board Resolution (if the cheque is issued by a company)
Authorizing signatory to issue cheques.
9. Memorandum of Association (MOA) & List of Directors
To establish accused directors' roles.
10. Proof of Directors' Involvement
 Emails/WhatsApp messages (with S. 65B certification).
 Minutes of meetings showing approval of the transaction.
III. Court Fee & Process Documents
11. Court Fee Payment Proof
 Challan receipt (online/offline payment as per state rates).
12. List of Witnesses & Documents
 Filed u/s 254 CrPC.
13. Power of Attorney (if the complainant is represented by an agent).
IV. Procedural Requirements (JMFC Specific)
NEW FORMAT AS PER DIRECTION OF S Court 25-09-25
- Copies for Accused: 2+ sets of all documents for summons.
- Index: Page-numbered bundle with a table of contents.
- Verification: The complaint must end with the "I solemnly affirm..." clause.
V. Supreme Court Mandates
1. Anvar P.V. v. P.K. Basheer (2014): Electronic evidence (bank memos, emails) requires S. 65B certification.
2. Dashrath Rathod (2014): Jurisdiction is the payee's bank branch

location.

3. Aneeta Hada (2012): For S. 141, the company must be arraigned as accused.

VI. Common Pitfalls & Solutions

Defect	Remedy
Unsigned dishonour memo	File bank manager's affidavit
Notice sent via ordinary post	Re-send via registered post + file delay condonation
Cheque copy unclear	Submit certified copy + affidavit

VII. Pro Tips

- Pre-Filing Audit: Use the [e-Courts Checklist Generator](https://ecourts.gov.in) to validate documents.
- Digital Backup: Scan all documents (password-protected PDFs).

Note: For state-specific variations (e.g., stamp duty, notary rules), consult the NI Act Practice Manual or seek assistance via WhatsApp (9082093332).

This checklist ensures compliance with JMFC procedural rules and minimizes dismissal risks. Always verify local court.

****

VAKALATNAMA FOR COMPLAINT'S SIDE

(Under Section 138/141 of the Negotiable Instruments Act, 1881)

IN THE COURT OF THE JUDICIAL MAGISTRATE FIRST CLASS (JMFC), [CITY/STATE]

Case Title: [Complainant Name] v. [Accused Name]

Complaint Case No.: [] of 202

I, [Complainant's Full Name], S/o, D/o, W/o [], aged [], residing at [Full Address], do hereby appoint and retain:

1. Advocate [Name], [CLC (R) Panel No.] / [Designated Advocate Name], enrolled with the Bar Council of [State], having an office at [Address], OR
2. The Legal Services Authority (Mumbai CLC Panel Advocate), to represent me in the above case.o represent me in the above case.

SPECIFIC POWERS CONFERRED:

1. General Authority:

To file, prosecute, and conduct the complaint case to its logical conclusion (trial, appeal, revision, execution).

To submit/amend pleadings, examine witnesses, and argue on my behalf.

2. ADR/Compounding Powers:

To initiate/participate in mediation/conciliation (ADR) through court or private forums.

To negotiate, settle, and compound the offense under Section 147 of the NI Act on mutually agreeable terms, including:

Accepting partial/full payment from the accused.

Withdrawing the complaint upon settlement.

To sign compounding applications and withdraw the case post settlement.

3. Financial Authority:

To receive and issue settlement amounts/cheques on my behalf (subject to final approval).

To execute settlement agreements and file satisfaction memos.

4. Miscellaneous:

To collect certified copies, file applications (e.g., for secondary evidence), and represent me before police/other forums if linked to this case.

DECLARATIONS:

I agree to be bound by the acts of my advocate(s) in this matter.

This Vakalatnama shall remain valid until express revocation in writing.

Date: [DD/MM/YYYY]

Place: [City]

Signature of Complainant:

Name: [Complainant's Name]

Contact: [Phone/Email]

17 CHAPTER NO. 17

NOTICE DRAFTS

1. GENERAL PRECAUTIONS
2. SAFEGUARDS AGAINST MISCONDUCT OR OVERSIGHT UNDER SECTION 138(B)
3. SIMPLE NOTICE FORMAT TO A COMPANY (M/S ABC PVT LTD)
4. NOTICE FOR DISHONOUR OF CHEQUE NO [XXX] FOR ₹[AMOUNT]
5. STANDARD NOTICE UNDER SECTION 138 OF THE NI ACT, 1881
6. STATUTORY NOTICE FROM A FINANCIAL INSTITUTION TO A BORROWER
7. NOTICE UNDER SECTION 138(B) FOR DISHONOUR OF CHEQUE NO
8. NOTICE FOR DISHONOUR OF CHEQUE ISSUED TOWARDS REPAYMENT OF FRIENDLY LOAN
9. NOTICE FOR DISHONOUR OF CHEQUE FOR UNPAID DIRECTOR'S FEES
10. NOTICE UNDER PSS ACT, 2007 FOR DISHONOUR OF ECS CHEQUES
11. Draft NOTICE From Flat Buyer To Builder For Dishonoured Buyback Cheque
12. NOTICE FOR DISHONOUR OF CHEQUE FOR OUTSTANDING DUES (VIA REGISTERED POST)
13. NOTICE For Dishonour Of Cheque No [Xxx] For ₹25,00,000/-.

GENERAL PRECAUTIONS FOR ACCUSED SIDE

NOTICE REPLY RELATED

When responding to a NOTICE under Section 138(b) of the Negotiable Instruments Act, 1881 (NI Act) for cheque dishonour, the recipient must take strategic precautions to avoid legal liability and strengthen their defense. Essential precautions based on judicial precedents and procedural requirements:

1. Verify Notice Compliance with Legal Requirements Check Validity of Notice Ensure the notice: Was sent within 30 days of cheque dishonour (as per proviso (b) to Section 138). Clearly specify the exact cheque amount (without including extraneous charges like legal fees unless justified). Mentions the correct reason for dishonour (e.g., 'insufficient funds' or 'signature mismatch'). Challenge Defects: If the notice demands an incorrect amount (e.g., ignores partial payments) or is timebarred, explicitly state this in your reply. In Dashrathbhai Trikambhai Patel v. Hitesh Mahendrabhai Patel (2022), the Supreme Court held that a notice demanding the full cheque amount despite partial repayment is invalid ('omnibus notice').

2. Address Legally Enforceable Debt: Dispute Liability: Deny the existence of a 'legally enforceable debt' if: The cheque was issued as security (not for immediate liability). The debt is timebarred or arose from an illegal transaction (e.g., gambling). Partial payment was made before cheque presentation (cite evidence like bank statements). Failure to endorse such payments on the cheque invalidates the notice. Avoid Admission: Do not acknowledge the debt unless legally advised. In Dilip Hariramani v. Bank of Baroda (2022), admissions in replies were used against the drawer.

3. Timely and Evidence Based Reply: 15Day Deadline: Reply within 15 days of receiving the notice to prevent the payee from filing a complaint. Proof of Service: Send the reply via: Registered Post AD (to create a rebuttable presumption of service). Email/WhatsApp (valid per Rajendra v. State of U.P. (2024)) with read receipts. Document Everything: Attach evidence (e.g., payment receipts, loan agreements) to counter the payee's claims.

4. Raise Specific Legal Defenses: In your reply, include: Signature Mismatch: Argue forgery if applicable and demand a handwriting expert examination (Lakshmi Dyechem v. State of Gujarat, 2012).

Account Closure: Cite Nepc Micon Ltd. v. Magma Leasing Ltd. (1999) to clarify that closure implies 'insufficient funds', but challenge if closure predated the cheque issue. Technical Dishonour: If the cheque bounced for nonfinancial reasons (e.g., overwriting), state that Section 138 is inapplicable.

5. Avoid Common Traps: Do Not Ignore: Even defective notices warrant a reply to prevent ex parte proceedings. No Vague Language: Use precise language (e.g., 'The notice is invalid as it ignores partial repayment of ₹4,09,315 made on [dates]'). Escalation Warning: State that frivolous complaints may lead to costs/defamation suits.

6. Structure Your Reply: Organize the reply as follows:

1. Introduction: Reference notice details (date, cheque number).

2. Factual Corrections: Dispute inaccuracies in the notice.

3. Legal Defenses: Cite noncompliance with Section 138(b) and case laws.

4. Consequence Warning: Demand withdrawal of the notice to avoid legal costs. Critical Precaution: Consult a lawyer immediately to: Draft a legally sound reply. Strategize for potential criminal proceedings. Ensure alignment with local High Court rulings (e.g., Punjab & Haryana High Court guidelines on moneylending debts). Key Insight: A welldrafted reply can deter litigation or secure acquittal by exposing flaws in the notice.

NOTICE: DRAFT

Under Section 138(b) Safeguards against Misconduct Or Oversight:

Critical Steps for Issuing a Statutory Demand Notice

(Payee to Drawer)

Objective: Ensure legal compliance, prevent procedural flaws, and create defensible evidence.

1. Trigger Event Confirmation:

Verify the cheque was dishonored (return memo from the bank stating "insufficient funds," "account closed," etc.).

Obtain the original cheque return memo from your bank immediately.

2. Strict Adherence to Timeline (Non Negotiable):

30Day Window: The notice must be sent within 30 calendar days from the date the payee receives the cheque return memo.

Calculate Precisely: Exclude the day of receiving the memo; count 30 days thereafter. Use a calendar tool to avoid miscalculation.

3. Drafting the Notice (Content Safeguards):

Cross Examination Mandatory Elements:

Full name & address of both Drawer (debtor) and Payee (creditor).

Specifics of the dishonored cheque (No., date, bank, branch, amount).

Explicit mention of dishonor (quote reason from memo).

Cross Examination Demand: Clearly state the demand for payment of the cheque amount.

15Day Ultimatum: Specify the drawer has 15 days from receipt to pay.

Cross Examination Consequence: State that failure to pay within 15 days will result in legal action under S. 138 NI Act.

Cross Examination Safeguards:

Cross Examination Accuracy: Crosscheck all details (names, addresses, cheque details, and amount) against original documents (cheque, agreement, memo).

Cross Examination Clarity: Use unambiguous language. Avoid threats beyond legal consequences.

Cross Examination Professional Tone: Maintain a formal, non abusive tone.

Cross Examination Attach Copy: Include a photocopy of the dishonored cheque and the bank return memo.

Legal Review: Highly recommended: Have a lawyer specializing in NI Act matters review the draft notice.

4. Dispatch & Delivery (Evidence Safeguards):

Cross Examination Authorized Modes Only (Crucial): Registered Post with Acknowledgement Due (RPAD): Primary & safest method.

Cross Examination Speed Post: An acceptable alternative under India Post.

Cross Examination Certificate of Posting (COP): Use only as a secondary precaution, never as the sole method. Notoriously weak evidence.

Cross Examination Safeguards: Simultaneous Dual Mailing: Send one notice via RPAD and another via Speed Post to the drawer's correct, known address (usually the address on the cheque or as per agreement). This mitigates risk if one service fails.

Cross Examination Accurate Addressing: Use the drawer's address meticulously as known. Avoid typos.

Cross Examination Post Office Protocol: Obtain dated postal receipts for RPAD/Speed Post/ immediately upon dispatch.

Cross Examination Preserve Originals: Safeguard all postal receipts.

Cross Examination Track Diligently: Track the RPAD/Speed Post consignment online daily.

Cross Examination Acknowledgement Due (RPAD): Ensure the AD card is returned. This is the best evidence of receipt.

Cross Examination Refusal Handling: If the notice is "refused" or "unclaimed," preserve the returned envelope unopened. This is deemed valid service by courts.

5. Post Dispatch Documentation & Preservation:

Cross Examination File Creation: Create a dedicated file for this specific cheque/default.

Cross Examination Store Securely: File originals/true copies of:

The signed statutory demand notice.

The dishonored cheque (copy).

The bank return memo.

All postal receipts (RPAD, Speed Post,

The returned RPAD Acknowledgement Due card (if received).

****

CHAPTER-04

SURETY BOND

A Surety Bond in the context of Sections 138/141 of the NI Act is not a mechanism to avoid trial or a substitute for conviction. Instead, it is primarily a tool related to the grant of bail and securing the presence of the accused during trial, often used at the anticipatory bail stage or after arrest.

Core Concept: Why Surety Bonds are Relevant

1. Nature of Offence: An offence under Section 138 is:

- Bail -able: The accused has a right to bail; it is not at the discretion of the court or police.
- Compoundable: The complaint can be permanently closed if the parties reach a settlement and the complainant agrees to withdraw the case.
- Non- cognizable: Police cannot arrest without a warrant.

2. The Risk: Despite being bail able, an accused can be arrested upon the issuance of a warrant by the court. To avoid arrest and jail time while the trial is ongoing, the accused seeks anticipatory or regular bail or May apply for recalling /Cancellation of Warrant even without personal attending court , discretion of court apply.

3. The Court's Concern: The court's primary concerns while granting bail are:

- Ensuring the accused's appearance during the trial and at the time of judgment.
- Preventing the accused from absconding.

Here is where the Surety Bond comes into play.

What is a Surety Bond?

A Surety Bond is a tripartite agreement involving:

1. The Court (Obligee): The entity requiring the bond.

2. The Accused (Principal Debtor): The person who is required to appear in court.

3. The Surety (Guarantor): A third party (often a friend or family member) who promises to the court that the accused will appear as required. The surety undertakes to pay a specified sum of money to the court if the accused fails to appear.

How it Works in 138 Cases

1. at the Anticipatory Bail Stage

When an accused apprehends arrest, they file for anticipatory bail. The court, while granting prearrest bail, imposes conditions. One standard condition is:

- "The applicant shall execute a personal bond and a surety bond for a sum of ₹X to the satisfaction of the trial court."

This means the accused must:

· Personal Bond: Promise to pay a certain amount themselves if they violate bail conditions.

- Surety Bond: Find another person (the surety) who is financially solvent and acceptable to the court, who will also promise to pay the court a specified amount if the accused absconds.

2. **After Arrest (Regular Bail)**

If arrested, the accused will be produced before a magistrate. The magistrate will grant bail on the condition of executing a personal bond and a surety bond for a specified amount.

Key Conditions Attached to the Bond

The court doesn't grant bail blindly. The execution of the bond comes with strict conditions, such as:

- The accused must appear before the court on every hearing date.
- The accused shall not tamper with evidence or influence witnesses.
- The accused shall not commit any similar offence during the bail period.

- The accused may be required to deposit a percentage of the cheque amount with the court (a common condition in NI Act cases).

Consequences for the Surety

The role of a surety is serious. If the accused absconds or jumps bail:

1. The court can issue a notice to the surety to produce the accused.

2. If the surety fails to produce the accused, the court can confiscate the amount guaranteed in the surety bond (known as forfeiture of the bond).

3. The court can initiate recovery proceedings against the surety for the forfeited amount, just like recovering a fine.

Distinction from Compounding and Settlement

It is critical to understand that a surety bond is not a settlement. It does not settle the underlying criminal complaint.

- Surety Bond: A guarantee for the accused's appearance. The criminal case continues.
- Settlement/Compounding: The complainant agrees to withdraw the case upon full payment (often with some interest/compensation). The case is permanently closed upon approval by the court.

Often, as a condition of bail, the court may ask the accused to deposit a part of the cheque amount with the court. This deposit is separate from the surety bond amount and can be used to settle the case later or returned based on the trial's outcome.

Status under Section 141 (Offences by Companies)

Section 141 makes every "person in charge of, and responsible for, the conduct of the business of the company" liable for the offence under Section 138.

- Director/Partner/Officer as Accused: When a director or partner is arrayed as an accused under Section 141, they can individually seek bail.
- Surety for Company Officials: The surety bond in such cases is

for the personal release of the official, not for the company's liability. The company itself, being a juristic person, cannot be arrested, but its officials can be.

- Stringent Conditions: Courts may be more stringent while granting bail to directors of companies, fearing a higher flight risk, and may demand higher surety amounts.

Summary

Aspect Explanation

Purpose To secure the release of an accused on bail and ensure their presence during trial in a cheque bounce case.

Legal Context A condition imposed by the court while granting bail (anticipatory or regular).

Key Function The surety acts as a guarantor to the court, promising a sum of money if the accused fails to appear.

Consequence If the accused absconds, the court can forfeit and recover the bond amount from the surety.

Not a Settlement It does not resolve the underlying criminal complaint under Section 138. The trial continues.

Relevance to S. 141 Applies to company officials accused in their personal capacity under this section.

In essence, a surety bond is a crucial judicial tool in the criminal process surrounding a cheque bounce case, acting as a safeguard for the court while upholding the accused's right to liberty during trial.

This is a critical procedural aspect of cases under Sections 138/141 of the Negotiable Instruments Act.

V- VAKALATNAMA

Vakalatnama Specifically Authorizing An Advocate To Plead "Not Guilty" and Vicariously LIABILITY defend your case under Sections 138/141 of the NI Act, while retaining all essential safeguards:

VAKALATNAMA WITH SPECIFIC POWER

"NOT GUILTY" PLEA AUTHORIZATION

IN THE COURT OF JMFC, [CITY/STATE]

Case Title: [X] v. [Your Name]

Case No.: [__] of 202

I, [Your Full Name], accused in the above case, hereby appoint [Advocate's Name] as my counsel with special emphasis on:

1. NOT GUILTY PLEA & DEFENSE STRATEGY

To enter a formal plea of "Not Guilty" on my behalf at the first hearing

To vigorously challenge all allegations through:

Technical Defenses:

Jurisdictional objections

Invalid statutory notice (u/s 138(b))

Cheque alterations (u/s 87 NI Act)

Substantive Defenses:

Rebutting presumption u/s 139 (no legally enforceable debt)

Proving the cheque was issued as security/without consideration

Establishing the complainant's unclean hands

2. EVIDENTIARY PROTECTION

To object to inadmissible evidence:

Uncertified electronic records (noncompliant with S.65B Evidence Act)

Improperly served notices

Hearsay testimony

To crossexamine the complainant/witnesses on:

Debt validity

Cheque handling chain

Notice delivery

3. LIMITED SETTLEMENT POWERS

Any settlement/compounding requires my prior written consent

May explore ADR only after consulting me

4. TRIAL MANAGEMENT

To seek exemption from personal appearance (where permissible)

To demand strict proof of all allegations

Special Instruction: My advocate SHALL NOT make any admission of liability without my express written authorization.

[Rest of the Vakalatnama remains unchanged regarding signatures, declarations, etc.]

Why This Matters?

1. Preserves Your Defense: Prevents inadvertent admissions by counsel

2. Strategic Focus: Targets both technical and substantive weaknesses in the complainant's case

3. Control Retained: Ensures you decide on settlements

CHECKLIST FOR FINANCIAL LOAN

Cheque Dishonour Cases Under Sections 138/141 Of The NI Act, Covering All Borrower Types (Individuals, Sole Proprietorships, And Companies):

FINANCIAL LOAN CHEQUE DISHONOUR PRE-NOTICE CHECKLIST

(For Complaints under Sections 138/141, NI Act)

I. ESSENTIAL ELEMENTS TO PROVE

1. Legally Enforceable Debt

Loan agreement with repayment terms

Sanction letter/disbursement proof

Acknowledgment of debt (promissory note, ledger confirmation)

2. Valid Cheque Issuance

Cheque signed by authorized person

For companies: Issued for the company's benefit (not personal debt)

3. Proper Dishonour

Return memo states "insufficient funds" or "account closed"

No material alterations on the cheque

4. Timely Action

Notice sent within 30 days of dishonour

Complaint filed within 30 days after the 15-day notice period

II. DOCUMENTARY REQUIREMENTS

| Category| Individual Borrower | Sole Proprietorship | Company Borrower|| Loan Documents Loan agreement Disbursement proof (bank transfer) Payment demand notices | same as individual + Business license/GST | same as individual + Board resolution authorizing loan MCA records |

| Cheque Records| Original cheque/copy Return memo Deposit slip | same as individual | Same as individual + List of authorized signatories |

| Borrower ID Proof | PAN/Aadhaar Address proof | Proprietor's PAN Shop Act license | CIN PAN Director's KYC |

| NOTICE | Draft notice Postal/email delivery proof | Same as individual | Must name the company AND directors |

III. SPECIAL CONSIDERATIONS FOR SECTION 141 (COMPANIES)

1. Director Liability

Cheque must be issued for the company's business

Directors must be actively involved in day-to-day operations

2. Defences Available

Director was not in charge of financial affairs

Cheque issued without company authorization

IV. CRITICAL ACTION POINTS

1. Pre-Notice Verification

Confirm cheque was issued towards loan repayment (not as security)

Verify borrower's current address for notice delivery

2. Notice Contents

Loan account number & outstanding

Cheque details & dishonour date

Clear 15-day payment demand

Warning of prosecution under S.138/141

3. Post-Notice Steps

Track payment for partial settlements

Prepare complaint with an affidavit of documents

V. COMMON PITFALLS TO AVOID

- Missing 30-day notice deadline
- Failing to mention the company name as Accused No.1 and all directors in company cases having vicarious liability
- Not preserving the original cheque/dishonour memo
- Claiming incorrect amounts (stick to cheque value)

VI. PENALTIES & RECOVERY

Criminal Case: Up to 2 years jail + 2x cheque amount fine

Civil Suit: For principal + interest (if cheque covers partial amount)

Director Liability: Personal assets may be attached for company cheques

Pro Tip: For company borrowers, attach:

- Latest MCA 21 form (list of directors)

- Board resolution authorizing loan
- Bank mandate for signatories

Bombay High Court

****

CHAPTER-05

Conversations Between Client And Advocate

1. **Advocate Client Consultation.**
2. **Between A Law Firm (Advocate) And A Client (Actor/Director).**
3. **Consultation: Director Vs. Production House.**
4. **A Banking Official And An Advocate Regarding Dishonored ECS**
5. **Conversation between CA and Advocate.**
6. **A multispecialty hospital lodged a complaint against Y.**
7. **Between the Flat Owner (Defaulter), AND ADVOCATE**

CONVERSATION FORM

Conversations before Issuance of Statutory Notice and Subsequently to File Complaint/138/141 NI Act.

Introduction:

Key Principles for Section 138/141 NI Act Complaints

Before the conversations, remember the strict sequence (Cause of Action Chain) for a Section 138 case:

1. Cheque Issued (for a legally enforceable debt/liability).

2. Cheque Presented to the bank within 3 months of issue or validity period.

3. Cheque Dishonoured (Returned unpaid by the bank).

4. Demand Notice issued to the drawer within 30 days of dishonour, demanding payment.

5. Drawer fails to pay the amount within 15 days of receiving the

notice.

6. Complaint Filed within 30 days of the expiry of the above 15-day period.

All conversations must help gather facts that satisfy this chain.

Templates for Advocate-Client Interaction

Template 1: Advocate-Client Consultation Prior to Sending Demand Notice (S. 138(b)

Participants: Mr./Ms. [Advocate Name] (Advocate) & Mr./Ms. [Client Name] (Client) Matter:Dishonour of Cheque(s) issued by [Name of Drawer]

Advocate: "Thank you for coming in, Mr./Ms. [Client Name]. I understand a cheque issued to you has been dishonoured. To proceed with a legal demand notice, I need to ask you some specific questions. Please have your documents ready."

Client: "Yes, I have everything here."

Advocate: "Perfect. Let's begin:

1. The Parties: What is the full name and complete address of the person/company who gave you the cheque?"

2. The Liability: What was this cheque for? Please describe the underlying transaction (e.g., loan repayment, fee for services, goods supplied, etc.). Do you have a contract, invoice, or agreement supporting this?"

3. The Instrument: Do you have the original dishonoured cheque? May I see it? What was the date on the cheque? What was the amount?"

4. Presentation & Dishonour: When did you deposit or present the cheque to your bank? (Client provides date). When did you receive the dishonour memo from your bank? (Client provides date). What was the reason for dishonour mentioned on the memo? ('Insufficient Funds' is crucial)."

5. Current Status: Have you contacted the drawer after the dishonour? Have they made any promises or part payments?"

6. Entity Cheque: If the drawer is a company, what is your role in it?

Are you a director? Shareholder? Or are you an external party?"

Client: "The cheque was from [Drawer's Name] for [Purpose, e.g., outstanding consultancy fees]. The date was [Date], and it was for ₹[Amount]. I presented it on [Presentation Date] and got the memo back on [Dishonour Date] stating 'Insufficient Funds'. I am not related to the company; I am an external vendor."

Advocate: "Based on this, the 30-day period to send the demand notice started on [Dishonour Date]. We must act quickly. I will draft a statutory demand notice under Section 138 of the NI Act. We will send it via registered AD post and courier to their official address. They will have 15 days from receipt to pay. If they fail, we can file a criminal complaint."

Template 2: Conversation Format - Law Firm (Advocate) & Client (Actor/Director)

Participants: [Senior Advocate] (Law Firm) & [Mr. ABC] (Film Director/Producer) Matter: Dishonour of Cheque from Production House against Acting Services.

Client (Mr. ABC): "My production house, [Production House Name], issued a cheque to [Actor Name] for his last film. It has bounced. The bank says 'Account Closed'. The actor is now threatening legal action."

Advocate: "I see. We need to strategize. First, confirm: was the cheque issued from the company's account or your personal account?"

Client: "It was from the company's account. I am the managing director."

Advocate: "Under Section 141 of the NI Act, every director in charge of the company's conduct at the time of the offence can be held liable. Were you actively involved in the day-to-day operations?"

Client: "Yes, completely."

Advocate: "We need to assess the defence. Was the cheque issued as an advance? Was there a breach of contract by the actor? Do you have a clause in the agreement about payments being subject to the film's completion?"

Client: "The cheque was for the final payment. The actor has completed all his work. We are facing a cash flow crisis."

Advocate: "A 'cash flow crisis' is not a legal defence to a S. 138 complaint. Our best course is to settle before a notice is sent or immediately upon receipt. If a complaint is filed, we will have to plead for compounding under Section 147 at the earliest stage to avoid a criminal record. I advise you to negotiate a settlement and issue a new cheque from a functional account immediately."

Template 3: Consultation - Director (Client) vs. Production House (Accused)

Participants: Advocate & Director (Client who received the cheque) Matter:Seeking recovery of dues from a production house.

Director (Client): "I directed a web series for [Production House Pvt. Ltd.]. My final payment cheque of ₹[Amount] has bounced. The reason is 'Payment Stopped by Drawer'."

Advocate: "'Payment Stopped' is a clear dishonour and falls under S. 138. This is a deliberate act. Do you have the agreement and the delivery acceptance email proving you fulfilled your obligations?"

Client: "Yes, I have both. I also have emails where they acknowledge the debt but ask for more time."

Advocate: "Excellent. Those emails are crucial evidence. We will send a strong demand notice. Since it's a company, we will send it to the company's registered office and to every director as per the MCA records. This will personalise the liability and force them to respond. Given their conduct, we should also immediately apply for attachment of their bank accounts after filing the complaint to pressure them for a quick settlement."

Templates for Professional Consultations

Template 4: Banking Official & Advocate regarding dishonoured ECS

Participants: [Mr. Sharma] (Bank Manager) & [Advocate Mehta] Matter:Recurring ECS Mandate dishonoured for a client.

Bank Manager: "Advocate Mehta, our client, [Lender Name], has an ECS mandate from [Borrower Name] for their loan EMI. The last two ECS presentations have failed due to 'Exceeds Arrangement'."

Advocate Mehta: "Thank you for informing me. An ECS dishonour is treated similarly to a cheque dishonour under the NI Act. Please ensure you send the official ECS return memo to our client immediately. This memo is equivalent to the cheque return memo. Our client will then need to issue a demand notice within 30 days of receiving that memo from you."

Bank Manager: "Understood. We will dispatch the memo today. Should we attempt the presentation again?"

Advocate Mehta: "You may, but from a legal standpoint, the cause of action has already accrued on the first dishonour. Please provide a statement of account reflecting the failed transactions as well."

Template 5: Conversation between a CA and an Advocate

Participants: [CA Ananya] (Chartered Accountant) & [Advocate Roy] Matter:Financial analysis of a company that issued bounced cheques.

CA Ananya: "Advocate Roy, as per your request, I've analysed the financials of [Accused Company]. Their net worth is negative, and the bank account from which the cheque was issued has been inactive for months."

Advocate Roy: "This is helpful. Does it appear to be a case of intentional cheating, or just insolvency?"

CA Ananya: "The directors have siphoned off funds through related party transactions. Look at these ledger entries. The insolvency is likely fraudulent. I can prepare a report tracing the funds to show that the debt was legally enforceable and the dishonour was wilful."

Advocate Roy: "Please do. This forensic report will be vital for opposing any bail application and to show the court that this is not a simple case of business failure but one of fraud."

Template 6: Multispecialty Hospital vs. Supplier/Patient

Participants: [Hospital Administrator] & [Advocate] Matter:Bounced cheque from a medical equipment supplier.

Hospital Admin: "We purchased equipment from [Supplier Pvt. Ltd.] and issued a post-dated cheque. They delivered faulty equipment. We stopped the cheque and now they are threatening us with a 138 case!"

Advocate: "A 'stop payment' instruction is a dishonour. However, a legally enforceable debt is a prerequisite. If you can prove the equipment was faulty and not as per the agreed specifications, the debt is disputed and may not be 'legally enforceable'. We have a defence."

Hospital Admin: "We have inspection reports from two independent engineers."

Advocate: "Perfect. If they send a demand notice, we will send a detailed reply refuting the liability and enclosing those reports. If they still file a complaint, we will use this to seek acquittal. Do not ignore their notice; a cogent reply is essential."

Template 7: Flat Owner (Defaulter), Housing Society Executive & Society's Advocate

Participants: Mr. Kapoor (Defaulter Owner), Ms. Desai (Society Secretary), Mr. Iyer (Society's Advocate) Matter:Recovery of outstanding maintenance via dishonoured cheque.

Ms. Desai (Secretary): "Mr. Kapoor, your cheque for maintenance dues has bounced. This is the second time."

Mr. Kapoor (Owner): "I know, I'm facing financial difficulties. The society can't file a criminal case for this!"

Mr. Iyer (Advocate): "Mr. Kapoor, I must correct you. Maintenance dues are a legally enforceable debt as per the Society bylaws and the Ownership Act. The dishonoured cheque creates a criminal liability under S. 138. The society is within its rights to file a complaint."

Mr. Kapoor: "What are my options?"

Mr. Iyer: "You have 15 days from receiving our NOTICE to pay the entire outstanding amount along with the bank charges and our legal fees. If you do that, the matter ends. If you cannot pay the lump sum, propose a written settlement with post-dated cheques from a confirmed account. If you do nothing, we will be compelled to file a criminal case, and the court can impose a fine double the cheque amount and even a prison sentence."

Ms. Desai: "We prefer to avoid litigation. Please give us a written proposal for settlement within a week."

CONVERATION FORM BUNCH

Conversation Form No.1

ADVOCATE-CLIENT CONSULTATION

2. Advocate Client Consultation Prior to Section 138(b) NI Act Demand Notice

Please adjust the following points based on your client's specific circumstances:

1. Documentary Evidence:

Provide written agreements or MOUs related to the transaction.

Include relevant communications (emails, WhatsApp) about the debt and cheque.

Submit the original dishonoured cheque and bank return memo.

2. Payment History:

Record any partial payments made by the debtor.

Confirm acknowledgment of the outstanding balance by the debtor.

3. Acknowledgment or Denial of Debt:

Present documentation of any formal denial of payment by the debtor.

Is there a written acknowledgment of the debt?

4. Evidence of Dues:

Along with the cheque, submit invoices or statements verifying the debt.

Ensure compliance with Section 63 of the Bharatiya Sakshya Adhiniyam concerning electronic documents.

III. Corporate Liability (If Applicable)

5. Section 141 NI Act (Corporate Entities):

Verify if the issuer is a Company, LLP, or Firm.

Identify the individual responsible for the cheque.

List any directors or officers involved in the dishonour and their roles.

Attach the company's incorporation documents if available.

IV. Strategic Considerations

6. Settlement Options:

Consider negotiating a settlement prior to issuing notice to reduce costs and duration.

7. Fee Structure and Costs:

Our Fees: Drafting and sending the notice costs [₹X]. In the event of litigation, fees will be [₹Y] per hearing or a total of [₹Z], with an initial retainer of [₹A].

Additional Costs: Include court fees and related expenses until resolution.

8. Time Frame:

Expect a minimum of 2 to 4 years for a final court ruling if ADR efforts are unsuccessful.

9. Be prepared to file a case within 45 days if there is no response or compliance with the notice.

Conversation Form No 2

LAW FIRM AND CLIENT (ACTOR/DIRECTOR) CONSULTATION

Conversation Format No. Between A Law Firm (Advocate) And A Client (Actor/Director) to collect critical facts before issuing a NOTICE under Sections 138 & 141 of the Negotiable Instruments Act.

I. Core Cheque Details

1. A: When was the cheque issued? (Date) C: [Date]

2. A: Exact amount? (₹) C: ₹[Amount]

3. A: Cheque number & issuing bank? C: No. [XXXX], [Bank Name, Branch]

4. A: Whose name is printed on the cheque? (Production house name) C: [Full Name of Production House] II. Dishonor Evidence

5. A: When did your bank notify you of dishonor? (Date) C: [Date]

6. A: Reason for return? (e.g., 'Insufficient Funds,' 'Account Closed') C: 'Insufficient Funds' (as per bank memo)

7. A: Do you have the original cheque and bank return memo? C: Yes, here they are. (Hands over documents) III. Underlying Transaction

8. A: What was this cheque for? (Fee/contractual payment?) C: My acting/directing fee for the project '[Project Name].'

9. A: Is there a written agreement/invoice? C: Yes, here's the contract/email trail confirming the amount. IV. Debtor Entity & Signatory

10. A: Full address of the production house? (Registered office) C: [Full Address]

11. A: Who signed the cheque? C: [Name], Designation: [e.g., 'Managing Director']

12. A: Is the signatory a director/partner? (Crucial for Section 141 liability) C: Yes, as per their website/MCA records. V. Post Dishonor Actions

13. A: Did you demand repayment after dishonor? (Verbally/written?) C: Yes, I sent an email on [Date] – no response.

14. A: Any partial payments/promises to pay? C: None. VI. Corporate Structure (Section 141)

15. A: Is the production house a Pvt Ltd/LLP/Partnership? C: Pvt Ltd Company.

16. A: Names of all directors/partners? (For notice liability) C: [Names] – I can share their website/MCA extract. VII. Critical Compliance Check

17. A: Today is [Current Date]. Your bank notified you on [Dishonor Date]. We have 30 days from that date to issue notice. We're within

the limit.

C: Understood. A: Based on this, we'll draft a notice: Demand ₹[Amount] within 15 days of receipt. Cite Sections 138 (dishonor) + 141 (director liability). Send to BOTH the company AND every director. C: What next if they ignore? A: We file a criminal complaint within 30 days after their 15day window ends. Directors can face jail (up to 2 years) + double cheque fine. Fact Summary Checklist for Notice Drafting | Item | Client's Input | | | | Cheque Date | [Date] | | Cheque Amount (₹) | ₹[Amount] | | Cheque No. & Bank | [No.], [Bank] | | Debtor (Company Name) | [Production House Name] | | Signatory (Name/Designation) | [Name], [Designation] | | Directors/Partners | [List Names] | | Registered Address | [Full Address] | | Dishonor Date | [Date] | | Dishonor Reason | 'Insufficient'

Conversation Form.3

Consultation: Director vs. Production House

Participants:

1. Mr. X (Director)

2. Adv. Y (Entertainment Law Specialist)

Setting: Advocate's Office / Virtual Consultation

1. Opening: Director Explains the Situation

Mr. X: "Advocate, I directed a film titled '[Movie Name]' for [Production House]. My contract stipulated a fee of ₹1.2 crore, payable in 3 instalments. They issued a cheque for the final ₹40 lakh, but it bounced due to 'insufficient funds'. I've emailed them thrice, but they're avoiding me. What can I do?"

Adv. Y: "Mr. X, let's methodically assess your case. First, confirm:

Do you have the original bounced cheque and the bank return memo?

Is there a written contract specifying payment terms?

Did you issue any formal payment reminder before this meeting?"

2. Document Verification & Legal Grounds

Mr. X: "Yes, I have:

1. The dishonoured cheque (No. 456, dated 15/03/2024, drawn on XYZ Bank).

2. Bank memo stating 'insufficient funds' (dated 20/03/2024).

3. Signed contract (Clause 7 mentions instalments).

4. Email reminders (attached)."

Adv. Menon: "Good. This is a clear case under Section 138 of the NI Act. However, before sending a legal notice, let's explore:

Option 1: A stern lawyer's letter demanding payment within 7 days (nonlegal notice).

Option 2: A statutory Section 138 notice – triggers criminal liability if unpaid in 15 days.

Which approach aligns with your goal – quick recovery or legal deterrence?"

3. Strategy Discussion

Mr. Kapoor: "I want my money, but I also want to set an example. The producer has a history of cheating artists. However, if they pay promptly, I'll avoid court."

Adv. Menon: "Understood. Here's the plan:

1. Step 1: We'll issue a hybrid notice – a stern letter (nonstatutory) giving 7 days to pay, mentioning our intent to file under Section 138. Often, this speeds up settlement.

2. Step 2: If they ignore it, we escalate to a formal 138 notice (attaching all proofs).

3. Step 3: Simultaneously, we'll draft a complaint for JMFC Court to file immediately after notice expiry."

4. Cost & Timeline Clarity

Mr. Kapoor: "How long will this take? And what are your fees?"

Adv. Menon: "Timeline:

Settlement: 2–4 weeks (if they respond to the hybrid notice).

Court case: 8–18 months (but we'll seek interim attachment of their assets).

Fees:

Notice drafting: ₹5,000–10,000.

Court case: ₹25,000 (lump sum) + 10% of recovered amount.

We'll also add 18% interest and litigation costs to your claim."

5. Director's Authorization & Next Steps

Adv. Menon: "To proceed, I need:

1. Your signed vakalatnama (to represent you).

2. Original documents for notarization.

3. A brief affidavit of facts.

Shall I draft the hybrid notice today?"

Mr. Kapoor: "Yes, please proceed. I'll also share the producer's other contact details – they've changed offices to avoid notices."

Adv. Menon: "Noted. We'll serve notices to all known addresses and publish in a newspaper if needed. Rest assured."

Key Takeaways from the Conversation:

1. Documents Reviewed: Contract, cheque, bank memo, communication trail.

2. Options Offered: Negotiation (hybrid notice) vs. legal action (Section 138).

3. Strategy: Graded escalation to maximize recovery chances.

4. Transparency: Clear timelines, fees, and risks explained.

Next Steps Template:

Draft hybrid notice → Send via email/registered post → Wait 7 days → Escalate to Section 138 notice if unpaid.

Question and Proposition: With regard to one cheque, whether it was lost, misplaced, or lost along with a bank return memo, legal notice, etc., if it was misplaced by the holder (payee), what practical advice can you provide? Before proceeding with the answer or advising on appropriate steps, please specify at which stage and in which scenario the cheque in question was misplaced or lost:

1. The cheque was originally misplaced by an individual who is the payee before presentation to the bank.

2. The cheque was misplaced from the corporate office before its

presentation.

3. The cheque and bank return memo were lost before issuing a notice.

4. The cheque, memo, and notice copy were lost before filing the case.

5. The cheque return memo, notice, dispatch postal receipt, and postal tracking report in the original were lost before the court took cognizance, meaning before verification and issuance of process.

6. All originals were misplaced before filing the affidavit of evidence and tendering the originals in court, meaning before marking exhibits.

7. Lost in any other way.

Conversation Form 4 BANKING OFFICIAL AND ADVOCATE REGARDING DISHONORED ECS

Conversation Format Between A Banking Official And An Advocate Regarding Dishonored ECS (Electronic Clearing Service) cheques issued as security (PDCs) under the Payment and Settlement Systems Act, 2007:

Conversation: Banking Official (Mr. Sharma) & Advocate (MS Desai)

Subject: Legal Action for Dishonored ECS Cheques (Security PDCs)

Mode: Phone Call / Office Meeting

Date: [DD/MM/YYYY]

1. Initial Context (Banking Official)

Mr. Sharma (Bank Manager):

"Advocate, we have a corporate client, 'XYZ Ltd', who issued 12 ECS cheques as Security PDCs against a credit facility. These were to cover future EMIs, but 3 cheques were dishonored due to 'insufficient funds'. The loan agreement clearly mentions these PDCs are for 'prospective liability'. What's our legal recourse under the Payment and Settlement Act?"

2. Advocate's Clarification

Adv. Desai:

"Mr. Sharma, let's break this down:

1. Nature of Cheques: Were these ECS mandates explicitly labeled as 'Security PDCs' in the loan arrangement?

2. Dishonor Reason: Confirm if the bounce memos cite 'Insufficient Funds' or 'Account Closed'.

3. Agreement Clause: Does the contract state that PDC dishonor constitutes a default event?"

Mr Sharma:

"Yes, the agreement's Clause 8 specifies PDCs as security for future EMIs. The bounce memos show 'Insufficient Funds'. We've already issued a recall notice but want to escalate legally."

3. Legal Strategy Discussion

Adv. Desai:

"Here's the actionable plan:

Step 1: Immediate Notice

Issue a demand notice under Section 25 of the Payment and Settlement Act, 2007 (for ECS dishonor) + Section 138 NI Act (since cheques are involved).

Highlight that PDCs were for 'discharge of liability' as per ICICI Bank v. Prakash Kaur (2007).

Step 2: Dual Action

Civil Suit: File for summary judgment under Order XXXVII CPC to recover the amount.

Criminal Complaint: Under Section 138 NI Act against the company and its directors.

Step 3: RBI Complaint

Notify the RBI's Banking Ombudsman for ECS mandate violation under RBI Circular No. DPSS.CO.CHD.No.1832/04.07.05/2018 19."

4. Banking Official's Queries

Mr. Sharma:

"Can we invoke SARFAESI Act simultaneously? The loan is secured by property."

Adv. Desai:

"Absolutely. Since PDC dishonor is a default event:

1. SARFAESI Action: Issue a Section 13(2) notice to take possession of collateral.

2. Parallel Proceedings: NI Act complaint won't affect SARFAESI proceedings (M.D. Frozen Foods v. Axis Bank, 2016)."

5. Documentation & Timeline

Adv. Desai:

"To proceed, I'll need:

1. Original loan agreement + PDC copies.

2. ECS dishonor memos from NPCI.

3. Board resolution authorizing legal action.

Timeline:

Notice can be sent within 30 days of dishonor.

Complaint must be filed within 1 month after notice expiry."

Mr. Sharma:

"We'll share the documents today. Draft the notice with a 15day payment window."

Key Legal Points Covered

1. ECS Cheques as PDCs:

Treated as 'security' but still attract Section 138 NI Act liability if dishonored (Sampelly Satyanarayana Rao v. Indian Renewable Energy, 2016).

2. Payment and Settlement Act:

Section 25: Penalizes unauthorized debit/ECS dishonor with fines up to ₹1 lakh per instance.

3. Dual Remedies:

Criminal action (NI Act) + Civil recovery (SARFAESI/Order XXXVII CPC).

4. RBI Compliance:

Mandatory reporting of ECS defaults to RBI under DPSS Circulars.

Next Steps Template

1. Draft Notice: Combine Section 138 NI Act + Section 25 Payment Act demands.

2. File Complaint: Before JMFC Court + Debt Recovery Tribunal (if SARFAESI invoked).

3. RBI Reporting: Submit ECS default details via the RBI's Complaint Management System.

Conversation Form 5 CONVERSATION BETWEEN CA AND ADVOCATE

Conversation between CA and Advocate: The Chartered Accountant A, whose cheque for twentyfive lakhs was returned unpaid, issued it against the rendering of professional services for the entire financial year to Company X. A conversation is needed between the CA, who is a client, and an esteemed advocate firm during this dialogue. CA (Client) and an Advocate from a reputed law firm regarding the dishonored cheque of ₹25 lakhs issued for professional services rendered to Company X. The conversation covers legal options, procedural steps, and strategic advice under the Negotiable Instruments Act, 1881: Dialogue: CA (Client) vs. Advocate Setting: Advocate's Office | Virtual Consultation

1. Initial Explanation by the CA (Client): CA: "Good morning. I'm a Chartered Accountant, and I provided yearlong financial advisory services to Company X. They issued a cheque for ₹25 lakhs as payment, but it was dishonored due to 'insufficient funds.' I've already sent a legal demand notice under Section 138 of the NI Act, but they haven't responded. What are my options now?"

2. Advocate's Clarification Questions: Advocate: "Thank you for the details. To proceed, I need to confirm a few points:

1. Do you have the original cheque, bank return memo (with dishonor reason), and proof of service of the demand notice (postal receipts/Aadharlinked tracking)?

2. Was the cheque issued for a legally enforceable debt? (i.e., Is there a contract/invoice for your services?) 3. Did you issue the demand notice within 30 days of dishonor?" CA: "Yes, I have all documents—the cheque, bank memo, and postal receipts. The services were under a signed contract (attached here). The notice was sent within 25 days of dishonor."

3. Advocate's Legal Strategy Breakdown: Advocate: "Understood. Here's the roadmap:

Step 1: File a Complaint – We'll draft a criminal complaint under Section 138 NI Act before the JMFC Court within 1 month of your notice expiry. Penalty: Up to 2 years imprisonment or a fine of twice the cheque amount.

Step 2: Parallel Recovery – We can initiate a summary suit under Order XXXVII CPC for speedy recovery without a lengthy trial.

Step 3: Negotiation Leverage – The legal threat often pushes defaulters to settle. Would you consider a onetime settlement if Company X offers?"

4. CA's Concerns & Advocate's Reassurance: CA: "How long will the case take? And what if Company X disputes the liability?" Advocate: "Timeline: Typically 6–18 months for resolution. However: Evidence Strength: Your contract, invoices, and bank memo make this a strong case. Dispute Handling: If they claim 'service deficiency,' we'll counter with your service delivery proofs (emails, approvals). Interim Relief: We can also seek attachment of Company X's assets during the case."

5. Fee Structure & Next Steps: Advocate: "Our fee for the 138 complaint is(depending on court location). For the recovery suit, it's 8–10% of the recovered amount. We'll need: 1. Your authorization letter. 2. Original documents for filing. Shall we proceed?" CA: "Agreed. Let's file the complaint immediately and explore settlement talks in parallel."

Key Legal Points Highlighted:

1. Documentation is Critical: Cheque + Return Memo + Demand

Notice + Contract = Strong Prima Facie Case.

2. Dual Strategy: Criminal prosecution (Section 138) + Civil recovery (Order XXXVII CPC).

3. Settlement Window: Negotiation can be pursued even after filing the complaint. Suggested Next Steps: Draft the complaint, file in the jurisdictional court (where the cheque was issued/presented). Let me know if you'd like to refine any part of this dialogue or need help with drafting the actual complaint.

Conversation Form No.6 MULTISPECIALTY HOSPITAL V/S PATIENT

A multispecialty hospital lodged a complaint against Y, the patient's father, following discharge and a cheque issuance for outstanding payments related to services, equipment, and medicine, which later bounced. A senior attorney reviewed the details and discussions before proceeding with the legal demand notice.

A multispecialty hospital lodged a complaint against Y, the patient's father, following discharge and a cheque issuance for outstanding payments related to services, equipment, and medicine, which later bounced.

Conversation Form 7 FLAT OWNER (DEFAULTER), HOUSING SOCIETY EXECUTIVE, AND SOCIETY'S ADVOCATE

between the Flat Owner (Defaulter), Housing Society Executive, Society's Advocate, and Society Matters Expert to address potential cheque dishonor and legal action:

1. Initial Notice from Society to Flat Owner (Official Letter/Email)

Subject: Urgent: Clear Outstanding Dues of ₹[Amount] to Avoid Legal Action

Content:

"Dear [Owner's Name],

Outstanding: Maintenance (₹) + Fines (₹) + Interest (₹) = Total ₹[X] as of [Date].

Cheque No. for ₹[X] (issued on) is likely to bounce due to insufficient clearance.

Immediate Options:

1. Clear dues in full by [Date] via NEFT/DD (Account: [Society's Bank Details]).

2. Submit a written settlement proposal to the Managing Committee.

Consequences of Non Payment:

NOTICE u/s 138 NI Act + complaint to Registrar Cooperative Societies.

Restriction on property transactions (if applicable under state laws).

Contact: [Secretary/Manager] at [Phone] or visit society office by [Date]."

2. Flat Owner's Discussion with Society Executive

Key Points to Address:

Clarify Dues:

"Can I get a detailed breakdown of fines and maintenance arrears?"

"Is there flexibility to waive penalties or pay in instalments?"

Negotiation:

"I propose to pay ₹[X] now and clear the balance by [Date]."

"Can the society accept a post dated cheque for the remaining amount?"

Warning:

Executive: "If the issued cheque bounces, we must initiate legal action per society bylaws."

3. Society's Internal Discussion (Executive + Advocate + Expert)

Checklist:

1. Verify Legal Standing:

Advocate: "Confirm if the byelaws allow recovery via 138 NI Act for maintenance dues."

Expert: "Check state cooperative society rules for additional remedies (e.g., lien on property)."

2. Documentation Review:

Ensure demand letters, meeting minutes, and cheque issuance proof are recorded.

3. Next Steps:

If dues are unpaid, issue a 15day NOTICE u/s 138 NI Act (via advocate).

File a complaint with the Registrar of Cooperative Societies simultaneously.

4. Advocate's Direct Communication with Flat Owner

Formal Notice/Phone Call:

"This is to inform you that the cheque issued for society dues was returned unpaid.

You have 15 days from [Date] to pay ₹[X] or face:

JMFC complaint (criminal case).

Attachment of property (if state laws permit).

Submit your reply in writing to avoid escalation."

5. Flat Owner's Last Chance Response

Suggested Reply (If Seeking Time):

"I acknowledge the dues and request 3 months to pay in instalments ([Proposed Plan]).

I will provide post-dated cheques as security.

Kindly confirm if the society accepts this to avoid legal action."

Critical Documents to Exchange

| Party | Documents to Provide

| Society |

1. Dues breakdown

2. Cheque return memo

3. Copy of byelaws (highlighting recovery clauses)

| Flat Owner

1. Payment proposal

2. Proof of financial hardship (if any)

3. Alternate security (if offering)

Key Legal Considerations

1. For Society:

Ensure bylaws authorize cheque payments for dues (to qualify u/s 138 NI Act).

Maharashtra Societies Act: Allows property attachment for dues (Section 101).

2. For Owner:

Negotiate before cheque bounce to avoid criminal liability.

Seek expert help if dues are disputed.

Next Steps if Deadlock Continues:

Society files JMFC complaint + Registrar complaint.

Owner may explore mediation through cooperative authorities.

Would you like templates for:

1. Settlement agreement?

2. NOTICE u/s 138?

3. Complaint to Registrar?

(This structured approach balances legal compliance with negotiation scope.

****

CHAPTER-06

Notice

NOTICE FOR DISHONOUR OF CHEQUE NO [XXX] FOR ₹[AMOUNT]

NOTICE NUMBER.4

Addressed To A Real Estate Development Company For A Bounced Cheque Issued As Part Of A Buyback Agreement:

[On Advocate's Letterhead] Date

To,

The Director,

[Developer Company Name],

[Registered Office Address].

SUBJECT: NOTICE UNDER SECTION 138 OF THE NEGOTIABLE INSTRUMENTS ACT, 1881 FOR DISHONOUR OF CHEQUE NO. [XXX] FOR ₹[AMOUNT]

Dear Sir/Madam,

1. Introduction:

I act as the duly appointed advocate for my client, Mr./Ms. [Complainant's Name], residing at [Address] ("Complainant"), and address you on their behalf.

2. Background:

On [Booking Date], the Complainant booked [Flat/Plot No.] in your project "[Project Name]" under a Booking Agreement.

Due to [reason: delay/failure to deliver/other breach], a Buyback Agreement was executed on [Cancellation Date], whereby your company agreed to refund ₹[Amount] and issued:

Cheque No. [XXX], dated [Cheque Date], for ₹[Amount], drawn on [Bank Name, Branch].

3. Dishonour of Cheque:

The cheque was presented for encashment on [Presentation Date] but was dishonoured with the remark "Insufficient Funds" (copy of return memo enclosed).

4. Legal Demand:

Under Section 138 of the Negotiable Instruments Act, 1881, and Section 141 (for company liability), you are hereby:

Notified of the dishonour.

Called upon to pay the cheque amount of ₹[Amount] within 15 days from the receipt of this notice.

5. Consequences of Nonpayment:

If payment is not made within 15 days, my client will:

Initiate criminal proceedings under Section 138 NI Act.

Seek punishment (imprisonment of up to 2 years and/or fine of up to twice the cheque amount).

Claim costs and interest under applicable laws.

6. Copy to:

Bank Manager, [Bank Name], [Branch] – for record.

Yours faithfully,

[Advocate's Name]

Encl.:

1. Copy of dishonoured cheque and return memo.

2. Copy of Buyback Agreement.

3. Postal tracking receipt (to be attached after sending).

Key Points to Include in the Notice:

1. Specific Details:

   Cheque number, date, amount, and bank.

   Clear reference to the buyback agreement (attach copy).

2. Legal Compliance:

   Sent within 30 days of dishonour (Section 138 proviso).

   Explicit 15day payment deadline.

3. Mode of Service:

   Send via Registered AD/Speed Post + Courier + Email (for proof).

   Retain postal receipts and tracking reports.

4. Section 141 NI Act (Liability of Directors):

   Name the Director(s) responsible for company operations to ensure personal liability.

IMPORTANT NOTE

As An usual Practice, and in terms of the implied authority vested with the Advocates to issue Notice as per the instance of Client/s Still its advisable that All pages of the Notice preferably be signed both by Client/s and Advocate to avoid facing any finger qua the issue of Admissibility in due course of law.

<u>Next Steps if No Reply:</u>

1. File a complaint under Section 138/141 NI Act after 15 days.

2. Attach:

   Original cheque and return memo.

   Proof of notice delivery.

   Buyback agreement.

STANDARD NOTICE UNDER SECTION 138 OF THE NI ACT, 1881

NOTICE NO.5

Example Format:

To, M/s. ABC Pvt. Ltd. (Registered Office Address)

Subject: NOTICE under Section 138 of the Negotiable Instruments Act, 1881

Dear Sir/Madam,

1. This notice is issued on behalf of Mr. X (the Complainant) concerning the dishonor of Cheque No. , dated, for ₹ drawn on Bank (Branch).

2. The said cheque was dishonored due to "Insufficient Funds" (or another reason) as per the Return Memo dated.

3. You are hereby called upon to pay the said amount within 15 days from the receipt of this notice, failing which legal action under Section 138 shall be initiated.

4. Please treat this as a formal notice under the law. Legal Implications: If the notice is not properly addressed to the company, it may be considered defective, and the complaint may be dismissed. The directors/officers in charge can also be made liable if they were responsible for the company's affairs when the cheque was issued. Conclusion: The notice must be issued in the name of the company, but it can also include responsible individuals (if applicable). Proper service and compliance with statutory timelines are crucial for a valid case under Section 138/141 of the NI Act.

STATUTORY NOTICE FROM A FINANCIAL INSTITUTION TO A BORROWER

NOTICE NO.6

STATUTORY NOTICE UNDER SECTION 138 OF THE NEGOTIABLE INSTRUMENTS ACT, 1881 (From a Financial Institution to Borrower/Drawer for Dishonored Cheque) '

NOTICE HEADER On Official Letterhead of

[Financial Institution Name]

Date: [Date]

Ref: [Loan Account No./File Reference]

To: Mr./Ms. [Drawer's Full Name]

[Drawer's Address]

Via: Registered AD/Speed Post with Acknowledgement From:

[Financial Institution Name],

through its Authorized Signatory

SUBJECT Notice under Section 138 of the Negotiable Instruments Act, 1881 for the dishonor of Cheque No. [Number] dated [Date] for ₹[Amount] towards part repayment of Loan Account No. [Account Number].

KEY FACTS

1. Loan Disbursement: On [Date], you availed a loan of ₹[Total Loan Amount] under Loan Account No. [Account Number] from our institution. As per the agreement dated [Date], repayment was due in [EMIs/lumpsum] by [Due Date].

2. Cheque Issuance: Towards part payment of outstanding dues, you issued Cheque No. [Number] dated [Date] for ₹[Amount] drawn on [Bank Name], [Branch].

3. Dishonor Event: Upon presentation on [Date], the cheque was dishonored vide [Bank Name]'s Return Memo dated [Date] (Ref: [Memo ID]) with the remarks: "[Reason: Insufficient Funds/Account Closed/Exceeds Arrangement]"

4. Statutory Compliance: This notice is issued within 30 days of dishonor (intimation received on [Date]). LEGAL DEMAND You are required to pay within 15 days of receiving this notice: | Component | Amount | | Dishonored Cheque Amount | ₹[Cheque Amount] | | Penal Interest (@ [Rate]% p.m. from cheque date) | ₹[Calculated Interest] | | NOTICE Costs | ₹[Amount] | | TOTAL | ₹[Total] | Payment Mode: Demand Draft/RTGS to:Cross Examination Account Name: [Financial Institution Name]Cross Examination Account No.: [Account Number]Cross Examination IFSC: [IFSC Code]Cross Examination Branch: [Branch Address] CONSEQUENCES OF NON

COMPLIANCE Failure to pay within 15 days will compel us to:

1. Initiate criminal proceedings under Section 138 NI Act (punishable with imprisonment of up to 2 years/fine of up to twice the cheque amount/both).

2. File a summary civil suit under Order XXXVII CPC for recovery of the total outstanding loan (₹[Total Dues]) + interest + costs.

3. Initiate proceedings under SARFAESI Act, 2002 (if applicable) for asset seizure.

4. Report default to credit bureaus (CIBIL/Experian), impacting your credit score.

ATTACHMENTS

1. Copy of dishonored Cheque No. [Number]

2. Bank Return Memo (Ref: [Memo ID])

3. Loan Statement (outstanding dues as of [Date]) SIGNATURE For [Financial Institution Name] [Authorized Signatory Name] [Designation] [Seal/Stamp] Contact: [Phone/Email] Copy to: Legal Department, [Financial Institution Name]

CRITICAL NOTES FOR FINANCIAL INSTITUTION

1. Dispatch Proof: Send notice via Registered AD and retain the postal receipt/Acknowledgment Due.

2. Timeline Compliance: File a criminal complaint within 30 days after the 15day notice period expires.

3. Documentation: Attach certified copies of: Loan agreement clauses confirming cheque issuance for debt discharge. Cheque return memo (original retained for court). Loan account statement reflecting cheque amounts as part payment.

4. Legal Strategy: Simultaneously initiate SARFAESI proceedings (if a secured loan) for parallel recovery. Submit the board resolution authorizing the signatory (for the institution's validity).

Discussion Format

Between:

Advocate (for Multispecialty Hospital)

&

Hospital Management/Billing Team

1. Introduction & Purpose

Advocate:

"We are initiating legal action under Section 138 of the Negotiable Instruments Act, 1881, for the dishonored cheque issued by Mr. Y (father of the patient). Before drafting the demand notice, let's clarify the facts, documents, and legal strategy."

2. Factual Discussion

A. Patient Admission & Discharge Details

Hospital Representative:

Patient Name:

Admission Date: | Discharge Date:

Treating Doctor: | Department:

Nature of Treatment: (e.g., Surgery/ICU/Therapy)

B. Outstanding Dues Breakdown

(Verify each component with supporting bills/receipts)

1. Hospital Services: ₹ (Room charges, nursing, doctor's fees)
2. Medical Equipment: ₹ (Ventilator, monitors, etc.)
3. Medicines/Consumables: ₹ (Pharmacy bills)
4. Other Charges: ₹ (Diagnostics, ambulance, etc.)

Total Outstanding: ₹

C. Cheque Details & Dishonor

Cheque No.: | Date: | Amount: ₹

Bank: | Account No.:

Dishonor Reason: "Insufficient Funds"/"Account Closed"

Return Memo Date: (Attach copy)

D. Prior Communication

Any written reminders/emails sent? (Attach copies)

Any verbal promises by Mr. Y to repay?

3. Legal Strategy Discussion

A. Grounds for Legal Notice

The cheque was issued for a legally enforceable debt (hospital services).

No dispute on liability (the patient was treated & discharged).

Dishonor confirmed by bank memo.

B. Demand Notice Drafting Points

Mention breakup of dues (hospital bills attached).

Give 15 days to repay (as per Section 138(b)).

Warn of criminal complaint + recovery suit if unpaid.

C. Additional Legal Options

1. Civil Suit for Recovery: If the cheque amount < total dues.
2. Consumer Court Complaint: Deficiency in service (if applicable).

4. Document Checklist

Hospital Must Provide:

Copy of dishonored cheque + return memo

Detailed final bill (signed by patient/relative at discharge)

Admission form/agreement (terms of payment)

All receipts/acknowledgments (if partial payment was made)

Email/SMS reminders (if any)

5. Next Steps

1. Advocate drafts NOTICE u/s 138 NI Act (sample format shared).
2. Hospital reviews & approves notice content.
3. Notice sent via Registered AD + Courier (tracking proof kept).
4. If no payment in 15 days, file complaint before JMFC.

Sample Key Sentences for Notice

"The cheque was issued in discharge of a legally enforceable debt for medical services availed by [Patient Name]. Despite repeated reminders, you failed to clear the dues, and the cheque was dishonored. Pay ₹ within 15 days, failing which criminal proceedings will be initiated."

Special Considerations for Hospitals

Medico legal angle: Ensure no patient care dispute (pure payment issue).

Ethical tone: Avoid aggressive language (maintain hospital reputation).

Tax compliance: Ensure bills are GST compliant for legal validity.

NOTICE UNDER SECTION 138(B) FOR DISHONOUR OF CHEQUE NO [XXX]

Notice Number.7

An advocate, namely X, by profession (MACT side), whose cheque was returned unpaid by his client due to the professional fee agreed upon with one person,

To:

Mr. Y (Client/Drawer)

[Full Address]

Date: [DD/MM/YYYY]

Subject: NOTICE u/s 138(b) of the Negotiable Instruments Act, 1881 for Dishonour of Cheque No. dated for ₹

1. INTRODUCTION

I, Advocate Z, am duly appointed by my client, Advocate X (hereinafter referred to as "the Payee"), to issue this NOTICE to you, Mr. Y (hereinafter referred to as "the Drawer"), under Section 138(b) of the Negotiable Instruments Act, 1881, for the dishonour of a cheque issued towards unpaid professional fees.

2. FACTUAL MATRIX

a) You, Mr. Y, had engaged the professional services of Advocate X for [briefly mention the nature of work, e.g., "a Motor Accident Claim Tribunal (MACT) case"].

b) In discharge of your liability towards unpaid professional fees, you issued a cheque bearing:

Cheque No.:

Date: [DD/MM/YYYY]

Amount: ₹

Bank: [Bank Name & Branch]

Account No.:

c) The said cheque was presented for encashment on [DD/MM/YYYY] but was dishonoured by your bank with the return memo dated [DD/MM/YYYY] citing the reason: "Insufficient

Funds"/"Account Closed"/[Other Reason]. A copy of the dishonoured cheque and return memo are enclosed.

d) The liability arises out of a fee agreement/[oral understanding] dated [DD/MM/YYYY] between you and Advocate X.

3. LEGAL DEMAND u/s 138(b)

a) Through this notice, you are legally demanded to pay the cheque amount of ₹ (Rupees only) within 15 days from the receipt of this notice.

b) Consequences of Non Payment:

Failure to pay will compel Advocate X to initiate criminal proceedings under:

Section 138 of the N.I. Act (Punishable with imprisonment of up to 2 years and/or fine).

Section 420 IPC (Cheating), if applicable.

You will also be liable for litigation costs and interest.

4. MODE OF PAYMENT

Pay via Demand Draft/Online Transfer to:

Account Name: Advocate X

Bank Details: [Account No., IFSC, Bank & Branch]

5. ENCLOSURES

1. Copy of the dishonoured cheque.

2. Copy of the bank return memo.

3. Copy of the fee agreement (if available).

6. CC

The Branch Manager, [Bank Name], [Branch Address] (for record).

NOTE: This notice is without prejudice to any other legal remedies available to my client.

Sincerely,

Advocate Z

[Stamp & Signature]

Key Points for Compliance:

1. Timeline:

Notice must be sent within 30 days of dishonour.

Complaint must be filed within 30 days after the 15day notice period expires.

2. Service:

Send via Registered AD/Speed Post with tracking. Retain proof of delivery.

3. Tone:

Professional and unambiguous. Avoid extraneous thr

NOTICE FOR DISHONOUR OF CHEQUE ISSUED TOWARDS REPAYMENT OF FRIENDLY LOAN

NOTICE NO.8

NOTICE Regarding Cheque Dishonour for a Friendly Loan

LEGAL NOTICE

UNDER SECTION 138 OF THE NEGOTIABLE INSTRUMENTS ACT, 1881

Via Registered AD with Acknowledgement Due

Date: 5th July 2025

To:

Mr. [Full Name of Drawer],

S/o [Father's Name],

[Full Address].

From:

[Your Full Name],

S/o [Your Father's Name],

[Your Full Address].

(Through Advocate: [Advocate's Name], [Bar Council No.], [Law Firm/Address])

Subject: NOTICE Under Section 138 of the Negotiable Instruments Act, 1881, for Dishonour of Cheque No. for ₹10,00,000 (Ten Lakh) Issued Towards Repayment of Friendly Loan.

KEY DEMANDS & CONSEQUENCES

| Demand | Deadline | Legal Consequence of NonCompliance |

| Payment of ₹10,00,000 (Principal) | 15 Days from Receipt | Criminal Complaint U/S 138 NI Act |

| Interest @ 2% P.M. (From Cheque Date Till Payment) | 15 Days from Receipt | Civil Recovery Suit U/Order XXXVII CPC |

| ₹5,000 (NOTICE Cost) | 15 Days from Receipt | Liability for Litigation Costs |

DETAILED FACTUAL BACKGROUND

1. Friendly Loan Agreement:

On [Date], you requested a friendly loan of ₹10,00,000 from me to address urgent personal needs, promising repayment on demand with monthly interest @ 2%.

Given our longstanding acquaintance (since [Year]), I disbursed the amount in cash/transfer on [Date] without formal documentation, trusting your integrity.

2. Issuance of Cheque:

Towards liability discharge, you issued Cheque No. dated [Date] for ₹10,00,000 drawn on [Bank Name], [Branch].

The cheque was expressly handed over as repayment security for the loan.

3. Dishonour Event:

Upon presentation on [Date], the cheque was dishonoured via Return Memo dated [Date] with remarks: "Insufficient Funds" (copy enclosed).

Bank intimation received on [Date], triggering my 30day statutory notice period.

4. Failure to Rectify:

Despite telephonic reminders on [Dates] and a personal meeting on [Date], you neglected repayment.

LEGAL VIOLATIONS

Section 138 NI Act: Dishonour constitutes a criminal offence punishable with imprisonment for up to 2 years or a fine of up to twice the cheque amount.

Breach of Trust: Issuing a cheque without ensuring the sufficiency of funds reflects dishonest intent, inviting liability under Section 420 IPC (Cheating).

Civil Liability: You remain liable for principal + interest (@ 2% p.m. since [Cheque Date]) + costs.

REMEDIAL DEMAND

Within 15 days of receiving this notice:

1. Pay ₹10,00,000 (Principal) + accrued interest (@ 2% p.m. from [Cheque Date]) + ₹5,000 (notice costs) via demand draft/RTGS to my account.

2. Provide written confirmation of payment to my advocate.

Failure to comply will compel me to:

File a criminal complaint U/S 138 NI Act before the competent Magistrate;

Initiate summary civil suit U/Order XXXVII CPC for recovery;

Seek costs and punitive damages.

ATTACHMENTS

1. Copy of dishonoured cheque.

2. Bank Return Memo (Reason: "Insufficient Funds").

3. Loan disbursement proof (if available).

Note: This notice is without prejudice to my other legal rights. A copy is retained for court proceedings.

Advocate's Signature

[Advocate's Name]

[Enrollment No.]

[Law Firm Address]

[Contact Details]

CRITICAL NEXT STEPS FOR YOU

1. Send via Registered AD: Ensure proof of delivery.

2. Preserve Evidence: Original cheque, return memo, loan transaction proofs (e.g., bank statements, witness details).

3. Timeline Compliance:

File complaint within 30 days after the 15day notice period expires.

4. Legal Consultation: If the drawer disputes the loan, strengthen your case with:

Witness affidavits confirming the transaction;

Documentary trail (messages/emails acknowledging debt).

NOTICE FOR DISHONOUR OF CHEQUE FOR UNPAID DIRECTOR'S FEES

LEGAL NOTICE:9

Under Section 138 Of The Negotiable Instruments Act, 1881

From:

[Director's Name]

[Director's Address]

[City, State, PIN Code]

[Contact Number]

[Email ID]

To,

[Producer's Name]

[Production House Name]

[Registered Office Address]

[City, State, PIN Code]

Date: [DD/MM/YYYY]

Subject: <u>NOTICE under Section 138 of the Negotiable Instruments Act, 1881 for Dishonor of Cheque No. [XXX] for Unpaid Director's Fees</u>

Through: Registered AD/Speed Post with Acknowledgment

Dear Sir/Madam,

1. INTRODUCTION

I, [Director's Name], hereby serve this NOTICE upon you in my capacity as the director of the film [Film Name], for which I was engaged by your production house, [Production House Name], under an agreement dated [Agreement Date].

2. BACKGROUND OF THE LIABILITY

As per the terms of our agreement, you were liable to pay me a total fee of ₹[Total Fee Amount] for my services as the director of the aforementioned film. The payment was to be made in [Number of Instalments] instalments, out of which you have failed to pay the final instalment of ₹[Unpaid Amount].

In discharge of this legally enforceable debt, you issued:

Cheque No.: [XXX]

Dated: [DD/MM/YYYY]

Amount: ₹[Unpaid Amount] (Rupees [Amount in Words] only)

Drawn on: [Bank Name], [Branch Name].

3. DISHONOR OF THE CHEQUE

Upon presentation, the aforementioned cheque was dishonored on [Date of Dishonor] due to "Insufficient Funds" (as per the Bank Return Memo dated [Date of Return Memo]). A copy of the dishonored cheque and the bank return memo are enclosed herewith for your reference.

4. STATUTORY DEMAND

Under Section 138(b) of the Negotiable Instruments Act, 1881, you are hereby called upon to:

Pay the cheque amount of ₹[Unpaid Amount] within 15 days from the receipt of this notice.

5.CONSEQUENCESOF NONCOMPLIANCE

Failure to comply with this demand will compel me to initiate legal proceedings against you under Section 138 of the Negotiable Instruments Act, 1881, which may result in:

Criminal prosecution punishable with imprisonment up to 2 years and/or a fine up to twice the cheque amount.

Civil recovery suit for the unpaid amount along with interest @ 18% p.a. from the date of dishonor until realization.

Costs of legal proceedings.

6. DOCUMENTS ENCLOSED

1. Copy of the dishonored cheque.

2. Copy of the bank return memo.

3. Copy of the agreement (if applicable).

4. Copy of payment reminders (if any).

7. FINAL NOTE

This notice is issued without prejudice to any other legal remedies available to me under any other law for the time being in force.

Yours faithfully,

[Director's Name]

[Contact Details]

Copy to:

1. [Advocate's Name], [Law Firm Name], [Address] – for records and further action.

Key Points to Remember:

1. Service of Notice: Ensure the notice is sent via registered post/speed post with acknowledgment due to maintain proof of delivery.

2. Timeline: The recipient has 15 days from the date of receipt to make the payment.

3. Next Steps: If the payment is not made within the stipulated time, file a complaint under Section 138 before the appropriate court within 30 days from the expiry of the 15day notice period.

NOTICE UNDER PSS ACT, 2007 FOR DISHONOUR OF ECS CHEQUES

NOTICE 10

under Section 25 of the Payment and Settlement Systems Act, 2007 (PSS Act) for dishonor of ECS (Electronic Clearing Service) cheques issued as security PDCs (Post Dated Cheques) by an accused enterprise to discharge prospective liability:

[Law Firm's Letterhead]

ADVOCATES & LEGAL CONSULTANTS

[Address] |

[Contact] |

[Email] |

[GSTIN/UIN]

Date: [DD/MM/YYYY]

To, The Managing Director,

[Accused Enterprise Name],

[Registered Office Address].

SUBJECT: NOTICE under section 25 of the payment and settlement systems act, 2007 for DISHONOR OF ECS cheques (security PDCS)

DATED [DATE(S)]

Through:

Registered AD/Speed Post with Acknowledgment Dear Sir/Madam,

1. Background of Liability Our client, [Creditor's Name], entered into an agreement dated [Agreement Date] with your enterprise for [Purpose of Transaction, e.g., supply of goods/loan facility]. As security for prospective liabilities, your enterprise issued: ECS Cheques (Security PDCs): Cheque No. [XXX], Dated [DD/MM/YYYY], Amount: ₹[X] Cheque No. [XXX], Dated [DD/MM/YYYY], Amount: ₹[X] (List all dishonored cheques)

Drawn on: [Bank Name], [Branch].

2. Dishonor of ECS Cheques The above cheques were presented for encashment on [Date(s)] but were dishonored due to: "Insufficient Funds" (Bank Return Memo(s) dated [Date(s)] enclosed). Or "Account Closed" (if applicable).

3. Statutory Demand under Section 25, PSS Act Under Section 25(1) of the PSS Act, read with CHAPTER NO. XVII of the Negotiable Instruments Act (NI Act), you are liable for: Criminal Offense: Dishonor of electronic funds transfer (ECS cheques) for discharge of debt/liability. Penalty: Imprisonment of up to 2 years or a fine of up to twice the cheque amount, or both. You are hereby demanded to:

1. Pay the total dishonored amount of ₹[Total Amount] within 15 days of receiving this notice.

2. Submit written confirmation of payment to our office.

4. Consequences of Non Compliance Failure to comply will compel our client to: File a criminal complaint under Section 25 PSS Act + Section 138 NI Act. Initiate civil recovery proceedings with 18% interest from the date of dishonour. Seek attachment of your enterprise's assets under interim relief provisions.

5. Documents Enclosed

1. Copy of dishonored cheques + Bank Return Memos.

2. Copy of Agreement (highlighting the PDC clause).

3. Proof of prior reminders (if any). Note: This notice is issued without prejudice to other legal remedies.

[Contact Details]

Copy to:

2. [Creditor's Name] – for records.

Key Legal Points:

1. Applicability of Section 25 PSS Act: Covers ECS cheques issued as security PDCs for prospective liability (if linked to a legally enforceable debt). Presumption of Liability: Under Section 25(2), the transfer is presumed for debt discharge unless disproven.

2. Notice Requirements: Must be sent within 30 days of dishonor. Payer gets 15 days to rectify post receipt.

3. Dual Liability: Criminal: Prosecution under PSS Act + NI Act (via Section 25(5)). Civil: Summary suit for recovery under Order XXXVII CPC.

4. Enterprise Liability: Directors/officers in charge are vicariously liable under Section 141 NI Act (applied via Section 25(5) PSS Act).

2. Defences Invalid: Lack of knowledge about insufficient funds is not a defense. Next Steps: File Complaint: Within 1 month after notice expiry (JMFC Court). RBI Reporting: Notify RBI's Banking Ombudsman for ECS default. For templates, refer to:

Draft NOTICE From Flat Buyer To Builder For Dishonoured Buyback Cheque

NOTICE 11

From Flat Buyer to Builder Whose Buyback Consideration is Dishonoured.

From: [Your Name]

Advocate for Mr./Ms. A

[Your Law Firm's Name]

[Your Office Address]

[City, State, PIN Code]

[Email Address]

[Contact Number]

[Date]

To: Builder X

[Designation, if applicable]

[Builder's Company Name]

[Registered Office Address]

[City, State, PIN Code]

Subject: NOTICE NUMBER

for Dishonour of Cheque Issued Towards Buyback Consideration

Demand for Immediate Payment. Dear Sir/Madam, Under instructions from and on behalf of our client, Mr./Ms. A (hereinafter referred to as 'Our Client'), we serve upon you this NOTICE regarding the dishonour of the cheque issued by you towards the buyback consideration under the Housing Project [Project Name] at [Project Location], pursuant to the mutual cancellation of the flat allotment. Background & Facts:4

1. Our Client had booked Flat No. [X], Tower [Y], in [Project Name] under an Allotment Letter/Buyer's Agreement dated

[Agreement Date].

2. Due to prolonged delays in construction and legal issues concerning the project, the parties mutually agreed to cancel the allotment via the Cancellation Agreement/Mutual Termination Letter dated [Cancellation Date].

3. As per the terms of cancellation, you agreed to refund the buyback consideration and issued a cheque bearing No. [Cheque No.], dated [Cheque Date], drawn on [Bank Name & Branch], for an amount of ₹[Amount in Figures & Words].

4. Upon presentation, the said cheque was dishonoured with the remarks '[Return Reason, e.g., "Insufficient Funds"/"Account Closed"]' via return memo dated [Return Memo Date].

5. Despite our Client's repeated requests, you have failed to make the payment, thereby violating the terms of the mutual cancellation agreement. Legal Violations: Your actions constitute: Breach of the Cancellation Agreement under the Indian Contract Act, 1872. An offence under Section 138 of the Negotiable Instruments Act, 1881 (Dishonour of Cheque). Deficiency in service and unfair trade practice under the Consumer Protection Act, 2019 (if applicable).

Demands: In view of the above, we call upon you to:

1. Immediately pay the due amount of ₹[Amount] along with interest @ [X]% p.a. from the due date till realization.

2. Compensate our Client for the financial loss, mental harassment, and legal costs incurred, quantified at ₹[Amount]. Notice Period & Consequences: You are granted 15 days from the receipt of this notice to comply with the demands. Failure to do so will compel our Client to initiate legal action, including but not limited to: Filing a criminal complaint under Section 138 of the Negotiable Instruments Act. Initiating a civil suit for recovery and breach of contract. Lodging a complaint before the Consumer Forum for deficiency in service. All costs and consequences shall be borne by you. Copy retained for future legal recourse.

Yours faithfully,

[Your Name]   Advocate for Mr./Ms. A

[Enclosures:

1. Copy of Dishonoured Cheque & Return Memo
2. Copy of Cancellation Agreement/Mutual Termination Letter
3. Copy of Allotment Letter/Buyer's Agreement (if applicable)]

Note: This is a draft for reference. Kindly consult your legal counsel for modifications based on specific facts and jurisdictional laws.

NOTICE FOR DISHONOUR OF CHEQUE FOR OUTSTANDING DUES (VIA REGISTERED POST)

NOTICE 12

to a flat owner whose cheese is dishonest issued by the cooperative housing society for outstanding maintenance charges, etc.

To: [Flat Owner's Name]

[Flat No. and Address]

[Cooperative Housing Society Name]

[Society Address] Date: [DD/MM/YYYY]

Subject: NOTICE for Dishonor of Cheque No. [XXX] dated [DD/MM/YYYY] for Outstanding Dues Via Registered Post/Speed Post Dear Sir/Madam,

1. Reference to Cheque and Liability You issued Cheque No. [XXX] dated [DD/MM/YYYY] for ₹[Amount] drawn on [Bank Name, Branch] in favor of [Society Name] towards: Outstanding maintenance charges: ₹[X] Fines/penalties: ₹[X] (specify reasons, e.g., late payment, rule violations).

2. Dishonor and Statutory Demand The cheque was presented for encashment on [DD/MM/YYYY] but was dishonored due to "[Reason: Insufficient Funds/Account Closed/etc.]" as per the bank's return memo dated [DD/MM/YYYY]. Under Section 138(b) of the NI Act, you are hereby demanded to pay: "The said amount" (cheque value): ₹[X] within 15 days of receiving this notice. Note: Additional claims (interest/costs) may be specified separately but cannot overshadow the cheque amount demand.

3. Consequences of NonPayment Failure to comply will compel the society to initiate legal proceedings under Section 138 of the NI Act, punishable with imprisonment of up to 2 years and/or a fine of up to twice the cheque amount.

4. Proof of Service This notice is sent to your registered address. Service on relatives/third parties without proof of your awareness is invalid. Authorized Signatory [Name] [Designation] [Cooperative

Housing Society Name] [Contact Details]

Key Legal Points to Include

1. Clarity of Demand: The notice must explicitly demand the cheque amount ("the said amount") as per Supreme Court rulings. Other dues (interest/fines) should be listed separately to avoid invalidation.

2. Timeline: The 15day window for payment starts from the date of receipt (not issuance) of the notice.

3. Service Validity: Ensure the notice is delivered to the drawer's official address. Service on relatives without proof of acknowledgment is insufficient.

4. Attachments: Include copies of the dishonored cheque, return memo, and ledger of dues for transparency.

NOTICE FOR DISHONOUR OF CHEQUE NO [XXX] FOR ₹25,00,000/-

NOTICE NO.13

on behalf of the Chartered Accountant (Client) to Company

[Law Firm's Letterhead]

ADVOCATE & LEGAL CONSULTANTS

[Address] | [Contact] | [Email] | [GSTIN/UIN]

Date: [DD/MM/YYYY]

To,

The Managing Director,

Company X,

[Registered Office Address].

SUBJECT:

LEGAL DEMAND NOTICE NUMBER

UNDER SECTION 138(b) OF THE NEGOTIABLE INSTRUMENTS ACT, 1881 FOR DISHONOR OF CHEQUE NO. [XXX] FOR ₹25,00,000/

From CA to Client

Through: Registered AD/Speed Post with Acknowledgment

Dear Sir/Madam,

1. Background of Liability

Our client, CA [Name], provided professional accounting/advisory services to your company for the financial year [YYYY YY] as per the agreement dated [DD/MM/YYYY]. In discharge of this legally enforceable debt, your company issued:

Cheque No. [XXX]

Dated: [DD/MM/YYYY]

Amount: ₹25,00,000/ (Twenty Five Lakhs)

Drawn on: [Bank Name], [Branch].

2. Dishonor of Cheque

Upon presentation, the cheque was dishonored on [DD/MM/YYYY] due to 'Insufficient Funds' (Bank Return Memo attached).

3. Statutory Demand

Under Section 138(b) of the NI Act, you are hereby called upon to:

Pay the cheque amount of ₹25,00,000/ within 15 days from receipt of this notice.

Failure to comply will compel our client to initiate:

Criminal proceedings (punishable with imprisonment up to 2 years/fine up to twice the cheque amount).

Civil recovery suit with interest (@18% p.a.) and costs.

4. Documents Enclosed

1. Copy of dishonored cheque.
2. Bank return memo.
3. Copy of service agreement/invoices.

5. Consequences of Nonpayment

Legal action will be initiated without further intimation.

Liability for additional costs (legal fees, interest, etc.).

Note: This notice is issued without prejudice to our client's other rights.

Yours faithfully,

[Advocate's Name]

Enrollment No.: [XXX]

For [Law Firm Name]

[Contact Details]

Copy to:

1. CA [Client Name] – for records.

Key Legal Requirements Addressed

1. Mandatory 15Day Notice: As per Section 138(c), NI Act.

2. Specific Demand: Only the cheque amount is demanded (other claims like interest can be pursued separately).

3. Proof of Service: Send via registered post (acknowledgment receipt is crucial evidence).

4. Annexures: Attach cheque copy, return memo, and proof of debt (agreement/invoices).

Next Steps if Unpaid:

File a complaint under Section 138 before the JMFC Court within 30 days after notice expiry.

Consider a parallel civil suit for recovery.

****

CHAPTER-07

WRITTEN ARGUMENTS And oral Points For Complainant in a Friendly loan cheque

---

In a "friendly loan" case under Section 138 of the Negotiable Instruments Act, the complainant's goal is to construct a clear, legally sound narrative that transforms an informal agreement into a legally enforceable debt. The defence will inevitably argue the loan was a gift, never existed, or was repaid in cash.

Here are the main points for argument and the evidence to support them, structured for a compelling presentation in court.

Overarching Legal Principle: Presumption under Section 139 NI Act

The complainant's entire strategy should be built around invoking Section 139, which states:

"It shall be presumed, unless the contrary is proved, that the holder of a cheque received the cheque, for the discharge, in whole or in part, of any debt or other liability."

This means the law presumes the cheque was for a valid debt. The burden of proof shifts to the accused to rebut this presumption. The complainant's job is to first establish a strong prima facie case to make this presumption operative.

Main Points for Argument & Supporting Evidence

The complainant must prove three core things: (1) the existence of a debt, (2) the issuance of the cheque for that debt, and (3) the dishonour of that cheque.

1. Point: Proving the Existence of a Legally Enforceable Debt/Loan

This is the foundation. The argument is that the transaction was a loan, not a gift.

· Supporting Evidence & Arguments:

· Loan Agreement or Promissory Note: This is the best evidence. Argue that even between friends, a written document shows intention to create a legally enforceable relationship.

· Witness Testimony: Testimony from a common friend, family member, or colleague who was aware of the loan transaction. ("I was present when X agreed to lend Y the money for his business.")

· Financial Capacity: Provide your own bank statements or financial records to show you had the capacity to lend the claimed amount. This counters the defence that you never had the money to lend.

· Circumstantial Evidence: Argue about the context. Was the accused buying a house/car? Starting a business? Facing a medical emergency? The timing of the loan request supports the probability of a debt. A gift of a large sum is highly improbable without a special occasion (like a wedding).

· Partial Repayment Evidence: If the accused made any partial payments (especially via bank transfer), this is the strongest admission of the debt's existence. Argue that one does not repay a gift.

2. Point: Proving the Cheque was Issued for the Discharge of this Specific Debt

The accused may admit to owing money but claim this particular cheque was for a different purpose or was issued as security.

· Supporting Evidence & Arguments:

· The Cheque Itself: The cheque is Exhibit No. 1. Highlight that it bears the accused's signature and is drawn from their active bank account.

· Accompanying Documents: Did the accused hand over the cheque along with a signed document? Even a simple receipt or an email saying "Here is my cheque for the loan" is crucial.

· Demand Notice Reply: If the accused replied to your statutory demand notice and did not deny the debt in their reply, or gave a vague excuse, this is a major point to argue. Silence or an evasive reply is an admission against interest.

· Pre litigation Communication: Text messages (WhatsApp/SMS) and emails are golden evidence. Any message from the accused saying, "I need more time to arrange the funds," "Please don't deposit the cheque yet," or "I will repay you soon," is a direct admission of liability. Argue that these messages corroborate your entire story.

3. Point: Proving Strict Compliance with the NI Act's Procedure

The technical procedure must be flawless. Any lapse can lead to acquittal.

· Supporting Evidence & Arguments:

· Cheque Return Memo: The bank's memo is conclusive proof of dishonour. It proves the "actus reus" of the offence.

· Proof of Dispatch & Delivery of Demand Notice: Argue that the demand notice was sent correctly.

· UPC/Acknowledgment Receipt: Show the court the postal receipts and the signed acknowledgment card (AD) proving the notice was delivered to the accused's correct address.

· Timing: Argue that the notice was sent within 30 days of receiving the cheque return memo and that the complaint was filed only after 15 days from the date of delivery of the notice, giving the accused the legally mandated time to pay.

4. Point: Attacking the Credibility of the Accused's Defence

Anticipate the defence and be ready to dismantle it.

· Against the "Gift" Defence: "My Lord, is it the accused's case that the complainant gifted him ₹5 lakhs with no occasion or reason? The accused has provided no evidence of any relationship or event that would justify such a large gift. This claim is a blatant afterthought to escape liability."

· Against the "Lost/Misused Cheque" Defence: "The accused claims the cheque was lost. Then why did he not issue a stop payment instruction to his bank? Why did he not file an FIR for the lost cheque? His inaction proves this defence is fabricated."

· Against the "Security Cheque" Defence: "Even if the cheque was issued as security (which is denied), it becomes enforceable the moment the underlying debt is not paid. The debt remains unpaid, and thus, the cheque is liable to be presented."

Summary: The Complainant's Checklist for Argument

1. Start with the Presumption: My Lord, Section 139 of the NI Act grants me a presumption in my favour.

2. Establish the Debt: I have shown the existence of a friendly loan through [Evidence: Witness, Context, My Financial Capacity].

3. Link the Cheque to the Debt: The accused issued the cheque for this loan, as supported by [Evidence: Their own messages/emails, partial repayment, lack of denial in notice reply].

4. Prove Dishonour & Procedure: The cheque was dishonoured (Return Memo), and I followed the strict procedure of the Act (Postal receipts, AD card, correct timelines).

5. Rebut the Defence: The accused's story of [gift/lost cheque] is unbelievable and unsupported by any evidence. They have failed to rebut the statutory presumption.

By building this layered argument, the complainant can effectively prove their case and secure a conviction.

****

CHAPTER-08

Synopsis as per direction of Supreme Court

Which shall be filled immediately after the index at the top of the file i.e. prior to formal complaint

JUDGEMENET DATED 25.09. 2025 IN SANJABIJ TARI VERSUS KISHORE S. BORCAR & Anr

Compliant under Section138 of the Negotiable Instruments Act,1881

I. Particulars of the parties

(i)Complainant :………………

(ii)Accused:………………………

(In the case where the accuse is a company or affirm then Registered Address, Name of the Managing Director/Partner, Name of the signatory ,Name of the Persons Vicariously liable)

II.Cheque Details

(i)Date…………………..

(iii)Amount:……………….

(IV)Drawn on Bank/Branch………………

(v)Account no……………………….

lll.Dishonour

(i)Date of presentation …………………

(ii)Date of Return/Dishonor Memo………………

(iii)Branch where cheque was dishonored………..

(iv)Reason for Dishonor……………………..

Iv.Statutory Notice

(i)Date of Notice…………………..

(ii)Mode of Service………………

(iii)Date of Dispatch and Tracking No……………..

(iv)Whether served…………………………

(vi)If not, reasons thereof……………………

(vii)Reply to the Legal Demand Notice, if any……………..

v.Cause of Action

(i)Date of accrual………..

(ii)Jurisdiction invoked under section 142(2)………………

(iii)Whether any other complaint under section 138 NI Act is pending between the same parties ,if yes, in which court and the date and the year of the institution .

VI. Relief Sought

(i)Summoning of the accused and trail under section 138 NI Act……………

(ii)Whether Award of the interim compensation under section 143A of NI Act sought …………………..

VII.Filed through:

Complainant/Authorize Representative

SCRUTINY OF COMPLAINT U/SEC 138 /141OF N.I ACT

General practice in CMM COURTS MUMBAI

CHECK LIST

Sr No.	Particulars	Check
1	Whether names and address of parties are described in title?	
2	Whether mobile number, email address of complainant is given?	
3	Whether mobile number, email address of accused is given?	
4	Whether the complaint is properly signed and verified by complainant or its power of attorney holder? Whether it is filed by authorized person or company?	
5	Whether the complainant has made disclosure on a sworn affidavit that no other court in respect of the same transaction?	
6	Whether it is properly stamped?	
7	Whether the necessary court fees stamps of the necessary postal charges for the services of the summons on the accused have been affixed to it?	

8	Whether the complainant has produced relevant documents (Cheque, Bank slip/Memo, Notice acknowledgment, jurisdiction proof, etc) with proper list thereof?	
9	Whether there is averment as to cause of action for filling a Complaint?	
10	Whether the grounds disclosing how the complaint is accompanied by application for condonation for delay and supporting affidavit?	
11	Whether it is indicated how the court has jurisdiction?	
12	If the person committing an offence under section 138 is a company, whether there is averment in the complaint how person accused was responsible for conduct of business of the company? Whether copies of Form-32 of the companies act, 1956 is Filed?	

Mandatory Synopsis as Per Supreme Court Directions

****

CHAPTER-09

X Y Z

JOINT COMPROMISE/ SETTLEMENT / TERMS DRAFT

IN THE COURT OF THE JUDICIAL MAGISTRATE FIRST CLASS at __

CC NO……..OF _____2025

ABC **...Complainant**

Versus

XYZ **...Accused**

JOINT COMPROMISE/COMPOUNDING

APPLICATION UNDER SECTION 147 OF THE NEGOTIABLE INSTRUMENTS ACT, 1881

Respectfully Showeth:

The Complainant and Accused named above most respectfully submit this Joint Compromise Application and beg to state as follows:

1. That the above-mentioned case filed by the Complainant under Section 138 of the Negotiable Instruments Act, 1881, is pending before this Hon'ble Court and is presently fixed for hearing on November 2025

2. That the parties have, without any coercion, pressure, or

undue influence from any side, voluntarily arrived at an amicable and mutual settlement of all their disputes, including the subject matter of the present case.

3. That as per the terms of the settlement, the Accused has undertaken to pay a sum of Rs. [Double the Cheque Amount] (being double the amount of the dishonoured cheque) to the Complainant as full and final settlement of all claims. The Complainant accepts this amount as full and final satisfaction.

4. That in view of this settlement, the Complainant has no objection to the compounding of the offence under Section 147 of the Negotiable Instruments Act, 1881, and the consequent acquittal of the Accused.

5. That the Complainant further agrees to apply for a refund of the court fees as per the relevant rules, to which the Accused has no objection.

6. That the Accused has deposited a surety amount of Rs. [Surety Amount, if any] in cash with the Court. The Complainant has no objection to the refund of this surety amount to the Accused upon the passing of the final order.

PRAYER

In view of the facts and circumstances stated above, it is most respectfully prayed that this Hon'ble Court may be pleased to:

a) Take this Joint Compromise Application on record;

b) Permit the compounding of the offence under Section 147 of the Negotiable Instruments Act, 1881;

c) Pass orders for the acquittal of the Accused in accordance with the law on compounding;

d) Dismiss/Withdraw the present case as "Withdrawn-Not Pressed";

e) Pass necessary directions for the refund of the court fee to the Complainant as per rules; and

f) Pass necessary directions for the refund of the cash surety amount to the Accused.

And for this act of kindness, the parties shall forever pray.

Place: Mumbai

Date:

(Accused: [Name])

VERIFICATION

We, the Complainant and Accused named above, do hereby solemnly declare and verify that the contents of this Joint Compromise Application are true and correct to our knowledge, that we have read and understood the same, and that nothing material has been concealed therefrom.

Dated......11/2025

Draft and identified the respective

Party as an Advocate

ADVOCATE VINOD K CHHA BRA

FOR COMPLAINANT

[Enrollment No.]

MAH/C/401 /1991

[Office Address]

SPA

SPECIAL POWER OF ATTORNEY

ACTUAL DRAFT

Know All Men by These Presents: I, Mr. Nitian Led, S/o [Father's Name], residing at [Full Address], do hereby appoint, constitute, and authorize: Name of Attorney Holder: [Full Name of Common Friend], Son/Wife/Daughter of: [Details], Residing at: [Full Address], as my true and lawful attorney to act on my behalf in Complaint Case No. 138 NI/CC pending before [Court/Forum Name] for the following purposes:

1. To appear, represent, and plead on my behalf before the concerned court/forum.

2. To sign, verify, and submit all necessary documents, affidavits, and pleadings.

3. To file and receive papers, applications, and orders.

4. To negotiate, settle, or compromise (if required) in the best interest of the case.

5. To take all necessary steps from the date of this authorization until the final decision, execution of the award, and full conclusion of the matter. This Special Power of Attorney is given voluntarily, with full understanding, and shall remain in force until the final disposal of the case or until revoked in writing.

IN WITNESS WHEREOF, I set my hand on this day of , 20 at [Location]. Executant (Principal):

Mr. Nitian Led

(Signature)

Witnesses:

1.Name:

Signature:

Address:

2.Name:

Signature:

Address:

- Note: Require Attestation from Notary Public

****

INDEX PART V

CHAPTER-01

Admission in 313 CrPC Statement:

---

1. Admission as Conclusive Proof of Debt (S. 138)

Rajesh Jain v. Ajay Singh (2016) 15 SCC 580:

"An admission by the accused in a 313 CrPC statement that the cheque was issued to discharge a liability is sufficient to prove the existence of a legally enforceable debt."

No further evidence is needed if the accused admits the debt/liability.

V.S. Krishnan v. West fort Hi Tech Hospital (2008) 3 SCC 363:

"Admission in pleadings or evidence dispenses with the need for the complainant to independently prove the debt."

2. Settlement Refusal Acquittal

K.M. Ibrahim v. K.P. Mohammed (2010) 1 SCC 798:

"The accused cannot demand acquittal merely because the complainant refuses to settle. Admission of liability shifts the burden to the accused to rebut the presumption under S. 139."

Damodar S. Prabhu v. Sayed Babalal H. (2010) 5 SCC 663:

"Courts may impose higher costs on accused who delay settlement, but refusa l to compound does not negate admission."

3. Conviction Based Solely on Admission

Rangappa v. Sri Mohan (2010) 11 SCC 441:

"Once the accused admits the issuance of the cheque, the presumption under S. 139 applies. The burden shifts to the accused to prove the cheque was not for a debt or liability."

If the accused admits liability during examination, it constitutes evidence under S. 313(4) CrPC and can form the basis for conviction.

Magistrate's Action Plan

1. Verify the Admission

Ensure the admission is clear, unambiguous, and covers:

(a) Issuance of the cheque,

(b) Existence of a legally enforceable debt,

(c) Liability for the amount.

Unpaid" suffices.

2. Check Rebuttal of S. 139 Presumption

Even with admission, the accused can rebut S. 139 by proving:

Cheque was stolen/forged,

Issued as security without liability,

Debt was time barred.

If no rebuttal: Conviction is mandatory.

3. Address Complainant's Refusal to Settle

Record the complainant's refusal to accept instalments.

Sentencing Options:

Order compensation under S. 357 CrPC (directing accused to pay the cheque amount + interest).

Impose symbolic imprisonment (e.g., 1 day) if compensation is paid.

For non payment: Apply S. 64 IPC (sentence till payment).

4. Judgment Drafting

Explicitly state:

"Accused admitted liability in [pleading/evidence/313 statement]. Despite the complainant's refusal to settle, the admission proves the debt under S. 138. The presumption under S. 139 remains unrebutted."

Pitfalls to Avoid

Assuming settlement refusal vitiates admission.

Ignoring the limited scope of admission (e.g., if the accused admits cheque issuance but disputes the debt).

Reference High Court Ruling:

Ashish Ghosh versus Ajay Ghosh CALCUTTA HIGH COURT)

Contrary :

****

CHAPTER-02

Co-operative Housing Societies:

Cheque Dishonors Cases Involving Cooperative Housing Societies: A Legal Perspective

Short Notes Compilation by Mr. Vinod Chhabra, Advocate, Bombay High Court, and Author of Cheque Law Reporter, Mumbai

In the realm of financial transactions, Cooperative Housing Societies (CHS) are not immune to disputes concerning dishonored cheques Understanding the legal landscape under the Negotiable Instruments Act, 1881 (NI Act) is crucial for protecting the society and its managing committee from criminal liability.

Point 1: Role and Liability of the Housing Society

A CHS, being a registered body corporate, can be named a party in a cheque dishonour case. A key legal principle is that the society itself is primarily liable only if the cheque was issued in its name and for discharging its own liability. If the society is merely facilitating a transaction between individual members—for instance, collecting a share transfer payment on a member's behalf—it may not be held liable under Section 138 if that cheque bounces.

Point 2: Personal Liability of Office Bearers and Officials

This is the area of greatest risk for managing committee members. Section 141 of the NI Act stipulates that when an offence is committed by a company or a body corporate, every person responsible for the conduct of its business at the time of the offence is deemed guilty.

Consequently, the Chairman, Treasurer, or any authorized signatory who signs a cheque on the society's behalf can be held personally liable for its dishonour. This liability is joint and several with the society. It is critical to note that this is not an automatic vicarious liability; it applies specifically to those who were "in charge of and responsible for" the conduct of the business concerning the dishonours transaction.

Direct Judicial Precedent: The Supreme Court of India in A.K. Singhania vs. Gujarat State Fertilizer Co. Ltd. & Anr has consistently affirmed the principles of Section 141. The Court has held that for prosecuting a person under Section 141, the complaint must contain specific allegations regarding the role of the director/officer, showing that they were in charge of and responsible for the company's conduct at the relevant time. Mere designation is not sufficient to fasten criminal liability.

Point 3: Rights and Liabilities of General Members

General members of the society are typically shielded from individual liability in such cases. A member cannot be prosecuted merely by virtue of their membership. Liability arises only if a member, in their capacity as an office-bearer (like a committee member), was responsible for authorizing or signing the cheque in question.

Point 4: Essential Precautions for Societies

To safeguard the society and its office bearers from legal entanglements, the following precautions are imperative:

1. Clear Authorization: Maintain a clear and updated record of who is authorized to sign cheques and for what purposes, as per the society's bye-laws.

2. Financial Diligence: Exercise due diligence to ensure sufficient funds are available in the society's account before issuing any cheque.

3. Transparent Procedures: Follow robust financial procedures and maintain transparency in all transactions with members. Ensure that all cheque issuances are backed by corresponding minutes or resolutions.

4. Adherence to Bye-laws: Strictly follow the society's bye-laws concerning financial management and member-related transactions. This includes ensuring that cheques are issued only for legitimate society expenses and liabilities.

Conclusion

While a CHS can face liability for a dishonoured cheque issued in its name, the greater personal risk lies with its office bearers who sign or authorize such instruments. The judiciary, as evidenced by the Supreme Court's stance, emphasizes the seriousness of such offences while requiring specific allegations against individuals. In this legal landscape, prudent financial management, strict adherence to authorized procedures, and active participation in any legal proceedings are the best defences for a society and its committee members against criminal prosecution under the NI Act.

Disclaimer: This Short article is for informational purposes only and does not constitute legal advice.

FAQs

Q: Is a Cooperative Housing Society (CHS) considered a company under the NI Act, and are its Chairman, Secretary, and others covered under Sections 138/141?

A: No, a CHS is not a company but a separate legal entity under cooperative law. However, Sections 138 and 141 of the NI Act apply to office bearers such as the Chairman and Secretary if they are responsible for issuing the dishonoures cheque They can be held liable if the offence occurred with their consent, connivance, or negligence, similar to officers in a company.

Q: What are key Supreme Court rulings on NI Act liability of society chairmen and secretaries?

A: The Supreme Court has clarified liability principles under Sections 138 and 141 for persons responsible for financial affairs. Chairmen and secretaries who issue dishonours cheques can be liable if they control the society's financial decisions. Non-executive members without direct responsibility are generally not liable. Liability is direct and joint if they signed or authorized the cheque.

Q: Can complaints under Section 138 be filed against society office bearers without naming the society?

A: The Supreme Court allows complaints against individuals like partners or office bearers without naming the entity if the individuals are in charge and responsible. For societies, naming the Chairman or Secretary responsible for cheque issuance can suffice, reflecting direct joint liability, unlike companies where liability is often vicarious.

These rulings signify that society chairmen and secretaries, while not in a company, face similar liabilities for dishonoured cheques under the NI Act if they are responsible for the cheque issuance and financial conduct.

Q: What is the limit for payments made by a Society?

Ans: As per Bye-law 146 of the CHS, all payments in excess of Rs. 1500/- shall be made by means of a crossed account payee cheque.

Query: CASH COMPONENT ABOVE 20,000/- WHETHER 138 NI ATTRACT.

Whether a complaint under Section 138 of the Negotiable Instruments Act (NI Act) is maintainable if the cheque was issued to recover a debt above Rs 20,000 that was paid completely in cash. **? ? ? ?**

Answer:

This issue arose from a Kerala High Court judgment that held a debt created by a cash transaction above Rs 20,000, in violation of Section 269SS of the Income-Tax Act, 1961, cannot be considered a "legally enforceable debt" under Section 138 of the NI Act unless a valid explanation is provided.

Key points from the Kerala High Court's ruling and the awaited Supreme Court decision:

Section 269SS of the Income-Tax Act prohibits transactions above Rs 20,000 in cash and mandates such transactions be made through an account transaction or cheque/draft.

According to the Kerala High Court, if a debt originates from a prohibited cash transaction above Rs 20,000, the complainant who later receives a cheque for that debt should have a valid explanation for the cash transaction, or else the criminal court cannot entertain a complaint under Section 138.

The Kerala High Court set aside convictions in such cases and ordered refunds of deposits related to these proceedings.

The accused in such cases must raise the defence that the cash transaction violated Section 269SS; otherwise, courts may presume a legally enforceable debt under Section 139 of the NI Act.

The case before the Supreme Court involves challenging this Kerala High Court ruling and determining the maintainability of Section 138 complaints in such contexts.

Thus, the Supreme Court's decision will clarify whether a cheque issued for a cash debt above Rs 20,000—presumably violating tax laws—can be the basis of a criminal complaint for cheque dishonour under Section 138 of the NI Act, especially when no valid explanation for the cash transaction is given

CHAPTER-03

(EX PARTE) JUDGMENT OF CONVICTION

Speculative outcome in the light of the facts of the case .

Present:

Shri/Smt. [Presiding Officer's Name], Judicial Magistrate First Class

FACTS OF THE CASE

1. The complainant filed this case under Section 138 of the Negotiable Instruments Act, 1881, alleging that the accused issued a cheque bearing No. dated for ₹ in discharge of a legally enforceable debt, which was dishonoured for 'Insufficient Funds' as per return memo dated from [Bank Name].

2. Despite the statutory demand notice dated (sent via registered post and acknowledged), the accused failed to make payment within 15 days, leading to this complaint.

3. The court took cognizance and issued summons, but the accused willfully evaded service. Subsequently: Bailable & NonBailable Warrants were issued but not executed. Proclamation under Section 82 CrPC was issued on , declaring the accused a Proclaimed Offender. Attachment under Section 83 CrPC was also initiated.

4. The complainant filed an application under Section 299 CrPC for recording evidence in the accused's absence, which was allowed.

5. The complainant submitted: Affidavit of Evidence (Ex. CW1/A) Original dishonoured cheque (Ex. CW1/1) Bank return memo (Ex. CW1/2) Postal receipts & NOTICE (Ex. CW1/3 to CW1/5) Other relevant documents COURT'S ANALYSIS & FINDINGS

1. Ingredients of Section 138 NI Act Proved: Cheque issuance in order to discharge enforceable debt (Ex. CW1/1) no rebuttal Dishonour for insufficiency of funds (Ex. CW1/2). Legal demand

notice served (Ex. CW1/3 to CW1/5). Accused failed to pay within 15 days of notice.

2. Accused's Absconding Status: The accused was duly proclaimed under Section 82 CrPC but failed to appear. His absence is willful and deliberate, justifying ex parte proceedings under Section 299 CrPC. 3. Evidence Conclusive: The complainant's unrebutted testimony and documents prove guilt beyond reasonable doubt.

FINAL ORDER

1. The accused is convicted under Section 138 of the Negotiable Instruments Act, 1881. Yes, in a Section 138 NI Act case, the court can finally decide and convict the accused even after proceeding under Section 299 CrPC (recording evidence in the absence of an absconding accused),

provided the following conditions are met:

1. Legal Position on Deciding the Case After Section 299 CrPC Proceedings Section 299 CrPC allows the court to record evidence in the absence of an absconding accused to prevent indefinite delays. Once the complainant's evidence is recorded ex parte and the court is satisfied that: The accused was duly served/proclaimed (under Sections 82/83 CrPC). The complainant has proved all ingredients of Section 138 NI Act (cheque issuance, dishonour, legal notice, non payment). The court can pronounce judgment (conviction or acquittal) based on the available evidence.

2. Key Conditions for Final Decision Proper service of summons/warrants – The court must be satisfied that the accused was given a fair opportunity to appear. Proclamation under Section 82 CrPC – The accused should have been declared an 'absconder' with a public notice. Evidence conclusively proves guilt – The complainant must establish: Cheque was issued by the accused. It was dishonoured for 'insufficient funds' or other valid reasons. A legal demand notice was served within 30 days of dishonour. The accused failed to pay within 15 days of notice. No reasonable defence – Since the accused is absent, the court relies solely on the complainant's evidence.

3. Can the Accused Challenge Later? If the accused is convicted ex parte, he can file: Application to set aside ex parte order (under Section 317 CrPC) if he later appears.

****

NOTE : Actual and Factual Judgement Of JMFC MUMBAI Passed In Favour Of Complainant In A Matter In Next Volume 2 Of Practical Guide Which Is Under Appeal By Accused: You may however open and access C.C NO, 43002398/SS/2019 CNR NO. MHMM170095052019

FAQS

Question

Does the account being blocked or not being used have an effect in the case of Section 138 of the NI Act?

Answer:

There is no rescue for the accused, even if the check is returned unpaid due to the account being closed or not in use.

(Reference: Bombay High Court :Dilip Vs Nishant Sahakari Gramin:09-12- 2011

Overlooking S. 141 liability (admission by one accused ≠ guilt of all directors).

COACHING & FAQS

What Works in Favour of the Complainant (Holder of the Cheque)?

- The Legal Presumption (Section 139): This is the complainant's biggest weapon. The law presumes the cheque was received for a debt or liability. The burden is on the accused to rebut this.
- Supporting Documentation: The complainant produces a loan agreement, a receipt, an email, or a ledger entry showing the transaction and the purpose of the cheque.

- Admission by Accused: If the accused, in their reply to the statutory notice or in their deposition, admits to taking the money but disputes the amount or terms, it strengthens the complainant's case that a debt exists.

QUESTION NO. 223

Is it permissible for the HIGH COURT to record and find, wherever there are factual disputes while dealing with a petition under section 482 Cr. P.C?

Answer: NO, It is not permissible for the High Court to record a finding wherever there are factual disputes.

(Reference : Supreme Court: Dr. Lakshman Vs. the State of Karnataka : 17-10-2019)

Quashing by High Court precise legal question regarding the inherent powers of the High Court under Section 482 of the CrPC to quash proceedings in a case under Section 138 of the Negotiable Instruments Act (the "cheque bounce" law).

Let's break this down in detail.

The Foundation: Section 482 CrPC

Section 482 of the Code of Criminal Procedure, 1973, preserves the inherent powers of the High Court to:

(a) give effect to any order under the CrPC,

(b) prevent abuse of the process of any court, and

(c) otherwise to secure the ends of justice.

This power is extraordinary, discretionary, and must be exercised sparingly and with caution. It is not an alternative remedy to a regular trial.

Quashing a Section 138 NI Act Case: The Key Grounds

The Supreme Court of India, in a catena of judgments, has outlined the specific circumstances under which a High Court can quash a complaint under Section 138 of the NI Act. These grounds are strict and narrowly interpreted.

Here are the specific grounds you are asking for:

Category 1: Grounds Based on Legal Deficiencies in the Complaint itself

These are the strongest grounds for quashing. If the complaint itself, even if taken at face value and presumed to be entirely true, does not disclose an offence, it must be quashed.

1. Absence of a Legal Debt or Liability: The foundational requirement for an offence under Section 138 is a "legally enforceable debt or liability." If the petitioner can demonstrate with documentary evidence (e.g., a settlement agreement, full payment receipt, a written contract showing the cheque was for security only) that no such debt exists, the proceedings can be quashed.

Example: 'A' gives a cheque to 'B' as security for a loan but never takes the loan. 'B' presents the cheque. Since no debt was ever created, the complaint is an abuse of process.

2. Nonfulfillment of Mandatory Procedural Conditions: The NI Act has strict procedural steps (issuing a demand notice within 30 days of bounce, waiting 15 days for payment, filing complaint within 30 days of the cause of action arising). If the complainant fails to adhere to these timelines prima facie evident from the complaint, it can be a ground for quashing.

3. Lack of Essential Ingredients: If a vital ingredient of the offence is missing from the complaint, it is liable to be quashed.

Example: The complaint does not allege that the cheque was drawn for the discharge of a debt. Or, it is clear the cheque was signed by an unauthorized person without the company's knowledge.

Category 2: Grounds Based on Settlement Between Parties

This is the most common and practical ground for quashing in NI Act cases.

1. Admissible Settlement under Section 147 of the NI Act: Section 147 makes the offence compoundable. If the parties have entered into a settlement and the petitioner has paid the agreed amount (or a substantial part of it), the High Court can quash the proceedings to secure the ends of justice.

- The Court will typically do this even if the settlement happens after the filing of the complaint or during appellate stages.

- The consent of the complainant is crucial for this.

Category 3: Grounds to Prevent Abuse of Process of Court

This is invoked when the continuation of proceedings would be manifestly unjust.

1. Patently Frivolous or Vexatious Complaints: If the complaint is shown to be maliciously filed with an ulterior motive to harass the accused, and no offence is made out, the High Court will quash it to prevent abuse of process.

Example: Filing a complaint on a cheque that was stolen or obtained by coercion.

2. Inordinate and Unexplained Delay: If the case has been pending for an excessively long time (e.g., 1015 years) due to no fault of the accused, and the trial has not commenced meaningfully, the High Court may quash it to secure the ends of justice, especially if the delay prejudices the accused's right to a fair trial.

What is NOT a Ground for Quashing under Section 482?

It is critical to understand what the High Court will not consider at this stage:

- Purely Factual Disputes: If the defence requires leading and testing evidence (e.g., "I already repaid the debt in cash," "the cheque was lost"), the High Court will not conduct a minitrial. It will relegate the accused to raise these defences during the trial. Quashing is not meant to shortcut the trial process.
- Merely because the case is weak: A seemingly weak prosecution case is not enough; it must be so weak that no conviction is possible.
- Alternative Remedy: The existence of an alternative remedy (like raising these issues before the trial court) is not an absolute bar, but the High Court will be reluctant to interfere if the petitioner has not availed of those remedies.

Important Caveat: The New BNSS

Please note that from July 1, 2024, the Code of Criminal Procedure, 1973 (CrPC) has been replaced by the Bharatiya Nagarik Suraksha Sanhita, 2023 (BNSS). The inherent powers of the High Court are now contained in Section 531 of the BNSS. The text and spirit of this section are identical to Section 482 CrPC. All the principles and grounds mentioned above will continue to apply under the new law.

Section 531 BNSS: "Nothing in this Sanhita shall be deemed to limit or affect the inherent powers of the High Court to make such orders as may be necessary to give effect to any order under this Sanhita, or to prevent abuse of the process of any Court or otherwise to secure the ends of justice."

Conclusion: The High Court's power to quash a 138 NI Act case is not to be used lightly. It is restricted to specific, welldefined grounds primarily concerning the absence of a legally enforceable debt, fatal procedural errors, or a valid settlement between the parties. It is not a tool to decide factual disputes that are rightfully meant for the trial court.

QUERIES, QUESTIONS & RESPONSED

Question No.252

Does any post-dated cheque issued as collateral security attract Section 138 of the NI Act.

Answer: When a Post dated cheque is issued as collateral security and the point of time, is on the date of issuance of the Cheque No subsisting liability, No 138 attracts.

(Reference: Gauhati High Court : Sri Don Ayengia Vs State of Assam : 02-04- 2014)

Scenarios & Specific Repercussions

Scenario 1: Blank Signed Cheque Given as Security

Risk: The holder may fill in arbitrary details (amount, date) and present it.

Drawer's Liability:

If the cheque bounces, criminal liability under Section 138 applies unless fraud is proven.

Courts presume the cheque was issued for a valid debt; the drawer must prove otherwise.

Defence Strategies:

File a police complaint for misuse if threats are received.

Issue stoppayment instructions to the bank immediately (though this may still lead to a bounce).

Challenge in court by proving:

No legally enforceable debt existed (e.g., cheque was for a gift, not a loan).

Fraudulent alteration (e.g., amount filled without consent).

Scenario 2: Duly Signed Filled Cheque Bounced

Drawer's Options:

Pay within 15 days of notice to avoid prosecution.

Negotiate settlement out of court (e.g., via mediation).

Corporate Liability:

Directors can be held personally liable if the cheque was issued for company transactions.

Scenario 3: PostDated or Stale Cheques

Post dated Cheques: Bounce treated similarly under Section 138.

Stale Cheques (>3 months old): Not enforceable; returnable by banks.

IV. Precautionary Measures for Drawers

1. Avoid Blank Cheques: Never issue signed blank cheques/stamp papers. Use formal agreements instead.

2. Stop Payment Orders: Valid for lost/stolen cheques but may not absolve liability if debt is proven.

3. Document Security:

Keep cheque records (dates, amounts).

Use secure methods (e.g., bank transfers).

- Blank cheque/Cheque not filled by accused

Dishonour of cheque - Blank cheque - Can be filled up by the Holder thereof. which will be a valid instrument in the eye of law. (MADRAS HIGH COURT. M.VENUGOPAL, J., Date of Decision/21.11.2012). (A.dhinakar Vs L.Kezhson).

- Blank cheque/Cheque not filled by accused

SC Dishonour of cheque - Blank cheque - If a signed blank cheque is voluntarily presented to a payee, towards some payment, payee may fill up the amount and other particulars - This in itself does not invalidate the cheque - Onus will still be on accused to prove that cheque was not in discharge of debt or liability by adducing evidence. (SUPREME COURT OF INDIA, R.BANUMATHI AND INDIRA BANERJEE, JJ., Date of Decision/06.02.2019). (Bir Singh Vs Mukesh Kumar)

BLANK CHEQUE VS. PRE- FILLED CHEQUE

Question No.35

Whether The Complaint Be Dismissed If The Fill-Up Cheque Is Filled With Different Ink And The Witness Cannot Explain It?

Answer:

Yes, It Was Held That The Trial Court Had Taken A Reasonable And Probable View While Dismissing The Complaint.

(Reference: Punjab And Haryana High Court: Subhash Chander Sharma Vs Ravinder alias Babli : 16-01-2020)

IMPORTANT CITATIONS

GENERAL PRECAUTIONS

NOTICE NO.1

When responding to a NOTICE under Section 138(b) of the Negotiable Instruments Act, 1881 (NI Act) for cheque dishonour, the recipient must take strategic precautions to avoid legal liability and strengthen their defense. Essential precautions based on judicial precedents and procedural requirements:

1. Verify Notice Compliance with Legal Requirements Check Validity of Notice Ensure the notice: Was sent within 30 days of cheque dishonour (as per proviso (b) to Section 138). Clearly specify the exact cheque amount (without including extraneous charges like legal fees unless justified). Mentions the correct reason for dishonour (e.g., 'insufficient funds' or 'signature mismatch'). Challenge Defects: If the notice demands an incorrect amount (e.g., ignores partial payments) or is timebarred, explicitly state this in your reply. In Dashrathbhai Trikambhai Patel v. Hitesh Mahendrabhai Patel (2022), the Supreme Court held that a notice demanding the full cheque amount despite partial repayment is invalid ('omnibus notice').

2. Address Legally Enforceable Debt: Dispute Liability: Deny the existence of a 'legally enforceable debt' if: The cheque was issued as security (not for immediate liability). The debt is timebarred or arose from an illegal transaction (e.g., gambling). Partial payment was made before cheque presentation (cite evidence like bank statements). Failure to endorse such payments on the cheque invalidates the notice. Avoid Admission: Do not acknowledge the debt unless legally advised. In Dilip Hariramani v. Bank of Baroda (2022), admissions in replies were used against the drawer.

3. Timely and Evidence Based Reply: 15Day Deadline: Reply within 15 days of receiving the notice to prevent the payee from filing a complaint. Proof of Service: Send the reply via: Registered Post AD (to create a rebuttable presumption of service). Email/WhatsApp (valid per Rajendra v. State of U.P. (2024)) with read receipts. Document Everything: Attach evidence (e.g., payment receipts, loan agreements) to counter the payee’s claims.

4. Raise Specific Legal Defenses: In your reply, include: Signature

Mismatch: Argue forgery if applicable and demand a handwriting expert examination (Lakshmi Dyechem v. State of Gujarat, 2012). Account Closure: Cite Nepc Micon Ltd. v. Magma Leasing Ltd. (1999) to clarify that closure implies 'insufficient funds', but challenge if closure predated the cheque issue. Technical Dishonour: If the cheque bounced for nonfinancial reasons (e.g., overwriting), state that Section 138 is inapplicable.

5. Avoid Common Traps: Do Not Ignore: Even defective notices warrant a reply to prevent ex parte proceedings. No Vague Language: Use precise language (e.g., 'The notice is invalid as it ignores partial repayment of ₹4,09,315 made on [dates]'). Escalation Warning: State that frivolous complaints may lead to costs/defamation suits.

6. Structure Your Reply: Organize the reply as follows:

1. Introduction: Reference notice details (date, cheque number).

2. Factual Corrections: Dispute inaccuracies in the notice.

3. Legal Defenses: Cite noncompliance with Section 138(b) and case laws.

4. Consequence Warning: Demand withdrawal of the notice to avoid legal costs. Critical Precaution: Consult a lawyer immediately to: Draft a legally sound reply. Strategize for potential criminal proceedings. Ensure alignment with local High Court rulings (e.g., Punjab & Haryana High Court guidelines on moneylending debts). Key Insight: A welldrafted reply can deter litigation or secure acquittal by exposing flaws in the notice.

QUASHING (SECTION 482 CRPC) PART II

<u>Grounds:</u>

Lack of specific averments in the complaint proving the accused was "in charge of and responsible for" the company's business when the offense occurred.

Unimpeachable evidence (e.g., resignation documents, proof of role exclusion) showing non-involvement in the cheque transaction.

Timeline: High Courts may decide within 36 months if the evidence is clear.

Question No.222

Is the locus standi of the complainant, authorized by the company, competent when the affidavit of the power of attorney holder, who has personal knowledge of the transactions, is on record.

Answer:

In answer, the State High Court quashed the orders of three subordinate courts in a quashing case, whereas the Supreme Court is of the considered opinion that the attorney holder, who was on record, claims to have personal knowledge of the transactions and is competent.

(Reference: Supreme Court: Mita India PVT. LTD. Vs Mahendra Jain

Q- Question

Whether to place a heavy burden on the accused to prove the debt ?

The Hon'ble Supreme Court held that the trial court committed an error in placing a heavy burden on the complainant to prove the debt. (Reference: Supreme Court: Pavan Dilprao Dike Vs Vishal Narendrabhai Parmar: 12-07-2019)

JUDGEMENT SUPPORTING DEFENCE

P-PROBABLE DEFENCE

FAQS CONCEPT "A"

Question

Is the lack of capability of the complainant to pay money a probable or a good defense for the accused in the case of Section 138 NI Act?

Answer:

The Calcutta State High Court held no.

(Reference: Calcutta High Court: Subrata Bose Vs Mithu Ghosh:07-11-2022)

P- PREPONDERANCE OF PROBABILITIES

THIS is an excellent question that gets to the very heart of how the legal machinery of Section 138 of the Negotiable Instruments Act, 1881 ("NI Act") operates.

The term "preponderance of probabilities" is not a standard legal phrase but is correctly understood as a reference to the "preponderance of probabilities", which is the standard of proof applied in civil cases, including those under Section 138 of the NI Act.

Let's break this down in terms of its scope, object, and application.

1. The Standard of Proof: "Preponderance of Probabilities"

- Meaning: This standard means that a fact is considered proven if it is more likely than not to be true. It is a balance of probabilities. If the evidence presented by one side is more convincing and has greater weight than the evidence presented by the other side, the court will rule in favor of the side with the superior evidence.
- Contrast with Criminal Standard: This is distinct from the criminal standard of "proof beyond a reasonable doubt," which requires a much higher degree of certainty. A cheque bounce case is a quasi criminal offence. While the proceedings are criminal in nature (as they can lead to imprisonment), the standard of proof for establishing the core liability is civil, i.e., preponderance of probabilities.

2. Object of Section 138 of the NI Act

The primary object of introducing Section 138 was to:

- Enhance the credibility of negotiable instruments, especially cheques, which are the backbone of commercial transactions.
- Prevent dishonesty on the part of the drawer of a cheque from sustaining liability.
- Promote financial discipline and ensure trust in the banking system.
- Provide a speedy and effective remedy to the payee for the loss suffered due to the dishonour of a cheque.

The standard of "preponderance of probabilities" aligns perfectly with this object. It allows the courts to decide cases based on a common sense assessment of the evidence (like the existence of a debt, the issuance of the cheque, and its subsequent dishonour) without requiring the draconian level of proof needed in a murder or

Question

Whether section 138/141 of the Negotiable Instrument Act is applicable if the cheque was issued by the Drawer/Accused from his respective bank account, which was closed before issuing the cheque, or the account was closed by the drawer after issuing the cheque to the payee?

Answer:

The bank account of the accused was closed by him either before or after the issuance of the impugned cheque. In both scenarios, if the cheque got dishonored, there would be no escape for the accused. Instead, the accused may be held guilty of committing another offense for issuing a cheque from a closed accounting standpoint.

****

CHAPTER-04

ORIGNAL CHEQUE OR DOCUMENTS LOST

WHAT TO DO

IF ORIGNAL CHEQUE ETC LOST OR MISPLACED

This is a critical situation, but the law provides a clear remedy. The advice and legal steps depend heavily on the specific stage at which the cheque was lost, as each scenario has different procedural requirements.

The overarching legal remedy for a lost cheque is provided under Section 45A of the Negotiable Instruments Act, 1881. This section allows a court to grant permission to the holder of a cheque to present a copy of the cheque as evidence, as if it were the original, provided certain conditions are met.

ADVICE and legal remedy of each scenarios:

The Overarching Legal Remedy: Section 45A of the NI Act

This is your primary weapon. To invoke Section 45A, you must satisfy the court on the following points:

1. The cheque was lost or destroyed: You must state this on oath.

2. It was lost/destroyed before it was presented: Or, if it was presented and then lost, that fact.

3. The loss was not due to your own fault or neglect: Or that of your agents. You must show you were prudent.

4. You apply to the drawer for a duplicate cheque: And the drawer refused to issue one.

The court, if satisfied, will make a formal order allowing you to use a copy of the cheque. This order is essential for proceeding with a case under Section 138 of the NI Act.

Stage-by-Stage Advice and Action Plan

Scenario 1 & 2: Cheque Misplaced by Payee (Individual/Corporate) BEFORE Presentation

This is the most straightforward scenario for Section 45A.

Immediate Practical Advice:

1. Inform the Drawer Immediately: Contact the person who gave you the cheque (the drawer) in writing (email + registered post). Formally state that the original cheque is lost and request them to issue a duplicate cheque. Mention your intention to invoke Section 45A if they refuse. This step is legally mandatory.

2. Thorough Search: Conduct a diligent search and document it.

3. Lodge a Police Complaint (FIR): This is highly advisable. It serves as official, third-party evidence that the cheque was genuinely lost and not in your possession, protecting you from any future misuse. It also strengthens your case when you approach the court under Section 45A.

4. Inform Your Bank: Notify your bank in writing about the loss of the cheque, providing them with the details (cheque number, account number, drawer's name). This puts them on alert in case someone tries to fraudulently present it.

· Legal Remedy:

If the drawer agrees to issue a duplicate cheque, present the new one.

If the drawer refuses (which is common, as it stops their liability on the original), you can proceed to file a complaint under Section 138.

Along with your complaint, file an Application under Section 45A of the NI Act, supported by an affidavit. In the affidavit, detail all the steps you took (search, police complaint, request to drawer, their refusal). The court will hear this application and, if convinced, pass an order allowing you to use a photocopy of the cheque for all legal purposes.

Scenario 3: Cheque & Bank Return Memo Lost BEFORE Issuing Legal Notice

Immediate Practical Advice:

1. Gather Secondary Evidence: This is crucial. Obtain a certified copy of the cheque transaction and the return memo from your bank. Banks maintain images of all processed cheques. Get a statement from your bank confirming that the specific cheque was presented and dishonoured.

2. Lodge a Police Complaint: For the loss of the entire set of documents.

3. Inform the Drawer: While not strictly required at this stage, it can be done to show bona fide.

Legal Remedy:

You can still issue the statutory legal demand notice under Section 138. Attach the photocopy of the cheque and the bank-certified copy of the return memo to the notice.

When filing the complaint in court, you will file an Application under Section 45A for the lost cheque and also plead that the bank's certified record is a valid substitute for the original return memo. The court has the power to admit such secondary evidence.

Scenario 4: Cheque, Memo, & Notice Copy Lost BEFORE Filing Case

Immediate Practical Advice:

1. Reconstruct the File: Collect all secondary evidence:

Photocopy of the cheque (from your records).

Certified bank statement/memo (from the bank).

Proof of sending the legal notice (this is VITAL). Retrieve the postal receipt, tracking report, and delivery confirmation from the postal service or courier company. This proves you complied with the mandatory notice period.

2. Lodge a Police Complaint for the loss of the documents.

Legal Remedy:

File your complaint under Section 138 by attaching all the secondary evidence.

File a detailed application under Section 45A for the cheque and a separate application requesting permission to rely on secondary evidence for the return memo and notice copy. Your affidavit must meticulously explain the loss and the steps taken to obtain certified copies.

Scenario 5: All Originals Lost BEFORE Court Takes Cognizance (Issuance of Process)

This is a delicate stage, as the court verifies your complaint and evidence before issuing summons.

Immediate Practical Advice:

1. Do Not Wait: Immediately bring this to the court's attention. Do not try to hide it.

2. File a Supplementary Affidavit/Application: File a formal application informing the court of the loss, along with an affidavit explaining the circumstances. Annex all the secondary evidence you have gathered (bank certificates, postal proofs, photocopies).

Legal Remedy:

The magistrate will consider your application under Section 45A and the general principles of evidence law for admitting secondary evidence.

If the magistrate is satisfied with your explanation and the secondary evidence is reliable, the court will take cognizance and issue process. The success here depends entirely on the strength of your secondary evidence and the credibility of your affidavit.

Scenario 6: All Originals Lost BEFORE Filing Affidavit of Evidence (Marking Exhibits)

This happens after the case is underway but before the final trial evidence is recorded.

Immediate Practical Advice:

1. File an Interlocutory Application: You must file an application before the trial court under Section 45A of the NI Act and Section 65 of the Indian Evidence Act, 1872 (which allows for secondary evidence when the original is lost).

2. Support with Strong Affidavit: The affidavit must explain the loss in detail and demonstrate the absence of bad faith.

Legal Remedy:

The court will hear your application. You will be cross-examined on your affidavit.

If the court is convinced, it will pass an order permitting you to exhibit the photocopies and certified copies as secondary evidence. This order is essential to proceed with your testimony.

Summary of Universal Steps

1. Act Immediately: Delay can be interpreted as negligence.
2. Document Everything: Keep a written record of every step you take.
3. Inform the Drawer in Writing (for pre-presentation loss): This is a legal prerequisite for Section 45A.
4. Lodge a Police Complaint (FIR): This is your strongest proof of the loss being genuine.
5. Gather Secondary Evidence: Bank certificates, postal receipts, and photocopies are your new best friends.
6. Use Section 45A: This is the specific legal provision designed for this exact problem. File a formal application supported by a truthful and detailed affidavit.

Disclaimer: This information is for educational purposes only and does not constitute legal advice. The success of an application under Section 45A depends on the specific facts of the case and the discretion of the court. It is strongly recommended that you consult with a Senior Expert to handle your specific situation.

HOW TO GET

E (EX PARTE) JUDGMENT OF CONVICTION

Present: Shri/Smt. [Presiding Officer's Name], Judicial Magistrate First Class FACTS OF THE CASE

1. The complainant filed this case under Section 138 of the Negotiable Instruments Act, 1881, alleging that the accused issued a cheque bearing No. dated for ₹ in discharge of a legally enforceable debt, which was dishonoured for 'Insufficient Funds' as per return memo dated from [Bank Name].

2. Despite the statutory demand notice dated (sent via registered post and acknowledged), the accused failed to make payment within 15 days, leading to this complaint.

3. The court took cognizance and issued summons, but the accused willfully evaded service. Subsequently: Bailable & NonBailable Warrants were issued but not executed. Proclamation under Section 82 CrPC was issued on , declaring the accused a Proclaimed Offender. Attachment under Section 83 CrPC was also initiated.

4. The complainant filed an application under Section 299 CrPC for recording evidence in the accused's absence, which was allowed.

5. The complainant submitted: Affidavit of Evidence (Ex. CW1/A) Original dishonoured cheque (Ex. CW1/1) Bank return memo (Ex. CW1/2) Postal receipts & NOTICE (Ex. CW1/3 to CW1/5) Other relevant documents COURT'S ANALYSIS & FINDINGS

1. Ingredients of Section 138 NI Act Proved: Cheque issuance in order to discharge enforceable debt (Ex. CW1/1) no rebuttal Dishonour for insufficiency of funds (Ex. CW1/2). Legal demand notice served (Ex. CW1/3 to CW1/5). Accused failed to pay within 15 days of notice.

2. Accused's Absconding Status: The accused was duly proclaimed under Section 82 CrPC but failed to appear. His absence is willful and deliberate, justifying ex parte proceedings under Section 299 CrPC. 3. Evidence Conclusive: The complainant's unrebutted testimony and documents prove guilt beyond reasonable doubt.

FINAL ORDER

2. The accused is convicted under Section 138 of the Negotiable Instruments Act, 1881. Yes, in a Section 138 NI Act case, the court can finally decide and convict the accused even after proceeding under Section 299 CrPC (recording evidence in the absence of an absconding accused),

provided the following conditions are met:

1. Legal Position on Deciding the Case After Section 299 CrPC Proceedings Section 299 CrPC allows the court to record evidence in the absence of an absconding accused to prevent indefinite delays. Once the complainant's evidence is recorded ex parte and the court is satisfied that: The accused was duly served/proclaimed (under Sections 82/83 CrPC). The complainant has proved all ingredients of Section 138 NI Act (cheque issuance, dishonour, legal notice, nonpayment). The court can pronounce judgment (conviction or acquittal) based on the available evidence.

2. Key Conditions for Final Decision Proper service of summons/warrants – The court must be satisfied that the accused was given a fair opportunity to appear. Proclamation under Section 82 CrPC – The accused should have been declared an 'absconder' with a public notice. Evidence conclusively proves guilt – The complainant must establish: Cheque was issued by the accused. It was dishonoured for 'insufficient funds' or other valid reasons. A legal demand notice was served within 30 days of dishonour. The accused failed to pay within 15 days of notice. No reasonable defence – Since the accused is absent, the court relies solely on the complainant's evidence.

3. Can the Accused Challenge Later? If the accused is convicted ex parte, he can file: Application to set aside ex parte order (under Section 317 CrPC) if he later appears.

Query

Whether a complaint under Section 138 of the Negotiable Instruments Act (NI Act) is maintainable if the cheque was issued to recover a debt above Rs 20,000 that was paid completely in cash. **? ? ? ?**

This issue arose from a Kerala High Court judgment that held a debt created by a cash transaction above Rs 20,000, in violation of Section 269SS of the Income-Tax Act, 1961, cannot be considered a "legally enforceable debt" under Section 138 of the NI Act unless a valid explanation is provided.

Key points from the Kerala High Court's ruling and the awaited Supreme Court decision:

Section 269SS of the Income-Tax Act prohibits transactions above Rs 20,000 in cash and mandates such transactions be made through an account transaction or cheque/draft.

According to the Kerala High Court, if a debt originates from a prohibited cash transaction above Rs 20,000, the complainant who later receives a cheque for that debt should have a valid explanation for the cash transaction, or else the criminal court cannot entertain a complaint under Section 138.

The Kerala High Court set aside convictions in such cases and ordered refunds of deposits related to these proceedings.

The accused in such cases must raise the defence that the cash transaction violated Section 269SS; otherwise, courts may presume a legally enforceable debt under Section 139 of the NI Act.

The case before the Supreme Court involves challenging this Kerala High Court ruling and determining the maintainability of Section 138 complaints in such contexts.

Thus, the Supreme Court's decision will clarify whether a cheque issued for a cash debt above Rs 20,000—presumably violating tax laws—can be the basis of a criminal complaint for cheque dishonour under Section 138 of the NI Act, especially when no valid explanation for the cash transaction is given

WHAT TO DO

Query: **?**

Defense and theory of Accused that check in question against no liability and a stolen check, also supported by police complaint, whereas the Name of the payee on the check is in the handwriting of accused, drawer himself **?**

✍Answer

The defence is critically undermined because the accused himself wrote the payee's name on the cheque.

This single fact makes the defence appear "fake and concocted" because:

- Legal Presumption: The law presumes a cheque is for a valid debt. The burden is on the accused to prove otherwise.
- Logical Implausibility: Why would the accused specifically fill in the payee's name if the cheque was stolen? This suggests intent and authorization, making the "theft" story highly improbable.
- Weak Alibi: A police complaint filed after the cheque bounced looks like a reactive, fabricated alibi rather than proof.

Conclusion:

The self-written payee's name is the core contradiction. To succeed, the accused must provide overwhelmingly strong evidence to explain this and rebut the legal presumption of debt, which is a very difficult task. The defence, as stated, is likely to fail.

Coaching Part:

The Practical Guide to the NI Act

.

Heading: How IBC Proceedings Affect a Complaint under Sections 138/141 of the NI Act1. The Core Conflict: IBC vs NI Act

NI Act Complaint (Sections 138/141):

This is a criminal proceeding for cheque bounce. It aims to hold the drawer (and company directors, if any) accountable for issuing a dishonored cheque.

IBC Proceeding:

This is a civil process for companies in financial distress. Its purpose is to either rescue the company or liquidate it in an organized way so all creditors are treated fairly.

Key Impact:

When the National Company Law Tribunal (NCLT) admits an IBC case, a moratorium (legal freeze) takes effect. This stops all lawsuits and recovery actions—including cheque bounce cases under Sections 138/141 of the NI Act. The focus shifts from punishing one debtor to collectively resolving the company's entire financial crisis.

2. The IBC Process in Simple TermsThink of the IBC as an emergency plan for companies on financial life support. The goal is to either revive the company or liquidate it fairly.

To be continued

QUREY????????????

The court found all three accused, A, B, and C, guilty. An order of compensation of 90 lakh is to be paid to the complainant, and in default, they will undergo six months of imprisonment. A is ready to pay his share of 30 lakh, but B and C do not contribute and have raised their hands. What should the court do in this scenario?

This is a classic situation in cases involving joint liability under the Negotiable Instruments Act. The court's course of action is well-defined by legal principles.

what the court is likely to do, based on your scenario:

The Legal Principle: Joint and Several Liability

When a court finds multiple accused persons guilty in a cheque dishonour case and orders them to pay a total compensation amount, they are typically held to be "jointly and severally liable."

This is a crucial legal concept which means:

- Jointly: They are all together responsible for paying the full amount.
- Severally: The complainant can recover the entire amount from any one of them, regardless of their individual share.

The court's order to pay ₹90 lakhs is against all three accused as a group. It is not three separate orders of ₹30 lakhs each.

What the Court Will Do in This Situation

Since Accused 'A' is ready to pay his share but Accused 'B' and 'C' are defaulting, the court will proceed as follows:

What the Court Will Do in This Situation

Since Accused 'A' is ready to pay his share but Accused 'B' and 'C' are defaulting, the court will proceed as follows:

1. The Compensation Order is for the Full Amount: The court will not accept a partial payment of only ₹30 lakhs from 'A' as a discharge of its order. The order is for ₹90 lakhs, and until that full amount is paid to the complainant, the order is not satisfied.

2. 'A' is Not Shielded from the Default Consequences: Because the liability is joint, the court will hold all three accused, including 'A', to

be in default until the full ₹90 lakhs is paid. The fact that 'A' was willing to pay his share is a matter between 'A', 'B', and 'C', but it does not absolve him from the court's order.

3. The Court Will Likely Initiate Default Proceedings Against All Three: Since the compensation has not been paid in full, the court will trigger the "default" clause. This means:

The court will issue a warrant for all three accused—A, B, and C—to undergo the six months' imprisonment as stipulated in the judgment.

· 'A' will be treated as being in default along with B and C.

What Are the Options and Likely Outcomes?

Given this strict legal position, here are the practical outcomes:

Given this strict legal position, here are the practical outcomes:

Option 1: All Three Go to Jail

If no one pays the full₹90 lakhs, the court will send all three accused to prison for six months. 'A's willingness to pay his share will not save him from this consequence.

Option 2: 'A' Pays the Entire ₹90 Lakhs to Avoid Jail

This is'A's most straightforward legal escape route. To avoid imprisonment, Accused 'A' can:

Pay the entire ₹90 lakhs to the complainant.

Once the full payment is made and proven to the court, the liability under the compensation order is extinguished. The court will then drop the imprisonment proceedings against all three accused.

What happens after 'A' pays the full amount?

After paying the full₹90 lakhs, 'A' does not simply lose the extra ₹60 lakhs. He acquires the legal right to sue his co-accused, 'B' and 'C', in a separate civil suit to recover the ₹60 lakhs that he paid on their behalf. This new case would be for "reimbursement" or "contribution."

Option 3: 'A' Approaches the Court with an Application

'A'can file an application before the court stating that he is willing and ready to pay his share of ₹30 lakhs, but his co-accused are refusing to pay. However, the court's response will be guided by the principle of joint liability.

Option 3: 'A' Approaches the Court with an Application

'A'can file an application before the court stating that he is willing and ready to pay his share of ₹30 lakhs, but his co-accused are refusing to pay. However, the court's response will be guided by the principle of joint liability.

The court may give a short adjournment to allow 'A' to try and arrange for the full payment.

The court is highly unlikely to modify its original order or accept a partial payment, as it would prejudice the rights of the complainant, who is the victim in the case.

Summary and Advice

The Court's Priority: The court's primary duty is to ensure the complainant gets the compensation awarded. The internal arrangement between the accused is not the court's concern.

'A's Best Course of Action: To avoid a six-month prison sentence, Accused 'A' should make every effort to pay the full ₹90 lakhs to the complainant. He should then immediately initiate a civil recovery suit against 'B' and 'C' for ₹60 lakhs.

The Reality for 'A': 'A' is in a difficult position because of the actions of his co-accused. The law, in this case, places the burden on him to pay the full amount to save himself from imprisonment and then seek his own legal remedy against the others.

In conclusion, the court will proceed to send all three accused to prison for six months for defaulting on the payment unless the full compensation of ₹90 lakhs is paid. 'A's willingness to pay only his share is not a valid defense against the joint liability order.

✍Just Authour opinion....not to be construed advice.

QUESTION IN THIS CASE IS WHETHER The accused

In HIS Case IN" A" COURT A can rely on the facts or proceedings of a separate, pending case (IN COURT B) filed by the complainant SAME IN BOTH COURT A AND B BUT ACCUSED ARE NOT THE SAME NOR THE TRANSACTION ARE SAME OR CONNECTED .

The logic says that to rebut the statutory presumptions under Sections 118 and 139 of the Negotiable Instruments Act, 1881. To be admissible, the accused must independently establish through credible evidence that the specifics of Case B have a direct bearing on the transaction in Case A.

IMPORTANT CITATIONS

FAQS CONCEPT PART "A"

QUESTION AND ANSWEER

Even if it is held that specific averments are necessary, whether in the absence of such averments, can the signatory of the cheque and/or the Managing Directors of Joint Managing Director, who admittedly would be in charge of the company and responsible to the company for the conduct of its business, be proceeded against?

Answer :

The answer to the question has to be in the affirmative. The question notes that the Managing Director or Joint Managing Director would be admittedly in charge of the company and responsible to the company for the conduct of its business. When that is so, holders of such positions in a company become liable under Section 141 of the Act. By virtue of the office they hold as Managing Director or Joint Managing Director, these persons are in charge of and responsible for the conduct of the business of the company. Therefore, they are covered under Section 141. As far as the signatory of a dishonored cheque is concerned, he is responsible for the incriminating act and will be covered under sub-section (2) of Section 141.

(Reference: Supreme Court : S.M.S Pharmaceuticals Ltd vs Neeta Bhalla And Anr:20-09-2005: Part of CLR Volume 2 page no. 177-198.)

Question N

Whether a complaint under section 138 Negotiable Instruments Act would be maintainable against the company if the statutory notice under section 138 Negotiable Instruments Act is issued only to its Managing Director and is not issued to the company which is maintaining the account from which the subject cheque is issued.

Answer :

Yes, Maintainable.

(Reference: Delhi High Court : DSC Ltd.Vs Dada Jeetu Buildcon Pvt. Ltd.,:16-11-2018: Part of CLR Volume 2 page no. 365-378.)

Question No.63

The entire amount of compensation, if deposited by the appellant, for the register of the Supreme Court, will have what effect?

Answer:

All proceedings emanating from the complaint are quashed. (Reference:. Supreme Court: Vikas Jalan Vs M/s Shreya Pet Pvt . Ltd. & Ors.: 07-03-2011)

Question No. 89

After the closing of the defense side witness, the accused wanted to examine at the Argument Stage, whether permissible at such a belated stage.

Answer :

Section 315 of CR.P.C . does not prescribe any time limit, so there is no legal bar expressly available to reject on the belated ground. Such an opportunity would normally not be denied. (Reference: Madras High Court :E.Vanitha Vs Smt.S.Lakshmi : 30-08-2017

www.ingramcontent.com/pod-product-compliance
Lightning Source LLC
Chambersburg PA
CBHW031334230926
51848CB00002B/233
9789364318648